30 v 96

For Lloyd and Sue

With profound
gratitude for
everything you
have taught me –

[signature]

TETHERED DEER

MARC BLECHER AND
VIVIENNE SHUE

Tethered Deer

GOVERNMENT AND ECONOMY
IN A CHINESE COUNTY

STANFORD UNIVERSITY PRESS
STANFORD, CALIFORNIA
1996

Stanford University Press
Stanford, California
© 1996 by the Board of Trustees of the
Leland Stanford Junior University
Printed in the United States of America

CIP data are at the end of the book

Stanford University Press Publications are
distributed exclusively by Stanford University Press
within the United States, Canada, and Mexico; they
are distributed exclusively by Cambridge University Press
throughout the rest of the world

For Ruthe and Saul Blecher,
who personify the pleasures of the
road less traveled,

and

for Georgi,
who brings us laughter

Acknowledgments

The research for this book began in 1979, when we were part of a team of five scholars that included Phyllis Andors, Stephen Andors, and Mitch Meisner. We were privileged to be able to undertake one of the earliest stints of field research in China by American social scientists. At the kind suggestion of Professor Paul T. K. Lin, the Chinese People's Association for Friendship with Foreign Countries and the Chinese Academy of Social Sciences jointly invited us to visit China to explore a subject of our choosing and to specify the kinds of localities in which we would like to study it. We wish to thank first the researchers of the Chinese Academy of Social Sciences and its Rural Research Institute, who met with us during that first visit, and the Chinese People's Association for Friendship with Foreign Countries, which served as a most generous host on that visit. In particular, we would like to express our thanks to Zhang Wenpu for issuing the invitation and overseeing the arrangements, and to Su Guang and Pu Ning, who accompanied us on our travels and assisted us with the fieldwork. We were indeed privileged to have their help.

Shulu county was just one of the localities we visited that summer—but we returned to Shulu in 1986, and again in 1990. Each time we were in the county, many people there took time from their busy schedules to meet with us, answer our countless questions, and respond to our requests for statistics and documentary materials. None of that very intense work could have been accomplished without the great and generous cooperation of the Shulu County People's Government, and in particular its Foreign Affairs Office. We wish to thank especially Zhi Yingbin, who handled the practical arrangements for us on all our visits to Shulu. We met with so many people in Shulu that it is not practical to thank them all by name here. But we are most grateful for their time and for the patience and grace with which they unfailingly bore our queries and demands. We would like most especially, however, to thank former mayor Liu Baolu, for sharing with us his fund of personal and professional knowledge, and for all the help we received through his good offices.

Generous grants from the Ford Foundation and the National Endowment for the Humanities helped defray our travel expenses in China, gather our research team during the initial phases of writing, and subsidize our research expenses. Further support for research was provided by Cornell University, Michigan State University, Oberlin College, and Yale University. Marc Blecher received several research leaves to work on this book: in 1982–83 from Oberlin College, and in the summer of 1987 and in 1988–89 from National Endowment for the Humanities grants #FT-29696-87 and #FB-25930-88, respectively. The Institute for Development Studies of the University of Sussex provided a most exhilarating environment for research, thinking, and writing by hosting him as a Visiting Fellow in 1982–83. Vivienne Shue held a junior faculty fellowship from Yale University during 1980–81, which allowed time for research on this project, and she is grateful also for grants from the Yale-China Association, the Yale University Council on East Asian Studies, and the Cornell University College of Arts and Sciences, which facilitated the fieldwork and research at early stages of the project.

This book began with five co-authors. Phyllis and Steve Andors and Mitch Meisner undertook the initial field research with us. We also worked together to produce the rough drafts, and met over fascinating weekends to probe the material and puzzle over the analysis. Steve served as our informal leader, and played key roles in putting the group together, coordinating arrangements with our Chinese hosts, and making our grant applications. Starting the project with these perceptive and energetic colleagues had many salutary effects on our work. By dividing into subgroups, we were able in 1979 to cover a great deal of ground in a rather short time. The intellectual companionship of Mitch, Phyllis, and Steve alerted us to a wider range of questions, issues, and perspectives than we could have raised on our own. It also imparted to our research agenda a scope whose ambition we did not appreciate at the time, and have come to recognize only after many years of struggling with the material. Ultimately we were unable to satisfy our curiosity about many questions with anything like the definitiveness that, perhaps somewhat naïvely, we had sought together in those early days. The audacious plans that grew so naturally out of our collaboration have made our subsequent task more arduous, and our publication date far later than we ever expected. But we also hope that the large questions our colleagues helped us raise have made this work more worthwhile for our readers; we know they have done so for us. Finally, though they might no longer recall their roles in making many of our initial discoveries, or recognize their early contributions to this work now in its final form so many years later, it is our great pleasure to acknowledge that we surely do.

We wrote the final draft of our manuscript with special sadness in our hearts knowing that the untimely death of Phyllis Andors meant she would never read what the two of us finally thought worth saying on the work we had all done together. It was the resilience of Phyllis's spirit that kept us going more than once, and that we shall always remember.

We were fortunate to have very able research assistance over many years from Cui Hong, Li Ning, Liu Zicheng, Wang Shaoguang, and Yue Ming. These talented people helped us in our fieldwork and in the sorting of our research materials. They saved us from many a delusion and often succeeded in opening new lines of inquiry for us with their own perceptive questions. We have learned a great deal from them and this work owes much to their energy and their dedication.

Christine Wong read the manuscript just before its final revision, and offered many discerning and constructive criticisms that have helped us correct some remaining errors and tighten the presentation. We are grateful to Daniel Kelliher, Mark Selden, and to Lynn T. White III, who read earlier versions of the work in progress, giving us many thoughtful comments. Remaining errors of fact or interpretation, we hasten to add, are of course our responsibility alone.

We are grateful to Kathleen Hartford and Elizabeth Remick for important bits of bibliographical assistance. Joel and Jacob Blecher lightened the load of statistical data inputting, and Ian Blecher helped polish a translation from the Chinese. In the days before personal computers, Vera Alferio, Karen Barnes, Jan Dahl, Pauline Farrar, and April Paramore typed and retyped various chapter drafts with accuracy, and good cheer. Michael Busch provided sustained cover under fire as well as professional and moral support leading to the completion of this project. Tracy Tucker helped keep communications moving smoothly during the final phases of production.

Muriel Bell took an early interest in this work, and then kept faith with us and with this manuscript when other editors, surely, would have flagged. We are pleased to record here our appreciation for all her many efforts to improve the ultimate product. Amy Klatzkin handled the production of the book expertly and with understanding. Ann Klefstad did a splendid job with the copyediting.

Henry and Sharon must have wondered many times over the years if they would ever see the end of this particular labor of love. We thank them here, once again, for all their love's labors.

M.B.
V.S.

Contents

1. Studying Government and Economy in Shulu: Goals and Methods — 1
2. Historical and Material Settings — 13
3. The Shulu County Government — 29
4. County Financial Structures and Relations — 46
5. Industry and Industrialization — 92
6. The County Government in Commercial Development — 122
7. The County Government in Urban Development — 155
8. The County Government in Rural Development — 170
9. Conclusion: Moving Structures and Changing Demeanors of the Local State — 202

Notes — 223
Index — 257

Errata

Map 7 (Hierarchy of central places in Shulu county, 1979) appears on page 144, and Map 8 (Markets and administrative centers, Shulu county, 1906) appears on page 25.

Illustrations

Figures

1. Leading Organs of Shulu Government in the 1980's 32
2. Administrative Expenses of County Government, 1949–89 38
3. Administrative Expenses as Percentage of Total Budgetary Expenses, 1949–89 38
4. Shulu County Budgetary Revenues and Expenditures, 1949–89 49
5. Shulu County Major Tax Revenues, 1949–89 55
6. Shulu County Industrial and Commercial Profit Revenues, 1965–89 61
7. Shulu County Major Budgetary Expenditures, 1949–89 69
8. Support for Agriculture as Percentage of Budgetary Expenditures, 1949–89 172
9. Budgetary Expenditures on Agriculture and Social Welfare, 1949–89 172
10. Breakdown of Budgetary Expenditures on Agriculture, 1965–81 173
11. Fruit Area and Production, 1949–87 189
12. Fruit Yields, 1970–87 189

Maps

1. Shulu County in National Context 4
2. Shulu County in Regional Context 6
3. Shulu County 7
4. Major Roads in Shulu County, 1906 15

5. Major Roads in Shulu County, 1970   *16*
6. Major Roads in Shulu County, 1980   *17*
7. Hierarchy of Central Places in Shulu County, 1979   *25*
8. Markets and Administrative Centers, Shulu County, 1906   *144*
9. Periodic Markets, Shulu County, 1986   *145*
10. Xinji City   *160*

Photographs follow page 121

Tables

1. Shulu County, Shijiazhuang Prefecture, Hebei Province, and National Basic Economic Indicators, 1978   8
2. Hierarchies of Settlements in Shulu County, 1979   24
3. Hierarchies of Settlements in Shulu County, 1986   27
4. Organization and Development of County Government Administration in Shulu, 1979–90   30
5. State Employees in Shulu, 1979 and 1989   35
6. Women as a Percentage of State Employees, 1979 and 1989   35
7. Town Government Administration, Xincheng *Zhen*, 1990   40
8. Shulu County Financial Revenue, 1949–89   50
9. Shulu County Budgetary Expenditures, 1949–89   52
10. Income Tax Rates, 1979   58
11. Financial Targets for Township and Village Industries, Shulu County, 1980–89   59
12. Shulu In-Budget Industry Profits and Profit Distribution, 1970–89   64
13. Township Financial Revenue and Expenditure Targets, 1986   73
14. Township Budgetary Revenues and Expenditures, 1986–89   74
15. Budgetary Expenditures of Town and Township Governments by Category, 1988–89   75
16. Township Budgetary, Extrabudgetary, and Other Revenues and Expenditures, 1988   76
17. Distribution of Profits in the Second Light Industry System   78

18. Shulu Second Light Industry Profits, Taxes, and Profit Distribution, 1958–89   *80*
19. Shulu Extrabudgetary Enterprise Profits and Profit Distribution, 1971–89   *84*
20. Labor Force in County Industry and Commerce, Shulu County, by Employment Category, 1949–90   *110*
21. Development of Shulu State-Run and Collective Trade, 1949–78   *124*
22. Shulu County Foreign Trade Bureau Export Purchases, 1974–89   *128*
23. Development of Shulu Collective Trade, 1979–89   *132*
24. Development of Shulu Trade Under the Commerce Bureau, 1979–89   *133*
25. Volume of Private Trade, Shulu County, 1979–89   *140*
26. Shulu County Foreign Trade Bureau Financial Breakdown, 1979–89   *147*
27. Development of Town and Township Industries, 1980–89   *183*
28. Gross Value of Output (GVO), Profits, and Profit Rate of County and Rural Industry, 1979–89   *184*

CHAPTER I

*Studying Government
and Economy in Shulu:
Goals and Methods*

China's most recent successes in economic development, when they are compared to the dilemmas and disappointments faced by many other "late-developing" and former state socialist countries, have commonly been traced by analysts to the unusual degree of developmental dynamism at intermediate levels of government in the Chinese system. Among state socialist systems, the Chinese state has typically been thought to display a more decentralized pattern of authority than most. China's village and township governments, its counties, and its provinces have been vested over the years with considerable financial and other resources, and sometimes with very appreciable latitude in deploying those resources. By and large, political leaders at these intermediate levels have used their resources and their administrative discretion in pursuit of local economic growth. Even during the last decade of the Mao period, when in other respects Chinese politics had produced so seemingly exaggerated a form of centralized party and personal dictatorship, leaders at regional and local levels of government often strove to overcome the developmental constraints posed by politically and ideologically driven economic policies emanating from the center—with visible success. Certainly in the Deng period, when those obstacles were gradually lifted, regional and local governments have been at the forefront of promoting, leading, and managing some of the most rapid economic development seen in any country during the 1980's and 1990's.

The administrative latitude and economic dynamism of China's intermediate levels of government have raised important questions and sparked lively academic debates. How could local governments achieve such room for maneuver within China's centralized Leninist state socialism? How and why were they able to do so when their counterparts within most other state socialist and authoritarian capitalist states were not? What roles have the various intermediate levels come to play? Has bureaucratic decentralization—in both the forms pursued under Mao and those pursued under Deng—proceeded differently in different parts of the country? Have local governments' economic initiatives advanced economic efficiency as well as growth? What implications have they had for developmental balance among sectors and regions? What does decentralization portend for China's political future? Has it proceeded so far as to threaten the very coherence of Chinese national government?

While we cannot adequately address, much less resolve, all of these questions here, we hope to contribute to the ongoing discussions about them with this detailed study of one locality in a part of China that, though politically and economically of enormous importance to the course of the country's development, has not been the main focus of recent scholarship.[1] This work focuses also on one of the intermediate levels of government—the county—that, in spite of its critical placement within the constellation of the Chinese state structure, has somehow escaped serious scrutiny in recent years.[2]

This, then, is a book about Shulu county, a rather unexceptional place on the north China plain. *Shulu* can be translated as "bound (or tethered) deer"—the meaning of this character *shu* is ambiguous. Our focus here is on Shulu county government institutions and activities, particularly with respect to the management and development of the local economy. We explore the internal structure of this local state apparatus, its relationships to government institutions above and below it in the wider Chinese polity, and the ways in which it has shaped the Shulu economy. Our argument is that, for all these issues, calling them "tethered" rather than "bound" better captures the overall tenor of the myriad relationships involved. We find definite latitude in the relationships of county government institutions with one another and with their institutional superiors and subordinates; this flexibility has provided Shulu county leaders with opportunities to exercise their political and administrative skills in the service of local economic development, under some adverse conditions in both the Mao and the Deng years.

Our work focuses on the years 1970 to 1990, encompassing the last decade of the Mao period and the first decade of the Deng reforms. Here too our metaphor remains the tether. For, contrary to many scholarly, popular, and political analyses that emphasize a sharp break—indeed a veritable sea change in Chinese political economy beginning in 1978—in Shulu we found not only great changes but also many enduring features in the county's government and economy. Even within a single policy, administrative decision, or local social phenomenon, we often found past and present closely intertwined. Although bonds to the past had loosened, China in the 1980's was still visibly tethered to the 1970's and to a great deal of earlier history as well. In particular, as we attempt to show in the chapters to come, Shulu county in the 1980's was not so much released from an earlier condition of bondage as it was enabled to stretch its political and economic tether a little further.

In 1979 the Chinese People's Association for Friendship with Foreign Countries and the Chinese Academy of Social Sciences jointly extended an invitation to Phyllis Andors, Stephen Andors, Mitch Meisner, and us to visit China for several weeks during the summer to conduct field research on a subject of our choice. All five members of the group having been trained in political science, and all then teaching Chinese politics in American colleges or universities, we found that a common concern was establishing a better understanding of the middle levels of the Chinese political system. Scholarship in our field had for many years focused on elite-centered macroanalyses of the political system. In response to this, we had each been among those who contributed to a wave of newer studies of politics at the grass roots. But the links between these two distant realms of political activity remained to be illuminated, and our 1979 invitation seemed to offer the opportunity to begin to do so. We married this preoccupation with the midlevels of the system to our common concern with issues of political economy. In the end, we would produce this study of how one county government has engaged in planning, administering, and regulating the economic development of the territory for which it is responsible, and how in the course of doing so it has related to prefectural, provincial, and central governments above it, to local governments below it, and to the society that both surrounds and suffuses it.

We chose to focus on the county (xian) level, for several reasons. First, throughout China's many dynastic changes, including its political crisis and collapse in the twentieth century, the county somehow remained a continuous unit of governance. In the 1930's, even many modernist-inspired efforts at developmental leadership and administration, which in many ways marked new departures for Chinese government, nonetheless remained anchored there.[3] In the 1960's and 1970's, the county was specifically identified in Maoist policy as the locus of political leadership of the process of self-reliant economic development.[4] The county's resilience and tenacious importance as a unit of administration through so many historical transfigurations and political maelstroms formed an interesting puzzle in its own right as well as an asset for anyone wishing to launch a study of the vast uncharted middle of the Chinese state.

Second, the county lay right on the interface of state and society in China. It had been for a long time the lowest level of unalloyed state organization and administration. Even in the Mao period, the people's commune immediately below it was partly a unit of local society, in the lim-

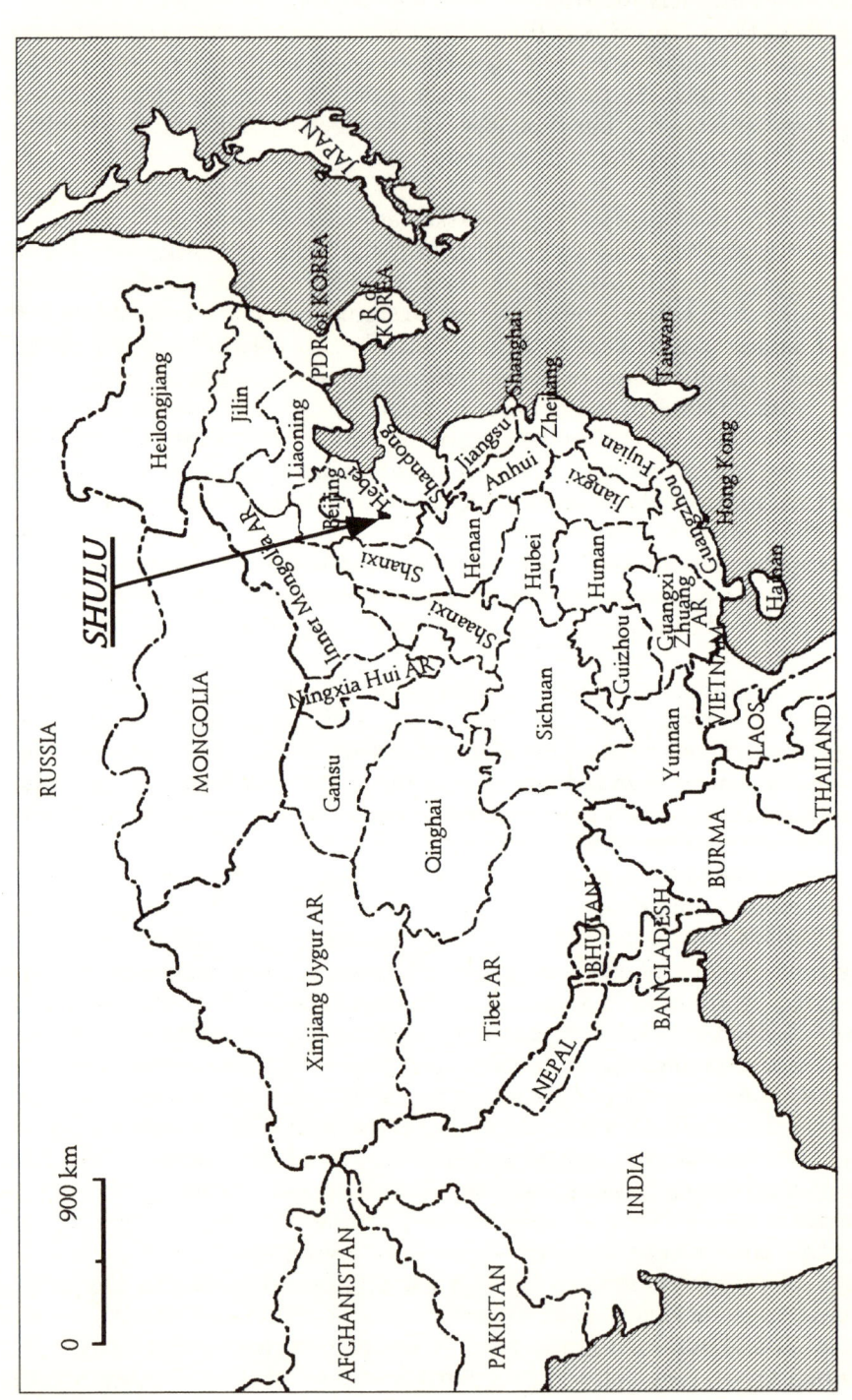

Map 1. Shulu county in national context

ited but important sense that many commune cadres and officials were local people whose interests and incomes were tied far more to the locality than to the wider state. The county is an administrative unit small enough to permit face-to-face relationships among its top leaders, local bureaucrats, and even quite a few ordinary citizens. In the county's institutions, activities, and politics we hoped to find a window on state-society relations in China—on the state's efforts to govern, administer, and transform society, and on the ways in which society constrained, posed problems for, made demands on, and perhaps even sought to influence the state.

Third, while frequently small and in some respects an intimate unit, a county is still large enough potentially to possess the intriguing and important forms of differentiation—between industry and agriculture, between urban and rural life, and between richer and poorer communities—that lie at the heart of the developmental process in China, both propelling and confounding that process now and into the foreseeable future. A county could, therefore, possibly provide a microcosm in which to analyze some of the dynamics and dilemmas of China's growth and the role of the state in advancing that growth.

Fourth, in 1979 some scholarly work had been or was being done on institutions, politics, and development at the provincial level, the other major intermediate locus of organization in the Chinese state.[5] But little or no work was focusing on the county level.

We made several stipulations about the county in which we were to conduct our field research. First, we sought a place in which standard Mandarin was spoken. Second, we wanted to work in a rural and not a suburban county, and one that was well within the middle range of China's economic development. Though we were well aware that no place in China can possibly be typical, and that national data were problematical and incomplete enough to preclude any strong assertion of typicality anyway, we still wanted our study of agriculture and rural society and of local political economy to focus on a place that faced constraints and problems similar to those facing many other parts of the countryside. Third, we insisted that the county in which we were to work not be a model unit. We had already learned from our own previous work and that of our colleagues how politics and development could be seriously distorted in model localities, and thus how research focused on places exposed to the glare of national publicity and elite political conflict could carry many difficulties as well as advantages.[6] Yet we also requested to work in a county with some industry, so that we could study its relationship to agriculture and to county government.

Our hosts obliged every one of these requests and stipulations by selecting Shulu county. It is situated on the north China plain, about 65 kilometers east of Shijiazhuang, the capital of Hebei province, and about 250 kilometers south-southwest of Beijing (see Maps 1–3). It can be reached from Shijiazhuang by rail or highway in one to two hours. In 1978

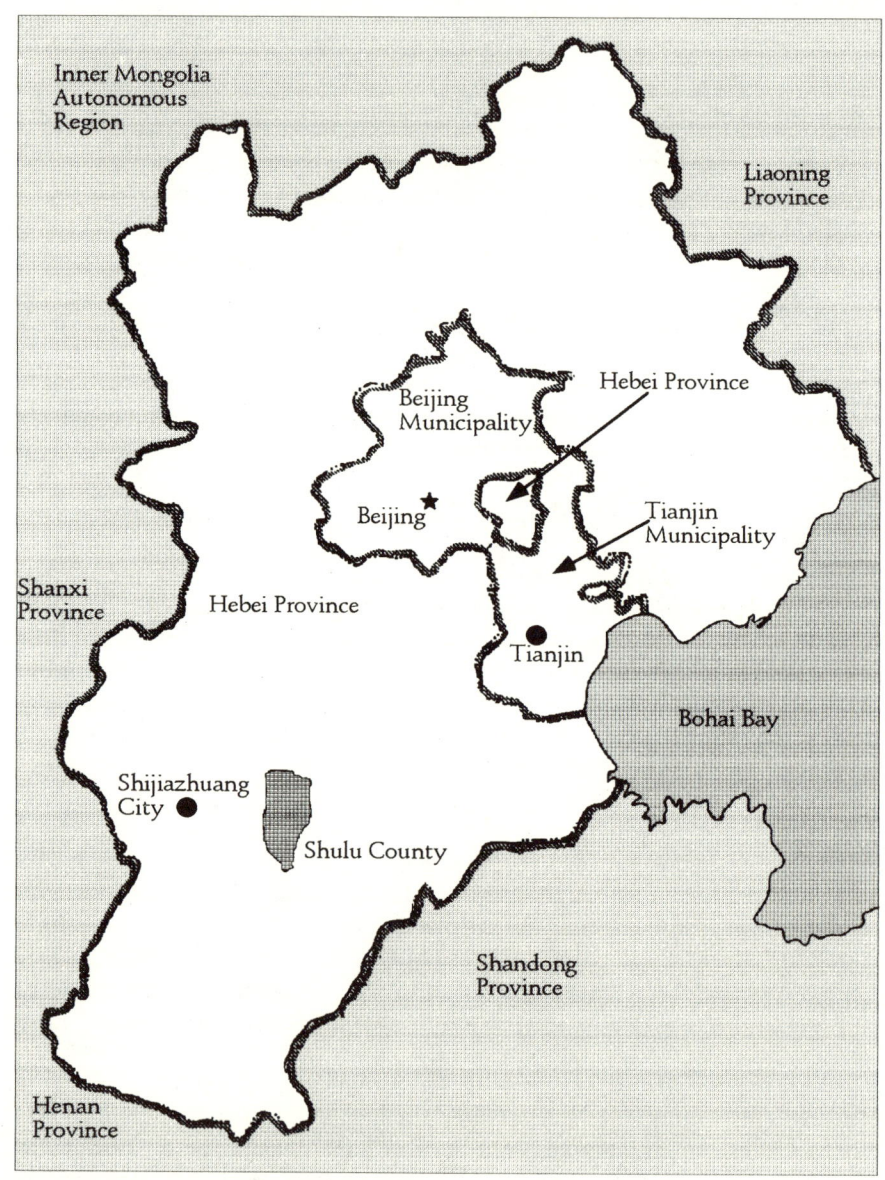

Map 2. Shulu county in regional context

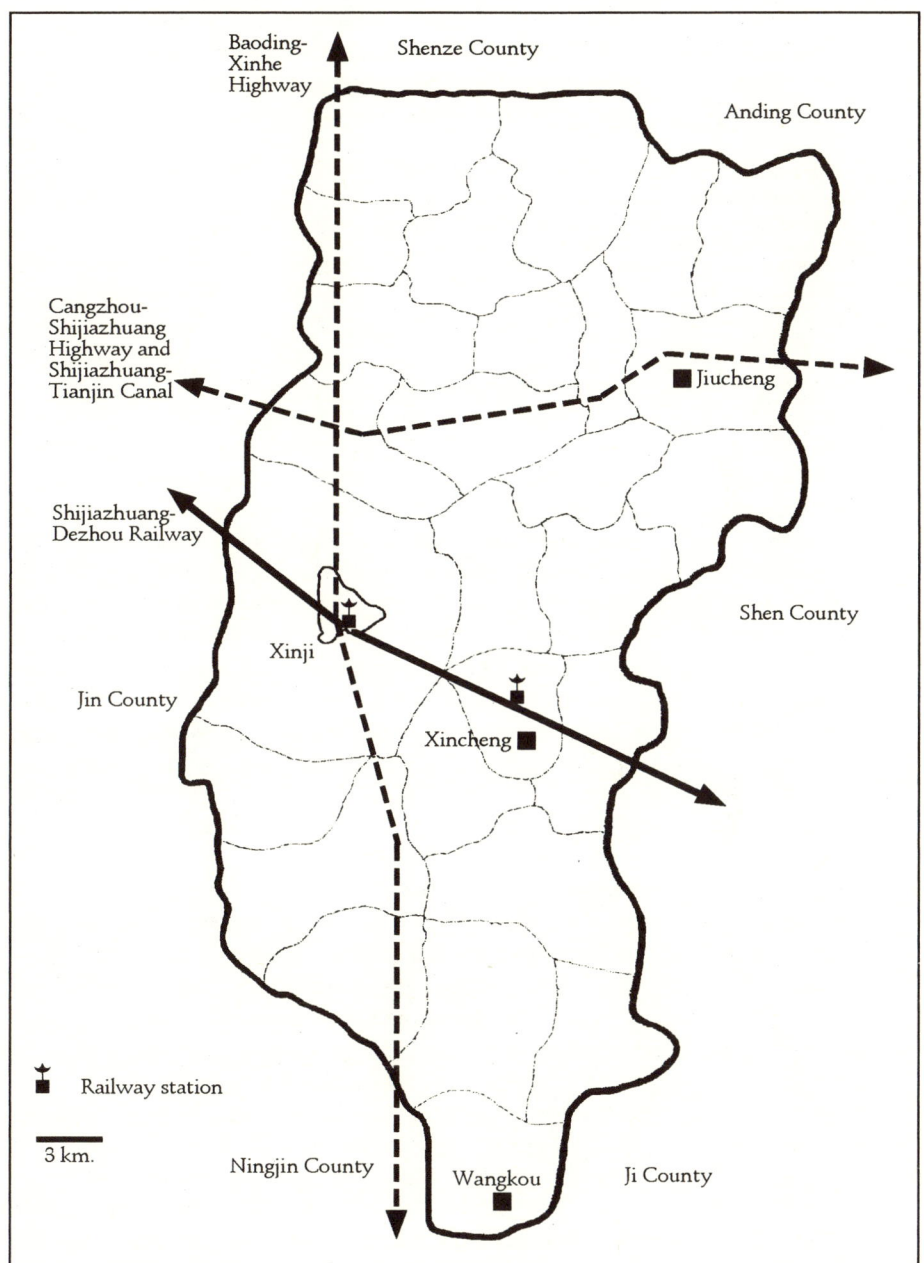

Map 3. Shulu county

TABLE 1
Shulu County, Shijiazhuang Prefecture, Hebei Province,
and National Basic Economic Indicators, 1978

	Shulu county	Shijiazhuang prefecture	Hebei province	China
Population per hectare of cultivated land	7.3	9.3	7.5	10
Grain production per capita (kg)	439	473	337	318
Cotton production per capita (kg)	10.6	5.3	2.0	2.1
Gross value of agricultural output per capita (yuan)	240	221	—	120
Gross value of industrial output per capita (yuan)	>302	142	—	445
Rural collective distributed income per capita (yuan)	88.4	84.5	75.7	74.0

NOTE: A dash indicates that no data were available.

it had half a million people, and a population density per unit of cultivated land that was about average for Hebei, though lower than prefectural or national averages (Table 1). Grain production per capita was above national and provincial averages, a function of Shulu's regional location, but it was lower in the context of its prefecture. The county had excelled historically in cotton production, and in 1979 had been designated a cotton production base area by Hebei province planners. While important, however, cotton accounted for only half as much cultivated land as grain, and produced only 13.6 percent of gross value of agricultural output (GVAO), compared to grain's 47.7 percent. Grain was by far the major crop, cotton an important but secondary specialty. Rural sidelines and enterprises were also relatively well developed, accounting for around one-third of GVAO. These combined lines of production gave Shulu a level of rural collective distributed income that was only a little higher than prefectural, provincial, or national averages. Including yearly income from private sources of around ¥14 per capita, Shulu's average annual per capita income of about ¥102 was well below the 1978 national average of ¥133.6 per year.

Where Shulu excelled, regionally speaking, was in industry. In 1978, gross value of industrial output per capita was over twice the prefectural average. Though Shulu was one of seventeen counties in the prefecture, with only 9 percent of the prefecture's population, it produced 13.1 percent of the prefecture's enterprise revenues in the state budget, and 14.2 percent of its total state revenues. Shulu accounted for no less than 41.7 percent of the prefecture's mostly industrial foreign export production. Despite these achievements, however, Shulu was no industrial paragon. Industrial output per capita was only two-thirds the national average. And Shulu industry's technological levels and product mix were still far from the cutting edge of Chinese industry, not to mention world industry.

Despite its industrial preeminence within Shijiazhuang prefecture, Shulu was not a model county, nor did it contain any subunits of national prominence or substantial notoriety. A small number of minor accolades received by Shulu and its subunits in the national press are the exceptions that only confirm the county's relative obscurity.[7] There is no evidence that Shulu has been the beneficiary of special largesse or attention within the Chinese state.

In 1979, our five-member research team spent twelve days in Shulu, sometimes working as a group and at other times dividing up to increase our coverage. Shulu officials asked us for the names of county government organs in whose work we were interested, and then arranged briefings with their representatives every morning and afternoon. In no case was a request rejected. The briefings were conducted in the presence of a representative of the Foreign Affairs Bureau of the county government and, in some cases, also of Hebei province, since our visit had been arranged through the Hebei provincial government. (The Provincial Foreign Affairs Bureau had also arranged briefings with officials of the prefecture and province offices in which we were interested, both before and after our trip to Shulu.) But despite the presence of their bureaucratic superiors, Shulu government officials were generally relaxed and spontaneous. More than once they aired their concerns about prefectural and provincial policies they felt would pose problems for Shulu. They were also not afraid to admit their ignorance about some of our questions, and when they did they were assiduous in doing subsequent searches through their files and getting back to us with their answers.

In addition to the briefings, we requested maps and detailed statistical records, and again almost all our requests were met. County officials also evinced a serious concern with statistical accuracy. The head of the Shulu Statistical Bureau began his first meeting with us with a long disquisition about the professional and even political importance of correct data. He explained gloomily how professional statistical work had been distorted and undervalued in years gone by—in particular during the Cultural Revolution decade. Throughout our work, other officials mentioned this problem from time to time, and they said they preferred, with regret, sometimes to give us no statistics rather than to pass along dubious ones.[8] We also had many opportunities to triangulate on key data by probing from several different sources, including briefings with various government offices at various levels as well as published materials. Where we encountered discrepancies, Shulu officials were patient in helping us resolve them. In addition to statistics, Shulu officials shared with us their own collection of news clippings, mostly from provincial newspapers.

We returned from our 1979 fieldwork and set about the task of organizing, explicating, and analyzing our findings. In the course of doing so, we found ourselves with more and bigger questions than we could answer on the basis of the information we had collected. Writing in the days when the economic reforms were dawning and the Maoist record in political economy was coming under attack, we wanted to know just how well or poorly the Shulu economy had done in the Mao period, and what positive and negative roles the county government had played in local development. As researchers who had worked on local affairs in Mao-period China, we wanted to establish just how much political and economic latitude the county government had enjoyed within the wider state, and how this was changing from the Mao to the Deng periods. How large was the surplus it produced, particularly in its relatively advanced industrial sector? How much of that surplus could the county government retain in Shulu? How much control did it have over the shape and planning of its development, and how did it exercise that control? Documentary research using the county's own clipping files as well as American libraries yielded some interesting sidelights and confirmation of many facts, but still not enough for us to be able to resolve some of these larger issues.

These frustrations eventually led the two of us back to Shulu in 1986.[9] The changes were startling. Even Shulu's name had changed. In May 1986 it was redesignated Xinji municipality (*shi*), under a national policy of identifying rural counties that had been relatively successful industrializers as prospective centers of further growth in their regions. Now Shulu was included directly as a line item in the Hebei province budget. It no longer reported to the prefecture. This appeared to put it in a slightly better position in its financial negotiations with higher levels of the state (see Chapter 4). But the redesignation did not involve any boundary modifications or perceptible changes in other administrative relationships. Meanwhile, the county seat of Xinji had blossomed into a burgeoning city replete with many new amenities and facilities, and bustling with commerce. Agriculture had grown apace, even though under the reforms the focus of state activity had clearly shifted to the urban areas. Industry was in the midst of complex readjustments.

Our findings in 1986, while extending those of 1979, did not contradict them. In many ways they confirmed the earlier data. For example, statistical series requested for 1979–86 generally dovetailed well with those through 1978 which we had received in 1979. And even though officials were very proud of what had been accomplished since 1979, they did not use the contrast to denounce or contradict what had gone before or what they had told us about it. Of course the 1986 work enabled us to correct mistakes that had been made in the 1979 research and clarify questions that had arisen in our attempts at analysis. The process of the research this time was the same as in 1979: briefings with representatives of government agencies of our choice every morning and afternoon, and collection of statistics and maps. By this time, though, our hosts had professionalized and systematized their work with us by insisting that we prepare outlines of our questions in advance, so that our interlocutors could come well prepared. Yet this did not appear to constrict or ritualize the information imparted to us. Officials were as willing as before to stop for explanations and detour for digressions. There was an air of somewhat greater informality in 1986 as well. For example, officials who brought sheaves of statistical tables for their own reference were without fail willing to hand them over to us to copy down and return the next day. (This also made our research far more efficient, as we no longer needed to use scarce time to take down data from briefings.)

On the basis of the 1986 research, the entire draft manuscript was completely reorganized and rewritten. We took one more opportunity to update our work in 1990, with the longest of our three field trips.[10] This time the changes were less stark than in 1986. The research atmosphere was not noticeably affected by the national political chill following the events of 1989. Our work proceeded with the same seriousness, efficiency, and apparent frankness of our earlier visits. Again the statistical data matched up well with previous series, and triangulated well.

All this having been said, we would like to make it clear also that we are most sharply aware of the limitations of our work. In all our visits, we have had only the most limited contact with the people of Shulu county, for example. We did not attempt to undertake our own social or economic surveys. Furthermore, we could probe only in the most indirect way the prevailing patterns of politics within the county government, or between it and the people of Shulu on the one hand and the other state and local organs it dealt with on a continual basis on the other. Our original aspiration to evaluate in a detailed and systematic way the economic and social policy performance of the Shulu county government ultimately had to be set aside because the sheer volume and depth of information that would be required proved impossible to gather even in the considerable span of time we were able to work in Shulu. Mindful of these and other limitations, we have consequently chosen a focus for this work appropriate to the kind of information and data that we could collect. This, then, is a book about the institutions of the Shulu county government: the roles they have played, the activities in which they have engaged, and the choices they have made to promote and shape economic development, and the effects of those roles, activities, and choices.

Chapter 2 sketches the historical and material bases of contemporary life in Shulu, and the patterns of human settlement and built environment as they have developed historically. Chapter 3 looks at the county government, focusing on its institutions, personnel, cost, and ethos. This leads directly to a study of the county government's finances in Chapter 4. We analyze them in terms of moving structures—looking at changing institutional arrangements—and of processes such as revenue and expenditure flows and the financial regulations that accompanied and shaped them. This in turn sets the stage for analyzing the Shulu county government's roles, activities, and choices in four arenas of economic and social life. Chapter 5 focuses on industry, including issues about the complex forms of ownership and structures of administration, the disposition of profits, and several aspects of labor and employment. Chapter 6 explores the county government's role in the institutions, development, rationalization, and regulation of commerce, encompassing collective, private, and foreign trade. The county government's roles in urban development—environmental protection, city planning, land use control, and housing and real estate regulation—are studied in Chapter 7. Chapter 8 takes up the county government's roles in rural development, including infrastructure development (water conservancy, road construction), rural industrialization, specialization (in orchard products), cropping, organization (the responsibility system), land use regulation, and migration control. Some of the most important themes and conclusions of the study are summarized in Chapter 9.

Insofar as was possible and appropriate, we have striven within each chapter and section to organize the discussion chronologically, so that the late Mao period (generally, 1970–78) and the early Deng period (1979–90) may be compared. We find here remarkable changes over time, of course. But there are many interesting continuities between the two periods as well.

CHAPTER 2

Historical and Material Settings

It is generally believed that a county government was founded in Shulu during the Han dynasty,[1] though local people are able to trace it back with confidence only as far as 1520, during the reign of the Zhengde emperor of the Ming. A minor controversy surrounds the derivation of the county's name. One version has it that a Tang emperor hunting in the area captured and tied up a deer (*shu lu*). But local people today tell a more exciting tale. Through the Tang Dynasty, the county was known as Lucheng.[2] But when An Lushan, the legendary leader of a violent and protracted peasant rebellion, was finally caught and incarcerated there, the place was renamed Shulu—the place where "Lu was restrained" (*shu lu*).[3]

Even before the Ming dynasty (1368–1644), the Shulu towns of Xinji, then known as Lianguandian, and Muqiu, a township in west central Shulu, were major national centers of fur and leather production. In the late Ming, when the imperial capital moved from Nanjing to Beijing, traffic passing between the two great cities provided another economic boon to the towns of Shulu. Through much of the Qing dynasty (1644–1911) Xinji prospered, mainly on the strength of its fur and leather sector, which eventually supported as many as 50,000 households.

By the late Qing dynasty, and apparently for quite a few centuries before, Shulu's borders were already its present ones.[4] But internally, intermediate structures of administration and transport have changed drastically. During the late Qing, Shulu was subdivided into eighteen districts (*tuan*) in addition to what was then the capital, Xincheng.[5] Of these, only six, and Xincheng itself, later became commune seats (and subsequently townships). In other words, fewer than one-fourth of the 1979 commune seats and present-day townships were administrative centers directly below the county level as recently as a century ago. And even the borders of these seven districts did not correspond very closely to those of the communes that later came to be centered on them. Moreover, by 1936 the eighteen *tuan* were gone, replaced by five *qu*.[6] Shulu, then, offers a precaution about Skinner's widely accepted analysis of the relationship of traditional and contemporary units of local governance at intermediate levels between the village and the county.[7] Skinner implicitly assumed historical continuity of the loci of townships, on the basis of which he posed the problem of whether and when the new rural institutions of the post-1949 period were aligned with them. In Shulu the old township structure itself had changed significantly, so there was little in the way of existing historical structures on which the new state could or was required to base new institutions. The post-1949 period was, then, not the first time that institutional transformations took place between the village and the county level.

The sharp discontinuity in historical structure is also reflected in shifting patterns of transport. Maps 4–6 depict the major roads of Shulu in 1906, 1970, and 1980, respectively. Reflecting the depth of the disruptions and dislocations Shulu has experienced this century, the roadway network seems to have been finer, and the towns of the county more directly connected with one another, in 1906 than they were in 1970. By then, for example, there were no direct linkages from Jiucheng, a major market town and Shulu's former capital, to the capital, Xinji, or to Xincheng, also a major market town and former capital. None of the roads connecting Shulu to other counties in 1906 still existed in 1970. In another major departure from the past, the Cangzhou-Shijiazhuang highway, a major inter- and intracounty route during the Anti-Japanese War and still today, does not even appear on the 1906 map. Clearly, the patterns of intra- and intercounty transport had changed markedly. (Yet map 6 shows that during the final decade of the Mao period, much was accomplished to extend and rationalize Shulu's road network.)[8] Down at the grass-roots or community level much greater continuity appears again, despite the heavy warfare before 1949 and the political reorganizations that occurred afterward. In 1906 there were 314 villages, and in 1936 there were 327; by 1979 there were 329. These relatively constant figures do not seem to mask changes such as the replacement of old settlements with new ones. Every single village mentioned in the Qing gazetteer can be found on contemporary maps.[9] Thus, over the past century Shulu county has not changed much in its overall shape or its pattern of village settlement, but there have been very great changes in the intermediate administrative structures and physical infrastructures.

These discontinuities probably owe a great deal to the warfare and

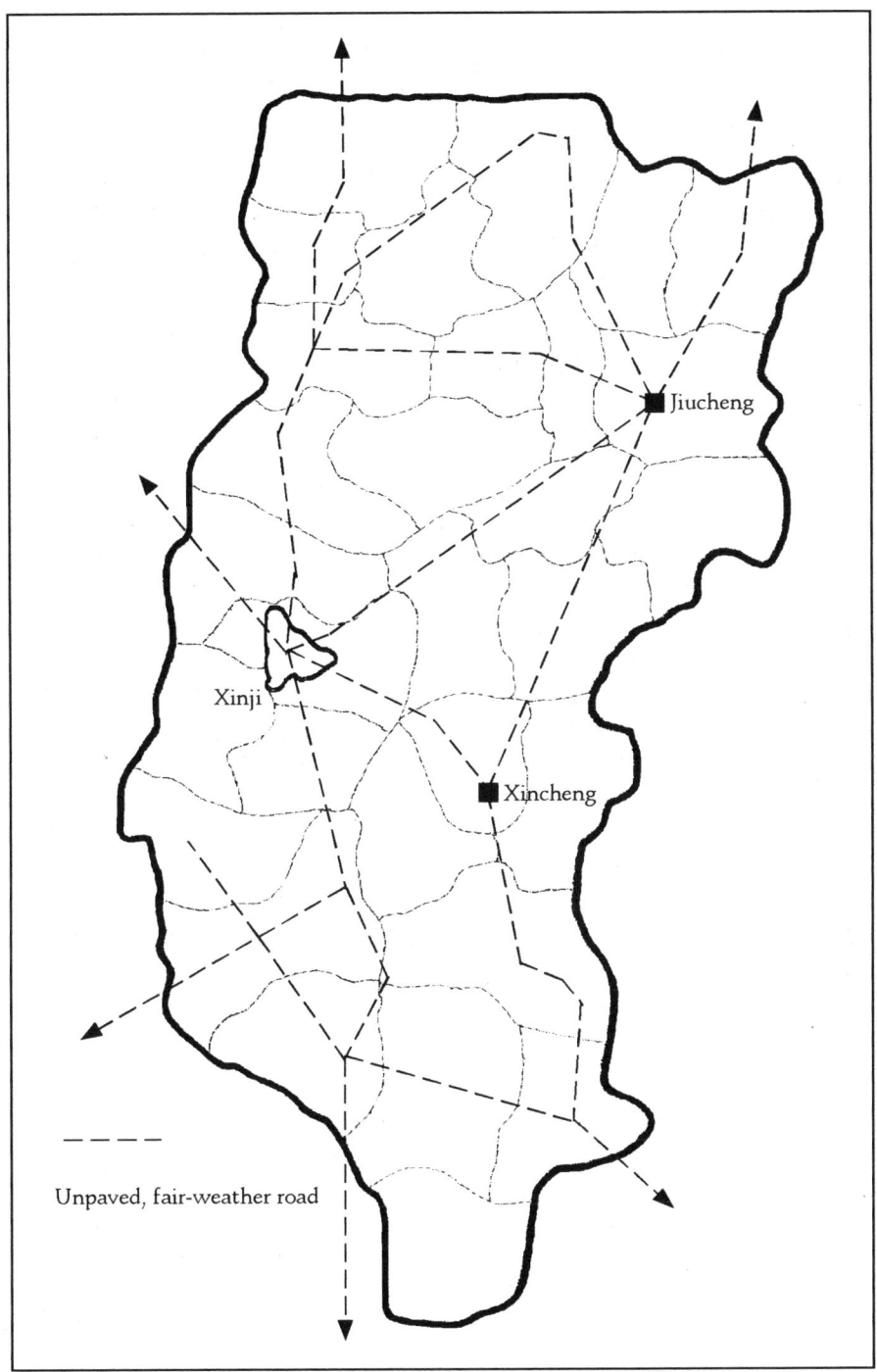

Map 4. Major roads in Shulu county, 1906
SOURCE: Information from *Shulu xiangtu zhi*, superimposed on a modern map of Shulu.

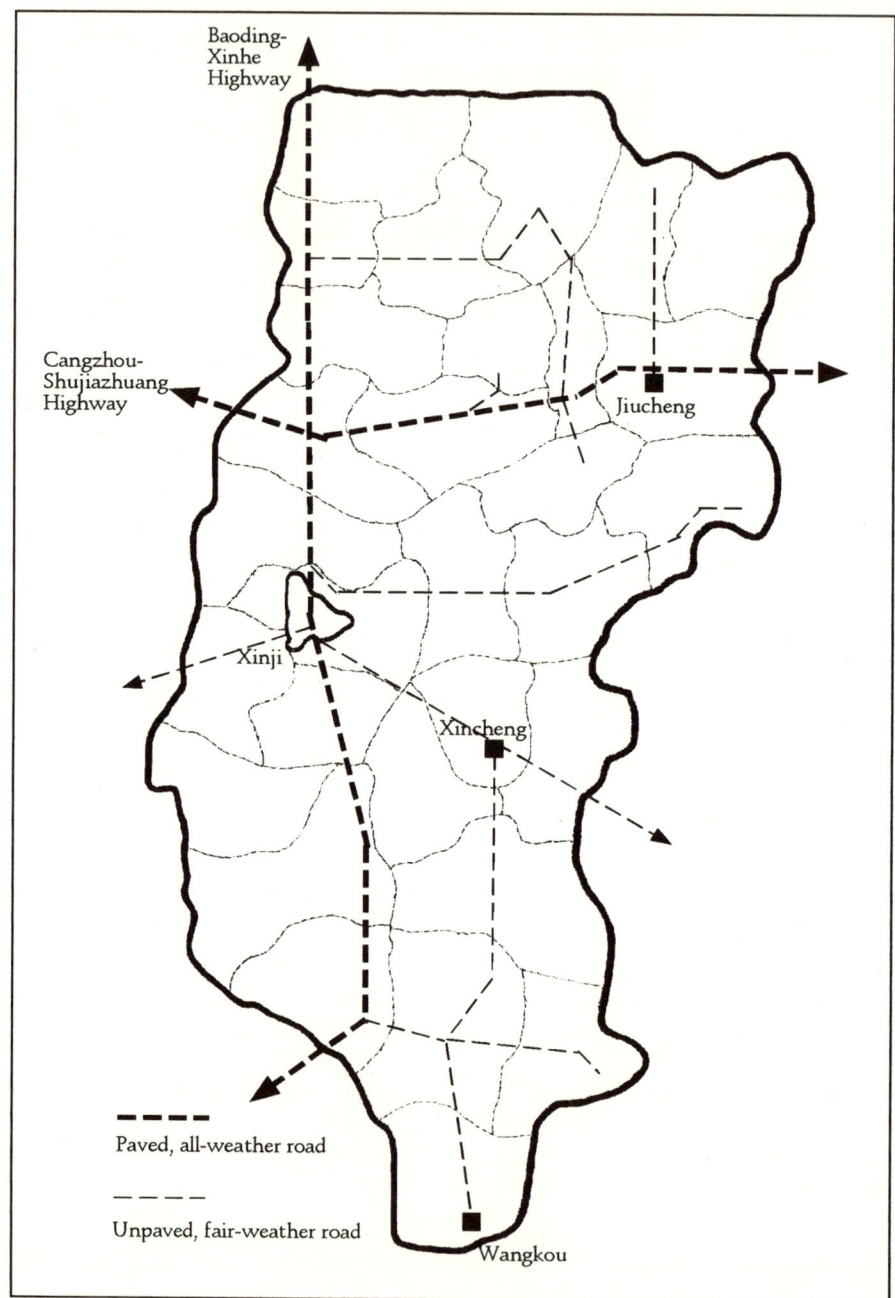

Map 5. Major roads in Shulu county, 1970

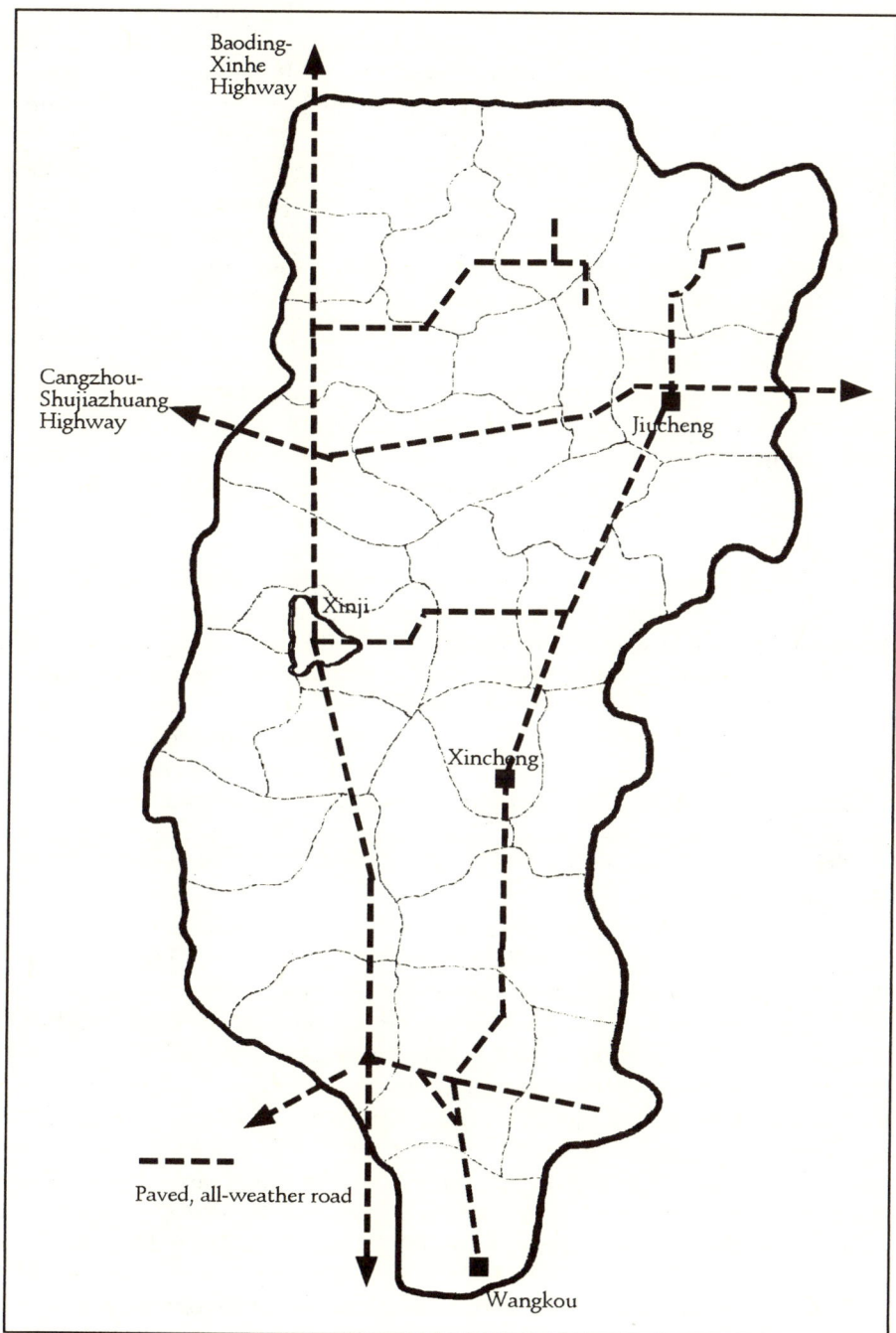

Map 6. Major roads in Shulu county, 1980

attendant political and economic crises that have been visited upon Shulu. The county was intimately involved in the Boxer Rebellion, the Chinese Revolution, and the civil and anti-Japanese wars associated with it. In 1901, Western forces allied against the Boxers thrust southward from Baoding, burning the former county seat of Jiucheng to the ground and killing over four thousand people there alone.[10] The first secret Communist Party organization in the county dates from 1932. Following the defeat of the Nationalist forces under the famous General Lü Zhengcao at the battle of Fanjiazhuang (in north central Shulu), a People's Self-Defense Army was established and later incorporated into the Eighth Route Army.

The Japanese occupation hit Shulu hard. In order to occupy Shijiazhuang, the Japanese first had to take Xinji. They bombed the town in 1937, driving out all but 3,000 of its 50,000 people. By early 1938, anti-Japanese mobilization committees and mass organizations of remaining workers, peasants, women, youth, and intellectuals were formed, and anti-Japanese military forces were established in every district (*qu*) and village of Shulu. In spring of 1939, Japanese soldiers again invaded Shulu, occupying Xincheng, Xinji, and Jiucheng. Communist-led forces occupied the smaller villages of northern and southern Shulu. The county was split. The patriotic forces redrew Shulu's boundaries, recombining parts of it with three other neighboring counties.[11] (Immediately after the cessation of hostilities, Shulu was reconstituted in its traditional shape.) During the Hundred Regiments offensive, the Japanese-sponsored puppet government drove out an anti-Japanese county government that had been headquartered at Xincheng. On May Day, 1942, the Japanese initiated their infamous May 1 Mopping Up Campaign in the Jizhong military region, which included Shulu. They used their standard tactic of encirclement, building fortified strongholds every five kilometers and pillboxes every one and one-half kilometer. From these citadels, the notorious "three-all policy" (*san guang zhengce*) of killing, burning, and looting entire villages was carried out, provoking terror and destruction that is still recalled by local people. Small bands of local irregulars along with units of the Eighth Route Army carried on a guerrilla war against the Japanese during 1943–44.

During the civil war that followed the end of the Anti-Japanese War, Shulu was a liberated rear area. Land reform began in the fall of 1947, apparently in advance of the promulgation of an outline land law by the North China Bureau of the Communist Party in the winter of 1947–48. Land reform was complete by the start of the growing season of 1948. Even more significant for future development, in the late 1940's the revolutionary government built in Shulu several industrial plants, many war-related,[12] and a school and university—the North China United University (Huabei Lianda)—that trained political and administrative cadres, teachers, and junior high school students. One factory would evolve into a large chemical factory that has been a leader in Shulu's modern industrialization. Huabei Lianda evolved into the Xinji Middle School, a national "keypoint" institution—that is, a school designated for investment of extra resources and for high admission standards—which has trained many of the technical specialists and professionals who have made valuable contributions to Shulu's economic development.

The Historical Economy and Its Implications for Modern Development

The material base of the Shulu county economy contains only a little to presage its modern development. It had a poor endowment of natural resources, serious soil problems in some areas, and a high population-to-land ratio. It was also very prone to military and natural disasters.[13] The authors of the county gazetteer described the local economy as in serious stagnation and even decline in the nineteenth century, with weak, empty markets and poor agricultural conditions.[14] Yet historical records also describe a certain development of specialized production and external commercial linkages that may have helped prepare this poor county for economic development once more modern inputs became available and Shulu began to develop links with growing regional, national, and even international economies.

In 1906, 60 percent of county cropland was planted to grain, much of it poor varieties.[15] Production was insufficient to meet local needs, so Shulu historically had imported grain from other parts of China. It paid for these imports partly by selling cotton, which it grew on 30 percent of its land. It also exported to other localities certain other specialized cash crops like peanuts, fruit, vegetables, and lumber, which occupied the remaining 10 percent of cultivated land. Early on, then, Shulu agriculture, though not prosperous, demonstrated a certain degree of specialization.[16] Historically, animal husbandry has been a problem in Shulu, posing a serious obstacle to the development of agriculture and also, curiously, to the very important local fur and leather tanning industry. Most large animals used for draft or for their hides had to be shipped in. Presumably this stemmed from a shortage or irregular supply of fodder due to the periodic floods and droughts to which the county has been prone.

Lacking a strong agricultural base to support its large population, Shulu attempted to adapt by developing manufacturing and some minor food processing. The absence of any significant raw materials forced it to procure its key manufacturing inputs from other parts of China. The most important county industry historically, and one that remains prominent today, was fur and leather goods.

> Our municipality was already known by the sixteenth century as a national center of fur and leather production, since it already monopolized 70 percent of national fur and leather production. In the Guangxu period [1871–1908], we processed 600,000 hides and 500,000 *jin* [=275 tons] of furs annually, turning out more than one hundred

types of products and exporting them to Japan, England and the United States.[17]

Skins and pelts were brought in from the Beijing area and even further away, "beyond the Great Wall."[18] Mainly these were processed into semi-finished items like pigskins, cowhides, horsetails and so forth, though some finished goods such as fur coats and brushes were produced and found their way into national and even international markets. So did wool products like carpets, blankets, hats, and flannel, until they were forced out of business by foreign competition.[19] For a time significant banking, including foreign currency exchanges, flourished. There was also some local agricultural product processing, such as cotton spinning and oil pressing, with products destined mainly for markets within the county. But these did not satisfy local demand, which had to be met by trade with other Chinese localities.

In short, Shulu had had a lively manufacturing sector, but one that was not articulated very well in Shulu's own agricultural or raw material inputs or to its final markets. For a relatively remote rural county, it was closely tied into regional, national, and international markets.[20] But China's generalized political, military, and economic crises during the first half of this century took their toll: while the 1906 gazetteer spoke of Xinji as being as thick with factories as "trees in a forest,"[21] with the onset of the Anti-Japanese War the economy was worse than decimated. The very same war, however, prompted the creation of small new industries that would lead with the coming of peace to the growth of a far more diversified and modern industrial base than Shulu had ever known before.

Overall, then, Shulu was not well endowed with an agricultural base or with natural resources that could enrich it historically or fuel its economic growth and modernization in more recent years. But two interrelated features of Shulu's historical economy helped position it for development in the state socialist period. The first was its elaborate links with regional, national, and international economies, based on specialized manufacturing industries that traded inputs and outputs with other places. These industries provided the capital and the entrepreneurial, informational, and personal impulses and linkages that were used to expand the material base of the economy—particularly in industry—when new technologies and markets came on the scene starting in the 1940's. Second, the county had a major production center and commercial entrepôt at Xinji. In 1936 it was almost as large as the next three largest towns in the county combined.[22] It contained the commercial, entrepreneurial, and transport linkages, and the skilled labor force, that could readily attract and generate investment and fuel economic growth. The Japanese invasion and the civil war that followed provided a turning point for the Shulu economy. They destroyed the old industrial economy, but also provided the seeds for recovery. These would only flourish, though, with the coming of sustained peace, the development of modern transportation, and the rise of a state capable of organizing the local economy, providing infrastructure and education, and developing linkages with the wider national and international economies, as sources of capital and technology and as markets.

Economic and Human Geography

The Shulu way of life remains essentially rural but is rapidly urbanizing. The land is flat and ocher to yellow in color. There is almost no grass anywhere. The powdery earth fills the wind with grit in dry weather and turns to ankle-deep mud after just a sprinkle of rain. Slender trees line almost every one of the county's string-straight roads and form windbreaks between vast fields, but are scarce elsewhere. Low farmhouses made of mud brick and thatch huddle in small groups with their backs to the traffic, a miscellaneous mixture of motorcycles, bicycles, trucks, and ox- or donkey-drawn carts. In appearance Shulu is indistinguishable from the rest of the north China plain except for its smattering of modern urban life in Xinji.

THE NATURAL BASE

Shulu agriculture is oriented largely to grain production, but with a strong historical specialization in cotton.[23] Located well out on the north China plain 65 kilometers east of Shijiazhuang, it is not a suburb. Its population density is too high to permit much commercial animal husbandry, even though its vibrant fur and leather industry could provide a very sizable market for hides and pelts. The rest of its industry does not provide much demand for agricultural products, though in 1990 local economic planners were attempting to promote some industrial growth in crop and crop by-product processing. Nonetheless, some vegetables and oil-bearing crops are produced for local demand, and fruit production for local, regional, and national markets existed even during the Mao period and has been expanding since, with an eye toward exports in the future.

Practically all of the county's arable land was already being cultivated in 1978, and 97 percent of it was irrigated.[24] Soil and water conditions vary significantly throughout Shulu. In the northernmost tier of six townships, water is generally sweet. In 1979 the water table was at a depth of about 20 meters, necessitating drilling to a depth of around 42 and sometimes 60 meters. Soil generally poses no problem except in the extreme northwest, the county's pocket of deepest poverty. In the central region water is also sweet, and lies approximately 15 meters below the surface. Soil conditions there are the best: land yields of grain and cotton in this region were the highest in the county in 1978, and the great bulk of cultivated land there could guarantee bumper harvests despite what officials termed "ordinary" waterlogging or one rainless year.[25]

The natural water and soil conditions of the 12 southern townships have posed much greater problems. The water table there is higher than in the north or center, causing seasonal flooding. Worse yet, subterranean water is alkaline, so it damages crops when it reaches their roots. Shulu lies on the western edge of a region known as the "Heilonggang" (Black Dragon Harbor), a fearsome name for an environment much less hospitable to residents of agricultural communities than it might be to the mythical beast. The Heilonggang had an average annual food-grain shortage of 352,000 tons between 1953 and 1973, and is therefore regarded by Chinese planners as a "drag" on Hebei agriculture.[26] The problems endemic to southern Shulu are those of the Heilonggang. They provide the conditions for its relatively low population density, both historically and at present. A major county-organized water conservancy project constructed in 1977–78 was directed especially at the problem of waterlogging and drainage in this area.[27]

BUILT ENVIRONMENT

On this natural base have been built a large number of settlements of various sizes and functions, transport and communications networks, and public facilities (see photographs).

Transport Arteries

Shulu is well connected by highway and rail to the wider region, and also possesses a developed set of internal roads. The Cangzhou-Shijiazhuang highway, recently widened to carry large truck traffic, and the Andong highway traverse the county in all four directions, linking it directly to the national roadway network.[28] The Shijiazhuang-Dezhou Railway has stations at Xinji and Xincheng towns, and by 1986 eighteen trains departed daily for final destinations of Tianjin, Dezhou, Shanghai, Changchun, Jinan, Xi'an, Taiyuan, Wuhan, Shijiazhuang and Changzhi. Shulu economic planners note that these arteries give the county developmental advantages by putting it in direct touch with Shanxi coal supplies and with what they called "the Shijiazhuang-Xinji-Hengshui-Dezhou-Jinan economic belt" as well as the major economic centers of Tianjin and Beijing.[29] Internally, by 1980 paved roads reached to twenty-three of the thirty communes of the county outside Xinji; by 1986 the network extended to every township and work had begun linking up smaller settlements.[30]

Patterns of Settlement and Administration

As noted in Chapter 1, population density in Shulu county is about average for Hebei province. It tends to be concentrated in the central region, where the county seat is located.[31] The pattern of built settlements is also thickest there.[32] The biggest population center is the city (*chengzhen*) of Xinji, the county seat. In 1982 it had a resident population of 44,771, about 9 percent of the county's total population of half a million. This included 31,704 urban (literally, "non-rural") people (*fei nongye renkou*) and 13,067 rural people (nongye renkou) who were members of the Xinji People's Commune.³³ With only 4.69 square kilometers of land in the built-up area, Xinji—even counting only legal residents³⁴—had a very high population density of 9,546 per square kilometer. That was around half the population density of downtown Shanghai.³⁵ This presented a serious problem to Xinji's urban administrators and planners. As of 1990, the population of the original city had nearly doubled since 1982, to 82,000. About 35 percent of these people continued to hold rural household registrations, and around 65 percent were classified as urban. Moreover, another 68,000 or so lived in four periurban *xiang* (townships) that had been incorporated in 1986 into the city of Xinji as urban administrative districts (*jiedao banshichu*).³⁶ In this way, Xinji became a diversified city with five urban administrative districts covering 122 square kilometers of rural and urban places, and agricultural, industrial, and commercial space. What could be called greater Xinji, then, was home to 150,000 people in 1990. Yet, largely because of systematic urban planning (see Chapter 7) and continued regulation of population movement (discussed in Chapter 8), in the late 1980's the main streets of Xinji, though bustling, were still very far from the level of overcrowding associated with China's major cities.³⁷ The exception was on special market fair days (*miao hui*), when pedestrian traffic downtown could be so thick as to bring even the most determined shopper to a dead halt. Xinji officials were making plans for the continued controlled growth of the urban population: the downtown of greater Xinji was not to exceed a population of 200,000 by the year 2000, but after that Xinji was slated in the Hebei provincial plan to grow gradually to become a "middle-sized city" with a downtown population of 400,000 to 500,000. Shulu, then, affords us a good example of the pattern of small-scale urbanization that has been both a characteristic of Chinese society and a continuing goal of its development planners.

The central region of the county also contains two other large towns—Jiucheng (Old City) and Xincheng (New City)—which have in the past served as county seats, the latter as recently as during the Anti-Japanese War. As late as the 1980's, these were the only settlements besides Xinji with somewhat complex patterns of crisscrossing downtown streets. The center of the county is also the area of thickest development of transportation infrastructure, including rail lines, highways, and bus routes.

Shulu contains a range of settlements, which can be graded along four scales: official Chinese geographical category, administrative function, marketing function, and size and complexity (Table 2). There has been a tendency for the four kinds of attributes to scale together, but their parity is only rough—those communities higher on one scale have not necessarily been higher on another. Moreover, the first two scales have changed with the advent of the Deng period, and the third has been reinvigorated, reflecting the recent relative emphasis on commerce as a criterion of a community's importance.

TABLE 2
Hierarchies of Settlements in Shulu County, 1979

Name	Official geographic designation	Administrative status	Market status	Size and complexity
Xinji	City (chengzhen)	County seat, county government local center, and seat of two communes	Intermediate	27,369 people; large, complex downtown
Jiucheng, Xincheng	Small cities or large towns (xiao chengzhen)	County government local center, commune seat, and former county seat	Intermediate	Several thousand people; small, complex downtown
Zhangguzhuang, Weibo, Hemujing, Nanzhiqiu, Guoxi	(Market) towns (zhen)	County government local center and commune seat	Standard	Small population; simple downtown
Xinleitou, Fanjiazhuang, Xixiaowang, Mazhuang, Mengjiazhuang	Villages (xiang cun)	Commune seat	Standard	Small population; simple downtown
18 others	Villages (xiang cun)	Commune seat	Local green market (yao dian) and general store only	Small population; simple downtown

THE LATE MAO PERIOD   In terms of official geographic categories, the Shulu county of 1978 contained the city (chengzhen) of Xinji, the two large towns (xiao chengzhen) of Jiucheng and Xincheng, ten market towns (zhen) and 316 rural villages and hamlets (xiang cun). In administrative terms, Xinji was the seat of county government and also the headquarters of two "rural" people's communes: Xinji Commune, an agricultural and industrial sideline production unit located entirely within the city, and Chengguan (City Gate) Commune, a more agricultural unit whose fields lay on the periphery and out into the suburbs of the city. The two large towns and ten market towns also served as commune headquarters, as did eighteen other villages around the county. In other words, commune headquarters in Shulu could be found at all four levels of the official geographic scale, from the city down to the village.

Moreover, in contrast with the commonplace that in the Mao period the commune was the level of administration immediately below the county, the Shulu county government maintained seven administrative subcenters scattered around the county outside of Xinji.[38] Two of these were the large towns of Jiucheng and Xincheng, and the other five were market towns (Map 7). All of these communities had served as headquarters of township (da xiang) governments before 1958, and also of the

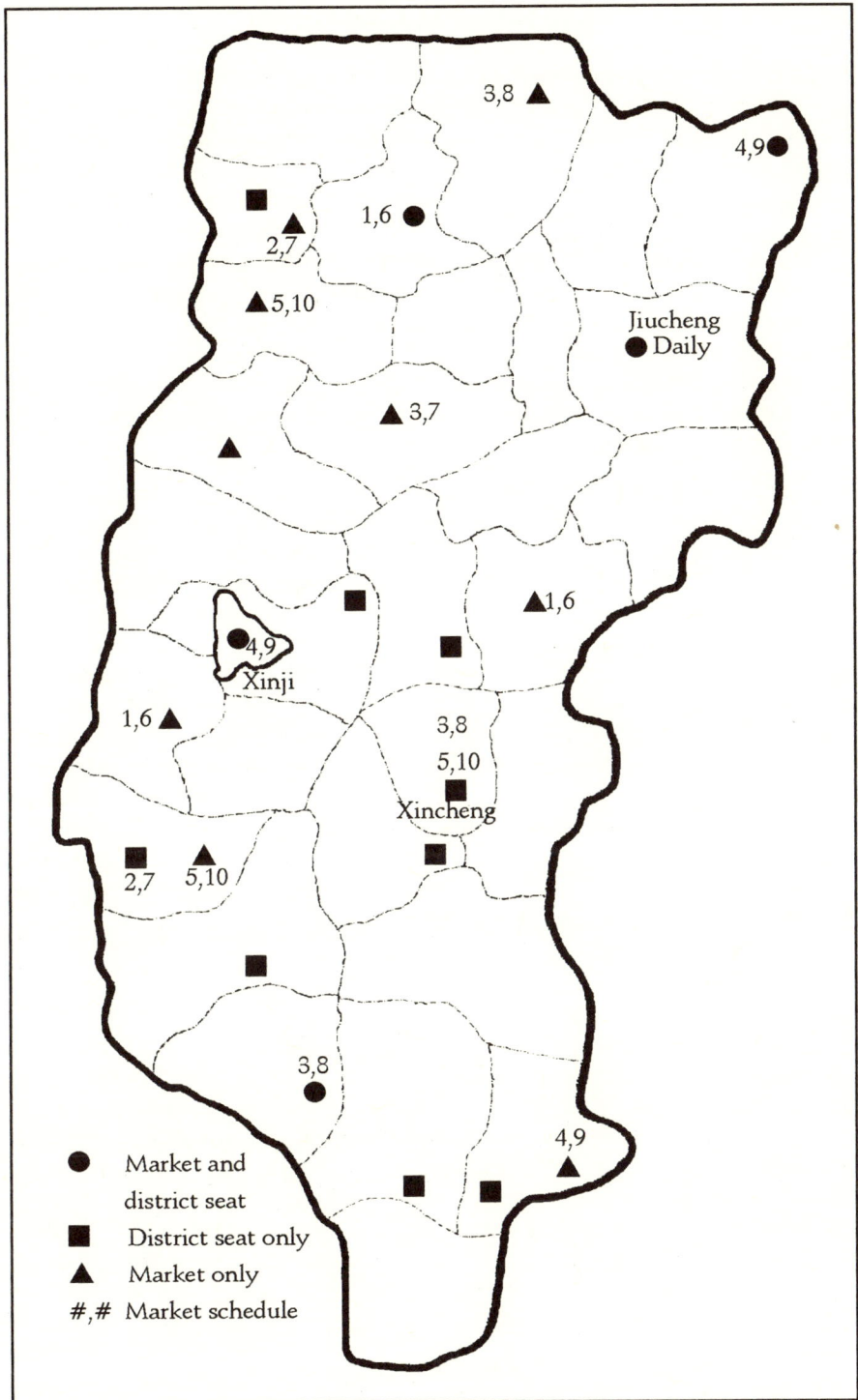

Map 7. Hierarchy of central places in Shulu county, 1979

original large communes formed in 1958. In 1979 all were still headquarters of the smaller communes that had been formed after the larger ones were subdivided. The historical continuity of these seven places is underscored by the fact that all six of them that had periodic markets in 1906 continued to have such fairs eighty years later. They even met on the very same schedules as before.[39]

Shulu contained thirteen markets in 1979. Those at Xinji, Jiucheng and Xincheng were classified as intermediate markets. Then there were ten more places with periodic markets, which were found at various levels of the other central place hierarchies. Only five of these, however, were designated in formal administrative terms as "market towns." Table 2 and Map 7 illustrate the situation as of 1979, before the major changes of the Deng reforms had begun.

THE DENG PERIOD By 1986, the situation had shifted. Xinji had annexed as "urban administrative districts" the four former communes (by then redubbed townships) surrounding it as well as the one that had existed inside its borders.[40] A major regional market had also been restored there. At the next level down in the official geographic hierarchy were six market towns (zhen), a designation assigned by the provincial authorities to the more economically developed of the townships. The two former county seats and large towns (xiao chengzhen) of Jiucheng and Xincheng were reclassified downward to market towns (zhen), and two other former market towns were demoted simply to townships (xiang).[41] Perhaps the very rapid growth of Xinji and its markets was acting as a magnet to draw business away from some of the more minor markets in its vicinity. Only Wangkou, the southernmost and formerly impoverished commune that has become an exemplar of the success of economic reform in the Deng period, had its designation raised from a village (cun) to a market town (zhen).[42] All the other former communes were simply converted into townships (xiang).

Table 3 and Map 7 summarize the situation. A comparison of Table 2 with Table 3 shows how the dissociation among the four hierarchies and the general complexity of the urban structure have increased in the Deng period. For example, three urban administrative districts had their own central settlements, while two did not. Both market towns and villages could have standard or local markets. In 1986 there were four levels of markets instead of three. Indeed, county officials said the restoration of markets in the early reform years occurred spontaneously and in accordance with preexisting patterns. This meant that they were not necessarily located in township centers or, despite their name, "market towns" (zhen). Administratively, two very distinct forms—urban administrative districts (banshichu) and township or town governments (xiang or zhen zhengfu)—existed directly below the county level, where in 1978 there had only been the commune.[43] Clearly the complications of uneven social

TABLE 3
Hierarchies of Settlements in Shulu County, 1986

Name	Official geographic designation	Administrative status	Market status	Size and complexity
Xinji	City (*shi*)	Seat of Xinji municipality; includes four surrounding administrative districts and one in the town	Central market (daily) and intermediate market (periodic)	130,000 legal residents plus thousands of documented and undocumented others; includes suburban rural areas
Chengdong, Xinghua	Parts of Xinji city	Administrative districts (*banshichu*)	Partake of Xinji city markets	Centers are parts of Xinji city urban area; also include suburban countryside
Chengxi, Chengnan, Chengbei	Parts of Xinji city	Administrative districts (*banshichu*)	Partake of Xinji city markets	Simple town centers up to 5 km from Xinji city center; include suburban countryside
Xincheng	Market town (*zhen*)	Township (*xiang*)	Intermediate[a]	Several thousand people; small, complex downtown
Jiucheng, Nanzhiqiu, Weibo, Zhangguzhuang	Market towns	Townships	Standard[b]	Small populations; simple downtowns
Wangkou	Market town	Township	Local[c]	Small population; simple downtown
Hemujing, Muqiu	Large villages (*xiang*)	Townships	Standard[b]	Small populations; simple downtowns
17 others	Villages (*xiang cun*)	Townships	Local[c]	Small populations; simple downtowns

[a] Shulu officials used the term "especially large market" (*te da jishi*).
[b] Officials used the term "big market" (*da ji*).
[c] Officials used the term "ordinary market" (*yiban jishi*).

development were more fully reflected in the central place hierarchy of 1986 than in that of 1979.

Public Facilities

By the end of the 1970's telecommunications reached at least to every commune seat, in the form of wired broadcast and telephone networks.[44] The county was dotted with ten hospitals and nine middle schools; by

1988, one more hospital and six schools had been added.[45] In 1978 Xinji contained a number of large stores, small specialized shops, a bus station, a social center, a small library, and an air-cooled (but not air-conditioned) theater. The main thoroughfare was paved, but many principal side streets were not. By 1986 the city had installed new sewers, widened and paved key roadways off the main artery, built a paved ring road around the downtown and underpasses to cross the railway, and put up large new downtown buildings including shops and, most dramatically, a large modern theater, a "workers' cultural palace," an enormous shopping center, and a large park replete with a little lake, a zoo, and amusement rides (see photographs).

Two examples capture parts of the situation outside Xinji. In 1978 Jiucheng, the second largest town, had a pre-1949 school building and a wide but unpaved main street, flanked by low buildings put up both before and after 1949 (see photographs). By 1986, a multistory township headquarters and a large new theater had been added. Plans were afoot to widen and pave main streets. In 1990, seven years after rapid growth there had begun to make Wangkou the exemplar of economic resuscitation under the Deng reforms, it still had the appearance of its historical poverty. The main street did not have a single building that looked as if it had been put up since 1949. On the contrary, the buildings were in various states of disrepair, collapse, and (in a first hopeful sign) demolition in anticipation of a major widening and reconstruction of the downtown street.

Summary

Shulu county is in many ways an unexceptional place. It is located well out on the north China plain, in a rural rather than suburban setting. Its economy is traditionally agricultural, and still today most of its residents make their living from the land. It has not been a model area or test site for particular policies, or the beneficiary of extraordinary state assistance.

Yet it does have several distinctive features. Shulu has had a historical comparative advantage in cotton, though under Maoist pricing and agricultural planning this actually proved to be more of a burden than a boon to economic development. More advantageous was its location astride a major railway and highway and the presence of a keypoint school that has trained technical specialists who have been a major force in the county's economic modernization. Its most significant economic features are its relatively advanced industry and the strong and burgeoning pattern of small-scale urbanization and commercialization, especially in the county seat of Xinji.

CHAPTER 3

The Shulu County Government

The organization of county government in Shulu was fairly simple, even spare, during the first thirty years following the Communist Party's victory in 1949. In 1979, when Shulu's population was already at about the half-million mark, the county government administrative apparatus was made up of only twenty major bureaus and departments, and it was staffed by a grand total of just 945 administrative cadres and 200 support workers. Though small in overall size and fairly streamlined in its organization during that earlier period, the county government, as detailed in several of the chapters to come, took on a most ambitious set of functions and goals. Even with its modest staff, the county government apparatus during the Mao period routinely undertook economic and social planning, resource mobilization, and other local development activities; furthermore, it carried out some very intricate coordinating functions and tasks. Consistent with Mao-period principles of administration, the local state apparatus in Shulu was simple in its design but sedulous in its tone and distinctly multifunctional in its operation.

Beginning around 1979, however, local state bureaucratic structures and operations in Shulu went through a period—schematically illustrated in Table 4—of unprecedentedly rapid expansion and elaboration. As detailed in the table, in the space of just ten years Shulu's major local government bureaus and offices grew to number 52. And by 1989 full-time administrative staff stood at 1,710 cadres and 527 additional support workers, very nearly double the force just a decade earlier.[1] This table illustrates a fairly steady process of bureaucratic growth, specialization of

TABLE 4
Organization and Development of County Government Administration in Shulu, 1979–90

End 1979	End 1985	1990
County Government Affairs Office	County Government Affairs Office	Municipality Government Affairs Office
Civil Affairs Bureau	Civil Affairs Bureau	Civil Affairs Bureau
	Labor and Personnel Bureau	Labor and Personnel Bureau
	Statistics Bureau	Statistics Bureau
	Price Bureau	Price Bureau
	Industry and Commerce Management Bureau	Industry and Commerce Management Bureau
Finance and Tax Bureau	Finance Bureau	Finance Bureau
	Tax Bureau	Tax Bureau
State Commerce Bureau	State Commerce Bureau	State Commerce Bureau
	Grain Bureau	Grain Bureau
	Auditing Bureau	Auditing Bureau
Urban Construction Bureau	Urban Construction Bureau	Urban Construction and Environmental Protection Commission
Planning Committee	Planning Committee/Economic Committee[a]	Economic Planning Committee
Transportation Bureau	Transportation Bureau	Transportation Bureau
Culture and Education Bureau	Cultural Affairs Bureau	Cultural Affairs Bureau
	Education Bureau	Education Bureau
Public Health Bureau	Public Health Bureau	Public Health Bureau
Agriculture and Forestry Bureau	Agriculture Bureau	Agriculture Bureau
Water Conservancy Bureau	Water Conservancy Bureau	Water Conservancy Bureau
Animal Husbandry Bureau	Forestry and Animal Husbandry Bureau	Forestry Bureau
		Animal Husbandry Bureau
Science Committee	Science Committee	Science Committee
Sports Committee	Sports Committee	Sports Committee
	Family Planning Committee	Family Planning Committee
	Township Industries Bureau	Township Industries Bureau
	Foreign Affairs Bureau	Foreign Affairs Bureau
Public Security Bureau	Public Security Bureau	Public Security Bureau
	Justice Bureau	Justice Bureau
Agricultural Machinery Bureau	Agricultural Machinery Bureau	Agricultural Machinery Bureau
	Broadcast Affairs Bureau	Broadcast and Television Bureau
	Earthquake Office	Earthquake Office
	Records Section	Records Bureau
Foreign Trade Bureau	Foreign Trade Company	Foreign Trade Company
Materials Bureau	Materials Company	Materials Company
Second Light Industry Bureau	Second Light Co-op Federation	
Hai River Headquarters		
		Standards and Measures Bureau
		External Economic Affairs Committee
		Land Management Bureau
		Structural Reform Office
		Public Sanitation Office

TABLE 4 (continued)

End 1979	End 1985	1990
		Investigations Bureau
		Nationalities and Religions Bureau
		Reception Section
		Staffing Office
		Real Estate Management Bureau
		Local Gazetteer Compilation Office
		Office of Economic Cooperation
		Huang-Huai-Hai Development Office
		Shenzhen Liaison Station
		Machinery and Building Materials Company
		Chemical Company
		Light Industries and Textiles Company
		Tobacco Grading, Pricing, and Sales Bureau
		Border Region Trade Company

^aAt this time, the Planning Committee and the Economic Committee—the successor to the Industry Bureau—were still formally distinct. But in practice they functioned in such close coordination that Shulu officials tended to refer to them as a single office called *jingjiwei* (literally, economic planning committee).

function, and intensification of activity in the Shulu government during recent years.

Note that Table 4 displays only what might be thought of as the administrative body of the local state bureaucracy. It details the changing structure of the Shulu county government only, which is placed in its schematic relationship to the other leading political institutions in Shulu in Figure 1. Table 4, therefore, does not diagram the full array of local political institutions in the county. Most particularly, this table does not include the various organs of either the Political Consultative Conference or the Communist Party itself.[2] Nor does it include any of the various units of community-level government in Shulu. What it does show, in skeletal outline, is what could be called the broad bureaucratic midsection of the local state and its authority. When understood in this light, what Table 4 plainly indicates is that the scope of activity undertaken by the local state bureaucratic apparatus was steadily elaborated and extended over the decade of the 1980's.

The most important change in the role of the local state that has come with the reforms, in Shulu as elsewhere in China, is that more and more economic activity has been permitted to take place outside the state plan. This has meant that the state itself has been directly responsible for a falling proportion of total local investment and receipts. Meanwhile, the

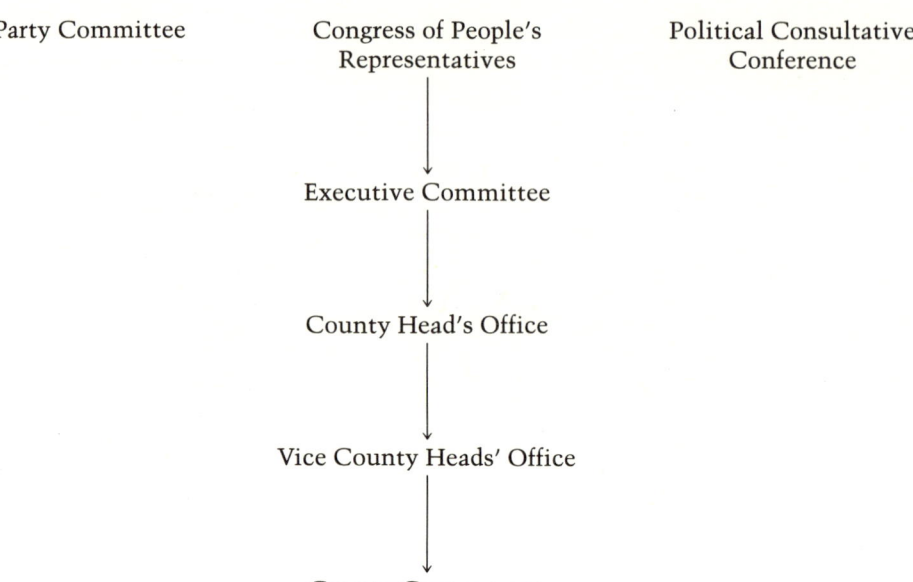

Fig. 1. Leading organs of Shulu government in the 1980's

local state apparatus of Shulu (as is also true elsewhere in China) has been becoming bigger, more complex, and, as we shall see in the section of this chapter below on subcounty government, more fully filled out at the bottom. At the same time, the actual work of this local state apparatus has been expanding to include numerous new tasks and responsibilities. But it is apparent that most of these new responsibilities, while they may often still be characterized aptly as "developmental" in tone and purpose, are not directive; they are, instead, heavily regulatory. That is, the Deng-period local state has come to rely less on issuing commands to subordinate organs and enterprises, and more on establishing the parameters within which they are permitted to operate. The regulatory thrust of much local state development during the Deng period in Shulu is discussed, in some of its specifics, in several of the topical chapters to come. We consider, for example, the county government's regulation of land use in Shulu (Chapters 7 and 8), its regulation and monitoring of urban development and environmental protection (Chapter 7), and its quite strict and comprehensive regulation of the expanding realm of private trade (Chapter 6). These and other examples illustrate how, with a greater proportion of local economic activity permitted to occur outside the scope of direct state planning, the local state in the 1980's was, somewhat ironically if not terribly surprisingly, called upon to take a much more active role in monitoring and regulating both the obviously beneficial and also the potentially disruptive activities of this burgeoning arena of unplanned endeavor. This dynamic, entailed in the very process of reform itself, has tended to produce the sprawling pattern of local state expansion recorded in Table 4.[3]

The Horizontal/Vertical Gridwork of Government

The administrative and political relationships of the congeries of bureaus and offices listed in Table 4 to each other and to higher levels of the state form a complex and differentiated web. County governments in China have generally been conceived of as the lowest level of unalloyed state organization in the entire system. The leading officials as well as the functional staff members of county governments are state cadres (*guojia ganbu*), which means they are in the state's personnel system and are on the state's payroll.[4] Most of a county's bureaucratic institutions have historically been the lowest-level branches of vertical (*tiaotiao*) administrative and political hierarchies that reach all the way up to what is universally referred to in China as "the center" (*zhongyang*)—the national government in Beijing. But county government is no mere transmission belt or local agency of higher powers. It holds itself responsible, and is held responsible by the higher levels of the state and also by those under its jurisdiction, for the coordination, integration, and development of the bounded area under its jurisdiction as a horizontal (*kuaikuai*) whole.

A county government's formal organization reflects these multiple roles and cross-pressures. And most departments at the county level are in fact woven into both the warp and woof of the fabric of Chinese government—they have both vertically and horizontally linked responsibilities. That is to say, they mediate between the county as a bounded local unit on the one hand and the higher levels of bureaucratically organized state authority on the other. The functions and identities of most county offices, therefore, can be seen as mixed. Some departments are especially tightly linked to a given vertical hierarchy, however, and they can be most usefully understood as vertically oriented. A few others have responsibilities that are mostly regional or locality-bounded, and they can be most usefully thought of as horizontally oriented. This categorization of county-level units is based upon the nature of a department's financial relationships as well as on functional considerations.[5]

Vertically oriented offices include those attached to what the Chinese call "systems" (*xitong*). These bureaus can be responsible for shepherding sizable amounts of money and other resources into and out of the county without their passing through the budget of the county government. For example, the Second Light Industry Bureau in Shulu collected a portion of the profits of the industries in the county that were in its orbit, and passed them on to its immediate administrative superior at Shijiazhuang prefecture. It also funneled investment capital downward from the province and prefecture to its enterprises. Other Shulu county offices engaged in similar transfers included the Materials Bureau, the Foreign Trade Bureau, and the Huang-Huai-Hai Development Office. Other vertically oriented agencies engage not so much in resource transfers as in the implementation of policies and programs set by higher levels of the state, such as the Civil Affairs Bureau, the Public Security Bureau, the Statistics Bureau, and the Family Planning Committee.

The horizontally oriented offices are those that engage primarily in the provision of services, or which provide administrative coordination on a countywide basis as determined locally, rather than focusing on the fulfillment of tasks specified by supervising agencies; their primary financial relationships are generally with the county government rather than with their supervising bureaus. In Shulu these include the Economic Planning Commission, the Urban Construction and Environmental Protection Commission, the Water Conservancy Bureau, and agencies involved in promotion of production and technology (such as the Science Committee, the Animal Husbandry Bureau, the Agriculture and Forestry bureaus), the Public Health Bureau, and the Sports Committee.

County government in Shulu is thus a complex set of institutions differentiated both functionally and administratively. County government is charged with the implementation and administration of all manner of national and provincial policies and guidelines as well as with providing service to and promoting the development of its locality. The often contradictory nature of these centrist and localist orientations has evidently produced interesting pressures and problems in Shulu. But it has also created a structure of options and opportunities that has contributed to the county government's flexibility and resilience. Shulu county officials have frequently, in fact, been able to mobilize both local and higher-level resources in creative ways. The deft handling of what are often partially conflicting vertical and horizontal responsibilities within the county administration, as we shall have many occasions to point out with concrete examples in the chapters to follow, has very often been at the heart of local politics in Shulu. Indeed, close study of the Shulu case suggests over and over again that just mastering the management of the vertical and horizontal cross-pressures that are concentrated at the county level is often tantamount to practicing the art of good government in the contemporary Chinese context.

The Overall State Employment Picture

Impressive as the indicators given above of the recent growth and development of the local state apparatus may be, lists of offices and figures for government administrative personnel alone do not really succeed in conveying the true scope and presence of the state—as organizer, regulator, development planner, and employer—in the local context. There have always been two other major categories of state employees besides those working in state government offices per se: those in state-managed institutions such as hospitals and schools (*shiye*), and those in state-owned enterprises, such as factories and department stores (*qiye*). In Shulu, state employees in these categories far outnumbered government administrative personnel. And including these other employees in the picture only serves to confirm that the generally rapid growth trend prevailing in the strictly administrative sphere of government was also being borne out in the other spheres of state-managed activity during the decade from 1979 to 1989 (Table 5).

Two other general observations are worth noting about state employment in Shulu, and especially about employment in government administration. First, with the exception of the *shiye* category, where many women have traditionally been able to find work as schoolteachers and health-care professionals, state employment is heavily the preserve of men. And especially as Table 6 makes clear, in the sphere of government administration, where political and other discretionary forms of power are concentrated, it was still in 1990 almost entirely a man's world.

TABLE 5
State Employees in Shulu, 1979 and 1989

State employees	1979	1989
Administrative (*xingzheng*)		
Cadres	945	1,710
Support	200	527
SUBTOTAL	1,145	2,237
Institutional and professional (*shiye*)		
Education	1,698	2,834
Health	306	632
Other	353	819
SUBTOTAL	2,357	4,285
In enterprises (*qiye*)		
State-owned	963	1,821
Collective[a]	73	359
SUBTOTAL	1,036	2,180
TOTAL	4,538	8,702

[a] State employees, usually with special technical skills or with experience in accounting or management, may be detailed to work in collective enterprises, if requested by the enterprise. These personnel continue to receive their state salaries and benefits while on assignment, however. Such transfers of technicians and specialists are one means by which the state has supported the rapid development of collective town- and village-run enterprises during the 1980's.

TABLE 6
Women as a Percentage of State Employees, 1979 and 1989

	1979	1989
Administrative (*xingzheng*)	7.8	8.4
Institutional and professional (*shiye*)	30.2	41.8
Enterprise (*qiye*)	19.4	20.1
All state employees	22.0	27.8

Second, almost everyone who works in Shulu county administration is a Shulu native. This pattern of overwhelmingly local recruitment into government work did not change during the 1980's; if anything, it intensified. In 1979, of the 1,145 Shulu government administrative personnel, only 68 (5.9 percent) came from outside the county. In 1989 just 74 (3.3 percent) of Shulu's 2,237 administrative workers were outsiders assigned to work in Shulu. Just occasionally local officials could be heard to gripe that somehow, of all the best and brightest Shulu students and young cadres selected for higher education and training in Shijiazhuang, Beijing, and beyond, not one had ever been posted back to Shulu, even though most had expressed willingness to return and put their talents to use at home. It was surely no accident, however, that Shulu tended to produce good talent for cadre training and a fair number of young people who were promoted to jobs at higher levels or selected for service elsewhere in the country. The county was fortunate to have within its borders, after all, the Xinji Middle School, a national keypoint institution. This school has been a valuable provincial resource, even a national one. Its graduates have been much more likely than most young people in China to take up official responsibilities outside their home district.

Education and Compensation of Administrative Personnel

Recent major changes on the administrative personnel front did, in fact, center on elaborate efforts to raise the educational level and the training of Shulu cadres. Shulu's efforts in this regard were made in conformity with various policies designed to improve the quality of government personnel that had been promulgated nationally during the 1980's. As late as 1986, over 44 percent of county-level administrative cadres had just a junior high school education or less. Another 43 percent had finished high school. Only 12 to 13 percent had completed two or more years of postsecondary education or technical training. By 1989, after targets had been set and a number of options allowing on-duty personnel to take time off to attend school and to study for equivalency exams had been put into effect, some 21.6 percent of county-level cadres had completed two or more years of postsecondary education, and 42 percent had high school equivalency ratings. Still, over 36 percent had only junior high school equivalency or less.

As for the wages of state administrative personnel, when the cadre grade system was phased out in 1985, Shulu was designated a class six locality. In 1990, cadres working in class six localities earned a basic wage of ¥39 per month. In Shulu everyone also received a standard ¥18 per month bonus and a series of flexible subsidies for items such as food, rent, transportation expenses, and compliance with the single-child family program.[6] There was also a locally determined system of subsidies for cadres working in hardship posts. Generally speaking, the further a work assignment put one from the county seat, the greater the hardship compensation. In Shulu, the worst hardship posts could bring in as much as one-third over the cadre's regular salary.[7]

As reform drove incomes in the private sector higher than those in state employment, Shulu officials were beginning to experience some difficulties attracting people to work in the government. But they did not see this as a very serious problem in 1990. They argued that the wage gap was offset by the greater income security, the lower risk, and the steadier pace of work in state employment. Moreover, Government Affairs Office officials hastened to add, since Chinese culture historically accords great honor to those who pursue an official career, many people can be expected to continue to choose to work in state administration more for the status and prestige than for the money anyway.

It is an ancient axiom of Chinese government, of course, that official administrative rank and position can be used to enhance personal income, in ways that range from the more or less legitimate to the thoroughly corrupt. This, plus the recently heightened public preoccupation with problems of official corruption in Deng-period China, naturally prompts concern about cadre corruption in Shulu. Although we did note occasional examples of gift-giving and other preferments (always small) offered to county officials as we made our way around Shulu in their company over the years, we were able to conduct no sustained investigation of corruption as such. Local officials acknowledged the problem as being a general and sometimes a quite serious one in China. Offices for carrying out both criminal prosecution and party discipline inspection were in operation in Shulu. The atmosphere surrounding this question appeared to be strict. In 1990, Shulu local television carried coverage of a mass rally for the public humiliation of convicted criminals and others who had abused managerial or other positions for personal gain.

The Cost of County Government

As Shulu county government has greatly expanded its scope of operations over the past forty years, expenditures on government administration have also risen quite steadily, from a mere ¥145,000 in 1949 to ¥8,940,000 in 1989. As Figure 2 shows, administrative expenditure grew rather slowly during the Mao period (at an average annual rate of 3.7 percent from 1952 to 1978),[8] but has taken off since: the annual rate was nearly 14 percent from 1978 to 1983,[9] and was an astonishing 21 percent per annum from 1978 to 1989. Figure 3, which tracks administrative expenses as a portion of total budgetary expenditure, also shows such expenses to have been ratcheted upward in the Deng period to over 20 percent; in the late Mao period it had hovered in the mid-teens. Thus the magnitude of Shulu government *institutions* as measured by administrative costs has grown significantly in the Deng period, outstripping even

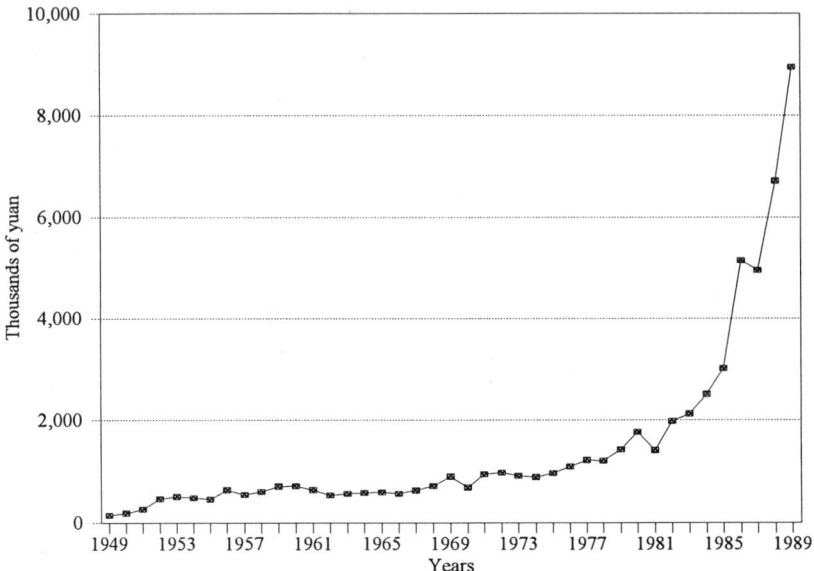

Fig. 2. Administrative expenses of county government, 1949–89

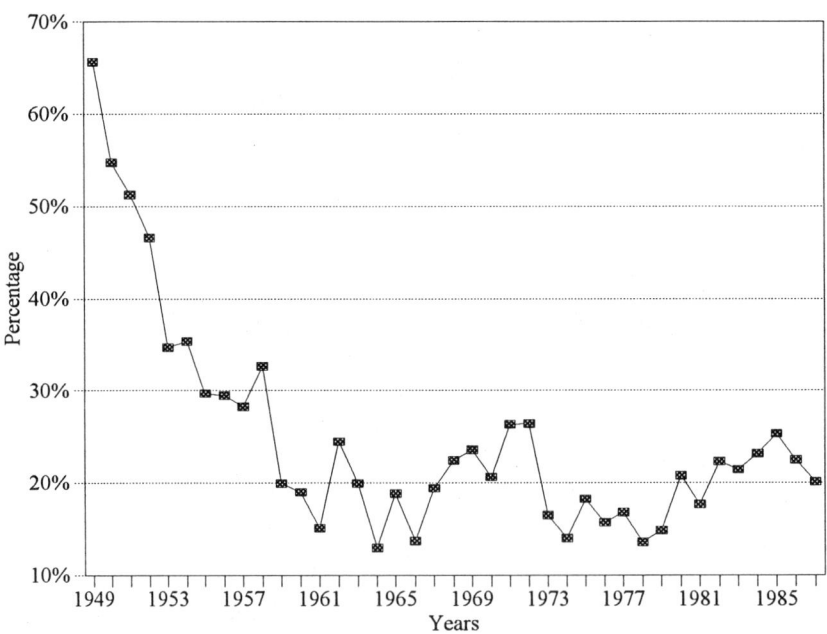

Fig. 3. Administrative expenses as percentage of total budgetary expenses, 1949–89

the general and already swift pace of growth of all government budgeted *activities*. And the costs of county government administration were even rising faster, though only moderately faster, than the overall rate of economic growth: in 1979, they came to .45 percent of gross output value, and in 1989 to .64 percent.

Subcounty Government

The remarkable pattern of growth in state administration size, density, and complexity evident at the county level in Shulu was indeed mirrored, though less markedly, at the subcounty level, that is, in the commune, and later in the township and town level as well.[10] Subcounty government administration was exceedingly spare, simple, and uniform in the late Mao period, with the people's commune model of organization then pervasive in both political and social life. Shulu's 31 people's communes and their 347 production brigades constituted virtually the whole of the subcounty structure of government in 1979.[11] Even many workers and other residents of the county seat holding nonagricultural household registrations could come, in effect, under commune jurisdiction at that time. Some people classified as nonrural residents lived in housing provided by the units that employed them, as was then, and is today, the customary arrangement in urban China. But many of them also were housed by and had their domestic lives organized through institutions and services of Xinji Commune, which occupied much of the land area of the county seat. There were no special residential sections of the city set aside for the non-commune households; they lived intermixed with commune households, either renting their homes from the commune or owning them outright. They also attended brigade-run schools and clinics. It is notable also that in this urban center, there were no urban residents' or neighborhood committees, or city government as such. Political work on a neighborhood level then was carried out by subunits of Xinji Commune, and disputes among residents, including those between commune members and nonmembers, were resolved by civil mediation committees (*minshi tiaojie weiyuanhui*) under the brigades.

There were a total of just 233 state administrative personnel working at the commune level in Shulu in 1979—only 7.5 administrative cadres per commune on average. This situation was much altered by 1989, when the analogous figure was 349, up about 50 percent. Town governments around Shulu were becoming more complex and differentiated at the end of the 1980's. By 1990 many were outfitted with their own branch offices (*suo*) of county administrative bureaus such as the Industry and Commerce Management Bureau, the Township Industries Bureau, the Finance Bureau, the Land Bureau, the Justice Bureau, and the Statistics Bureau. Especially noteworthy here was the extension of finance control—in effect a budgetary function—down to the town and township level. This gave the town and township governments a strong interest in collecting

TABLE 7
Town Government Administration, Xincheng Zhen, 1990

Government offices	Staff	Year established[a]
Civil Affairs	1	—
Militia	1	—
Justice	1	—
Police Station	3	—
Enterprise Office	6	—
Women's Association	1	—
Communist Youth League	1	—
Economic Management Station	1	1984
Legal Services	1	1985
Family Planning Work Station	5	1987
Finance Office	6	1988
Land Management Office	2	1988
Urban Construction Leading Group	2	1988

[a]Dates given only for those offices established after the Mao period (ending 1978).

taxes levied at higher levels by entitling them to a share of the target and over-target revenues.[12]

By 1990, in the town of Xincheng, for example, there were some thirteen separate administrative offices in the *zhen* government. A listing of these offices is shown in Table 7 with the number of full-time staff working in each office in 1990 and with the year each office was established (for those created since the commune period). Clearly, the local state apparatus was filling out its functions and offices not only at the county level but also at the next level down, closer to the lives of ordinary people. Again, as with the county government, this sketch of the administrative structure of government at the *zhen* level does not capture the full picture of the state's local presence. There may have been only 31 people officially working in Xincheng's government administrative offices, but there were another 5 people responsible for Party work, another 99 on the state payroll in state-managed institutions (*shiye*) in Xincheng, and 657 more working in state-run enterprises located in Xincheng. In addition, the local state's profile in the *zhen* was kept quite conspicuous by the existence in Xincheng of numerous branch offices (*fenzhi jigou*) of higher-level state units.[13] Thus the formal presence of state power out in the Shulu countryside, away from the main urban and government center of Xinji, remained at least as palpable in 1990 as it had been before the reforms, if not more so.[14]

The processes of urbanization have also picked up considerable speed in Shulu in the Deng period. The entire county was redesignated a municipality in 1986, and at that time the boundaries of Xinji, the county seat, were redrawn to allow for expected urban growth. Several other townships (*xiang*) contiguous with Xinji were, at the same time, annexed into the new urban center itself and were redesignated as urban administrative districts (*banshichu*). These were conceived as transitional governmental forms slated one day to evolve into something like city precincts.[15] The urban administrative districts had traded some of the formal political independence that went with their previous township status for the privilege of annexation into Xinji. Townships and towns (*xiang* or *zhen*) each elect a people's congress (*renmin daibiao dahui*), which in turn appoints the town's or township's leading officials. But the urban administrative districts do not have their own elected people's congresses; district residents vote, instead, in the Xinji-wide elections. A district's leading cadres are, subsequently, appointed to fixed terms of office by the Xinji people's congress.[16] In return, the advantages they received from incorporation into Xinji, and in particular inclusion in its urban plan,[17] included roadways financed completely by the Shulu government,[18] priority over towns and townships in the distribution of electricity (a very scarce resource in Shulu as elsewhere in so much of China), access to the corps of technical specialists serving Xinji in its planned urban development, and preferential access to credit (especially for starting new enterprises, which was one of the most difficult types of credit to obtain in the 1980's).

Like towns and townships, these urban administrative districts were developing increasingly complex and complete administrative structures in 1990.[19] And cadres working in these offices were under pressure from the Shulu government to demonstrate their professional competence and to improve the quality of their work.[20] In both the main urban setting and in small towns around Shulu by 1990, then, subcounty government and administration was in the midst of significant expansion, elaboration, and upgrading.

The Ethos of County Government in Shulu

In some parts of China, cadres working in local government have been able to accumulate enviable discretionary budgets and even more enviable personal fortunes over the last ten years. They have built ostentatious new homes for their families, their chauffeurs drive them around in foreign-made autos, and their day-to-day work has taken on a distinctly entrepreneurial wheeling-and-dealing character. The official duties of these local cadres may generate impressive incomes for their units, which often now have more the air of small profit-seeking corporations than that of professional civil service administration. Their unofficial (or after-hours) individual and family ventures, in turn, may be even more lucrative, and even more intensely preoccupying. Little of this kind of behavior and deportment was to be found in Shulu, however.

Shulu in the 1980's was a pretty "conservative" place, to use the common quasi-political categorization. There can be little doubt that the county and its government would instantly have been classified that way by most Chinese and most China watchers at the time. But since the term "conservative" has generally been contrasted with "forward-looking" and has been used as a whip to help bring laggards in line with the latest reform thinking in Deng's China, we suspect that Shulu government officials, if confronted with that label, while immediately understanding why they were so branded would nonetheless have vigorously rejected the insult. If, on the other hand, it were pointed out to them that much about the way they handled local affairs was reminiscent of the Mao period, they would have been neither insulted nor embarrassed, but would no doubt have readily agreed. Even as late as 1990, Shulu government cadres, unlike officials in many other Chinese localities, apparently saw little need to distance themselves from many of the developmental values and goals they thought of as Maoist. Of course they were duly critical of the excesses of radical politics, especially the extremism of the Cultural Revolution. But they did not spend much time disparaging their own past. They were as likely to point out accomplishments made using Maoist policies and methods as accomplishments made under reform.

Shulu government officials were by no means ignorant of what was going on in the rest of the country; they were well abreast of prevailing trends in political restructuring, economic reform, and social change. Furthermore, in our many interviews and more casual conversations and correspondence with them over the years from 1979 to 1990, they gave every evidence of pressing forward on the local scene with many of the reforms—encouraging markets, implementing incentives, and permitting privatization—that emanated, in fits and starts, from the center under Deng Xiaoping. If they had deep disagreements with the main lines of central policy, they did not ever reveal them. But their enthusiasm for reform did appear to be tempered by two quite different—and, in the context of China's recent political history, somewhat contradictory—sensibilities.

First, unlike some of the other large and small Chinese localities in which we have lived and worked over recent years, Shulu government officials had not by 1990 let go of all the old vocabulary and ethos of revolutionary socialist asceticism, service to the people, and political control of social and economic life, which had been such prominent themes in Party life and state administration in the days of Mao. The longevity of this set of political values in Shulu was, we came to believe, at least in part a product of the county's history as a node of early Communist organization and struggle and as a site of a revolutionary base area government. If there are still "conservatives" in China in the 1990's who cling to a peasant-Communist work style and to Maoist social values—and we know there are—then we should not be surprised if many of these people are to be found on the north China plain. Its bloody history of war and revolution is still alive in the minds of elderly villagers and Party cadres, who occasionally shared with us their vintage tales of horror and heroism. And Shulu county officials, themselves drawn overwhelmingly from among these local people, reflected those old partisan values, expressed themselves naturally using scraps drawn out of that old political vocabulary, and apparently saw little to be gained by separating themselves from their people and their roots in the ways they chose to justify and explain their programs and plans for reform.

Second, in both the Mao and Deng periods, Shulu's leadership was particularly sensitive to the positive role of specialized expertise, both in governance and in economic development. The well-known keypoint Xinji Middle School may have helped in imparting something of a technical orientation to the staff of the Shulu county government. This orientation may also have been a product of the fact that as early as 1947 Shulu was the site of a textile dyeing factory—not a traditional artisanal workshop, but a plant whose mass production of army uniforms and use of modern chemical dyes augured the advent of a new industrial age. Maoism, in some of its more extreme variants, deemphasized and even disdained the positive contribution that technological knowledge and sophistication could make to development. But Shulu was never placed at that particular radical forefront of Maoist theory and practice. Thus Shulu officials tended to marry easily the peasant-Communist values of community and public service, of personal sacrifice, of unified leadership, and of political control and overall integration of the economy to a decidedly modernist emphasis on scientific and technical knowledge and skill.

We met over the years with scores of county government officials in Shulu and, with but a few exceptions, we found them to project an attitude of straightforward professionalism about their work, to display general competence in their assigned areas of responsibility, and to stress the importance of unity in achieving their aims. In these respects they differed rather markedly from local government cadres we had encountered in a number of other localities where we had carried out similar fieldwork. Again and again, when pressed to give an account of the reasons for some success in administrative problem-solving or in economic development, Shulu officials cited first the unity and purpose of the local leadership and the local cadre corps and the efforts of one and all to achieve close coordination. They often gave us concrete examples of extensive consultations among the various agencies of the government in approaching a particular problem, as we shall see in chapters to follow. But they were reluctant, sometimes to the point of dead silence, even to respond to any of our countless questions about disagreement and conflict within the local government, or between the county and provincial or central authorities. We did not conclude from this that there were no conflicts. Rather, we understood that our informants chose to stress instead the ability of local government personnel to focus first and foremost on the public's business, and to strive to overcome disagreements and other divisions for the sake of the larger good. The revolutionary-era demand on cadres for more or less continuous personal sacrifice may finally have been set aside in the 1980's, but the ethos of public service and shared benefit remained quite palpable in Shulu.

This was reflected in a relative lack of ostentation on the part of local officials, both in their public actions and their private demeanor. New government buildings were going up in Xinji as part of the urban construction program, for example. But these, by and large, were modest in size and functional in their design, and they paled in comparison to newly built local public works projects such as the county's new shopping center, community center, and public auditorium. The Shulu government's official fleet of vehicles did grow steadily over the decade, but, with the possible exception of the local motorcycle police, there was nothing flashy about this equipment. In fact, top county Party and government leaders commented with grudging acceptance about how difficult the shortage of cars made their work. The pace of official business and the pressure to produce high-quality results on time did seem to be gradually heightening over the period from 1979 to 1990. Local cadres liked to joke about how they needed always to wear running shoes to work. But this general quickening of the pulse seemed to be offset as well by a clear preference for sober deliberateness in work style and self-presentation. As a group, the many men and women with whom we talked in the Shulu government projected, in 1990 as they had in 1979, an air of professional seriousness and a disinclination to be carried away.

Shulu officials projected also a certain sense of commitment, even in the 1980's, to achieving local economic development without severe social inequality. Officials at all levels in the county raised with us spontaneously the importance of seeing to it that various households or different localities advanced together toward economic development—or at least of seeing to it that none were left very far behind. Their concerns on this score seemed to convey something more than mere fealty to an ideologically correct formulation or slogan. (And indeed, by the 1980's such egalitarian formulations were no longer the ones being pressed by top-level Chinese leaders.) In later chapters we shall have the opportunity to explore several examples of the ways in which Shulu government officials went about trying to put this commitment into practice.[21]

Shulu officials appeared to operate, further, on the assumption that it is the responsibility of local government to find a way either to prevent or to solve all manner of economic and social problems. Healthy social initiatives of all kinds, they would often imply, should be expected to come from the public sphere, not the private one. Initiatives that did emerge in the private sector were, as a matter of general course, to be "linked up with" local state organization and routine.[22] Thus we found Shulu officials not to have any working concept of civil society, as it is generally understood in the West, and not to comprehend what lay behind our many disconcerted inquiries about the dominating role of the local state in shaping social life. A dominant role for the state they plainly regarded as the natural state of affairs. Shulu county officials represented themselves as open-minded and amenable to new ideas, deriving from whatever quarter, but they also displayed no doubt whatsoever about the importance of their leadership, and a considerable capacity for certitude about the correctness of their direction.

Although they would occasionally express some quiet pride in local accomplishments, Shulu officials seemed acutely conscious of their relative economic and technical backwardness, and were aware that a long road to genuine modernization and development still lay ahead of them. They seemed to like to portray themselves, in fact, as rather simple, unsophisticated, yet serious and energetic people. All this, of course, may have been an act put on for our benefit. But if it was an act, it was sustained over a very long period of time, by a very large and rotating cast of characters, in circumstances ranging from tense negotiations to tedious briefings to jovial dinner parties to idle one-on-one chats. The values and concerns repeatedly expressed, therefore, we took to be ones these local government officials chose to emphasize to us. That there were other aspects of their work in local government that they chose likewise not to emphasize, we never doubted. We understood their self-presentation, nonetheless, not as a mere façade, but as a reflection of certain important components of the more complex reality of the county government in which they worked.

CHAPTER 4

County Financial Structures and Relations

In any complex economy, patterns of financial authority are an important key to understanding the distribution of power among administrative levels and units throughout the system. Control over the budget is very often the control that really matters. We might suppose that this is a truism of political economy more important in market-based systems than in command systems, since keeping control over the disposition of scarce goods and materials is often at least as decisive, where "the plan" reigns, as finding the money to pay for those goods. Yet even in Mao-period China, when political leaders have sought to decentralize or to recentralize economic decision-making powers, they did not neglect accompanying reforms in the fiscal system—tightening or loosening budgetary powers accordingly.

Thus in most of our attempts to analyze the evolving political relationships between center and locality in China since 1949 we are accustomed to including, as an indicator of their relative strengths, variations in their shares of fiscal responsibility. Unfortunately, for many years following the Great Leap Forward little was known outside China about the precise mechanisms of revenue collection and sharing or about the division of supervisory and allocational responsibilities among units at the center, the provincial level, and the localities. We could see only the bare outlines of what we knew must be intricate processes. We were constrained to speak vaguely of fiscal "powers" and "tasks" being delegated to county governments or taken away from them without much detailed knowledge of how this was done institutionally and procedurally or of what real differences such reforms might make.

In this chapter, we lift a corner of the veil obscuring the financial aspects of China's local administrative and political system. We develop a triple-stranded model of the fiscal structure of the county and its relations to units above and below. The three strands, or revenue/expenditure pathways, discussed below are the state budget, the vertical systems, and the extrabudgetary fund. This model in turn raises questions about the integration of the functions of vertically linked (*tiaotiao*) or ministerial offices and of horizontally based (*kuaikuai*) or region-regarding offices within the institutional framework of a single county government. Our hope is that this exploration of some of the fiscal aspects of the local gridwork of vertical and horizontal government offices may help ground future considerations of the political, economic, and social effects of this distinctively crisscrossed structure of Chinese administration.

The questions that animated this aspect of our Shulu investigations were initially rather simple. How much of its revenue was the county obliged to give up to higher levels of government? How much autonomy did the county have in spending the monies left to it, or allocated to it? And finally, were expenditures made by the county becoming more important or less important (relative to spending by higher or lower levels of state organization) than they had been in the past? That is, were county cadres gaining or losing as responsible economic decision makers in the Deng period? These very straightforward questions reflected our initially far too simple and solidary assumptions about the structure and functions of a county as a revenue-generating and -spending unit. In hot pursuit of comprehensive generalizations, we became ensnared instead in a jungle of revenue-related units and systems, evolving procedures and conventions, ad hoc policies and piecemeal reforms. No aspect of our work in Shulu was to convince us more pointedly of the exceeding complexity of county organization than our repeatedly frustrating, if absorbing, forays into the forest of local finance.

In the end, only partial answers to those too-simple questions have been our reward. In fact, the major thrust of the analysis to follow is to demonstrate how the "answers" to such questions would be likely to differ depending on which of the three major revenue/expenditure pathways in the county's triple-stranded fiscal structure were under examination. Assuming (safely, we believe) that such a multistranded pattern of fiscal flows has been characteristic of other counties as well, then we must accept that meaningful answers to simple questions like those above for local governments in China as a whole can never be attempted on the basis of official state budget data alone. Many more detailed local studies, sensitive to the multistrandedness of financial affairs, will have to be done. It is our hope that this chapter will provide a framework for such work.

First Pathway: The State Budget

We begin with the official state budget because, while it was only one of three important fiscal pathways into and out of the county, it was always the most comprehensive one. The state budget has consisted of revenue and expenditure sides, each in turn subdivided into a multitude of specific budget lines, the major subcategories of which appear in Tables 8 and 9.[1]

A quick glance at Figure 4 reveals that Shulu has consistently produced a revenue surplus for the state: budgetary revenues have always substantially exceeded expenditures in the county. Roughly speaking, county budgetary revenues and expenditures have moved in tandem over time, but the connection between them has actually been indirect.[2] County expenditures were not, in any case, taken straight out of county revenues. Instead, revenues were collected by various county agencies and passed upward to higher levels of the state administration; expenditure funds were, in turn, allocated to the county from above. The state budget process was thus a tightly centralized and explicitly hierarchical fiscal pathway.[3] On this ladder of financial authority, throughout the Mao period, the county level of government consistently occupied the bottom rung.[4]

As a percentage of revenues collected, Shulu's actual budgetary expenditures have fluctuated irregularly over the years, from a low of 14.5 percent in 1951 to a high of 73 percent in 1964. Between 1949 and 1989, on average, the county was permitted to spend locally exactly one-third, just 33.3 percent, of what it collected through the state budgetary pathway. It is worth noting, however, that the revenue share trend moved in the county's favor over time. For the decade 1969–1979, Shulu budgetary expenditures averaged 26.3 percent of revenues, while for the decade 1979–1989 this average rose to 40.3 percent. But due to the overall pattern of fiscal decline that characterized the Deng years, a rising revenue share rate did not necessarily mean that a county's budget was more adequate to its needs than before.[5]

During the Mao period, county Finance Bureau officials explained, revenue and expenditure targets for the various budget lines and subcategories were set in detailed annual negotiations between county and prefecture representatives. Once these targets were negotiated, county officials lacked authority to move funds across budget lines without explicit approval from above. The county government then proceeded to carry out most of its financial planning and administrative operations within the context of those targets. Since expenditure funds were not derived directly from revenues, a system of rewards and penalties was devised to encourage the county government actually to meet, and if possible to exceed, the targets. If the county collected surplus revenues it was permitted to keep a certain percentage of them. Before 1977 it was generally supposed to keep

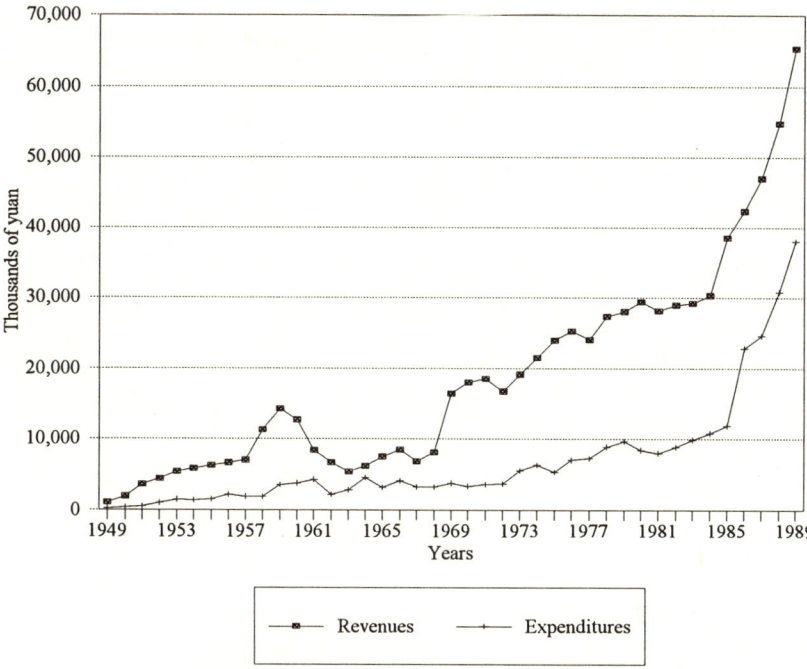

Fig. 4. Shulu county budgetary revenues and expenditures, 1949–89

15 percent of the over-target surplus; but in 1978, as part of the first phase of finance reforms under Deng, this was raised to 30 percent.[6]

As the reforms progressed, however, and a financial contracting (*baogan*) system took effect in 1980, the situation changed once more. All revenue sources were then divided into two different categories—fixed and adjusted—and an overall revenue-sharing formula was stipulated for each category for each county.[7] Shulu was allowed to keep just 23.2 percent of all the target revenues it collected in the first category and just 15 percent of all revenues in the second. Because of its relative prosperity, Shulu received the lowest revenue share rate of all the counties in its prefecture at that time. Some nearby counties classified as "poor, mountainous, and old revolutionary base area counties," for example, were granted target revenue retention rates of 100 percent or more. County officials did not complain about this low base retention rate. But they did say that over-target revenue collections were not well apportioned, from the county's point of view, at that time. Shulu was permitted to keep only 5 percent of the surplus it collected and was compelled to send all the rest up to higher levels.

But soon enough the ground rules were to change again. In 1982, the two distinct revenue categories, fixed and adjusted, were collapsed once more and Shulu was granted a single comprehensive revenue share rate of 20.9 percent. Almost immediately still more budget reforms were to be

TABLE 8
Shulu County Financial Revenue, 1949–89
(in thousands of yuan)

	Enterprise profits				Taxes on industry and commerce						
Year	Industry	Commerce	Other	Subtotal[a]	Industrial and commercial tax	Income tax	Other taxes	Subtotal	Agricultural tax	Other revenues	Total revenues
1949					64	3	28	95	1,038	2	1,135
1950					351	6	69	426	1,439	75	1,940
1951					1,308	173	377	1,858	1,654	69	3,581
1952					1,758	312	508	2,578	1,774	83	4,435
1953					2,354	714	157	3,225	2,092	112	5,429
1954					2,198	891	199	3,288	2,099	485	5,872
1955					2,642	755	194	3,591	2,149	567	6,307
1956				8	2,828	978	151	3,957	2,436	236	6,637
1957				4	3,142	1,286	135	4,563	2,125	311	7,003
1958				3,938	3,370	853	171	4,394	2,486	508	11,326
1959				7,993	3,372	224	185	3,781	2,421	60	14,255
1960				5,839	4,106	157	201	4,464	2,241	178	12,722
1961				3,420	2,995	360	267	3,622	1,317	68	8,427
1962				834	3,543	550	360	4,453	1,378	78	6,743
1963				492	2,969	718	450	4,137	768	40	5,437
1964				632	3,121	665	318	4,104	1,459	26	6,221
1965	256	978	75	1,309	2,932	1,136	394	4,462	1,488	242	7,501
1966	51	3,278	3	3,332	2,312	1,057	232	3,601	1,571	50	8,554
1967	(44)	2,719	8	2,683	1,761	433	175	2,369	1,753	19	6,824
1968	5	3,227	44	3,276	2,393	508	169	3,070	1,780	54	8,180
1969	6,283	4,780	236	11,299	2,757	669	111	3,537	1,664	8	16,508
1970	7,800	3,512	199	11,511	3,627	981	101	4,709	1,796	39	18,055

Year										
1971	7,288	2,957	142	10,387	5,170	1,133	121	6,424	1,726	12	18,549
1972	2,595	4,659	34	7,288	5,895	1,734	113	7,742	1,773	17	16,820
1973	3,377	4,405	7	7,789	7,565	2,027	45	9,637	1,754	15	19,195
1974	3,391	5,350	43	8,784	8,472	2,465	45	10,982	1,745	11	21,522
1975	3,748	5,026	35	8,809	9,724	3,582	44	13,350	1,744	23	23,926
1976	4,445	4,328	91	8,864	10,997	3,607	47	14,651	1,744	22	25,281
1977	2,350	4,348	69	6,767	12,295	3,758	40	16,093	1,128	22	24,010
1978	3,219	4,672	34	7,925	13,196	4,385	6	17,587	1,759	33	27,304
1979	4,236	4,012	1	8,249	13,123	4,548	2	17,673	2,044	6	27,972
1980	4,278	4,646	86	9,010	13,887	4,482	2	18,371	2,024	3	29,408
1981	2,968	5,620	24	8,612	14,045	3,343	2	17,390	2,054	54	28,110
1982	2,224	5,741	56	8,021	14,870	3,902	29	18,801	2,054	71	28,947
1983	929	7,315	217	7,385	15,805	3,671	102	19,578	2,078	138	29,179
1984	1,743	5,243	528	6,508	16,981	4,742	37	21,760	2,023	40	30,331
1985	7,161	606	801	7,814	19,992	6,121	787	26,900	2,738	83	38,546
1986	6,297	610	373	7,280	22,284	8,174	1,564	32,022	2,684	347	42,333
1987	7,032	491	406	7,929	24,863	7,697	3,107	35,667	2,669	714	46,979
1988	8,113	543	545	9,201	30,278	7,932	3,412	41,622	2,887	1,056	54,766
1989	8,291	621	572	9,484	33,439	10,287	5,369	49,095	5,297	1,456	65,332

NOTE: Parentheses indicate negative numbers.

[a] Enterprise profit subtotals for 1983–85 also include a small deduction for a coal price subsidy to offset increasing energy costs.

TABLE 9
Shulu County Budgetary Expenditures, 1949–89
(in thousands of yuan)

Year	Support for agriculture					Support for rusticated and unemployed youth	Pensions, welfare, and emergency relief	Government administration	Culture
	Basic construction and technical improvement	Agriculture, forestry, water conservancy, weather prediction, and mechanization	Small-scale water conservancy	Support for communes	Subtotal				
1949					2			145	
1950					11			189	
1951					12			266	
1952					23			469	
1953					31			510	
1954					16			489	
1955					68			456	
1956					60			637	
1957					62			546	
1958					140			605	
1959					1,623			708	
1960					1,231			716	
1961					2,054			644	
1962					366			534	
1963					705			564	
1964					740			588	
1965	1	108	462	20	590	51	580	599	15
1966	81	96	321	25	442	39	1,190	563	26
1967	26	62	49	243	354	5	684	631	33
1968	10	78	543	180	801	35	455	720	32
1969	563	61	60	150	271	355	386	901	73
1970	428	65		300	365		372	688	61
1971	357	90	89	60	239		322	945	73
1972	109	162	90	128	380		371	975	73
1973	70	272	1,246	165	1,683		639	917	80
1974	32	226	1,206	653	2,085	645	395	891	98
1975	416	367	75	160	602	473	410	970	68
1976	86	298	1,157	723	2,178	654	533	1,103	86
1977	210	391	1,027	906	2,324	276	751	1,223	80
1978	901	540	1,699	345	2,584	20	1,160	1,204	177
1979	374	1,317	1,707	260	3,284	2	638	1,426	116
1980	13	543	1,213	155	1,911	5	840	1,764	82
1981	6	387	898		1,285		870	1,413	115
1982					1,156	20	894	1,976	95
1983	79				768	173	746	2,123	467
1984	193				838	162	983	2,507	237
1985	516				386		1,119	3,017	172
1986	2,311				1,028		1,523	4,937	409
1987	279				2,248		1,764	5,005	592
1988	687				1,288	30	1,868	6,867	338
1989	442				2,676	10	2,010	9,060	594

NOTE: Parentheses indicate negative number.

Cultural and educational activities						Urban mainte-nance and environ-mental protection	Meat price subsidies	Other	Total expen-ditures
Educa-tion	Broad-casting	Science and earth-quake predic-tion	Health and family planning	Sports	Subtotal				
					74				221
					145				345
					241				519
					514				1,006
					930				1,471
					877				1,382
					1,011				1,535
					1,459			7	2,163
					1,297			27	1,932
					1,080			28	1,853
					1,206			14	3,551
					1,791			32	3,770
					1,559			13	4,270
					1,254			26	2,180
					1,506			54	2,829
					3,165			50	4,543
896		2	217		1,130			234	3,185
1,153	5	3	247		1,434			376	4,125
1,091	5	2	262		1,393			164	3,257
871	7		213		1,123			65	3,209
948	53		183		1,257			85	3,818
953	28		235		1,277			204	3,334
1,292	41		251	7	1,664			59	3,586
1,316	35		380	4	1,808			53	3,696
1,633	29	5	435	7	2,189			66	5,564
1,606	43	9	508	9	2,273			54	6,375
1,727	43	19	527	8	2,392			66	5,329
1,707	73	16	505	12	2,399			91	7,044
1,837	23	16	485	8	2,449			46	7,279
2,130	25	18	570	8	2,928			72	8,869
2,240	27	19	839	16	3,257			648	9,629
2,565	88	20	918	14	3,687			269	8,489
2,535	78	24	936	16	3,704			722	8,000
2,975	79	29	1,303	16	4,476			311	8,854
3,067	84	49	1,676	27	5,370	110		537	9,906
3,567	113	53	1,876	24	5,870	30		251	10,834
3,915	137	63	1,399	27	5,713	847	357	(57)	11,898
4,794	369	86	2,573	362	8,593	1,499	1,291	1,683	22,865
5,423	361	52	2,267	371	9,066	2,431	1,321	2,487	24,601
7,562	997	85	3,323	343	12,648	2,845	1,636	2,944	30,813
8,101	915	108	3,824	529	14,071	3,374	1,642	4,702	37,987

phased in, reforms associated with what was potentially a significant centrally mandated move from budgetary reliance on industrial and commercial profit remission to a more fully tax-based finance system (*ligaishui*).[8] Under the new *ligaishui* regime, Shulu cadres said they were looking forward to possibly keeping as much as 40 percent of their over-target revenue collections. They began to make preparations for local enterprises to pay taxes instead of forwarding their profits directly into the budget. But in Shulu as elsewhere in China, the *ligaishui* reforms were never actually put fully into effect. Instead, Shulu continued to operate under a comprehensive fiscal contracting system, one that now came to include annual stepwise increases in the county's base financial target (*shangjie dizeng baogan*). It was agreed in 1985 that Shulu would have to render to higher levels 5.5 percent more in financial revenues each year than the year before. All revenues collected over and above this annually rising target were to remain at the disposal of the county.[9] In 1985, Shulu had remitted ¥27.4 million in budgetary collections to higher levels of the state. Thus for 1986 target remissions were set at ¥28.9, exactly 5.5 percent higher; and for 1987, they were set 5.5 percent higher than that. Despite all the talk of replacing profit remission with orderly tax levies and despite the earlier announced determination to shift from a system of negotiated targets to a tax-based system of assessments, a negotiated stepwise contracting system remained in effect in Shulu through the late 1980's and into the 1990's.

Our close look at Shulu's experience made it plain enough in any case that, whatever the particular set of regulations in effect at any given time, state budgeting procedures in practice had never been quite as cut-and-dried as all the written regulations would have made it seem. By the early 1980's, with the onset of the economic reforms, however, seeking to comprehend central-local fiscal relations also meant taking aim at a rapidly moving target.

BUDGETARY REVENUES

On the revenue side of Shulu county's state budget (Table 8) there have been just two major sources of income: taxes and enterprise profits.

Taxes

Tax revenues collected by the county government were divided into four major categories: the industry and commerce tax, income tax, agriculture tax, and other taxes. Figure 5 depicts data in Table 8 to illustrate changes in Shulu's tax revenues in these four categories from 1949 to 1989.

AGRICULTURE TAX   The agriculture tax, assessed as a percentage of a hypothetical normal annual grain yield fixed many years ago, has remained quite stable in absolute terms in Shulu, as elsewhere in China. Sometime before the 1958 tax reform the hypothetical average yield was set for Shulu at 1.02 tons of millet (the conversion grain) per hectare, a considerable underestimate of true yields even at the time. At a tax rate in

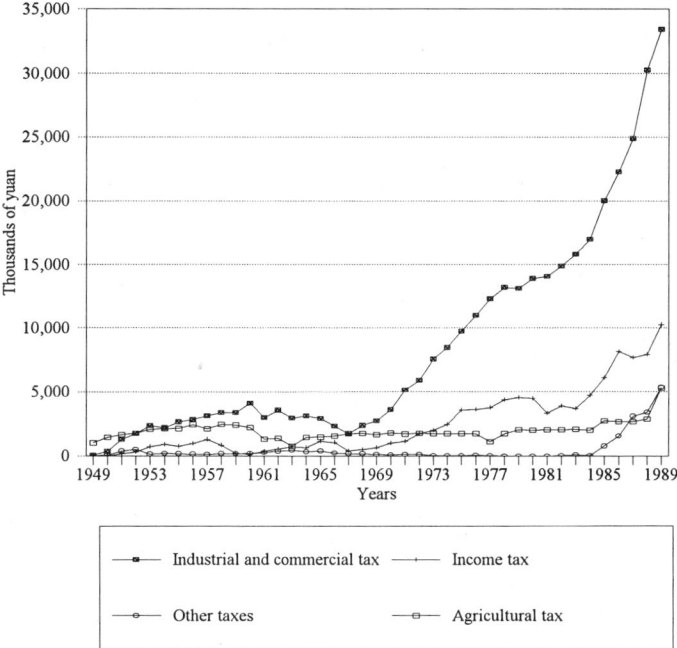

Fig. 5. Shulu county major tax revenues, 1949–89

1958 that was estimated at 9.6 percent, using 70,000 hectares as the cultivated area figure for that year, and with the price of millet at ¥254.55 per ton, the county would have paid about ¥1.75 million in agricultural tax, plus the prevailing local surtaxes. In 1978, twenty years later, when actual per hectare output had more than sextupled to 6.3 tons, Shulu paid almost exactly the same agricultural tax—¥1.76 million—and thus the effective rate of taxation had dropped dramatically to 1.6 percent (using constant prices). This seeming tax restraint where agriculture was concerned was, of course, more than offset by the fact that, in Shulu as in the rest of China, state procurement prices for agricultural commodities were artificially depressed from the 1950's through the 1970's, constituting a very heavy if indirect tax on that sector as a whole.[10]

Only in 1985 do we see the beginning of what could be an upward trend in the county's direct revenue collections from agriculture, which, in the context of all the other dramatic revenue upheavals going on at the time, was still of negligible financial significance. It may be a trend to note for other reasons, however. The more aggressive collection of the agriculture tax in 1985 was apparently linked to the 1984 establishment—in Shulu as in other counties across the nation—of township-level finance and tax assignments (*xiang caizheng*). This development, an important change in the context of county finance, is discussed further below.[11]

TAXES ON LOCAL INDUSTRY AND COMMERCE The other two major tax revenue sources in the budget were the income tax and the unified industry and commerce tax. To help clarify the scope and importance of these lucrative taxes on industries and enterprises, we must begin with a breakdown by category of the fifty or so county-level industries and review the tax liability of each category.[12]

Group 1. First, there were several local state-run (*difang guoying*) industrial enterprises. These enterprises were owned by the state and administered by the county government in its capacity as agent of the central state. Taxes and profits derived from these enterprises were entered directly on the revenue side of the county budget. This group of enterprises included the most important heavy and light industries run by the county, such as a large chemical plant, a cylinder-head factory, a petrochemical plant, a phosphate fertilizer factory, a fur and leather tanning plant, a glassworks, a brick works, and a textile plant. The number of plants counted in this category varied somewhat over time (as indicated in Table 8 below), with significant consequences for county finances. For example, the highly profitable chemical and cylinder-head facilities were removed from county administration in 1971 and put under prefecture management. Their profits and taxes went with them, out of the county's budget and into the prefecture's. This had a marked impact on county tax and profit revenues, as discussed further below.

Group 2. Next there was a group of "collective" (*jiti*) enterprises under the management of the county's Second Light Industry Bureau. These included a wood-furniture factory, a printing factory, a plasticware plant, and a paper mill.[13] As will be explained further, these enterprises were partly in and partly out of the county's state budget. They were subject to tax, and their taxes were recorded on the revenue side of the state budget. But their net profits went in large measure into the vertical ministerial system (*xitong*) of the Second Light Industry Ministry by way of its county-level bureau.[14]

Group 3. Similarly, there were several other enterprises operated directly by various county bureaus (such as the Water Conservancy Bureau, which had its own cement-pipe plant, or the Health Bureau, which had its own pharmaceuticals plant, and the Transportation Bureau, which had its own factory turning out asphalt felt). Like the factories under Second Light, this group paid some tax, but turned most of their net profits over to their parent bureau at the county level, which in turn sent some of this up to its vertical system superiors and kept some for local investment and expenditure.

Group 4. There were also some plants located in Shulu that were run by higher-level state authorities. This included a power-generating plant and a grain-processing plant that was attached to the Hebei province Grain Bureau. The taxes and profits of the grain-processing plant entered the province's budget directly. (This administrative peculiarity probably dated back to the Chinese authorities' 1953 move to centralize and control very tightly everything to do with grain collections, processing, and rationing, so as to prevent grain speculation and hoarding.) There were also a large cylinder-head factory and a chemical plant located in Shulu that for some of the time, as mentioned above, were run by Shijiazhuang prefecture authorities, and their taxes and profits entered the prefecture budget directly.

Group 5. Finally, there were several other county-run extrabudgetary (*xian ban yusuanwai*) enterprises in Shulu. Included in this group were a large rubber-products factory, a cement plant, an agricultural machinery factory, and a shop manufacturing electronic component parts.[15] These enterprises paid income tax, which appeared on the revenue side of the state budget, but placed all of their net profits into the county's own extrabudgetary fund.[16] Thus they were also partly in and partly out of the state budget. In contrast to the regular local state-run (*difang guoying*) enterprises, which the county administered for the larger state of which it was a part, the county-run extrabudgetary enterprises were run by the county for itself. Where the profits of these enterprises were concerned, our dualistic conceptualization of the county as a horizontally demarcated unit of local governance as well as a bureaucratic level within the vertical hierarchy of state organization acquired material significance.

To sum up, then, Shulu's approximately fifty county enterprises constituted a complex composite. It is sometimes hard to see just what they had in common (except that they were not in the rural collective sector). They differed in character of socialist ownership (understood here in the limited sense of claim on profits): some were treated as if owned outright by the county itself, while others were owned by the central state for which the county was acting only as the administering authority. Some were run by the entire county government as a unit, some by specific bureaus of regular state ministries that had offices in the county government, others by bureaus of vertical ministerial systems, and still others by agencies of the prefecture or province themselves. Applying to the enterprises in all these categories the commonly employed general term "state-sector" enterprises would mask their heterogeneity. We therefore—as did our informants in Shulu—refer to them all simply as county or county-level enterprises.

In addition to these five groups of county-level enterprises, Shulu was dotted with literally hundreds of smaller collective industries and commercial enterprises run by townships (formerly communes) and villages (formerly brigades) (*xiang, cun, zhen qiye*).[17] These industries and commercial enterprises paid taxes into the county budget too, but at much lower rates than those applied to county-run enterprises. We shall return, in the section on town-level finance below, to a brief consideration of the financial contributions of these small enterprises to the county coffers.

We can return now to our review of budgetary revenues, bearing in mind that several different systems for collecting taxes and for sharing and

TABLE 10
Income Tax Rates, 1979

Enterprise gross profits (yuan)	Tax rate (%)	Enterprise gross profits (yuan)	Tax rate (%)
<300	7	2,500–10,000	35
300–600	10	10,000–30,000	40
600–1,000	20	30,000–80,000	50
1,000–2,500	30	>80,000	55

redistributing enterprise profits have been applied to the fifty or so county enterprises in Shulu over the years. These differences are of considerable importance in analyzing the evolving fiscal structure of the county.

Generally speaking, from the mid-1960's through the 1970's, local state-run (*difang guoying*) industries and state-run commercial enterprises in Shulu (groups 1, 3, and 4 above) paid only one tax, the unified industry and commerce tax. This is a turnover tax proportional to output value; by 1979 it encompassed forty-four taxable product categories and sixteen tax rates.[18] As illustrated in Figure 5, since 1967 industry and commerce tax receipts had risen steeply and had become far and away the most important revenue source of all taxes levied in the county.[19]

For the county-run extrabudgetary (*xian ban yusuanwai*) industries (group 5 above) and for all "collective" (*jiti*) industries—that is, for group 2 above as well as for town- and village-run collective enterprises—the most important tax was not the industry and commerce tax but the income tax (*suode shui*). This was a progressive tax on profits divided into eight grades. Income tax rates in 1979 are listed in Table 10.[20] In the late 1970's and early 1980's the average rate actually paid by Shulu's collective industries under the administrative leadership of the Second Light Industry Bureau was at the high end of the scale, between 50 and 55 percent.

Commune- and brigade-run (later called town/township- and village-run) industries in Shulu paid this income tax too, but their rate scale was much lower, through the 1970's reportedly averaging around 15 percent of profits. As the breakdown of financial targets for township and village industries detailed in Table 11 indicates, during the first half of the 1980's the income tax burden on these enterprises was actually averaging a little less—around 11 to 12 percent.[21] From 1986 to 1988, the effective income tax rate on these town- and village-run enterprises stayed between 14 and 15 percent. But in 1989 it rose suddenly to more than 18 percent.

Looking back at Figure 5 we can see that by 1973, income tax revenues to the county, derived primarily from these "collective" industries run at the county level and below, exceeded agricultural tax revenues. They rose steadily thereafter, except for a noticeable decline during 1980–83 when all Shulu industries, including its Second Light industries, were going through a very rocky period of adjustment to the Deng reforms.

TABLE 11
Financial Targets for Township and Village Industries, Shulu County, 1980–89
(in thousands of yuan)

Year	Gross receipts	Expenditures	State taxes		Net profits			Total wages	Fixed capital	Liquid capital used by year's end	Unused bank loans at year's end
			All taxes	Income tax	Total profits	Portion remitted upward	Portion retained at enterprise				
1980	25,890	18,810	1,180	430	5,900						
1981	28,190	21,280	1,210	590	5,700						
1982	32,010	24,970	1,580	940	5,460						
1983	34,940	26,750	1,870	1,240	6,320						
1984	88,530	64,160	7,060	3,230	17,310	6,010	8,310	10,230	17,210		
Township only	47,100	35,470	4,630	2,390	7,000	2,170	3,720	5,110	12,630		
1985	135,230	98,800	9,400	3,780	27,030	6,480	11,510	18,550	22,410		
Township only	60,620	47,940	4,880	2,520	7,800	1,870	4,940	7,420	15,500		
1986	170,350	128,820	8,880	3,780	29,780	6,840	22,940	20,670	80,500	69,860	39,170
Township only	68,950	55,700	3,500	1,160	8,450	1,980	6,470	8,280	44,600	42,760	24,530
1987	235,310	188,950	9,320	3,270	23,380	5,580	15,920	25,300	103,600	119,930	66,250
Township only	90,940	76,540	3,740	1,000	7,130	1,380	5,530	9,260	61,340	61,630	43,310
1988	352,070	293,700	11,370	3,990	39,180	7,870	29,640	31,020	128,220	181,300	101,000
Township only	136,800	115,140	5,220	1,970	13,380	2,590	9,880	11,930	72,060	99,680	65,440
1989	362,080	312,260	9,770	2,030	26,650	5,560	22,150	32,770	173,760	248,980	13,460
Township only	139,890	123,250	4,980	1,380	7,070	1,540	12,590	12,850	101,020	144,700	9,740

Before leaving this general discussion of tax revenues, it is worth pausing to consider just how many new taxes made their appearance in Shulu during the 1980's. As noted earlier, the industry and commerce tax levied during the 1960's and 1970's was the product of a deliberate process of "tax simplification" that had eliminated a number of petty and not-so-petty taxes levied by both central and local governments prior to liberation in 1949 and through the 1950's. In 1979, during our first set of interviews in Shulu, we were told that further tax simplifications were planned for the future. The reality, however, has clearly turned out otherwise. A host of new taxes, central and local, many of them wryly reminiscent of the variety of pre-1949 levies, have come to Shulu as part of the reform program. New taxes have included, most prominently, the adjustment tax (*tiaojieshui*, introduced to help make up state revenue losses that came with the *ligaishui* effort and later largely eliminated); the commodity tax (*chanpinshui*); the business tax (*yingyeshui*); and the value-added tax (*zengzhishui*). These taxes were all nationally authorized and levied locally in close coordination with higher levels of government. Added also in the 1980's was a bonus tax (*jiangjinshui*) levied on state-run industries and state administrative units, and also a new state-run enterprise income tax (*suodeshui*) that paralleled the income tax levied on collective enterprises. Collective enterprises were also liable for a bonus tax, and all enterprises were subject to a new urban construction and environmental protection tax (*chengshi weihu jiansheshui*). In addition, the 1980's saw the reintroduction in Shulu of an animal trade tax, a construction tax, a motor vehicles and boat tax, a real estate tax, a tax on income from private enterprise, a market trade tax, a slaughter tax, a deed tax, a land-use tax, and new agricultural taxes such as the *nonglin techan nongyeshui*, a tax on producers of specific fruits, vegetables, and aquatic products. County revenues from the new land-use tax and the deed tax are recorded under the heading of "Other Revenues" in Table 8. These new taxes were in part responsible for the late-1980's swelling of collections in this column, which over the years since 1949 had otherwise consisted of the proceeds from government license and registration fees, fines (including pollution fines after 1982), official confiscations of property, and other sundry receipts.[22]

With so many new and newly revived taxes coming onto the books, not surprisingly, Shulu county officials also found it necessary to tighten up their local tax-evasion and late-tax-payment penalties. Deng-period liberalization and reform of the local economy certainly did not imply any relaxation of vigilance where state extraction was concerned.

Enterprise Profits

After taxes on industry and commerce, the next most important source of monies listed on the revenue side of the Shulu state budget was the net (that is, after-tax) profits of the local state-run (*difang guoying*) industries and of several other state-run commercial enterprises in the county.[23] A

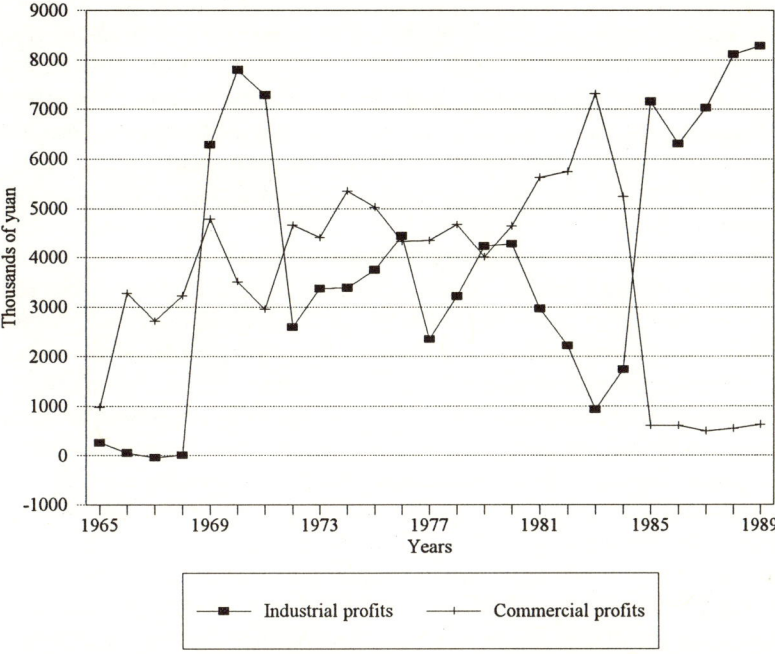

Fig. 6. Shulu county industrial and commercial profit revenues, 1965–89

time series of these revenues is charted in Figure 6. This category of revenues represents a large portion of county-level industries' profit remissions, but it does not reflect all such remissions. The enterprises run directly by county bureaus (group 3 above), which might have been expected to fall into this category, giving up their profits to the county, did not in fact turn their profits in to the County Finance Bureau, but to their own respective bureaus for forwarding to higher levels of their vertical system. These profits did not appear in the official budget revenues. Likewise, the enterprises under Second Light turned most of their profits after taxes (using a profit-sharing formula discussed below) over to the Second Light Industry Bureau, and these profits also did not appear in the state budget for the county. The county-run extrabudgetary industries, as their name suggests, turned their profits after taxes in to the county's extrabudgetary fund. These too, therefore, did not appear in the county's state budget.

Figure 6 shows a number of steep dips and rises in the commercial enterprise profits collected by the county over the years. The general trend over the two decades from the early 1960's to the early 1980's, nevertheless, was a fitfully rising one. Only in 1984, with the implementation of some of the most dramatic economic reforms, did the bottom fall out of county budgetary collections from commercial enterprise profits. In that year, as discussed further in Chapter 6, the county's major state-run commercial enterprises, operating under the leadership of the Shulu Commerce Bureau, were decisively pried away from their embrace of the local (formally "collectively" owned and operated) Supply and Marketing Co-op network (*gongxiaoshe*) enterprises. The liberated co-op enterprises were immediately made liable for payment of some seventeen different business taxes as well as the income tax, but they no longer were required to remit their profits directly to the local government. And the detached state-run commercial enterprises, now standing alone in 1984, were also reorganized into semi-independent companies that would pay taxes to the state rather than turn their profits directly in to the county government. The fiscal effects of these bold reforms of the nation's domestic trade system are reflected in the dramatic shift of budgetary receipts from commercial enterprise profits to taxes levied on commercial companies in Shulu. In the realm of commerce, then, at least at one level, the frequently articulated reform ideal of *ligaishui*—switching from a profit-based to a tax-based system of state finance—was partly realized in the 1980's.

Looking still at Figure 6, we can also see some steep dips and rises in the county's budgetary revenues from industrial profits over the years. These ups and downs, first of all, reflect fairly faithfully broader national patterns in the decentralization and recentralization of administrative control over industries. Before 1958 all profits of state-run enterprises were remitted directly to higher levels, without going through the county budget. But in the celebrated decentralization of 1958, higher administrative levels turned leadership of many of these enterprises over to the county. Simultaneously, a number of previously collective enterprises were transformed into state-run enterprises under the county. This accounts for the nearly ¥8 million in Shulu county revenue from enterprise profits in 1959. In the early 1960's, during the "readjustment" following the economic and administrative disasters of the Great Leap Forward, some of the larger county factories reverted to upper-level leadership and others reverted to collective ownership.[24] Thus county state budget revenues from all enterprise profits in 1963 were down to ¥492,000, a mere 6 percent of the 1959 figure. By 1965, county authorities in Shulu retained under their jurisdiction only one farm-machinery factory and one brick-and-tile factory, both of which were producing and providing services almost exclusively for local demand.

The rise in county budgetary revenue from industrial profits again in 1969 is attributable to yet another administrative reorganization which brought under county leadership several factories previously operating under prefectural or provincial control.[25] Then in 1971 two large plants, producing chemicals and cylinder heads, were taken over once more by the prefecture. This caused a sharp drop in county budgetary revenues in 1971-72. Then again, in 1977, a power-generating station went from county to prefectural administrative control, which caused another decline in the county's state budget revenues in this category. In 1984 the cylinder-head factory was returned to Shulu jurisdiction, resulting in an upward profit trend. And in 1985, the important chemical factory was returned, producing a dramatic rise in county industrial profit revenues.

Thus when more factories came under county administrative control, county budgetary revenues from profits rose; and each time a factory was claimed or reclaimed by a higher level of government, the county budget showed a decline in profit revenues. We might expect, therefore, that county authorities would automatically seek to keep as many profitable enterprises under their ægis as possible, and would regret decisions made at higher levels to take back administrative authority over established enterprises. In interviews with Shulu county officials, however, this expectation was not borne out. This can best be explained by looking back at Table 8 for the years when county budgetary revenues from industrial profits declined due to loss of control over one or more plants, noting that the negative effect on overall budgetary revenues in each case was minimal. In 1971 and 1972 when the county lost its valuable chemical plant and cylinder-head factory, the blow to total county budgetary revenues was neither very severe nor very long-lasting. Likewise when Shulu's power plant was transferred to prefectural control in 1977, the effect on total county state budget revenues was hardly perceptible. Probably more important from the point of view of county officials is the fact that while county revenues sometimes suffered slightly in these upward reorganizations of factory control, levels of county budgetary expenditures were not permitted to fall. Figure 4 shows that 1971 and 1972 saw no drops in what the county had available to spend. Likewise in 1977 the loss of revenue from the power plant did not interrupt the upward curve in Shulu county's total expenditures. In one way or another, during the budget negotiations the county's revenue losses were made up to it and its level of expenditures—surely the bottom line for county cadres—was supported.

The great bulk of the county's budgetary revenues from industrial profits came thus from a shifting but always small group of local state-run industries. The relationship of these industries to the county's financial affairs was so intimate, in fact, that county cadres tended to refer to these enterprises in conversation as "in-budget" (*yusuannei*) more often and more naturally than they would refer to them by their official designation, "local state-run" (*difang guoying*). Even so, not absolutely all the profits of these factories were remitted to the County Finance Bureau to be recorded in the budget. A detailed breakdown of the calculation and distribution of the profits of these local state-run (or "in-budget") industries appears in Table 12. In this table, the left-side calculation of real profits generally balances out.[26] But the right-side accounting of debt repayments, tax payments, pollution cleanup payments, and other allocations from profits does not always balance satisfactorily—especially not in the 1980's. This

TABLE 12

Shulu In-Budget Industry Profits and Profit Distribution, 1970–89

(in thousands of yuan)

Year	No. of enter- prises	Gross receipts	Sales tax	Production costs	Merchan- dising costs	Technical upgrading expenses	Profits from sales[a]	Other profits
1970	7	25,810	1,780	15,929			8,101	44
1971	7	31,082	3,031	20,128			7,923	45
1972	5	16,251	1,596	11,983			2,672	31
1973	6	23,642	2,530	16,635			4,477	80
1974	7	25,840	2,628	19,272			3,940	76
1975	9	31,078	2,836	23,699			4,543	72
1976	9	34,207	3,114	26,029			5,064	74
1977	8	31,308	3,000	25,306			3,002	144
1978	9	37,852	2,848	29,373			5,631	157
1979	9	43,419	2,704	34,665			7,080	406
1980	9	45,709	2,774	36,414			6,521	226
1981	9	43,362	2,497	35,970	13		4,882	214
1982	9	39,504	2,212	34,418	22		2,852	120
1983	9	37,646	1,795	33,976	15	3	1,857	194
1984	10[c]	47,211	2,309	41,223	129	6	3,544	429
1985	11[d]	98,766	7,224	77,219	159	102	14,062	355
1986	11	113,690	8,074	89,601	132	57	15,826	533
1987	11	127,260	9,132	101,978	280	40	15,830	437
1988	11	159,802	11,233	124,522	2,997	12	21,038	786
1989	11	197,920	15,580	157,622	3,866		20,852	759

[a] Gross receipts minus sales tax, production costs, merchandising costs, and technical upgrading expenditures equals profits from sales.
[b] Profits from sales plus other profits minus nonbusiness income equals real profits.
[c] Cylinder-head plant returned to county in 1984.
[d] Chemical plant returned to county in 1985.

table shows what actually happened to the profits of these several industries in Shulu. There are several points worth noting here.

Looking at the two rightmost columns we can see first that starting in the early 1970's a small percentage of profits was generally retained within the factories themselves to be put toward workers' welfare funds. Then with the onset of the economic reforms in 1978, and as part of a national incentive program, factories overfulfilling their planned targets were allowed to retain a certain percentage of over-target profits for distribution to workers.[27] Factory-retained profits jumped up in 1979 as a result; but in Shulu that year it was decided that only 5 percent of all such over-target profit retentions would revert to factory workers directly. The Industry Bureau at the county level would control the rest, using it as a cushion against losses in the industrial sector of the local economy and also as a source of extra investment funds for industry.[28] Starting also in 1978 was a program of withholding and diverting in-budget industry profits to certain county-run enterprises—primarily to extrabudgetary industries. No explanation was offered for this ad hoc move which appeared to constitute a de-

					Profit distribution				
Non-business income	Real profits[b]	Debt re-payment	Workers' welfare and bonuses	Pollu-tion clean-up	Income tax	Adjust-ment tax	Portion remitted to county	Portion retained at enter-prises	County-run enter-prises
161	7,984	355					7,629		
114	7,854	100					7,754		
22	2,681	100					2,581		
42	4,515	242					3,566	707	
70	3,946						3,547	399	
111	4,504	292					3,898	314	
112	5,026	510					4,212	304	
96	3,050	370					2,439	241	
282	5,506	320					2,884	250	2,052
179	7,307	167					4,510	836	1,794
136	7,782	729					4,351	817	1,885
70	5,166	91		30			3,018	788	1,239
135	2,837						1,975	14	848
67	1,984				1,077	351		556	
451	3,522	325	19		1,733	421		1,024	
786	13,631	3,710	500	801	5,331	2,193		2,629	
136	15,271	3,550	369		5,935	2,413		2,537	
1,374	16,306	4,068	352		7,192	2,934		1,655	
334	19,889	5,390	389		6,447	1,406		5,413	
1,112	19,701	4,329	265		6,430	842	1,417	6,550	

liberate subsidy to some of the county's own extrabudgetary industries, that were also about to become caught up in the wrenching readjustments brought on by economic reform. In 1978, however, the Shulu extrabudgetary fund did not get the full benefit of the deal intended because, as county cadres clearly indicated, this special cash reservoir was then subject to raiding by prefecture-level officials. But before this program was terminated in 1985, more than ¥7 million was estimated to have been successfully transferred from the state budgetary pathway to the extrabudgetary pathway in Shulu.[29] (See the discussion in the section on the extrabudgetary fiscal pathway below.)

Table 12 records rising real profits for Shulu's eleven in-budget industries from 1985 through 1989. But it also shows that these enterprises came to depend heavily on credit during that period. Under the impact of the reforms, no longer receiving state grants and subsidies to cover all their operations, these factories were obliged to secure loans to stay in business. Since first priority in the disposition of profits went to debt repayment, second priority to payment of state taxes, and third priority to securing the enterprise's own profit share, the county's Finance Bureau would have been the last on the list of claimants to be satisfied. And as the table shows, after 1982 there was little if anything left of these enterprises' profits to be forwarded to the county government. In 1983 also the county began the transition to making its claims against the earnings of these industries in the form of taxes rather than by direct collection of their profits. As with commerce, then, in industry an apparent switch had been made from a profit-based to a tax-based system of public finance. Still, the way these tax programs were administered at the local level certainly made that change seem more rhetorical than real.[30] Tax targets were sent down annually to each county-level bureau with industrial enterprises under its jurisdiction. The bureau then divided the targets out among its enterprises. Starting in 1987, the tax collection targets for industrial enterprises had been rising by 10 percent annually. As Zheng Lanying, former Finance Bureau chief, tried to explain it: "Since they are the major taxpayers, the enterprises are given targets that go up faster than the 5.5 percent overall target rise for the county budget."[31] If an enterprise managed to exceed its targeted taxability, it was permitted to keep just 20 percent of the surplus, the remaining 80 percent going again to the County Finance Bureau. As Zheng himself admitted, "Actually this is the old profit contracting system, but it's called *ligaishui*." Whatever it was called, whether enterprise profits or taxes, the overall trajectory of county-level revenue collections from industry and commerce was sharply upward in the late 1980's.

BUDGETARY EXPENDITURES

While Shulu county's budgetary revenues may have been growing very quickly—more than doubling during the decade of the 1980's—county-budgeted expenditures over the same period expanded even more dramatically: they more than quadrupled. Expenditure targets (by category) were set, along with revenue targets, in the important budget negotiations which took place between county officials and prefecture officials each year.[32] Shulu's budgetary expenditures from 1949-1989 are detailed in Table 9. As the table shows, the county's chief spending responsibilities over the years were concentrated in the realms of support for agriculture, urban construction, education, health, social welfare, and government administration. In looking at this expenditure side of the county's budget, it is important to bear in mind, then, what elements of necessary spending and investment are simply missing from it. The overwhelming proportion of the county's budgetary revenues, as explained earlier, derived from its industries and commercial enterprises. Yet there were no expenditures for capital investment or working capital of enterprises entered in the state budget for the county; there were also virtually no expenditures for capital construction or investment in industry.[33] Outlays for these purposes, along with outlays for technical renovation, for geologic exploration, for debt servicing, and for national defense, all came from the central budget.

This basic division of responsibilities between central and local budgets remained in effect both before and after the Mao period.[34] Funds for industrial development reached the county, and ultimately the enterprises themselves, by other fiscal pathways, not primarily through the county's state budget.

On what did the county spend its budgeted resources, then? By 1986 there were some thirty-four distinct lines in the Shulu county budget. As illustrated in Figure 7, those loosely grouped under the heading of cultural and educational activities made up the largest expenditure category. The great bulk of the funds here were allocated for education, but under this category also came public health clinics and services (including immunization and epidemic control programs, pre- and postnatal care programs, and free medical care coverage for state employees), along with family planning, sports, science and earthquake prediction, and radio and TV broadcasting. The county's education budget included disbursements over the years for kindergartens, primary and secondary schools, technical schools, "people-run" schools, retraining programs, night schools and anti-illiteracy programs. The important Xinji Middle School was funded through the county budget in the early years, but in 1978 it was designated a national keypoint school and it received some special allocations out of higher-level budgets for buildings, equipment, and the library that year. Then, in 1980, the school began to receive steady allocations from higher-level budgets, reducing but not eliminating the county's own responsibility for funding it. A major overhaul of education finance was introduced in 1984, reapportioning responsibilities for different types of schools across different levels of government. The county budget was to fund senior middle schools, normal institutions, and retraining institutions, while the burden for junior middle schools was shifted to town and township budgets and for primary schools, to village budgets. An education surtax, to back up with new funds at all levels these re-allotted responsibilities, began to be levied only in 1986.[35]

Outlays in support of agriculture made up another important budget category, but here the pattern of expenditure over the years was far more erratic. Included in this category were lines for animal husbandry, agricultural machinery, forestry, irrigation, aquatic products, weather prediction, and support for rural enterprises. Budget outlays in support of agriculture fluctuated over the years because they operated as a cushion for the county's rural communities in times of harvest failure. (Note the emergency expenditures in support of Shulu farmers from 1959 to 1961 and again in 1977, a year of disastrous flood.) Fluctuations in this category also reflect county government attempts to stabilize and improve agricultural production through occasional major investments in irrigation, drainage, and other agricultural infrastructure. The 1978 peak in expenditure, for example, represents part of the state's contribution to the big waterworks project undertaken in southern Shulu that year.[36] Farm input subsidies and additional agricultural technology supports account for the better part of the rising trend in expenditures in this category after 1985.

Expenditures for governmental operations rose generally yet remained relatively modest in the context of county finance during the first three decades. But new outlays for economic administration and management, for the work of the Industry and Commerce Management Bureau and the Tax Bureau, as well as for the local police force and judicial and procuratorial offices, all contributed to a major upward leap in the cost of local government during the 1980's. The rising relative cost of local government when compared to the other standard categories of budgetary commitment in Shulu has, in fact, been one of the most dramatic trends of the Deng period.[37] Included in regular expenditures made under this category were not only all wages for administrative personnel, but a host of salary supplements and benefits to local cadres and their families. Standard salary supplements covered support for aging staff members, special dietary needs of ailing staff members, reimbursements for visits by family members living far away, lunch expenses, subsidies for families with disproportionate numbers of women and children, and subsidies for Muslims with special dietary needs. After 1988, these were augmented by special grain price subsidies to cadres and staff, other food subsidies, coal subsidies, rent subsidies, bicycle repair subsidies, and more. The list of special welfare benefits for cadres and administrative staff included labor insurance and disability payments, funeral expenses, single-child family subsidies, widows' and widowers' pensions, medical allowances, travel reimbursements, post and telephone allowances, allowances for gas and repairs on motor vehicles, home leave allowances, allowances for baths and haircuts, and subsidies for those who agreed to retire early.[38]

The other most important county budget categories, as shown in Figure 7, have been pensions, welfare, and emergency relief, including death and injury benefits to workers in enterprises and their dependents, retirement benefits, social relief, disaster assistance, and basic construction and technical improvement, including temporary construction expenses, scientific tests and experiments, and technical-administrative assistance to enterprises. New lines, initially with rather small outlays, were added to the budget in the 1980's—for environmental protection, for the maintenance of urban public facilities, to subsidize meat purchases by consumers, for the support and training of unemployed youth,[39] and for the operation of a Communist Party school.

Under the residual category of "other expenditures," disbursements were made for a wide variety of uses over the years including provision of special egg, meat, and coal price subsidies to state employees, covering the costs of assisting the military in its conscription activities locally, meeting equipment and training expenses for local militia forces, provision of special subsidies to Hui nationality people living in the county, and covering the costs of various mass activities associated with political cam-

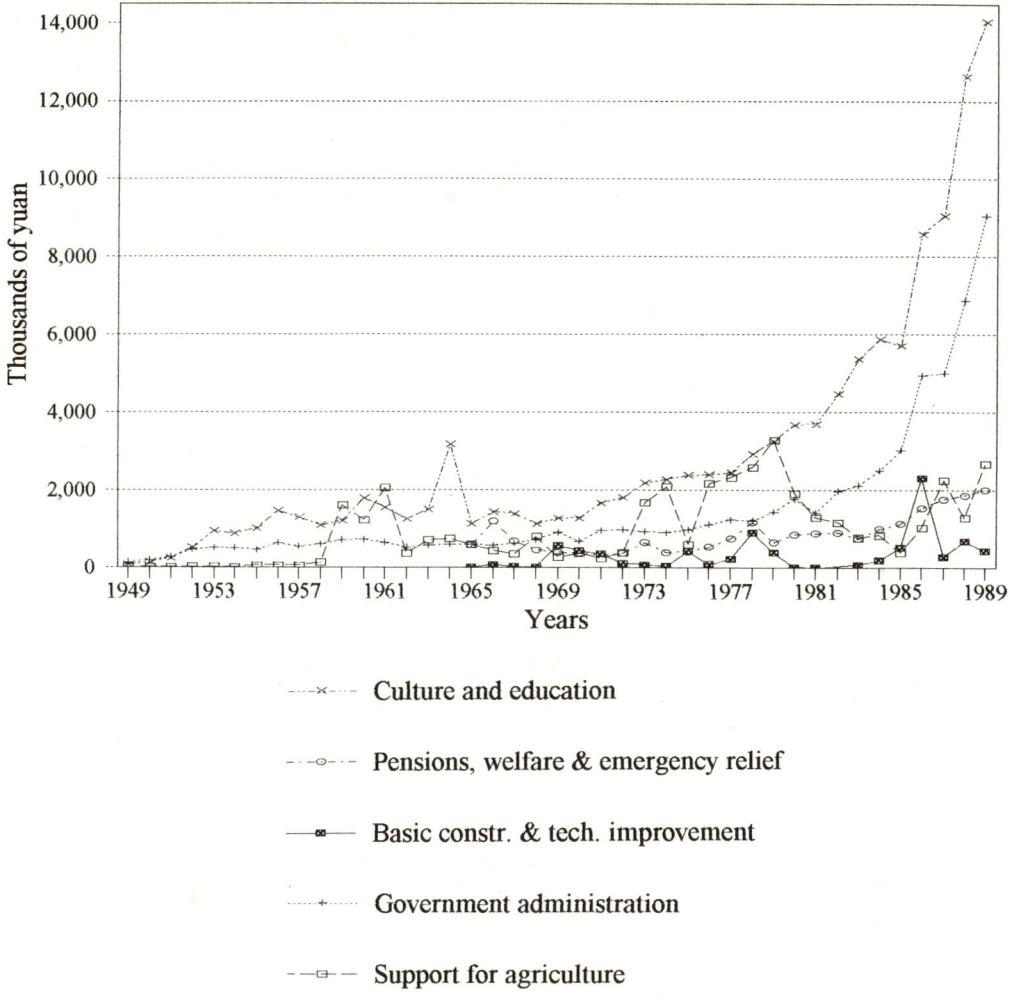

Fig. 7. Shulu county major budgetary expenditures, 1949–89

paigns, such as the Socialist Education Movement in the early 1960's and the Cultural Revolution a few years later. This category also included expenditures made to compensate people for political injustices done to them over the years (*luoshi zhengce zhichu*), and for the costs of cadre retraining.[40]

Analysts of the economic reforms commonly note that China's central budget has come under heavy strain during this period of general fiscal restructuring and relative revenue decline.[41] Some have noted also that local government budgets have also been heavily burdened due to rising prices and expanded regulatory and other local administrative responsibilities.[42]

Besides costly new policies and standards set to apply in the fields of education and health that fall to the localities to finance, demands on local government budgets have gone up because of inflation; the consequent demand to provide price subsidies for meat, grain, and other daily necessities to urban residents; and also because of rising administrative costs, traceable in part to institutional growth and in part to rising labor costs. In Shulu, where we were able to detect very little evidence of county government extravagance or waste as compared to other localities known to us, it seemed clear enough that the local budget was indeed fairly tight during the 1980's. It is interesting to note, then, that Shulu county officials did not often gripe or engage in complaint about the absolute size of the expenditure allocations they were given.

They did have grievances concerning some other aspects of the budgetary process affecting their expenditures. For example, before the reforms, in the normal course of the annual state budget negotiations, the county had routinely been assigned what were called "special projects expenditures." These were, in effect, grants from the province to cover necessary local outlays and investments. By 1979 these grants amounted to almost 40 percent of all Shulu's annual budgeted expenditures. In 1979, as a key part of the reform effort, this automatic grant-giving was terminated. A competitive application procedure was set up instead to distribute what grants the province could still afford to make to counties. Shulu's applications, we sensed from the finance cadres' diffidence on the matter, had suffered lengthy delays in the review process and were not often fully funded.

To cope with the sudden disappearance of the special projects grants on which it depended so heavily for expenditure allocations, Shulu officials appear to have entered into a series of deficit financing arrangements in the early 1980's. Local governments in China are not, technically, permitted to borrow; and yet that is how local officials described what they in fact were obliged to do in those years.[43] According to one set of official estimates produced for our information, Shulu county borrowing ranged from ¥2.1 million to ¥2.9 million annually between 1980 and 1984. This represented from 25 percent to 30 percent of total county budgetary expenditures during that period. In 1986, local officials stressed, with some patent concern and irritation, that such loans to local governments were authorized for productive purposes only and that they absolutely had to be repaid on schedule. They plainly chafed under the pressures of this new system, which they referred to as a way of "borrowing against the future," and which seemed to violate their sense of how intergovernmental financial relations should be ordered.

By 1990, however, Finance Bureau officials were treating the matter as closed. The very concept of distinguishing between budgetary grants on the one hand and loans to the county for budgetary spending on the other hand had proved to be "not actually feasible in reality," it was said.[44] The issue was never very fully aired in our discussions, but the clear implication, we thought, was that Shulu had not by any means actually repaid all the loans it had taken out for budgetary expenditure. By 1990, former bureau director Zheng Lanying was at pains to point out that the county itself had sometimes also been on the receiving end of "enforced borrowings" and of debts owed to it by higher levels of government that were never made good during the fiscal tumult of the 1980's. The screws had been put to Shulu's monetary reserves by "higher levels" in 1981 and 1982, and again in 1987, he explained. Although the amounts involved seemed nearly negligible in the context of overall county budgetary activity,[45] it was with evident resentment and distaste that Zheng dwelt upon the details of these past examples of bad faith at higher levels.[46]

Whatever little rip-offs Shulu county had actually sustained while riding the fiscal reform rollercoaster of the 1980's it certainly seemed in no position generally to complain about a lack of higher-level care and concern. In part this was due to the fact that special projects grants authorizations to Shulu went up sharply when, effective in 1986, the county was selected for promotion to municipality (*shi*) status. This administrative change clearly signified that Shulu had been given the green light for especially rapid development by superiors in the Hebei provincial government. The fiscal effects of this decision can be noted in the fact that budgetary expenditures in Shulu between 1986 and 1989 were permitted to grow 3 percent per year faster than budgetary revenues. And then, as of 1990, a change of even greater long-term potential benefit to the locality came into effect. As a full-fledged municipality, Shulu began to report directly to the province on financial matters. Local cadres no longer needed to go through prefecture-level officials; Shulu became incorporated into the provincial rather than the prefectural budget. This change in the reporting system would, Shulu finance officials acknowledged, likely carry some benefits. "It may help us keep our 5.5 percent revenue target down from year to year. And, if we need some special help, it may be easier for us to negotiate a good deal with the province than with the prefecture. Provincial level officials have more room for maneuver in their funds and so they may be able to give more consideration to our needs if we approach them."[47] These were only guesses, put forward with an air of mild skepticism, in fact, by Shulu officials. They were pretty safe guesses, surely. But Shulu cadres did not like being put in the position of seeming to give their administrative promotion to municipality status much of the credit for local successes. It was local effort they tended to find cause to praise and not the wise and helpful decisions of bureaucratic superiors.

TOWN-LEVEL FINANCE

As noted earlier, the budget and tax reforms brought with them an extension of state financial organization down to the level of town and township governments (*xiang* and *zhen*) in Shulu, as in other counties around the country. This extension of responsibility for finance and tax planning and administration down one more level in 1984 was significant because it clearly reflected a nationwide effort to push the state's revenue-capturing apparatus closer to rural people.[48] Before the 1984 reform, township cadres had little if any incentive to collect taxes from residents in their communities, however legitimate or reasonable those taxes may have been, because all such revenues passed immediately out of their hands to be entered directly in the county's budget. The establishment of township finance and tax assignments was a device designed to give cadres material incentives to make local collections.

Under the new system, township governments were permitted to keep and to spend within their communities a negotiated percentage of the total revenue they collected each year for the county. The Shulu County Finance Bureau, receiving its annual tax and profit collection targets from Shijiazhuang prefecture and being responsible for dividing them up among all the townships and other units in the county, proceeded by negotiating target figures for receipts and for revenue share rates with each township government. These targets and share rates were subject to change from year to year, based in part on the previous year's performance and in part on the townships' relative ability to pay. Table 13 lists the 1986 revenue targets and share rates for every township in Shulu. It shows that township revenue retention rates varied very considerably: poorer communities kept as much as 60 to 65 percent, while richer townships retained as little as 5 to 10 percent.

The former director of the Shulu Finance Bureau, Zheng Lanying, reported that there was bitter conflict and controversy in the late 1980's entailed in the process of setting and resetting annual targets and share rates for each one of the townships.[49] Finally, starting in 1989, a system of three-year fixed targets was put in place around the county. This system included the further incentive mechanism of allowing each township government to keep the lion's share of any over-target collections it could make. As of 1989, wealthier townships were keeping 80 percent of over-target collections and turning 20 percent in to the county finance bureau; average townships kept 90 percent and turned in 10 percent; the poorest communities were allowed to keep 100 percent of their over-target collections.[50]

Table 14 shows the actual budgetary revenues and expenditures of each township in Shulu from 1986 through 1989. The table reveals the rising trend in both total budgetary collections and expenditures made at the *xiang* and *zhen* levels of government administration. Director Zheng explained that the town-level finance offices had initially functioned just as "collection agencies for the county," but that the development and elaboration of their local budget planning, expenditure monitoring, and economic advisory functions through the late 1980's had already made

TABLE 13
Township Financial Revenue and Expenditure Targets, 1986

Township	Revenue base target (yuan)	Sources (yuan)		Revenue share rate (%)	Township expenditure target (yuan)
		Industry and commerce taxes	Agricultural tax		
Jiucheng	442,400	323,000	119,400	47.38	209,400
Hezhuang	166,700	75,000	91,700	48.71	81,200
Junqi	133,000	60,000	73,000	59.32	78,900
Tiangongying	173,000	41,000	132,000	61.45	106,300
Zhangguzhuang	216,700	82,000	134,700	65.90	142,800
Renci	220,100	140,000	80,100	43.75	96,300
Xiaoxinzhuang	315,400	175,000	140,400	45.02	142,000
Zhonglixiang	260,800	101,000	159,800	49.08	128,000
Fanjiazhuang	262,700	136,000	126,700	52.26	137,300
Weibo	307,100	186,000	121,100	40.51	124,400
Xinleitou	520,100	391,000	129,000	20.80	108,200
Nanlücun	185,700	122,000	63,700	41.63	77,300
Xinghua (Xinji)	2,273,000	2,708,000	65,000	4.42	122,500
Chengdong (Chengguan)	357,000	300,000	57,900	28.36	101,500
Chengbei (Angucheng)	541,400	374,000	167,400	23.97	129,800
Chengxi (Tianjiazhuang)	357,900	261,000	96,700	30.53	109,200
Chengnan (Ziyuezhuang)	320,900	252,000	68,900	24.93	80,000
Hemujing	626,200	531,000	95,200	21.62	135,400
Dashizhuang	281,700	174,000	107,700	38.02	107,100
Houying	181,400	105,000	76,400	53.47	97,000
Xizebei	188,500	86,000	102,500	60.95	114,900
Xincheng	539,700	472,000	67,700	19.05	102,700
Dalizhuang	382,200	301,000	81,200	20.33	77,700
Yijianfang	251,700	161,000	90,700	31.82	80,100
Mazhuang	370,400	251,000	119,400	27.46	101,700
Xixiaowang	225,500	117,000	108,500	51.44	116,000
Muqiu	321,200	235,000	86,200	32.44	104,200
Nanzhiqiu	657,200	559,000	98,200	19.13	125,700
Guoxi	374,200	263,000	117,200	33.59	125,700
Mengjiazhuang	155,700	99,000	56,700	39.37	61,300
Wangkou	946,100	826,000	120,100	8.60	81,400

NOTE: If income target is exceeded, 60 percent of surplus stays with the township office.

them into what he referred to as "small finance bureaus serving the township governments."[51] With all these new and rising revenues, town-level budgets were indeed becoming more elaborate and comprehensive.[52] Like the county government above them, most town and township governments by 1989 were also assembling detailed formal annual budgets with expenditure lines for culture, education, agriculture, agricultural machinery, animal husbandry, public health, medical care, broadcasting, family planning, and pensions. In 1988 and 1989, the budgetary expenditures of

TABLE 14
Township Budgetary Revenues and Expenditures, 1986–89
(in thousands of yuan)

Township	1986 Revenues	1986 Expenditures	1987 Revenues	1987 Expenditures	1988 Revenues	1988 Expenditures	1989 Revenues	1989 Expenditures
Jiucheng	442	120	538	189	589	241	458	277
Junqi	133	50	183	97	195	122	239	163
Hezhuang	155	48	189	99	191	131	220	183
Tiangongying	173	73	258	122	243	162	278	202
Zhangguzhuang	217	94	297	116	284	151	252	199
Zhonglixiang	261	74	343	152	333	198	362	250
Renci	220	72	282	110	303	140	280	173
Xiaoxinzhuang	315	85	379	169	361	210	401	246
Weibo	307	42	421	141	454	183	510	275
Nanlücun	186	49	231	90	233	113	266	135
Fanjiazhuang	232	63	273	139	268	171	302	209
Xinleitou	520	64	667	130	701	155	791	239
Xinghua (Xinji)	2,773	68	3,446	195	3,629	308	4,228	448
Chengdong (Chengguan)	358	58	448	103	495	118	543	170
Chengbei (Angucheng)	541	82	690	159	702	213	777	251
Chengxi (Tianjiazhuang)	358	64	493	139	530	175	580	217
Chengnan (Ziyuezhuang)	321	46	346	85	417	123	450	163
Muqiu	321	61	434	126	408	156	440	188
Hemujing	626	82	763	119	790	161	923	233
Dashizhuang	282	74	322	131	341	168	360	237
Houying	181	64	219	120	214	142	188	158
Xizebei	188	59	240	131	248	170	207	180
Xincheng	540	103	310	101	588	144	651	181
Dalizhuang	382	53	337	92	446	133	299	98
Yijianfang	252	52	296	99	302	126	337	159
Mazhuang	370	64	421	124	455	163	483	206
Xixiaowang	223	71	281	140	312	183	310	249
Nanzhiqiu	657	73	786	122	912	159	908	267
Guoxi	374	67	444	129	274	124	335	155
Mengjiazhuang	156	46	198	69	153	81	212	119
Wangkou	946	54	1,055	79	1,217	127	1,115	152
TOTAL	13,010	2,075	15,590	3,817	16,588	4,951	17,705	6,382

all town and township governments in Shulu broke down as shown in Table 15.

The trends toward rationalization and comprehensiveness that characterized the development of the state budgetary process at the county level through the 1980's had clearly reached down to touch the township level by the end of the decade. This in turn was contributing to greater regularity and professionalism at the grass-roots level of administration around the county.

TABLE 15
Budgetary Expenditures of Town and Township
Governments by Category, 1988–89

(in thousands of yuan)

	1988	1989
Agriculture, forestry, and animal husbandry	63	85
Culture, education, and health	3,073	3,201
Pensions, welfare, and benefits	939	1,072
Government administration	876	1,704
Other government expenses	—	321

Town and township governments had by 1989 already started levying surtaxes of their own on the industrial, commercial, and agriculture taxes they collected. These extra collections they deposited in town government "extrabudgetary" funds. And these funds, like the extrabudgetary fund of the county government itself (to be discussed below), were held as a cushion to give town officials additional financial flexibility and some greater autonomy in addressing local emergencies and other needs.[53] Table 16 displays budgetary and extrabudgetary revenues and expenditures, as well as other (self-generated) revenues and expenditures, for every township in Shulu for the year 1988. Self-generated revenues were made up primarily of profits from town and township enterprises, income from contracting (chengbao fei), special levies for public works and public welfare, and fines charged against households exceeding the birth limit. The table shows that, in gross terms, town and township governments were keeping and spending just under one-third of what they collected in budgetary revenues. It shows also that total expenditures made through the state budgetary pathway at the town and township level in 1988 had already exceeded expenditures made out of other self-generated township revenues.

Second Pathway: Fiscal Responsibilities of Vertical Systems

After taxes and some profits were turned over to the Shulu County Finance Bureau and entered in the state budget, there remained significant sums routinely transferred into and out of the county by means other than the state budget process. For the most part these monies were profits of commercial and industrial enterprises run by certain county bureaus. Such profits were clearly regarded as being attached to those bureaus and the vertical ministerial systems (xitong) to which they belonged. They were collected by the bureaus and then, applying the profit-sharing formula currently in use in that xitong, divided up among the enterprise itself, the bureau at the county level, and the bureau at prefectural level. In Shulu, especially during the late 1970's, the amounts involved in these intrasystem transfers were significant and the uses to which these monies were put

TABLE 16
Township Budgetary, Extrabudgetary, and Other Revenues and Expenditures, 1988
(in thousands of yuan)

Township	Revenues						Expenditures			
	Budgetary revenues			Extra-budgetary revenues	Self-generated revenues	Total revenues	Budgetary expenditures	Extra-budgetary expenditures	Expenditures from self-generated funds	Total expenditures
	Industry and commerce tax	Agriculture tax	Subtotal							
Jiucheng	479	110	589	38	10	637	241	38	10	289
Junqi	128	67	195	11	63	269	122	4	63	189
Hezhuang	108	83	191	9	25	225	131		29	160
Tiangongying	121	122	243	10		253	162	11	1	174
Zhangguzhuang	163	121	284	14	425	723	151	20	199	370
Zhonglixiang	186	147	333	37	53	423	198		137	335
Renci	229	74	303	6	187	496	140	11	190	341
Xiaoxinzhuang	231	130	361	12		373	210	12		222
Weibo	342	112	454	17	273	744	183	15	214	412
Nanliicun	175	58	233	32	37	302	113	25	39	177
Fanjiazhuang	151	117	268	44	113	425	171	14	114	299
Xinleitou	582	119	701	22	263	986	155	24	250	429
Xinghua (Xinji)	3,578	51	3,629	67	427	4,123	308	85	391	784
Chengdong (Chengguan)	442	53	495	5	101	601	118		113	231
Chengbei (Angucheng)	547	155	702	47	198	947	213	27	198	438
Chengxi (Tianjiazhuang)	441	89	530	33	137	700	175	26	163	364
Chengnan (Ziyuezhuan)	354	63	417	5	294	716	123		272	395

Muqiu	329	79	408	63	78	549	156	63	111	330
Hemujing	702	88	790	9	113	912	161		72	233
Dashizhuang	242	99	341	33	165	539	168	29	188	385
Houying	144	70	214	17	186	417	142	12	175	329
Xizebei	154	94	248	5		253	170	1		171
Xincheng	526	62	588	5	357	950	144	26	296	466
Dalizhuang	371	75	446	14	153	613	133	11	128	272
Yijianfang	219	83	302	6	97	405	126	9	186	321
Mazhuang	345	110	455	23	188	666	163	11	175	349
Xixiaowang	212	100	312	91	221	624	183	45	201	429
Nanzhiqiu	822	90	912	64	120	1,096	159	51	239	449
Guoxi	171	103	274	12	134	420	124	13	140	277
Mengjiazhuang	101	52	153	4	60	217	81	11	67	159
Wangkou	1,106	111	1,217	11	386	1,614	127	11	363	501
TOTAL	13,701	2,887	16,588	766	4,864	22,218	4,951	605	4,724	10,280

SOURCE: Xinji shi caizheng zhi, 286–89.

(once divided among the administrative levels) were essentially the responsibility of *xitong* officials only. To some extent they were able to make allocations of funds based on their own investigations and plans, without requiring permission from other county authorities. In practice, however, consultation and coordination with other county offices were the rule in Shulu; and where very large amounts were involved, a good deal of horizontal and vertical coordination was required for a project to succeed. Over the years in Shulu county, many enterprises were established by different county bureaus and managed, to one degree or another, as units in vertical systems. Here we consider just one of the more important examples of *xitong* fiscal transfers affecting the county economy: the Second Light Industry Bureau.

THE SECOND LIGHT INDUSTRY BUREAU

The clearest example of how ministerial fiscal pathways have affected Shulu's finance and economic development is in the operations of this bureau and its constellation of "collective" industries (group 2 above).[54] Through most of the 1960's, 1970's, and early 1980's, these industries paid an average of 40 to 55 percent of their profits in income tax to the Shulu Finance and Tax Bureau. After-tax profits were then apportioned among the enterprises themselves, the Second Light Industry Ministry Bureau at the county level, and the Second Light Bureau at the prefecture level, according to general formulas that were subject to change over time, as displayed in Table 17.[55]

One way to look at these formulas is to note that the first two rows represent monies that remained in Shulu county for use there. And the trend over time, clearly visible if we take this point of view, was for a greater percentage of profits to be left within the county: 60 percent before 1968; 82 percent during the 1970's, and 90 percent by 1986. The reslicing of the pie at the end of the 1960's gave county-level Second Light system authorities greater control over funds at the expense both of factory-level officials and of prefectural *xitong* officials. The renegotiations of the 1980's, on the other hand, gave greater control to individual enterprises at the expense of company superiors at both county and prefectural levels.

TABLE 17
Distribution of Profits in the Second Light Industry System

	Percentage of net profits retained		
	Before 1968	After 1968	1986
Enterprises	12	10	40
Shulu County Second Light Industry Bureau	48	72	50
Shijiazhuang Prefecture Second Light Industry Bureau	40	18	10

Between 1979 and 1985, as the light industry xitong adjusted (poorly) to the changed economic environment that came in the wake of the early reforms, the situation became highly volatile. The data we have for this period show not only declining profits, but considerable managerial confusion in the xitong and apparent frequent resort to ad hoc arrangements regarding profit distribution, investments, and the scramble to cover losses.[56]

Regardless of the vicissitudes of this awkward transitional period, however, it was the Second Light Industry Bureau at the county level that from the 1960's through the 1980's always enjoyed the largest profit share. And the county bureau used those funds almost exclusively for reinvestment and capital construction in the enterprises in its orbit. These funds—unlike the county's extrabudgetary funds discussed below—absolutely could not be used for other county projects, but only for further development of light industry in Shulu under the bureau's direction. During the decade of the 1970's, county bureau officials disbursed funds to enterprises in response to their applications, but could give out only a very modest ¥10,000 for a single project on their own authority. When an investment was to exceed ¥10,000, the Shulu bureau was required to seek approval from the county and prefecture planning committees.[57] County Second Light officials stressed, however, that most of their projects were coordinated with the Shulu Planning Committee, and that the real decisions were made at the county level, not by the prefecture committee. This is one point at which the concerns of the county as a comprehensively developing regional or horizontal unit (kuaikuai) could be brought to bear on the use of funds within its boundaries by vertical (tiaotiao) systems. While such coordination within the county was certainly essential for planned local development, fiscal responsibilities nevertheless remained separate and distinct.

In order to provide some idea of the magnitude of Second Light's financial flows in the context of general county finance over the years, Table 18 lists real profits of all Shulu enterprises in the Second Light xitong for every year from 1958–89. In thinking about the significance of these profits and their xitong flow patterns, we must recall first that from 1958–68 approximately 50 percent of real profits entered the county budgetary process each year as income tax and, second, that only about 60 percent of profits after taxes actually remained within the county, either in the enterprises or at the county Second Light Bureau. The profits of this constellation of factories, in any case, were small and unreliable over those years. Second Light profit retentions were of decidedly negligible importance, then, in the context of overall county spending during that period.

But from 1968–78, the percentage of profits retained within the county improved considerably, while taxation rates remained steady. Profit levels themselves also rose during the decade, contributing to making Second Light investments and expenditures a much more important element in overall county finance. The late 1970's were good years for the Second

TABLE 18
Shulu Second Light Industry Profits, Taxes, and
Profit Distribution, 1958–89
(in thousands of yuan)

Year	Real profits	Income tax	Profits remitted upward	Profits retained at enterprises
1958	42			
1959	127			
1960	247			
1961	131			
1962	61			
1963	37			
1964	107			
1965	142			
1966	55			
1967	24			
1968	77			
1969	194			
1970	237			
1971	240			
1972	398			
1973	668			
1974	915			
1975	1,308			
1976	1,556			
1977	1,312			
1978	1,604			
1979	1,545	734	279	327
1980	1,300	599	229	314
1981	565	317		260
1982	483	273	83	218
1983	768	320	84	286
1984	835	327	36	284
1985	810	226	34	249
1986	1,043	251	34	298
1987	1,475	244	31	271
1988	2,581	411	52	401
1989	3,223	551	49	441

Light system in Shulu (Table 18). By 1979, profits retained by the county (¥279,000) plus profits retained by enterprises in Shulu's Second Light system (¥327,000) totaled ¥606,000, a figure equivalent to 6.3 percent of all budgetary expenditures that year.

Between 1979 and 1985, however, profits dropped off very sharply, restoring this income source to relative insignificance once again in the then-surging pattern of county finance. In 1984, for example, Second Light *xitong* profits retained by the county (¥36,000) plus profits retained by enterprises (¥284,000) came to only ¥320,000, or just under 3 percent of total budgetary expenditures that year. And by 1989, Second Light profits retained in Shulu, although apparently beginning a recovery from their disastrous slump earlier in the decade, had nonetheless fallen to a figure equivalent to just 1.3 percent of total budgetary expenditures that year. Once loan repayments and debt service deductions were made from the real profits column in Table 18 during the late 1980's, there evidently remained little to divide up within the *xitong* for new spending or investment.

It was almost surely during the late 1970's, then, that the locally retained profits of this particular vertical system made their greatest contribution to investment and growth in Shulu county. This was probably true of other *xitong* as well. But a comprehensive understanding of the patterns of all other vertical system earnings and monetary flows and their contributions to county finance must remain a matter for further investigation. The tax liabilities and profit-sharing formulas in use for the additional enterprises run by other bureaus in the county were not detailed by local officials. After paying taxes these industries apparently went through a process similar to the one at Second Light with their respective parent bureaus. They then received their funds for operations and expansion through their own systems. But the actual significance of these enterprises and their profits in the context of overall county finance would be difficult to gauge precisely because of the many fluctuations in their operations and management. There were only six such bureau-run factories in Shulu in 1979. These had grown to fourteen in 1986. But by 1990, some of those fourteen had been closed down and some had been taken under the administrative wing of Second Light. New ones had been opened at the same time, specializing in the production of fodder, edible oils, enriched wheat flour, and veterinary medicines, to keep the grand total at fourteen enterprises. Real profits of enterprises in this group were reported at ¥6.7 million for 1989. This, it should be noted, is more than double the real profits reported by the constellation of Second Light industries that year. But, as with Second Light, loan repayments and interest likely claimed the better part of such reported profits. With the reforms of the middle and late 1980's came changing roles for credit and capital fees in the development of the economy. These too would need to be reflected in any more complete analysis of vertical system industry performance.[58]

One lesson, at least, leaps out from our work here. The financial structure and standing of a county cannot be estimated accurately without reference to vertical system transfers such as those of the Second Light Industry Bureau in Shulu. The patterns of vertical system activity are likely to have varied enormously from county to county. And even within a given county, the guidelines and regulations governing *xitong* activities were subject to nearly continual changes and readjustments over the years. The state budget arena may always have been the most significant one for county finance, but it was certainly not the only one. Especially in the decade of the 1970's, other arenas of financial activity were becoming capable of making important contributions to local patterns of development and growth.

Third Pathway: The County Extrabudgetary Fund

The third distinct fiscal process was the one governing monies belonging in the county's extrabudgetary (*yusuanwai*) fund. This fund was derived from several curiously different types of sources, and county receipts in this category fluctuated considerably over the years. But all those monies that did find their way into the extrabudgetary fund were retained by the county government itself, in the hands of the Finance Bureau, and were available for use on projects determined by the county government itself, without control by higher levels. This, therefore, was the revenue source that gave county government leaders most of what autonomy and flexibility they had in planning for local needs and in meeting the unplanned demands imposed by misfortunes or emergencies.[59]

EXTRABUDGETARY REVENUES

Annual extrabudgetary statistics as precise as those for budgetary revenues and expenditures in Shulu were not available. But the Finance Bureau director, Zheng, was able to work out a series of careful estimates covering extrabudgetary collections and disbursements in several major categories for the period 1961 to 1988, as follows.

Local Surtaxes

A good part of Shulu's extrabudgetary revenue was derived through the county's legal levy of a surtax on some, but not all, of the standard in-budget taxes it was obliged to collect for the provincial and the central governments above it. On the industrial and commercial tax, for example, Shulu county collected a 1 percent surtax almost every year from 1954 to 1985.[60] This surtax was not applied to all categories of the industrial and commercial tax—only to the larger ones. Between 1961 and 1985, the county extrabudgetary fund received some ¥2,150,000 from this surtax.[61]

A surtax was also levied on the agriculture tax in Shulu. This was a local grain tax generally dedicated to use by commune-level authorities in the 1960's and 1970's. The commune-level accountants, Director Zheng said, "did not always keep very clear records,"[62] so confident estimates of actual collections could only be made starting in 1982. (It is interesting to note that it was only with decollectivization in Shulu in the winter of 1982–83 that the county government apparently acquired a sure grasp of local surtax collection and expenditure levels in rural areas.) From 1982 to 1988, then, total collections in this surtax category were estimated at ¥1,503,000.

Starting in 1979, Shulu county also levied a surtax on local enterprises making heavy use of public utilities such as water and electricity.[63] By 1988, total collections in this category were put at ¥3,085,000. Then, starting in July of 1986, in line with national policy, Shulu began collecting a local education surtax. This surtax was figured at 1 percent of the combined commodities tax, value-added tax, and business tax collections in the county. By the end of fiscal 1988, levies in this new category amounted to just ¥483,000.

On these estimates, then, between 1961 and 1988 more than ¥7.2 million entered the Shulu county extrabudgetary fund in the form of local surtax collections. As explained further below, most of these monies were eventually disbursed for public projects with a direct connection to the revenue source.

Enterprise Profits

The county extrabudgetary fund acquired even more sizable revenues over the years from the profits of certain, but not all, of its locally operated industrial enterprises. The various special arrangements governing the apportionment of these profits, as detailed below, do at times appear to defy any obvious logic. On balance, however, they worked to produce improved extrabudgetary revenues to the county during the 1970's and into the early 1980's.

THE "FIVE SMALL" INDUSTRIES   National policy in the early 1970's encouraged local governments to develop five specific types of small industries turning out products for use in agriculture. Revenue-share rates for local state-run industries in the "five small" category initially called for 40 percent of profits to be forwarded to higher levels of the state while leaving 60 percent of profits in the county's budget. Starting in 1973, however, official policy mandated that the 60 percent left at the county level should be placed into the county's extrabudgetary fund. In Shulu, there were at least three factories established that qualified for this incentive program before it ended in 1979: a phosphate fertilizer plant, a chemical fertilizer plant, and a petrochemicals factory.[64] Between 1973 and 1978, under the "five small" program, an estimated total of ¥2,529,000 entered the Shulu county extrabudgetary fund.

THE EXTRABUDGETARY ENTERPRISES   Another and even more important group of enterprises turning profits in to the county extrabudgetary fund were, in fact, so completely defined by this distinctive financial relationship to the county that they were commonly referred to simply as the "extrabudgetary enterprises" (*yusuanwai qiye*). These included an agricultural machinery plant, a cement factory, a beet-sugar refinery, and a brickworks. By far the most important factory in this category, financially speaking, was a large rubber-products plant turning out conveyor belts and tires (see photographs). These extrabudgetary factories were all classified as state-run (*difang guoying*); their raw materials and output were included in the state plan, and their workers enjoyed the same wage scales and fringe benefits as regular state workers. But in some ways these plants were treated more like collective industries than like regular local state-run "in-budget" factories.[65] They paid an income tax on their profits, for example—the same tax applied to the "collective" industries under the Second Light Industry Bureau as well as to the more truly collective industries run by communes (townships) and brigades (villages). This tax was not to exceed 55 percent of profits. The remaining 45 percent (or more) was turned over to the county government. The Shulu Finance Bureau made the collections and the county planning committee, in consultation with other county offices, made allocations and decisions about expenditures from the fund.

Of all county-level factories and enterprises in Shulu, then, these extrabudgetary enterprises most closely approximated the concept of ownership by the government of Shulu county itself. The after-tax profits of these extrabudgetary enterprises were regarded by county representatives as the property of the county itself, and as long as the county's decisions on how to use them were legal, those decisions could not be overruled by higher levels. These funds were expressly available, then, for expenditure by the county as a horizontal (*kuaikuai*) administrative unit.

In 1971 and 1972, while the first factories in this category were just getting on their feet, there were little profits to speak of. None were turned in to the county government extrabudgetary fund (Table 19). From 1973 until 1983, the extrabudgetary fund did realize all profits of these enter-

TABLE 19
Shulu Extrabudgetary Enterprise Profits and Profit Distribution, 1971–89
(in thousands of yuan)

Year	No. of enterprises	Gross receipts	Sales tax	Production costs	Profits from sales	Real profits	Income tax	Portion remitted to county	Profits retained at enterprises
1971	2	380	5	365	10	80			
1972	5	1,904	155	1,506	243	214			
1973	6	9,579	989	6,867	1,723	1,740	867	873	
1974	6	11,740	1,141	8,631	1,968	1,969	867	1,102	
1975	8	13,232	1,302	9,761	2,169	2,194	1,217	977	
1976	8	15,456	1,563	11,897	1,996	2,038	1,089	949	
1977	8	15,456	1,576	11,943	1,946	1,861	1,031	830	
1978	9	17,391	1,712	13,165	2,514	2,531	1,349	1,182	
1979	9	16,682	1,528	12,304	2,796	2,592	1,440	1,152	
1980	9	16,879	1,498	13,269	2,112	2,074	1,098	976	
1981	9	16,284	1,467	13,421	1,396	1,476	802	674	
1982	10	18,337	1,715	14,890	1,620	1,585	880	705	
1983	10	17,708	1,798	14,750	1,030	1,105	668	437	
1984	11	16,310	1,643	13,313	1,256	1,313	663	354	163
1985	11	20,767	1,521	17,209	1,743	1,875	639	275	693
1986	9	18,022	1,708	14,853	1,402	1,475	641	259	284
1987	9	28,123	2,169	23,610	1,670	1,670	662	196	259
1988	9	37,378	2,754	30,315	2,353	2,303	956	203	499
1989	9	40,888	3,271	32,093	3,392	2,944	651	137	394

prises after taxes. Then, starting with 1984, a profit-sharing ratio was introduced that put just 70 percent of real profits into the county extrabudgetary fund and left 30 percent in the enterprises themselves. This was changed again, to a 50–50 division, in 1985. And in 1988, it was changed yet again, to leave 70 percent at the enterprises and 30 percent at the county. Total monies from this source entered in the extrabudgetary fund from 1973 through 1988 were estimated at ¥9,741,000.[66]

Table 19 provides a breakdown of Shulu extrabudgetary industry profits from 1971 to 1989. It shows that real profits grew steadily in the first half of the 1970's, remained solid in the mid-1970's, and peaked (along with net profits retained by the county) in 1978 and 1979. Thereafter, in the difficult readjustments of the early 1980's, profits fell dramatically, recovering only slowly during the second half of the 1980's. Net county retentions never did recover from the 1980's reforms. They reached their alltime low at the very end of the series.

There had been some discussion in 1979 of converting Shulu's extrabudgetary factories into ordinary in-budget local state-run enterprises.[67] But in the end, no satisfactory terms could be agreed to with officials at the prefecture level. The prefecture was eager to take the highly profitable rubber factory and one or two others that were doing well into the budget, but was insistent on leaving Shulu to manage the more precarious-to-floundering enterprises in the group on the old extrabudgetary basis. The county balked, and no deal was ever made. Local cadres were perhaps still banking in 1979–80 on the then relatively good profit performance of these enterprises to provide reliable revenues. They may have reasoned that by allowing their lucrative extrabudgetary industries to be integrated into the budgetary system, they could be trading away the greatest measure of fiscal independence the county possessed for at best only somewhat larger retained revenues in the short run. As it turned out, however, they might have done better to make a settlement on the terms that were offered, for Shulu's extrabudgetary enterprises, like many other local state-run enterprises, were to fall on hard times in the early 1980's. The all-important rubber factory, for instance, which turned in to the county ¥700,000 in profits in 1980, was reduced to handing in just ¥140,000 in 1985. The sugar refinery and an auto-parts factory in this group had to be closed down.

The Deng period's moves away from planning and toward more marketlike methods for obtaining inputs and selling products were to affect profitability in this group of Shulu factories just as adversely as they affected profitability in those factories within the state budget and those under Second Light. Administrative systems as ad hoc and differentiated as those that evolved in Chinese local finance in the 1970's are most difficult to reform without also setting in motion certain vitiating unintended effects.

IN-BUDGET INDUSTRIAL PROFIT CONTRIBUTIONS The "five small" and the extrabudgetary enterprises were not the only local state-run plants putting a portion of their profits into the county's extrabudgetary fund. Starting in 1979, some 30 percent of total in-budget industry real profits were earmarked for transfer to the extrabudgetary fund as well.[68] Just 70 percent of in-budget industry profits were thenceforward to remain within the state budgetary pathway. This variation from the normal procedure was estimated to have yielded a total of ¥7,139,000 in additional county extrabudgetary receipts between 1979 and 1984. As of 1985, however, as suddenly as it had been started, this system of diverting funds from the budgetary to the extrabudgetary pathway was stopped. The budgetary pathway received, once again, 100 percent of in-budget industry profits. The special contributions to the extrabudgetary fund were terminated.

Depreciation and Other Sources

In addition, during the period 1973-84, the county extrabudgetary fund netted an estimated total of ¥2,281,000 in "depreciation funds" authorized by higher-level industry officials. But this subsidy to in-budget enterprises stopped being paid into the county extrabudgetary fund in 1985, at the same time that contributions from in-budget enterprise profits ceased.[69] Then, in the years 1986, 1987, and 1988, the extrabudgetary fund also realized some earnings on Shulu county's obligatory purchase of state bonds. This amounted to some ¥975,000 in extrabudgetary income over those three years. And finally, in 1988, the fund also started to receive some revenue-sharing income from the collection of the new national agricultural and forestry special products tax. This came to just ¥294,000 that year, but promised to become a rising source of extrabudgetary income in Shulu, a leading fruit-producing county.

Summary of Extrabudgetary Revenue Collections

Surveying the entire extrabudgetary revenue picture for 1961 through 1988, then, the estimated total came to over ¥30 million. The single biggest source was the ¥9.7 million derived from the county's own extrabudgetary enterprise profits. That was followed by ¥9.4 million from in-budget industry contributions and depreciation allowances. Another ¥8.5 million was collected from taxes and bond earnings. And ¥2.5 million came from the early "five small" industries profit sharing program. The overall pattern of collections suggests that county extrabudgetary income varied substantially over the years. But this pathway—especially during the late 1970's and early 1980's—clearly represented a very significant contribution to overall county monies available for use.

EXTRABUDGETARY EXPENDITURES

The extrabudgetary fund was, as stated earlier, subject to expenditure by the county government as a horizontal (*kuaikuai*) administrative unit. It was in this sense that these funds differed most plainly from *xitong* profits retained within the county—that is, the second pathway. Those monies were not available for disbursement by the county as a horizontal administrative unit, but only by specific vertically linked offices within the county government. At the very least, those offices received clear priority guidelines from higher levels on how they ought to allocate their retained funds. County-level bureau cadres had to file reports to their vertical system superiors on how such funds were spent. If a county bureau deviated from its *xitong* priorities, it could be overruled by higher-level offices. As with funds in the state budget—the first pathway—earmarking and accounts monitoring by upper levels in the second pathway were the rule. Thus it was by the high degree of autonomy the county had in determining its use that the extrabudgetary fund was most clearly distinguishable from funds moving through the other pathways of county finance.

As with revenues, detailed records of expenditures were not available for this fund. But in the way Shulu officials discussed their general use of extrabudgetary monies it was clear that they maintained a fairly close connection between revenue sources and the projects they selected for expenditure. In some cases, especially where special surtax revenues were concerned, they were constrained to do so by law—but in other cases, they apparently chose to do so.

Extrabudgetary revenues collected as public utilities and industrial and commercial surtaxes, for example, were spent primarily on construction and maintenance of the county's urban district (Xinji). Money credited in these categories was spent on such necessities as city street lighting, garbage collection, and so on. In 1975 some ¥200,000 in this category was used to establish a water supply company for the city district. After 1979 even higher expenditures from this category of funds were made to equip a fire station and to open a new primary school in the urban district. Of the approximately ¥5 million of extrabudgetary revenue collected in these two surtax categories between 1961 and 1988, an estimated ¥4,141,000 was eventually spent on urban maintenance and projects such as these. Extrabudgetary revenues from the agriculture and the education surtaxes, similarly, were spent primarily on projects in those realms: that is, on roads, bridges, and other rural infrastructure repairs; and on schools and other educational units across the county, respectively.

Extrabudgetary revenues from industrial profits, while explicitly regarded as a kind of flexible financial reserve fund (*jidong caili*) for the county, were nonetheless mostly spent on furthering the development of local industry. These funds were used first to make up the losses of any of the county's factories that were running in the red, whether they were in or out of the state budget.[70] After such variable obligations were met, funds left over were generally used for technical improvements and for further capital investment in both the county's in-budget and its extrabudgetary industries.[71] Extrabudgetary funds in this category were sometimes also drawn upon for public projects. In 1975, for example, some ¥230,000 in this category was spent on renovating the county's guest house; and in 1982, ¥750,000 was allocated to build a large theater in the downtown area. Still, it is clear that county finance authorities liked to keep at least some funds in this category on hand for emergency demands. In 1981 and 1982, for example, when higher-level government officials made enforced "borrowings" from Shulu resources, it was to this category of extrabudgetary reserves that local officials turned to cover the assessments. Extrabudgetary revenues from enterprise profits were, so to speak, the county government's ace in the hole. Local cadres turned to these funds when, as was so often the case, the rules were changed in the fast game of poker they played with higher-level finance officials.

It is logical to suppose that local units with large extrabudgetary revenues like Shulu might have had these taken into account in negotiations over its state budget targets.[72] But our data suggest no long-term direct relationship of that sort—and despite the accounts of occasional raids by higher levels, county officials never hinted that any standardized trade-off had to take place between their two budgets. Still, counties like Shulu probably did find it more difficult than counties with smaller extrabudgetary resources to win large higher-level subsidies outside normal budgetary expenditures for special projects such as the water conservation project of 1978.[73] They may well have been expected by higher levels to make larger commitments from their own funds before requesting financial assistance from outside. Healthy extrabudgetary receipts gave counties the wherewithal to exercise some local entrepreneurial initiative, but such resources may also have concentrated and intensified for them the risks that are incurred in committing venture capital.

Conclusions: Segmentation, Negotiation, and Adaptation in County Finance

Detailed as it may appear in some respects, what we have been able to report here concerning Shulu county's financial structures and processes still leaves many intriguing questions unanswered. We believe that our triple-stranded model does succeed in capturing all the most important financial flow patterns that have affected the county's economic development over time. Even so, an absolutely complete accounting still eludes us, and this prevents our offering genuinely definitive answers to the general questions about county finance with which we opened this chapter. Nevertheless, certain interesting inferences and conclusions can be drawn from the data.

This discussion of county financial organization has indirectly illustrated some of the built-in tensions that have existed between the horizontally oriented offices and the vertically linked offices at the county level, or for that matter at any level of government administration in China. In the Chinese effort to achieve simultaneous economic efficiency, growth, and fairness in development, this built-in tension in administration has presented some advantages as well as some recognized disadvantages. The triple-stranded system outlined for Shulu leaves plenty of room for jurisdictional quarrels, incompatible priorities, departmental protectionism, and general lack of coordination. While a county's fiscal structure may appear from this discussion to have been fairly tightly controlled and regulated, how tightly integrated it was and how comprehensively it served local needs still depended heavily on the specific set of opportunities or lack of opportunities a given county faced, as well as on the ability of county officials themselves to work competently and creatively within this highly segmented system.

Also, the Shulu experience makes it plain that we cannot look at the state budget pathway alone if we wish to estimate trends over time in a Chinese county's financial performance. County governments are points at which several rather different types of fiscal processes have come to intersect over the years since 1949. While the most comprehensive pathway, the state budget, may well have operated very similarly from locality to locality all across the country, individual counties have no doubt each had their own particular patterns of *xitong* financial flows and extrabudgetary resources that have significantly affected their options for local expenditure and thus for local economic development.

We cannot help but note the rather ad hoc manner in which each of the three pathways has been managed in Shulu over the years. Profitable factories were moved in and out of the county budget seemingly at will. Profit-share rates were established, revised, revised again, and occasionally ignored entirely when pressing problems or special opportunities seemed to warrant it. Base targets and above-target incentive schemes were overtly manipulated as means not only to promote production and development but also to fine-tune the many complex institutional and procedural interrelationships that made up the constellation of county finance. And when changes with important financial consequences such as these did take place, we frequently find also that compensatory adjustments were made somewhere else in the system to keep the county from losing or profiting unduly overall.

Again, in our view, this rough balance was not so much the result of any master plan as it was a product of the continual efforts of local cadres to support, defend, and, when possible, advance the financial interests of the county while they adapted perforce to systems and circumstances over which their control was partial at best. Tethered always to central investment and development policies by ornate administrative systems, county cadres nonetheless always retained at least some scope for local initiative and bureaucratic resourcefulness. To utilize to maximum local advantage what play still remained in the administrative ties and policy lines that bound them to the center was often the name of the game in county finance.

Finance cadres negotiated with administrative superiors through the state budget pathway. County-level Second Light system cadres negotiated with their *xitong* superiors. Shulu factory managers and township heads negotiated month by month and year by year with county leaders for special projects and other considerations. And everybody went to the banks to talk about credit. The invisibility (to our eyes) of most of these processes of lobbying and persuasion, along with the pervasive price distortions in the Chinese economy and the more or less continuous revisions over the years of investment, tax, credit, and profit-sharing systems, all make it nearly impossible to trace just what proportion of what might be conceived of as the county's "surplus" was "extracted" by higher levels of the state from year to year. Only with respect to the state budget pathway are we here able to use the data to offer some precise estimates. Shulu county kept, on average, 33.3 percent of what it collected. But how did the fluctuating financial flows through the other two pathways affect the overall picture? Our guess was that they worked generally to bolster the county's own share of its total surplus: in some years—especially during the 1970's—very substantially; and in other years less so.

One related inference that fairly leaps from the data we do have is that revenues remaining within the county by means of the second and third pathways grew substantially during the period of the middle to late 1970's. By 1986, these two pathways had once again dropped to relative insignificance in county finance because the industrial plants from which their revenues largely derived had suffered so severely in the early reform period. But during the late 1970's their importance relative to the state budget pathway clearly had been very much greater. At that time, the economy generally was far more stagnant, and state budget procedures were more rigid. In those circumstances, county receipts through the second and third pathways plainly provided county leaders with their greatest room for maneuver in local funding. In fact, the very development of these two pathways as important financial channels, it now seems apparent, was the product of local cadres' adaptations to the tight restrictions that prevailed in other areas of possible entrepreneurship and economic growth at the time. The Mao-period political economy, and the spareness of the state budgetary pathway at that time, produced a number of such cleverly arcane offshoots and adaptations. Then, when the ground rules of the prevailing political economy were radically altered in the reform era, the salience and the efficacy of these special adaptations faded quickly.

The industrial enterprises on which the second and third fiscal pathways primarily rested were, first of all, to become less viable in the changed investment, input, and market conditions after 1979. Those formerly key enterprises were to become less crucial then as well, as the economy generally started to boom and better revenue-generating possibilities opened up. Those economic adaptations that had arisen in peculiar response to the exigencies of Mao-period central planning procedures and property-ownership regulations suddenly lost much of their underlying rationale and immediate value. At the same time, the state budget pathway was enormously enhanced and expanded through the 1980's, not only in real cash terms but in functional terms as well. The clear result was that the structures and processes of the official state budget pathway dominated the local finance of Shulu county more in the late 1980's than had been the case in the late 1970's.

Through all of this, the Shulu political economy certainly appeared to have maintained its resilience. When the development of largely self-reliant locally managed industries was the key to success in the Mao-period economic environment, Shulu county became a leader in its prefecture in the area of small-scale and medium-scale industrial growth. And when comprehensive and competitive bureaucratic negotiations for scarce state budget allocations and for preferential revenue retentions became the name of the Deng-period development game Shulu managed to get itself promoted to municipality status and, by 1990, was no longer even reporting to prefecture-level officials but directly to Hebei provincial authorities on its financial matters. The necessary change of gears had plainly not come without cost in the county. But after a decade of sometimes wrenching reforms, Shulu had not only fallen in step with the new thrust of policies issuing from the center—it remained out ahead, in the front rank at least, in Hebei.

CHAPTER 5

Industry and Industrialization

Shulu has a long history of manufacture. As we have seen, it was a major center of the fur and leather industry at least six hundred years ago. In the late nineteenth century its most famous products were being sold internationally. But the Japanese invasion devastated the Shulu economy, even as it provided the impetus for its eventual recovery, as the Communist base area government in the region established armaments, explosives, alkali, and soap factories in the county. In the 1950's the alkali plant became known as the Xinji Chemical Factory, which eventually became the world's second-largest producer of barium salts. It was this foundation that helped Shulu develop a significant specialization in chemical production as the anchor of its modern industry.

Today Shulu is relatively advanced in industry as rural counties go, though it is not exceptional. As of 1978 it was already the most industrialized of the seventeen counties in Shijiazhuang prefecture.[1] Gross value of industrial output (GVIO) had since 1971 exceeded gross value of agricultural output (GVAO); in 1978 the ratio was around 1.25:1 by official reckoning, and almost 2:1 if the industrial output of brigade-level enterprises were included. Yet at the end of the Mao period Shulu was a below-average industrializer by national standards, turning out only around ¥300 in GVIO per capita compared with ¥445 for China as a whole. By 1986 GVIO had reached ¥960 per capita, surpassing the national average of ¥854 and the Hebei average of ¥901.[2] Industry contributed 60 percent to gross output value.[3] The leading products of county industry were, in order of their

GVIO, industrial chemicals and textiles (at over ¥5,000,000 each), followed by fur and leather products at about half that figure, supplemented by significant machinery, building materials, and handicrafts sectors (most prominent among which was the production of fireworks).[4] By 1989, industry stood as an even larger component of the Shulu economy, accounting for a full 76 percent of total output value. Per-capita GVIO was ¥1,889 in 1989, compared with ¥1,745 for Hebei and ¥1,980 for the country as a whole.[5] The greatest growth since 1986 occurred in the machinery and clothing sectors, which more than doubled their output, and in chemicals, textiles, fur and leather, and building materials, which increased their output value about 60 percent each.

Rural industrial production has been an important part of Shulu's output in both the Mao and Deng periods. By 1989 rural industries turned out an astonishing 70 percent of Shulu's GVIO, and their profits were three and one-fourth times those of state industry. This major sector is discussed in Chapter 8. Here, however, we concentrate on what in Chapter 4 we called county industry. This chapter focuses on several aspects of the relationship of Shulu industry to the state, in particular to the county government: forms of ownership and administration, profit disposition, and policies and practices governing labor and employment (including the changing official categories of labor and the problems they engendered, labor cost control policies, and labor recruitment and allocation). In each case, we proceed from the Mao period to the Deng years, contrasting the two.

Along the way, we highlight those findings about practices in Shulu that help illuminate larger questions or challenge our assumptions about Chinese industry. These fall under two general rubrics. First, we will continue the theme developed in Chapter 4 by exploring further the complex variegation of the structures of industrial ownership and administration that coexisted within even this very small place, and that are often concealed by the implicitly monolithic term "state sector." Second, we will highlight the continuities between the Mao and Deng periods, the limits to market reform, and the continuing, in some ways even growing, presence of the state in Shulu's industrial economy.

Patterns of Socialist Ownership and Administration

Discussions of Chinese industry have tended to dichotomize it as state-run or collective. The situation in Shulu reveals that this conceptualization is only a starting point that conceals a great deal of very significant and often confusing differentiation within the category of "state-run industry," in both the Mao and the Deng periods. And since "state-run industry" is widely regarded by specialists as well as many Chinese analysts and political leaders as a major target of or obstacle to reform, a textured understanding of its heterogeneity is crucial in addressing wider questions concerning the future of China's political economy.

Shulu's "state-run" enterprises varied along several related dimensions: their levels (county, prefecture, province, or central) and bureaucratic loci of ownership; their levels and loci of administrative and planning control, which are not always coterminous with ownership; their historical origins (including the key question of their original investment sources); and the disposition of their surplus. The terms "state-run-industry" or "state sector" that have in the past been common to the literature on Chinese industry and state socialism more generally carry the connotation of the highly centralized and monolithic organization and administration emphasized in those literatures.[6] By contrast, the term "collective industry" all too often connotes only small rural firms or urban workshops owned by township and village authorities. Yet in Shulu, we found that "state-run" enterprises took several forms, not all of which were under tight central control. Likewise, "collective" firms could be quite large and subject to direct control by organs of the county government, which, after all, is not a collective, but the lowest level of unalloyed state authority. We will therefore use the less encumbered term "county industry" to refer to the universe of firms we are scrutinizing. In trying to counter the centralizing and nondifferentiating tendencies of previous work on Chinese industry, of course we do not wish to commit the opposite mistake of presuming too much decentralization or localized control. The Shulu county government was very much a part of the centralized state. "But we *are* the state!" county cadres more than once replied to our probings into their relations with the prefecture, province, and center. In using the term "county industry," then, we should keep their words ringing in our ears, while also keeping open in our minds the question of how the state, including the county government, was and is organized vis-à-vis the industries of Shulu county.

Shulu's county industry contained forty-eight enterprises in 1978—a number that ebbed and flowed slightly over the next decade. Chapter 4 laid out a basic description of these various industrial categories as well as an analysis of their administrative relationships from a financial point of view. Here we build on that discussion by asking a somewhat different set of questions: How did enterprises come to find themselves in one category or another? Did these categories correspond to particular production lines or sectors, to scale, to economic performance levels, technological levels, or to an enterprise's relationship to agriculture? And have the categories themselves, or the ways enterprises are grouped into them, changed over time from the late Mao period through the first decade of the Deng years?

THE MAO PERIOD

In the Mao period, Shulu industry was organized into five categories: local state-run enterprises, factories administered by the Second Light Industry Bureau, plants run by county government bureaus, plants run by higher-level government authorities (prefectures, provinces, or the center), and county-run extrabudgetary (*yusuan wai*) plants. In Chapter 4, these categories were developed for our analysis of finance. Here we use them to organize our examination of industry.

Local State-Run Industry

Shulu's local state-run enterprises were the mainstay of the centralized state industrial structure at the county level. County officials had little autonomy or entrepreneurial latitude in administering these industrial enterprises; instead, they acted primarily as agents for prefectural and provincial authorities in their management. Prototypically, the investment capital for these plants had originally been allocated downward from higher levels of the state; but as we shall see when we consider the case of the Shulu Fur and Leather Tanning Factory this category could also include firms that had been built up gradually by the locality itself from humble origins and indigenous accumulation. Thus the commonly heard principle of Chinese state socialist organization—"sheijian, sheiguan, sheiyong" (whoever builds the plant can manage it and have the use of its output)[7]—did not necessarily apply in practice. For whether a local state-run firm had been financed by the central state budget or by local accumulation, its taxes and profits were remitted to higher levels through the Finance and Tax Bureau, which entered them into the revenue side of the county's state budget.

These several plants were among the largest in the county, averaging profits of ¥612,000 in 1978, more than double the county average of ¥294,500.[8] They were turning out some of the heaviest industrial products and using some of the most advanced technology in the county. The mainstay of Shulu industry in the socialist period has been chemical production. This production line was begun with the establishment in 1947 by the Communist government of a plant turning out vulcanized alkali, an ingredient used in the making of dyes that, in turn, were needed for the manufacture of military uniforms during the civil war. The Xinji Chemical Factory subsequently went into production of barium salts, of which it would become the second-largest producer in the world by 1990.[9]

There were nine local state-run enterprises in Shulu in 1978. But that number had varied a great deal in the first half of the 1970's, from as few as five to as many as nine (Table 12). Some of this movement reflected the political uncertainties and penchant for reorganization that were characteristic of the Cultural Revolution decade. For example, in 1971 two large plants, a chemicals factory and a cylinder-head factory, were transferred back to ownership and management by Shijiazhuang prefecture (to which they had belonged in the past). In 1977 a power plant followed. But the change in the number of Shulu county's local state-run factories also reflected the industrial expansion of the late Mao period. Three of the heavier local state-run enterprises—a petrochemical factory and two fertilizer plants—had only been established since 1972.

Second Light Industry Bureau Enterprises

The Second Ministry of Light Industry was established in 1965 to replace the Central General Bureau of Handicraft Industry, as many of the former handicraft industries under the old bureau had now become upgraded in technology, complexity, or volume of production.[10] Some of these, including a carpentry shop, a clothing factory, and a shoe factory, were upgraded handicrafts enterprises that had started production before 1949. Others, including a printing factory, a hand tools shop, and a small chemical plant, had been founded in the 1950's. Still others, producing items as disparate as hardware, jade carvings, and tar paper, were founded in the 1970's. Some, such as the plants producing chemicals, bottled oxygen (for use in welding), and plastics, probably came under the Second Light Industry Bureau during the bureaucratic streamlinings and consolidations of the Cultural Revolution.[11]

There were eighteen factories under Shulu Second Light in 1978.[12] In general, they were smaller, less profitable, and more labor-intensive than the county averages.[13] While some rather large and important industrial enterprises have been grouped under Second Light, bigger and more profitable plants developed under its wing could also find themselves moved into the more centralized local state-run group. The Shulu Fur and Leather Tanning Factory is a case in point. With peace and national unification in 1949 a local historical sideline specialty in the production of tanned hides and leather goods was quickly revived in the county; within a few years there were 130 fur and leather enterprises in Shulu. These were consolidated into twelve tanning and fur-processing cooperatives by 1953. Then in 1956 the antecedent to the present-day fur and leather factory was set up as a large "collective" enterprise by amalgamating all the co-ops and combining them with the remaining privately owned fur and leather processing concerns, and with one government-run plant that had been established by the liberated area government in 1946. Its origins in the handicraft and collective sectors brought this new unified plant under Second Light. But in September 1958, at the dawn of the Great Leap Forward, the factory was transferred from collective to state ownership, and it has been administered as a local state-run enterprise ever since.

The Shulu case helps illuminate the ways in which county government authorities had greater control over Second Light plants and their profits than over the local state-run plants.[14] Local state-run enterprises were simply administered by county-level offices on behalf of higher levels of the state. Their after-tax profits were remitted to those higher levels of the government. But, as shown in Chapter 4, the Second Light Industry Ministry at the county level retained the lion's share of the after-tax profits of the factories in its own orbit for reinvestment, sharing the rest with its prefecture-level superiors and with its enterprises. The monies retained by the Shulu Second Light Industry Bureau could be used for the development of the specific enterprises that had generated them, but Second Light could also move these funds around among the other factories under its leadership. A certain amount of financial and planning discretion rested with county officials of this bureau, then, which was not the case with the local state-run plants.[15] Still, they could not operate with great autonomy. Because of its vertical "system" (xitong) organization, Second Light Industry Ministry officials at the county level, the lowest level in the system hierarchy, were subject to higher-level guidance regarding use of the funds under their control: they were required to seek the approval of their prefecture superiors for investments exceeding ¥10,000. Moreover, most of their projects were coordinated horizontally with the Shulu Planning Committee.

County Bureau-Run Enterprises

The next category of county industry—and a rather heterogeneous one in terms of origin, ownership, and control—is the enterprises run directly by county bureaus.[16] There were fourteen of them in 1986. Some of these, like the local state-run industries, were established on the initiative of various bureaus as responses to their own functional needs, and as such were firmly in the hands of agencies of the centralized state rather than the county government. For example, a cement-pipe factory was established by the water conservancy bureau to produce pipe for projects installed and run by the bureau. A pharmaceuticals factory was established by the Public Health Bureau to produce medicines that it could not obtain in other ways. But others were established by local bureaus of vertically oriented state ministries in order to absorb their excess labor or solve other local problems. And some were even established originally outside the state sector and then absorbed into it. A combination of these latter two processes can be seen in Shulu's asphalt felt factory, which was referred to as being under the "collective ownership" of the Transportation Bureau.

What a hybrid and apparently oxymoronic term like "collective ownership by a state bureau" means becomes clear from its historical development. This enterprise began life as a transportation company established by several porters in the early 1950's. It came under the supervision of the Transportation Bureau, probably in 1956 as part of the collectivization of small enterprises. The bureau used it to employ older workers who reached retirement age and could not be kept on the state administrative payroll any longer. As such workers became more numerous, the enterprise looked for new lines of production, and in 1976, long before the reforms would come to Shulu, it took an entrepreneurial step, hitting upon production of asphalt roofing paper as a solution to its problems. Shulu officials referred to it as a "collective" factory, then, because it began as a private partnership that was collectivized (albeit under the administrative leadership of a vertically organized state bureau), and because investments in its development were made by the bureau acting as a local entity on its own, rather than as part of its work in the transportation ministry system.[17] As we shall see in the discussion of the Deng period below, this same enterprise was later to become independent enough from its parent bureau that responsibility for its administration would eventually be moved to the new Light Industry and Textiles Company.[18] At the time of its establishment, the enterprise's chief product was probably related to the work of its parent bureau on the input side: the Transportation Bureau had access to asphalt since it was responsible for carrying out road repairs.

Thus the category of industries run directly by state bureaus exemplifies several distinct dynamics of Chinese state socialist development. It reflects the tendency in many state socialist countries for enterprises and economic bureaus to supply their own inputs and services in the face of difficulties in acquiring them through the planned economy.[19] Enterprise self-reliance was often carried to illogical extremes in pursuit of this particular Maoist antimarket ideal. This category of enterprises also served as a way for factories and bureaus to expand into production lines that had only an attenuated relationship to the main bureaucratic unit's original function. In the Deng period this device has been resorted to with increasing frequency and avidity and has now become a far more commonplace way for enterprises and agencies to increase their profits than was the case during the earlier period. But it is interesting to note that this sort of bureau-led enterprise creation could occur well before the onset of the reforms. And it is significant to note further that in the late Mao period, the impetus for creating such an enterprise could have little to do with profit-making: the profits realized by such factories in Shulu were then usually meager at best. In the case of the asphalt paper plant, the impetus lay clearly in the concern of the state (or at least of local state officials) with pursuing the socialist political objective of providing for the needs of its locality—here, its desire to supply employment for retired workers.[20]

Plants Run by Higher-Level Authorities

A handful of industries located in Shulu were run by the Shijiazhuang prefecture or the Hebei province governments. County authorities maintained no financial relations with these enterprises whatsoever; indeed, neither their capital expenditures nor their profit or tax revenues were entered into the county's state budget. The reasons for their control by higher-level state organizations had to do either with their high level of development or their special character. The chemical and cylinder-head factories exemplify the first reason: these two plants had become very large and technologically rather sophisticated by the early 1970's. It appeared that they had outgrown the capacity of the county Industry Bureau to administer them effectively. By contrast, the electricity generating station and the grain mill were run by the prefecture and the province, respectively, for functionally specific reasons. The former was linked into the regional power grid, and may also have been regarded as of such strategic significance as to require more centralized administration. The grain mill's situation was, similarly, a result of the 1953 decision to centralize and keep under very tight control everything concerning grain collections, processing, and marketing. Shulu also had, inside its boundaries, an oil field and a refinery operated by North China Petroleum, a central government agency. Administration of this installation fell entirely beyond the jurisdiction of the county government; it was kept under centralized administration in accord with official Communist Party doctrine that natural resources such as oil are the property of the Chinese nation as a whole rather than of the localities in which they happen to be situated.

County-Run Extrabudgetary Plants

Finally, as we have seen in Chapter 4, in 1979 Shulu county ran nine enterprises whose profits did not enter the state budget or the vertical ministerial systems, but rather were retained in the county's extrabudgetary fund and the enterprises themselves.[21] A special conference was convened in Shulu in 1970 by Hebei province industry officials to discuss the development of a three-level (county, commune, and brigade) network of agricultural machinery repair and manufacturing plants in the area.[22] Following the conference, and building in most cases on already existing enterprises of varying origins and ownership categories, several plants were designated part of this network and placed in a special status as county "extrabudgetary enterprises." For example, the rubber products plant had formerly belonged to the Second Light Industry orbit (and the Second Light *xitong* had to be compensated by the county when the factory was reclassified as an extrabudgetary enterprise and was changed from "collective" ownership status to "ownership by the whole people"). The cement factory had been set up originally by the Water Conservancy Bureau and some of its well-drilling teams. The brickworks had originally been a Xincheng Commune enterprise. But new extrabudgetary factories were developed as well. The sugar refinery was established with direct higher-level state allocations and with county-level contributions deriving from the "five small" program.[23]

As we have seen in Chapter 4, in terms of administration and planning the extrabudgetary factories were hybrids. Like the local state-run plants, they were included in the state plan for material allocation and procurement, and they employed regular state workers. Financially, however, these plants were treated very differently. Likewise, although they were placed under the administration of the Shulu Industry Bureau, the county planning committee also took an active role in overseeing their development.

The extrabudgetary enterprises thus reflect a confluence of central and county-level initiatives to strengthen local industrialization. They were made possible by the commitment of central state authorities in the 1970's to allow sizable manufacturing installations to accumulate under the leadership of county-level authorities, who were also granted significant autonomy to use the surpluses generated for local ends.[24] This policy created an opportunity for Shulu leaders to bring under one financially advantageous administrative umbrella a group of local firms that had developed from different roots over the years. The ability of county leaders to utilize such an opportunity for local benefit is a factor that helps explain why some counties were more economically successful than others during the Mao period.

THE DENG PERIOD

After ten years of reform, the administrative structure of county industry and the composition of its various categories remained largely intact, but novel developments were beginning to occur at the edges of this structure. Despite reformist impulses to the contrary, the number of enterprises in each category, and the financial relations between the enterprises in each category and the various government agencies charged with administering them, had not changed very significantly. What changes did occur are interesting, though, in illustrating the various tendencies toward expansion, consolidation, and transformation that were taking place in the Shulu economy in the Deng period. Meanwhile, new kinds of relationships were being forged between township and village industries and county industrial enterprises.

County Industry: Variations on a Theme

There was little change in the number of local state-run enterprises between 1979 and 1990. But this masks more complex processes that were afoot, reflecting in turn several of the principles and impulses associated with the new economic reforms. The agricultural machinery factory, referred to as a crankshaft factory, was apparently becoming more specialized in production. The dyeing and weaving plant was closed after showing no profits for five of the first seven years of reform. Administrative decentralization to lower-level horizontal bureaucratic coordinating authorities[25] was also taking place, as the chemical and cylinder-head plants were both returned to county jurisdiction by the prefecture.[26]

Over the 1980's the number of county extrabudgetary enterprises grew from nine to eleven, and then shrank back again with the closure of unprofitable firms. This troubled sector would soon see an interesting new development in ownership and control, as a rural collective-sector firm would come to the rescue of one of its enterprises.[27] Then one new extrabudgetary enterprise would be added by 1990. Finally, the vehicle repair shop that had been operated by the Transportation Bureau was moved into the category of county extrabudgetary enterprises in 1988.

But probably the most complicated story of all took place in the constellation of industries run by Second Light, reflecting through its unfolding some of the larger dynamics of industrial restructuring in the Deng period. A paper mill and a ball-bearing plant were shut, the latter closing caused, said Shulu officials, by the opening of a much larger province-run plant in nearby Shijiazhuang City. Furthermore, the 1979 merger of Second Light's two chemical plants into one reflected a trend toward industrial consolidation that was to go on through the early 1980's. In the second half of the decade, as part of a higher-level reorganization of the Second Light Industry Ministry, however, the Shulu bureau became a local office of a new national Light Industry and Textiles Company (a *gongsi*). And in connection with this, the tide turned back again toward expansion, elaboration, and transformation of Second Light firms, with the total number in Shulu growing from sixteen to twenty.[28]

There was even greater activity in creating and reorganizing industrial firms in the category of enterprises under direct management of government bureaus. There were twelve of these enterprises in 1986, compared with only eight in 1979. The establishment of so many new ventures reflects the growing business activities of state agencies under the impact of the reforms. Much of this growth resonated with the rapid expansion of the agricultural economy after the establishment of the rural responsibility system in Shulu in the winter of 1982-83: new factories were established in 1986 to provide freezing services and to process edible oils, fodder, enriched wheat flour, and cornstarch. But some of the new development still appeared to grow out of the old Maoist—indeed, generic—state socialist logic of self-supply: for example, the nationally renowned Xinji Middle School opened a workshop making school supplies. Subsequently the number of enterprises in this category declined again, but this reflected their success rather than failure. Three thriving plants were transferred to other agencies,[29] while another new enterprise was opened.[30]

In addition to these changes in the composition of the various administrative and supervisory categories of Shulu industry due to expansion, subdivision, contraction, and reorganization, the ways in which the state organized itself to supervise these firms were also modified after 1978. Horizontal organizational and administrative forms received increased weight. Administrative decentralization was taking place. Specifically, the Shulu Economic Planning Commission expanded its role greatly. It gained control over the county extrabudgetary enterprises, which had been so critical locally in providing revenues for Shulu's extrabudgetary fund. It took over leadership of both the in-budget and extrabudgetary county industrial enterprises formerly administered in the Industry Bureau *xitong*. The Economic Planning Commission also began to exercise considerable power over enterprises under the Second Light Industry Bureau, including taking a leading role in closing down unprofitable ones and reassigning their workers to other plants under its purview.

From 1980 through June 1986, the Shulu Second Light Industry Bureau, which also became a company in this period, was put under the leadership of the economic and planning committees, as part of a general administrative streamlining and simplification that was being encouraged nationwide.[31] In Shulu, the development of market forces and the relative contraction of state economic planning and material allocation left many firms—particularly the smaller ones—in the lurch. As the Economic Planning Commission devoted its limited administrative resources to the generally larger local state-run enterprises, the smaller factories in other categories, like those under Second Light, experienced shortages of raw materials, skilled workers, and capital equipment, for all of which they had previously relied on their administrators to supply them through the state plan. Second Light officials complained in late 1986, "This was a result of thinking only about administrative reform, but not enough about production."[32] They blamed this for much of the pervasive problem of reduced profits in Shulu industry.[33] But the Economic Planning Commission analyzed the problem differently, attributing the reduced profits to "the effects of the market," specifically to declining ex-factory prices and rising input prices.[34] This suggests a tension in the reform project: to the extent that efforts to rationalize state administration—which has been one aspect of reform—occur, they can harm the development of smaller, already troubled, or potentially more dynamic county-level firms that are less tightly connected to the central state, which is another reform goal.

Light industries' difficulties in adjusting to market forces continued through the remainder of the 1980's. By 1990, however, a major restructuring was underway, in the name of rationalizing administrative responsibility by industrial subsector. This brought under the Light Industry and Textile Company's management several light-industry and textile-producing enterprises, some of which had not formerly been collectively owned and had been run instead by other state agencies. The former Second Light apparatus, therefore, was gradually diversifying its operations and adding enterprises to its stable. Whether the injection of new blood into the old Second Light would eventually work to enliven and strengthen its competitiveness or would, instead, only burden it with new ailing members remained to be seen.

Collective Enterprises and the State: Toward New Forms of Ownership, Planning, and Control

New currents were at work in Shulu, as elsewhere in the country, promoting the expansion of small firms—specifically, the expansion of collective enterprises run by former communes and brigades, now towns (*zhen*) and townships (*xiang*), and by their constituent villages (*cun*), as well as by urban administrative districts (*banshichu*) and their constituent residents' committees (*jumin weiyuanhui*). Rural collective industry and its development are discussed in Chapter 8. But an instance of a new kind of relationship between a township industry and the county and even the provincial government merits some discussion here. One impresario of this new development was the Shulu Economic Planning Commission, a key horizontally oriented organ. A review of one of its success stories will help demonstrate the capacity of county government to undertake structural innovation for the purposes of protecting its economic interests and promoting local development.

As noted above, the onset of reform created economic difficulties for Shulu's county-run extrabudgetary enterprises, three of which faced closure by 1986. Over the years, the Xinji Agricultural Machinery Repair and Production Plant had accumulated losses of ¥1,000,000 and had run up debts of ¥560,000. It suffered from low production quality, poor management, and a cash flow so weak that by 1989 it had not paid its workers any wages for six months. In 1987, three farmers contracted to run the factory, but their managerial ineptitude prevented them from solving the many problems the enterprise faced. Since any profits it would have made, and any losses that would have to be covered, would affect the extrabudgetary fund, this imminent factory failure was the county government's problem. Local government leaders were also concerned about what to do with the employees of money-losing plants like this one; whether they were ultimately retained, transferred, or dismissed, it was the county government that would bear many of the economic and political costs.

It was in this context that the Economic Planning Commission hit upon the idea of contracting the county's Agricultural Machinery Repair and Production Plant to the Wangkou Town Appliance Factory. Wangkou town, located in the extreme south of the county, was one of Shulu's reform-period success stories. This was due in no small part to the sprightly entrepreneurship displayed by the managers of this former commune's rural industries, especially several fireworks plants and the appliance factory. Ji Yongchang, the manager of the Wangkou appliance plant, was nevertheless reluctant at first. He would be taking on, after all, an enterprise that had been deeply in the red for many years, and had a large accumulated debt. As such, it could not attract new loans that would be required to help solve the plant's problems. So a way had to be found to make the deal attractive to him and his Wangkou colleagues. Moreover, the distribution of risk had to be balanced so that the Wangkou plant would bear enough to provide an incentive to succeed but not so much as to sour it on the deal. Finally, there were legal and administrative issues associated with the fact that, if consummated, the new arrangement would put a county industry firm under the management of a rural collective-sector unit. Who would own the plant? Under what scale would it be taxed? Would its workers remain state employees?

Tough negotiations resulted in the formation in March 1989 of a limited partnership, a form of management and ownership new to Shulu. (The Wangkou managers had resisted a merger, because they didn't want to take on all the debt of the Xinji Agricultural Machinery Plant.) The partnership was to run for fifteen years. Wangkou would supply the management team (though some of the plant's own managers were kept on), but the plant would retain its Communist Party committee and its standing labor union organization. The plant got a three-year tax holiday, which cost the county government little since the plant was losing money anyway and had paid no taxes at all in 1986 and 1987. The Wangkou firm would invest ¥300,000 in the Xinji plant, on which it was guaranteed payment of interest by the Shulu county government even if the venture lost money. Profits would be split evenly between the county government and the Wangkou plant. But the preexisting capital would remain the property of the county government. The Xinji plant would also be given some preference in distribution of inputs by the Shulu Economic Planning Commission.

The knottiest problem in the negotiations for this deal had to do with the Xinji plant's workers, who feared that the new arrangement would jeopardize their privileged status as regular state workers, lowering them to the level of rural contract workers.[35] To assuage these fears, a meeting between the Wangkou managers and the plant workers was held. The partnership agreement specified that no presently employed workers could be dismissed. The local government further guaranteed that the county plant's employees would retain their status as regular state workers. And to sweeten the pot even further, the Wangkou management agreed to pay the workers two months' back wages. But the workers also bore significant costs. They subsidized the deal to the tune of four months' more back wages that would not be paid. They would also now be subjected to a piecerate wage system and to "strengthened management" by the Wangkou directors. But these more stringent work requirements were softened for the plant's older workers, who were given "lower quotas so as to get rid of discontent and to preserve stability."[36]

Wangkou factory manager Ji maintained that he finally went along with the new arrangement "out of a sense of responsibility to the [county] government."[37] But the takeover of the Xinji plant was also a shrewd move for Wangkou. The partnership turned gross profits of ¥150,000 in 1989 (compared with a ¥134,300 loss in 1988), and net profits of ¥94,400. For 1990, gross profits of over ¥300,000 were projected by the middle of the year. Wangkou also got the opportunity to expand its operations and establish a beachhead in the county's urban center, Xinji, something it probably could not have done otherwise in view of the tight restrictions on land use there.[38]

This move attracted the attention of provincial officials who, within the year, were in the midst of working out a new arrangement to provide financing and raw materials to the Wangkou Town Appliance Factory (as well as other rising stars in the rural collective sector) in return for a role in marketing their output. In 1990 a new type of relationship between rural collective enterprises and higher levels of the state—known as "raising the [administrative] level of management" (tiji guanli)—was being mooted. It was to involve inclusion of the enterprise in the state plan for material allocation, and would add to this inclusion financial assistance. Prefecture governments as well as that of Hebei province would identify collective firms with especially strong records of development and/or export production. A necessary condition for being raised to provincial management in Hebei was output value in excess of ¥10,000,000 or exports over ¥5,000,000. The higher-level governments would provide these firms with priority allocations of raw materials and energy (which was especially scarce) as well as preferred loans. In return, the prefecture and provincial governments would presumably gain first claim on the distribution of the factories' output. In Shulu, the pacesetting Wangkou Town Appliance Factory was selected for the provincial plan.

State administrative and material support for rural collective industry is nothing new, of course. From 1979–81, Mao-period controls barring these firms from many lines of production were lifted, tax concessions were granted, and administrative support was strengthened by incorporating some of these firms into state-planned material allocation. Following a period of retrenchment, in 1984–85 the state returned once again to a more encouraging posture by increasing financial support through expanding credit available to rural collective firms and permitting them to issue bonds and stocks.[39] What seemed different about *tiji guanli* was that it was more selective and market-driven. It was not so much a policy to help rural enterprises in general as a modality for a state agency at the provincial level to attach itself to enterprises that had emerged successfully from a previous set of stimulative policies. In that sense, it may represent an example of a provincial government agency becoming something of a market actor, in this case by utilizing to advantage the diminished powers it still had in economic planning and material allocation. Alternatively, in 1990, a time of retrenchment in state policy toward rural enterprises, *tiji guanli* may have been driven by an effort to reassert or strengthen state planning by hitching it to the rising stars of the rural collective sector. In either case, *tiji guanli* conforms to the tendency now recognized in significant elements of China's state sector to defy the expectations of many observers by actually becoming more competitive and market-oriented, with attendant gains in profitability and efficiency.[40]

Tiji guanli also seemed to have implications for county government and its relationships with the province. A direct relationship between a rural collective firm and the province was quite novel. In 1990, Shulu county authorities appeared happy to have helped forge a relationship between a leader of their rural collective industrial sector and the provincial authorities. They obviously expected Wangkou to benefit, in ways that the county government would find salutary. But it also seemed possible that expanding such relationships would undermine the influence of county authorities over their leading small-industrial performers, or would harm their ability to mobilize resources from those industries. *Tiji guanli* could, then, carry the seeds of new kinds of political conflict within the Chinese state.

Control Over County Industry Profits

A prominent object of reform in state socialist systems has been to loosen the control exercised by the central state over industrial profits. It is widely argued by reformers in China and elsewhere that decentralization of control over profits is necessary to provide incentives for more efficient production. But of course reallocation of control can take different forms. "Enterprise decentralization" gives more control to firms, which is a prerequisite for expanding the role of the market. By contrast, "administrative decentralization" gives more power to lower-level government agencies, which is a way to fine-tune the planned economy. Reallocation of control can also be carried out to different degrees, and it can come with more or fewer limitations and stipulations. Decentralizing control over profits has been, then, a policy direction that is fraught with significance for the economic restructuring of state socialist systems. It has also opened up new terrain for political bargaining and contention.

THE MAO PERIOD

In the Mao period, industrial profit control, though strictly governed by centrally determined policies and guidelines, was nonetheless characterized by a degree of administrative decentralization. It permitted very little enterprise decentralization, however. As we have seen, before 1978 enterprise decentralization in Shulu was minimal. Industrial enterprises under the Second Light Industry Bureau were permitted to retain a small percentage of after-tax profits under their own discretion.[41] In-budget industries were retaining a very small portion of their profits.[42] As for administrative decentralization, certain portions of the profits of Shulu plants were retained by the specialized county industrial bureaus supervising them. But the discretion of these bureaus over expenditure of these funds was in many cases hedged in by central state guidelines and by regulations generated at higher levels of their ministerial systems. Between one and three percent of the net profits of local state-run enterprises was kept within the county, presumably at the Industry Bureau, but these monies were to be used specifically for workers' welfare funds. Thus the greatest area of local discretion over industry profits existed in the county-run extrabudgetary enterprises, which (after paying taxes, of course) turned over all remaining profits to the county government for disposition as it saw fit.

As shown in Chapter 4, reform and readjustment of industrial profit control systems were hardly new to the Deng period. A 1972 reform left 60 percent of the net profits of local state-run factories established thereafter in the hands of the county Industry Bureau, which could use them for reinvestment in those factories only. In 1968 the county Second Light Industry Bureau increased its proportion of retained profits from 48 percent to 72 percent of after-tax profits. These funds could be used only for reinvestment in those plants or to start new ones. But this apparently broad discretion was circumscribed by a regulation that any expenditures in excess of ¥10,000 required the approval of prefecture Second Light authorities and of the county Planning Committee. In any event, this discretion was not being exercised by the factories themselves, but by county-level authorities.

THE DENG PERIOD

If Maoist political economy attempted to reform centralized planning through decentralization to local governments, including county governments, the Deng reform project promised marketization. This implied decentralization to enterprises. The reformist leadership also hoped that enterprise decentralization would increase efficiency. The experience in Shulu county demonstrates both the limits and the contentiousness of enterprise decentralization in the Deng period.

In 1978 a small step toward granting enterprises more resources was attempted. In a nationwide move, local state-run enterprises were to be permitted to retain a portion of their over-target profits up to a maximum of 5 percent of the value of their annual payroll. The proceeds were to be used for improving "workers' welfare." Presumably the profit retention percentage was tied to payroll size to equalize somewhat the amount of retained profits per worker. This implicit egalitarianism was the source of the reform's problems. Specifically, some larger but less profitable factories were being permitted to retain more than many smaller, leaner ones. Complaints were then heard in Shulu from the enterprises that were disadvantaged by the reform. These complaints resonated with the reformist thrust toward encouraging and rewarding higher labor productivity.

The response, interestingly, was not to extend enterprise decentralization further by adopting a new formula that would allow factories to keep a portion of their above-quota profits regardless of size. A move was made, instead, in the direction of administrative decentralization by having the profits aggregated and held at the county level and giving the county government authority to distribute them back to the eligible factories. In addition, the county government was to be permitted to utilize the funds for technical innovations as well as workers' welfare. Clearly the intended emphasis was not toward egalitarianism but toward improving production; yet in this case the mechanism was to be local state discretion, rather than material incentives or "market" forces.[43] This local permutation of the reform appeared to be as controversial as the one it replaced: in mid-1979 there was talk in Shulu of a return to some version of the 1978 enterprise decentralization. As early as mid-1979, then, at the very outset of the Deng period, administrative decentralization at the county level had been strengthened, while the higher levels of the state had flirted only tentatively with what was proving to be a very contentious effort at enterprise decentralization. At any rate, the county government in Shulu was keeping a generally tight rein on industrial profits.

Moreover, there were definite limits even to administrative decentralization to the county level. With the important exception of industrial profits going into the extrabudgetary fund, even those profits retained by the county government were subject to various restrictions. These included expenditure priorities set by the vertical bureaucratic systems (*xitong*), upper limits on per-item outlays, and requirements for clearance with other county and higher-level agencies. Although financial contracting came to Shulu as early as 1980, the negotiations over the county budget and its over-target profit retentions were plainly conducted much as before. The county government gained little actual leeway through the early financial reforms. Even in 1985, with the implementation of the policy of converting enterprise profit remissions into taxes (*li gai shui*), budget practices changed little and afforded the county government no greater measure of flexibility in spending its over-target revenue collections. Enterprises paid "taxes," but the county's financial relations with higher levels of the state still operated according to "contracted" profit levels based on 1983 financial figures.

As for enterprise decentralization, profit retention rates were to have been changed in favor of enterprises in the course of the continuing reform. Enterprises under the Second Light Industry Bureau, for example, were supposed to be keeping about 40 percent of net profits after 1985, as compared with only 10 percent in earlier years.[44] County-run extrabudgetary enterprises, which in the Mao period had remitted all of their after-tax profits to the extrabudgetary fund, and from 1978–84 had been permitted to retain 30 percent for themselves, were now entitled to keep half. County in-budget industries also were supposed to be permitted to keep larger percentages of their profits at the enterprise level by the mid-1980's. But in view of their increased tax and debt repayment responsibilities, many of these state-run factories seemed not actually to be left with all that much more than before.[45] It is interesting to note that actual factory-level rates of profit retention were virtually identical for in-budget and extrabudgetary enterprises during the latter half of the 1980's. Using the data recorded in Tables 12 and 19 we calculate that the percentage of in-budget industry real profits kept at the enterprise level between 1985 and 1989 was just 21.3 percent per year on average; and for extrabudgetary industrial enterprises that figure was identical, an annual average of 21.3 percent. It was precisely in these two categories of county industry, of course, that profits had been highest and most sustained over time.

Over a decade into the Deng period, then, state authorities had not relinquished control to enterprises over significant industrial profits. Profit shares retained by enterprises were growing compared with the Mao period, but they still came only to around one-fifth of real profits, which is a good deal less than the proportions mooted in policy pronouncements. Structural reform of Shulu county industry, then, still looked much more like the administrative decentralization of a state-run economy than the rise of a competitive market.

Labor and Employment

The industrial labor force in Shulu's county-run industries has grown significantly during the socialist period, from a few hundred in 1949 to almost 20,000 in 1990.[46] This growth has been accompanied by two structural changes in the terms of employment, each a response to different budgetary, administrative, and political pressures to limit the expansion of the labor force. From the mid-1960's to the end of the Mao period, strictures on the movement of rural people to urban areas made it difficult for urban enterprises to find the workers needed to fuel the industrial expansion that was taking place at the time. And in the Deng period, the reformist emphasis on promoting growth in the collective and private sectors and on reducing the financial drag of state enterprises nationally eventually brought about limitations on the hiring of new workers in state firms.

In the face of these difficulties, the Shulu county government, committed throughout the Mao and Deng periods to development of its state industrial and commercial enterprises, had to find fresh ways to expand the labor force in county industry. In the Mao period, its answer (though not its alone) was the hiring of peasants as temporary contract laborers. This went far toward meeting Shulu's growing requirements for labor, but in turn created new political pressures resulting from the way in which it divided the labor force. In the 1980's, temporary contract labor gave way first to a return to expanded regular employment. But when, after a few years, this too ran up against economic and political limits, the Shulu county government moved to utilize a new category of employment known as contract system employees (*hetongzhi zhigong*). This in turn posed new political difficulties for it to solve.

Specifically, through 1957, the end of the first Five Year Plan, the expansion of the labor force involved simply adding regular state workers (Table 20). But the second wave of expansion of the Shulu labor force largely involved the employment of farmers on a temporary contract basis (explicated below). These contract workers comprised 76 percent of the net increment to the labor force from 1964 to 1976. By 1976, rural contract workers actually outnumbered regular workers in Shulu's industrial labor force; by 1978, their proportion had increased still further.[47] This expansion had occurred despite serious popular political conflict arising from in-

TABLE 20
Labor Force in County Industry and Commerce, Shulu County, by Employment Category, 1949–90

Year	Regular workers	Temporary contract workers	Contract system employees	Total
1949	≈500			≈500
1957	6,248			6,248
1964	4,846	304		5,150
1976	6,986	7,130		14,116
1986	15,078	5,976	220	21,274
1990	16,695	4,706	4,522	25,923

equalities in pay and employment terms between the regular and contract workers.

Temporary contract labor was, as we shall see, an innovation that grew up in the specific institutional environment of the Mao period. It used the structure afforded by the people's communes in order to find a way to expand the county industry labor force while still restricting the size of the urban population, which was a key Maoist goal. So it is not surprising that once the institutional bases and the social policies of that period were replaced with very different ones, the temporary contract labor system began to atrophy. The Deng period saw the renewed expansion of the regular labor force, which, after having the lid kept on it during the last decade or more of the Mao period, more than doubled between 1978 and 1986 (Table 20). This reflected a triple conjuncture: the expanded power of local governments to manage their own affairs; the tremendous pressure and opportunity to expand the industrial and commercial economy; and the infeasibility, leading to obsolescence, of the temporary contract labor system, which depended completely for its administration and financing on the declining and eventually defunct people's communes.

In this context, the extant temporary contract workers, who in the 1980's were still very numerous (almost six thousand in 1986; see Table 20), posed an administrative anomaly and a gnawing political problem. Their terms of employment had been formally arranged through, and some of their income was to be funneled to, people's communes, which no longer existed. And they were employed on terms that were formally "temporary" (although many had had their jobs for a decade or more) and materially quite inferior to regular workers.

The solution to these problems awaited the formulation by the central state of a new employment policy directed at a different problem. Concerned about the burgeoning costs of expanding regular state employment, and in general motivated by the desire to remove the disincentive effects of workers' holding guaranteed jobs (the "iron rice bowl"), in September 1986 the state promulgated a policy according to which all new hirings were to take place in a category known as "contract system employment."

Moreover, in Shulu, which was chosen to pilot the new system before its wide-scale introduction, temporary contract workers and even some existing regular state workers were to be put into this category. Beijing policymakers did not intend temporary contract workers to be absorbed into the new category. But this happened in Shulu because, as detailed in the section on contract system labor below, these workers had a great deal of seniority and considerable skill, and they made up a very significant part of the county industrial labor force. The new system provided the unintended opportunity to resolve the problems posed by the anachronistic temporary contract labor system. This process, though not unproblematic, was well under way by 1990 (Table 20).

The complex changes the process entailed are explored in the following subsections, organized by each evolving category of labor and employment.

TEMPORARY CONTRACT WORKERS:
PEASANT LABOR FOR INDUSTRY

"Temporary contract workers" (linshi hetong gong) are farmers who were hired, mostly between 1964 and 1976, by county industrial enterprises through contracts with their rural collective units. In formal terms, the collectives made contracts with the enterprises to supply them with labor, for which they received monies to cover the cost of the work points which the collectives credited to the workers. The contract workers were still members of their rural collectives, rather than employees of the factories in the city. In terms of the household registration system, by which Chinese citizens are classified as either rural residents (nongye hukou) or nonrural ones (fei nongye hukou), they remained rural residents.[48] This meant, among other things, that they were not entitled to regular urban housing or employment in an urban area. Thus, although "temporary contract work" was often not very temporary at all—in Shulu most contract workers have been employed this way for many years—the contract workers have maintained their permanent homes in their villages. Their families have remained behind there, and the workers visit home periodically—in Shulu usually weekly or monthly—living the rest of the time (indeed, most of the time) in factory dormitories.[49]

From the point of view of the county government, one advantage of contract labor has been the relief it provided from the responsibility of providing food, housing, education, and other services for the contract workers and their families. Shulu officials also said that the major reason for requiring contract workers to maintain their rural household registrations was to relieve the state of the burden of supplying them with commodity grain.[50] Moreover, contract labor provided the Shulu county government with a solution to its labor recruitment problem. In the 1970's and 1980's the Shulu Economic Planning Commission operated under a very strict quota from higher-level state agencies mandating the size of the regular urban industrial labor force. That quota had not been revised upward for quite some time, because of the central state's unwillingness to increase the number of people depending on commodity grain supplies. Yet Shulu industry had been growing and was continuing to do so, and for this it had required and continued to require more workers. Expansion of the contract labor force was the solution to this contradiction in the 1960's and 1970's.

There were other advantages for the county government and the enterprises in employing contract workers (and other disadvantages for the workers). In 1978, Shulu contract workers averaged annual salaries of ¥455, compared with the regular workers' ¥571. They also drew fewer fringe benefits, such as free medical insurance, workers' compensation, pensions, and sick leave. In at least one Shulu plant, they were given less favorable piece-rate quotas, and were not even provided with the same protective clothing as regular workers. By housing them in dormitories and keeping their families in the village, pressure on scarce urban housing and land was reduced. Employing enterprises and the planning and administrative agencies that supervised them also gained managerial flexibility. Contract workers are easier to dismiss (simply by failing to renew the contract) than the regular labor force, which is accustomed to its "iron rice bowl" and is in a better position to threaten the state politically should its security come under attack. Contract workers also proved more pliable on the job. As the director of the Shulu Labor Bureau put it, "The temporary contract workers often listened to the manager better than the regular workers did. First, they were glad to have jobs in the factory. Second, they were hoping to convert their status to regular workers" so they had to be obedient.[51] Moreover, employment of farmers as contract workers in county industry provided the state with a way of reducing rural underemployment or unemployment in a planned and controlled way, avoiding the risks of massive and uncontrolled desertion of the rural areas that might result from opening up an unrestricted labor market. The contract labor system, then, has had strong attractions for industrial managers and urban government officials.

Yet it also set up a complex web of inequalities: between contract workers and their neighbors still engaged in farming, and between contract workers and regular industrial workers. Contract labor was a source of controversy and of discontent. In 1972, there was a national policy to change the classification of contract workers to regular workers, perhaps as a result of agitation by contract workers during the Cultural Revolution.[52] Its adoption in Shulu's Fur and Leather Tannery met so much resistance from the regular workers, however, that it was soon dropped. It is easy to see how the policy would be opposed both by the regular workers (who feared the dilution of their privileged position by its extension to peasant contract workers) and by factory managers and industrial administrators, who benefited from the lower wages and potentially more flexible terms on which the contract workers could be employed. Thus contract workers hired in 1972 or later were specifically denied the opportunity to become regular workers, and this stricture was still in effect in 1990. To assuage their unhappiness, a compromise was struck. Previously, contract workers received only 50 percent of their wages directly, with the rest going to their rural collective units, which in turn awarded them work points that were often worth less than the other half. But after 1972, contract workers could choose to be paid all of their salaries directly, except for ¥3 to ¥4, which went to their rural collective units.[53] This compromise was still in effect in 1979.

By 1986, in recognition of the fact that many temporary contract workers had been employed in state industry for up to two decades, the distinction between them and regular workers had narrowed further. With the decline of rural collectives under the responsibility systems, there were no more work points, so now all contract workers received their salaries directly. They had also become eligible to receive sick pay at a rate of 50 percent of their salary (compared with up to 100 percent for regular workers), full provision of medical care, and a ¥2.5 monthly grain subsidy (compared with ¥5 for regular workers).[54] In the Fur and Leather Tanning Factory, they now received the same protective clothing and the same piece work quotas and rates. To accommodate the needs of contract workers who wished to return to their home villages each day to work on agricultural plots, many factories had adjusted their schedules by skipping the lunch break and closing earlier.

But efforts to equalize the employment terms of regular and contract workers point to ongoing political conflict. Wage differentials persisted because of the regular workers' generally greater seniority. To ameliorate them, a proposal was made to set middle-level salary scales (such as level three on the eight-grade wage scale) for the contract workers ¥10 above those of regular workers. Protests from Labor Bureau officials on behalf of regular workers or out of anticipated fear of their reaction forced this down to ¥5. But even when this lower scale was enacted, howls of protest were heard from the regular workers. Moreover, contract workers still lacked lifetime job tenure and retirement pensions. This could only have grated on them even more sharply as the ranks of regular workers swelled with new hirees who were entitled to these treasured job security provisions (Table 20).

NEW DEVELOPMENTS IN EMPLOYMENT

Shulu officials found a solution to this festering discontent in the national policy enacted in October 1986 of putting all newly hired workers on a new kind of contract system (not to be confused with the one discussed above).[55] Shulu had been a test site for this program, as part of which it had already begun to convert some existing temporary contract workers to the new form of contract system work before the policy was adopted nationally. Labor Bureau officials were anticipating in 1986 that this new category of contract employment would gradually absorb those in the old category, while that of regular workers would also disappear through long-term attrition. Actual developments over the subsequent four years, however, during which the regular labor force was expanded by 21 percent (see Table 20), ran utterly counter to this expectation.

A second development—in response to the rising stature of temporary contract workers as well as increasing pressure on enterprises to cut costs—was the division in 1986 of the temporary contract workers into two subcategories: "in-plan" and "out-of-plan temporary contract workers" (*jihuanei* and *jihuawai linshi hetonggong*). The in-plan category took in 80 percent of the former temporary contract workers. The remainder—including seasonal workers and those temporary contract workers near retirement—were assigned to the out-of-plan category.

Thus by 1987 the structure of employment in Shulu's county enterprises was more, not less, administratively complex than it had been in the Mao period or in the early years of reform. Where in the past there were two categories—regular workers and temporary contract workers—now there were four: regular workers, contract system workers, and in-plan and out-of-plan temporary contract workers.

Regular Workers

One purpose of the 1986 reform was the eventual elimination of the category of regular state employment, with its employment guarantees and fringe benefits that were seen by the Deng leadership as labor disincentives. It may well be that over several decades the category of regular state workers will disappear, if only by attrition. But official policy and Shulu officials' statements to the contrary notwithstanding, there was no evidence of any atrophy of regular state employment in Shulu as of 1990. Indeed, if anything it had expanded since 1986, as we have seen. Shulu Labor Bureau officials said in 1990 that most regular workers were indeed signing contracts. Moreover, they claimed that the workers appreciated the contracts' specification of their duties, responsibilities, and incentives.[56] But even if job specification was often turned against the workers, they defended themselves in other ways from the efforts of the reform to discipline labor: any contracts the workers may have signed have not affected their overall classification as regular state workers or the benefits they derive from that classification. As of 1990, these still included protection from layoff, retirement fund contributions by the factory of 20 percent of wages, retirement benefits of up to 100 percent of salary, full medical coverage for the workers themselves and 50 percent for their families, funeral benefits of up to half of the average monthly salary in the factory, and disability benefits on a scale of up to 100 percent of salary depending on the length of the disability and the worker's experience.⁵⁷ In Shulu, these benefits also continued to include, for workers hired before 1959 only, the right to pass their jobs on to their children under certain circumstances.⁵⁸

Contract Employment

In 1990 there were three different types of contract employment in Shulu. They were similar in some ways. Shulu Labor Bureau officials asserted that regular and contract workers doing the same job and located at the same level on the seniority scale received the same wage. Even assuming this to be the case, there were a number of significant differences in wages, benefits, and job security between regular workers on the one hand and the various categories of contract workers on the other. All three categories of contract workers, including contract-system workers, tended to be toward the lower end of the eight-grade wage scale; thus their incomes were lower in general. In contrast to regular workers, they were all subject to dismissal as well. This was no abstract possibility. In 1983, for example, the Shulu Petrochemical Plant, in financial straits due to a 50 percent drop in the market price of a lubricating oil it produced, fired a full 10 percent of all the temporary contract workers in the county—around six hundred people—sending them back to their villages. This palpable job insecurity aside, contract workers all received fewer benefits. But these were differentiated among various categories of contract employment. So also were the workers' career backgrounds and modes of recruitment into the labor force.

CONTRACT-SYSTEM LABOR Contract-system labor was intended by central policy makers eventually to replace regular state employment. It was to eliminate some privileges, such as guaranteed lifetime employment and the capacity to bequeath jobs to children, in order to discipline and motivate the labor force. It would therefore amount to a downgrading of the terms of employment in state industry and commerce, though the policy was of course not promulgated as such. Some regular state workers were to be brought under this new category, and all new hirees were. In Shulu, though, the policy amounted to an upgrading of the terms of employment, because all the recruits into the contract system were former temporary contract workers.⁵⁹ Shulu Labor Bureau officials defended this reclassification by noting that these temporary contract workers "have been working for a long time, and have become skilled, experienced, middle-level workers. We want to take care of them and their retirement. This is what we do in a socialist country."⁶⁰

To be sure, there were significant differences between contract-system and regular state employment. Contract-system workers could be dismissed, and an unemployment benefits plan was even worked out for them.⁶¹ They received no funeral benefits, and their families received no medical benefits. They had to finance 15 percent of the contribution their factories made to the retirement fund. Yet despite this, their retirement and sick pay/disability benefits were so inferior[62] that they were awarded a 17 percent wage increment to make up for the difference.[63]

But the inferior benefits and job security of the contract-system workers were still an improvement compared with their previous situation under temporary contract employment, to which we will turn directly. To put the matter differently, the fact that all of Shulu's contract-system workers were recruited from among the ranks of temporary contract workers meant that they could experience contract-system employment as an improvement. This could help ameliorate the effects of or deflect their attention away from the differential between contract-system work and regular state employment. Shulu Labor Bureau officials asserted that "on the whole, the implementation of the contract labor system has been smooth,"[64] and there are good reasons to believe them.

IN-PLAN TEMPORARY CONTRACT LABOR   According to officials of the Labor Bureau, "the new category is not much different from the old temporary contract workers category: the only difference is that now they are in line to become regular contract workers when the opportunity permits."[65] In 1990, the category of in-plan temporary contract workers included all those in the old category of temporary contract workers who had not been reclassified as contract-system workers. In addition, it included newly recruited workers (of whom there were 1,120 in 1989 alone). In Shulu, then, new workers were not being recruited directly into regular contract employment, as the national policy envisioned they would be. Instead, regular contract employment was being used to mollify the longstanding complaints of former temporary contract workers. Meanwhile, new workers were being placed into the very same category that had incubated those complaints for over two decades in Shulu.

If the creation of contract-system employment helped reduce the political pressure on the fault line between regular state employment and contract work, it only increased that between contract-system and temporary contract employment. Temporary contract workers received no medical benefits even for themselves, not to mention funeral, retirement, sick pay/disability, or unemployment benefits. These were sufficiently expensive—the 17 percent increment was singled out as especially costly—that the Shulu government and enterprises could not afford to convert all of the "in-plan" temporary contract workers to contract-system employment, though the very concept of "in-plan" referred to the objective of doing so in the future when finances would permit.[66] These differentials were so valued by the workers themselves as to cause keen competition among workers for conversion to contract-system work. This often led to bitter complaints by workers to and through the labor unions about fairness in selecting one worker or group of workers over others.

OUT-OF-PLAN TEMPORARY CONTRACT LABOR   There was still in 1989 an employment category even lower than temporary contract labor. Out-of-plan temporary contract workers had become the new truly temporary employees. In the Fur and Leather Tanning Factory, they were seasonal workers who were employed for just a few months at a stretch, as well as people who before 1980 had worked for the enterprise at home on a putting-out basis. The factory management brought them into the factory "in order to improve management."[67] Specifically, under the putting-out system, these workers had been switching high-quality hides and pelts given to them by the factory for poor-quality ones, using the former in their own production or for resale. Bringing them into the factory to work was the response to this problem. These out-of-plan temporary contract workers were, of course, not on the state payroll; in fact, in the Fur and Leather Tanning Factory they were not on the payroll at all. They were employed by the Xinji Labor Service Company, which assigned them to the factory. The factory in turn paid the company a sum of money equivalent to their wages, which were equal to those of other regular and contract workers (though all the out-of-plan temporary contract workers were paid at level one on the wage scale). The company kept 10 percent for its trouble, so the out-of-plan temporary contract workers were in fact receiving 90 percent of the wages of their equivalent co-workers.[68]

The factory benefited from this arrangement in three ways. First, it did not have to pay them above level one on the wage scale. Second, it gained flexibility. Out-of-plan temporary contract workers could be added and released at will, the latter at minimal political risk to the factory since the workers were not employees of the factory anyway. Third, it did not have to provide the out-of-plan temporary contract workers with any benefits: they were entitled to no pensions, sick pay, health care, or even protective clothing. Disability benefits for them were in theory provided by the Labor Service Company.

THE DILEMMAS OF EMPLOYMENT

This overview of the recent history of employment systems in Shulu—in particular the rise of not one but three forms of "contract labor" alongside regular state employment—depicts the dilemmas of industrial employment in China. On the one hand are the forces driving the state and enterprises to economize on labor by reducing their wage bills and costs of labor force reproduction (such as housing, food supply, education, and medical care). This propelled the rise of temporary contract labor in the mid-1960's. On the other were the forces of industrialization in Shulu and places like it, which created an intense need for expansion of the labor force. This produced a burgeoning class of contract workers subordinate to but in the closest possible contact with regular workers over a long period of time.[69] The structural problem posed by this cleavage, combined with the political outrage contract workers expressed in the Cultural Revolution, forced adjustments in their terms of employment. These in turn undermined the attainment of the cost-saving objectives that had called contract labor into being in the first place.

At the same time pressures toward raising labor productivity (which could be accomplished partly by reducing labor costs) were only increasing as the Deng period proceeded. These in turn conjured up two new forms of contract labor intended to downgrade the privileges, benefits, and costs of labor. Yet these too resulted in the opposite. In Shulu, the newly minted category of contract-system labor actually raised the benefits to and costs of employing over 4,500 of Shulu's 40,000 workers in county industry. And if this mollified that phalanx, it only caused renewed disputation among those who were left behind. Meanwhile, in a concomitant development, by replacing the old two-tiered structure of employment with a four-tiered one, the result was a structure of social cleavage and of economic administration still more complex, segmented, and inegalitarian than the one produced in the Mao period in Shulu.

LABOR COSTS

The failure of the repeated efforts to economize by changing the structure of employment set the context for, and may well have prompted, another approach toward reducing labor costs. Expansion of the labor force and wage increases in county enterprises began in 1985 to be more closely regulated and more strictly based upon economic indicators. The total size of the state enterprises' wages in all of Shijiazhuang prefecture was to be linked to economic efficiency, the indicator for which was to be total taxes on real profits (*shixian lirun shui*) collected by the prefecture government. This would provide the financial parameters for labor force expansion and wage increases.

Specifically, beginning in 1986, the increase in the number of workers that a county enterprise could employ was no longer set according to planning targets—that is, by some combination of bureaucratic politics and routine. It could only increase in accordance with the rise in output, profits, and taxes. (No county industry enterprise could hire workers without approval from the Labor Bureau.)[70] For every 1 percent rise in the average of increases of industrial output, profits, and taxes, a county enterprise could be permitted to increase the size of its labor force 0.3 percent. In an especially interesting development, the same formula was applied in reverse: firms whose economic performance declined would have to shed labor.

Wage increases were linked to the same index. For every 1 percent increase in the index, the total wage bill could rise 0.3 percent to 0.7 percent. Whether a particular firm fell within this range in a given year was a complex matter involving subjective judgments as well as objective criteria. Five factors were to be taken into account. First was the quality of management, which is vague enough to permit some fudging of the remaining four. Second, priority in wage increases was to be given to productive over commercial enterprises. Third was the economic environment specific to the firm. If, in the opinion of the Shulu Economic Planning Commission and the Finance Bureau, it was relatively easy to increase profits, then a smaller wage increase could be permitted, and vice versa. Fourth was the average wage in the firm. Old firms with a preponderance of older and therefore higher-paid workers qualified only for lower wage increases. Finally, wage increases had to conform to a formula affecting the size but also the distribution of raises. If the total wage bill increased less than 7 percent, 10 to 20 percent of the workers could receive a raise; if the wage bill rose between 7 percent and 12 percent, 15 to 25 percent of the workers could get raises; and if the wage bill rose more than 12 percent, 20 to 30 percent of the workers could get raises.

THE STATE "LABOR MARKET": GOVERNMENT REGULATION OF RECRUITMENT AND HIRING

Chinese reality can play tricks with some of the most basic and potentially germane categories that analysts bring to it. The distinction between plan and market is one of the most common and fundamental ones in the lexicon of socialist political economy, particularly in a time of reform. But in Shulu there is an office—an administrative organ housed in a government building—known as the "labor market" (*laodong shichang*). It has nothing whatsoever in common with the standard meaning of "market" as a place of voluntary and relatively unrestricted exchange between buyer and seller. In Shulu the "labor market" was the government agency in charge of regulating labor recruitment and hiring—and the regulation it dispensed was getting tighter, not looser, in 1990.

In Shulu as of 1990, the state remained committed to limiting the size of employment rolls in county industry, suggesting that reform had not proceeded so far as to make the enterprises themselves responsible for their labor costs. Thus the process by which an enterprise could add workers to its staff was utterly state-centered. First it had to receive the approval of the Labor Bureau to expand the size of its payroll, according to the criteria discussed above. Once it had done so, it wrote job descriptions specifying the conditions of employment and required qualifications. These required the approval of the Labor Bureau. This agency also took the next steps in the recruitment process, advertising openings or, if only a handful of workers were to be hired, contacting applicants whose names were already on file. It also administered examinations and, if job candidates passed, actually conducted any job training that was necessary, according to a plan submitted by the hiring enterprise but approved by the bureau. Nowhere in this process of recruitment, selection, or training did the hiring enterprise play any direct role. (The Labor Bureau even undertook to make introductions to private firms seeking employees.) And once the worker was finally to be hired, the Labor Arbitration Department, an office under the Labor Bureau, had to approve the terms, conditions of work, and remuneration in the contract.

The Labor Bureau had its own priorities in the recruitment and selection of workers. In 1990 it was emphasizing the hiring of unemployed youth from Xinji City, in order to make up for the fact that in the recent past rural people had gotten preference in new hirings.[71] It also gave preference to Shulu people over outsiders, though its officials professed that it sometimes resorted to the latter to fill undesirable jobs such as construction work!

In order more effectively to regulate labor recruitment and promote its new goal of giving preference to urban people, the Shulu Labor Bureau had, in 1990, come up with its own new procedures. It was taking stock of Shulu's available "labor resources," which included "urban unemployed youth, rural surplus labor, qualified retirees, and people from outside Xinji who are living here."[72] It planned to register them and provide them with a certificate entitling them to take employment. Enterprises were strictly forbidden to hire anyone without such a certificate. In part the regulations were intended to have the effect of tightening up any loopholes that may have afforded enterprises some flexibility and discretion in hiring workers. For example, the new policy was an effort to prevent enterprises from hiring relatives of existing employees. It also had wider uses in the construction and implementation of Shulu's economic plans, by collecting detailed information on the number of unemployed persons in various categories. This information could presumably be used for other purposes as well (such as social control).

Conclusion: Variety and Continuity in County Industry

This chapter has focused on several aspects of Shulu industry that throw light on larger questions about Chinese industry. Two general observations are important to reemphasize in conclusion. The first is the variety of the structures of ownership and administration that the existing conceptualization of "state sector" can hide from view. While these textures have been noted before,[73] in Shulu we see how they developed over a long period of time and over a putatively sharp change from Mao-period political control to Deng-period reform. We see also how densely they could be commingled even within a small place, and how they could come to interact. In both the Mao and Deng periods, there have been five different types of ownership and attendant methods of surplus and profit appropriation within what we here refer to as county industry. These reflect the broad range of enterprises' historical origins and levels of development of industrial productive forces. Meanwhile, a variety of administrative agencies—some oriented vertically toward higher levels of the state (each in different ways, no less), and others horizontally oriented toward countywide, sectoral, or local constituencies and concerns (also in diverse ways)—oversaw, supervised, regulated, and planned industrial activity in Shulu. Moreover, a new and direct relationship could be seen lately emerging between rural collective-sector industries and levels of the state reaching upward as far as the province. Thrusts toward centralization and decentralization have mingled intimately and intricately.

Second are the continuities bridging the Rubicon that China is generally thought to have crossed from the Mao to the Deng period. State control of industry was decentralized in important ways to the county level, but it was not given over to enterprises or to the market. The structure of ownership and administration did not change significantly from one period to the other. It was not until 1990 that a novel development in socialist ownership and administration—the linkage between Wangkou's rural collective industry on the one hand and a county enterprise and the provincial government on the other—began to appear, and even then only in embryonic form. An effort in the early Deng period to transfer some significant control over profits from government bureaus to enterprises faltered. Policies aimed at labor reform evinced negative dynamics and delays, first as efforts to convert contract workers to regular workers were reversed, and later as a new contract system aimed at downgrading the privileges of workers in county enterprises actually upgraded them. There had been no serious challenge to the primacy of the state in industry. Privatization of county or collective firms had not proceeded far forward in Shulu by 1990. The state plan in materials supply and procurement retained at least some of its former power and importance—enough, at least, to be used as one of provincial officials' inducements to forge new linkages with the most dynamic rural collective-sector enterprises. The state was actively regulating the expansion of factories' labor costs. Even the "labor market" turned out to be the name of an agency within the Labor Bureau. In industry, then, the Deng period in Shulu represented less a break with the patterns of state domination that characterized the Mao period than an elaboration and set of variations upon those patterns. Into the second decade of the Chinese reforms, in Shulu at any rate, the state was as broadly and deeply involved in the industrial economy as ever, perhaps even more than in the Mao period.

Town and country in Shulu: farmland abutting industrial Xinji, 1979.

Town and country in Shulu: sheep grazing alongside urban apartments, Xinji, 1990.

Commerce, 1979: Xinji's sleepy main downtown vegetable market.

The Hebei Yiji Market. This panorama includes one of the market's two sides. Partially shaded by the clock tower, rows of open market stalls are interspersed with rows of two-story buildings containing shops on the ground floor and residences above.

Commerce, 1986: The bustling Hebei Yiji Market. Two large traditional Chinese-style gates flank the even larger Western-style gate replete with clock tower, a quintessential symbol of modernity. (Co-author Vivienne Shue and colleague Wang Shaoguang appear in the foreground; co-author Marc Blecher is behind the camera.)

Rock sculpture at the central crossroads inside the main gate of Hebei Yiji.

Commerce, 1990: New department store with glass facade.

The Andong Highway, Xinji's main north-south thoroughfare, 1979.

Liberation Avenue, Xinji's main east-west thoroughfare, newly widened into a boulevard, fronting Hebei Yiji and the People's Park, 1986.

The People's Park, across Liberation Avenue from Hebei Yiji, under construction, 1986. A lotus-shaped fountain greets visitors. The large quadrant at the rear is being dug out for a lake, and in the front are flower gardens. The park also includes a zoo and amusement rides.

Amusement ride in People's Park.

New urban amenities, 1986: *above*, public auditorium, fronting the Andong Highway; *below*, directly across the street, the Workers' Cultural Center.

Brightly painted wrought-iron fences around sidewalk plantings in downtown Xinji, featuring a deer motif.

The Golden Deer, a massive statue in the middle of Xinji's main intersection.

Sluice gates of the water conservancy project.

A trunk canal of the southern Shulu water conservancy project, built in 1977–78.

A large rural town: central Jiucheng, 1979.

Jiucheng on market day, 1986. The building facades still sported carved slogans dating from the Great Leap Forward, with some key characters chiseled out.

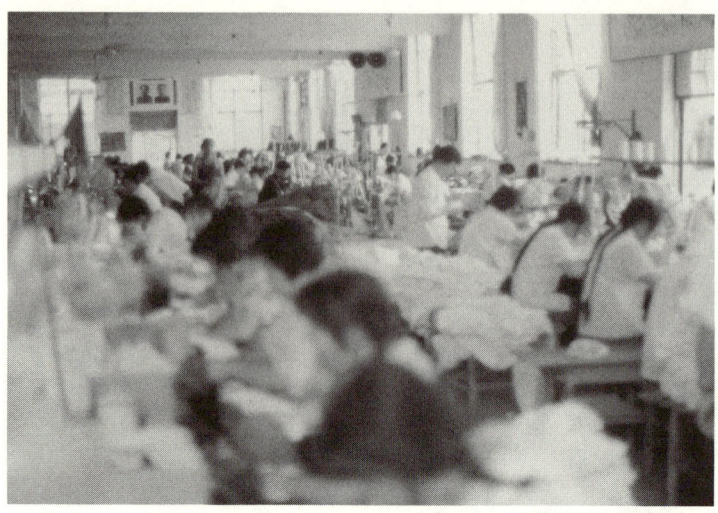

Industrial technology, 1979: The Shulu Textile Plant, a modern local state-run enterprise engaged in export production.

Industrial technology, 1979: The Chengguan Commune Lock Factory's sand foundry, for casting padlock casings.

Industrial technology, 1986: The Jiucheng Cotton Mill, owned by the Shulu Supply and Marketing Co-op. This spinning machine displays the nameplate of the British factory that built it in 1930. It began its Chinese service in Shanghai, and then moved to Wuxi, coming to Shulu only in 1984. Similar British equipment in this plant dated from 1921.

Industrial technology, 1979: The Shulu Rubber Products Factory, a county-run extrabudgetary enterprise (formerly under the Second Light Industry System).

CHAPTER 6

The County Government in Commercial Development

According to the fundamentals of Marxist analysis, the economic activities of the bourgeoisie depend upon the unruly networks and marketplaces of "free" domestic and foreign trade. Twentieth-century revolutionary socialist regimes, in their heyday some decades ago, it follows, typically put heavy emphasis on regulating these trade networks and marketplaces, subjecting them, in short, to strict party-state management and control. The evolving reform-socialist regimes of the 1980's and 1990's, in turn, hopeful of finding ways to allow their economies to benefit from the energy of "free entrepreneurship," have typically looked for means to restore competitiveness to commercial relations and to enliven both their domestic and foreign market activities. In this broad sphere of commercial management and reform, perhaps no socialist state has followed a more spectacularly extreme zigzag course over the years than the Chinese. Virtually all trade arrangements were subjected to progressively tightening centralization and regulation over the course of the Mao era, only to be followed by a swift loosening of regulations and a dramatic decentralization of commercial planning and management in the reform period.

Trends in Shulu county commerce, of course, have generally conformed to these broader policy changes affecting the nation at large. But in *both* the Mao period and the reform period, the county government itself has had enormously important and demanding regulatory and developmental tasks to perform. If anything, in fact, the scope of county government commercial activity and responsibility appears to have been widening, not shrinking, to cope with the intent and with the sometimes unexpected consequences of the recent "market" reforms.

In this chapter, we once again survey the major developments in Shulu during both the Mao period and after, dividing for discussion the commercial responsibilities of the Shulu county government into several key sectors: state and collective trade; small private (or "free") trade; and the Shulu foreign trade sector. We conclude with a brief discussion of some interesting barter trade and other special-purpose trade arrangements that have also emerged in recent years to plug a few of the remaining gaps in the Shulu commercial economy as it has evolved under the uncertain conditions of piecemeal and partial market reform.

The Mao Period

> Many of the initiatives which in a planned economy might be expected to originate with the planners, or in a market economy with private entrepreneurs, in China come from the commercial departments at different levels of the administration, especially those of the province, municipality and *hsien* [xian, or county]. The commercial departments seem to be the repository of much of the business ability with which Chinese society is so richly endowed.
>
> — Audrey Donnithorne, "China's Cellular Economy"

As of 1979, Shulu state-managed commerce certainly evinced the activity and energy evoked in the astute observation quoted above. Though surely some of the economic excesses of the Mao period must have taken their toll in Shulu as elsewhere, by 1979 the tone in which county commerce cadres described both their previous and their present work suggested more of confident professionalism and determination to improve than it did either the bureaucratic sclerosis or the mobilizational anarchy so often associated by Western analysts with China's prereform political economy. Yet in 1979 Shulu county commerce was still very much constrained within the limits of the prereform political-ideological and organizational framework.

STATE-RUN COMMERCE

Once, early in the 1950's, there had been a meaningful distinction between "state-run" and "collective" commerce. "State-run" meant commerce coordinated through the state plan, and generally it encompassed the wholesale and retail trade of state-owned and state-operated enterprises: that is, enterprises "owned by the whole people." "Collective," on the other hand, referred to trade involving the entire vast network of farmer-shareholder-owned rural supply and marketing cooperatives, and it encompassed also trade carried out by the myriad of small non-state-owned yet collectivized industries that were still operating as semi-independent enterprises in the 1950's. As that decade wore on, however, the state sector expanded at the expense of the collective. More and more

TABLE 21
*Development of Shulu State-Run
and Collective Trade, 1949–78*
(in thousands of yuan)

Year	Total purchases	Total sales
1949	8,430	8,120
1956	16,250	27,700
1966	31,090	44,030
1978	41,260	109,020

NOTE: All figures are in current prices.

"collective" trade came to be encompassed within the state plan; more and more state restrictions were applied to collective commerce; and finally, with the Great Leap Forward, the distinction between collective and state-run commerce was effectively collapsed. Formerly collective industries came under the direct guidance and supervision of state offices such as the Second Light Industry Bureau. And the entire rural supply and marketing co-op network was effectively merged with state-run commercial activity, and placed under the control of the Commerce Bureau. Table 21 displays a few statistics indicating both the overall size and the pattern of growth in this subsector of the Shulu commercial economy.

Not surprisingly, given its history of steady expansion and merger, by the late 1970's the Shulu Commerce Bureau was one of the county government's largest departments. It then employed nearly one-fourth of the total government staff of leading officials and supervised some 469 wholesale and retail units in the county, staffed by over 9,000 persons (including those working in the commune and brigade supply and marketing co-ops).[1] The Shulu Commerce Bureau received targets from higher levels of the commerce bureau system (*xitong*) for purchases to be made in the county. It was responsible for making the mandated local purchases and for forwarding the goods to wholesalers and retailers in Shulu and beyond. It was also responsible for estimating the market for products of all kinds that needed to be brought into the county for sale to local producers and consumers.

Like so many units of the county government, the Commerce Bureau played roles both vertical and horizontal. On the one hand, it was one of the chief agents and protectors of the state's managerial prerogatives and of its efforts to plan and dominate the local economy. It upheld the state's many price and commodity flow regulations, keeping detailed records of its own transactions in important commodities and reporting them to bureaucratic superiors in their own tightly regulated vertical system.[2] On the other hand, the Commerce Bureau was in a position either to promote development of the local commercial economy or to let opportunities pass. It sought outside markets for Shulu products, and conveyed useful market information and tips on popular demand to local units setting up enterprises. It made important contacts and helped arrange for resources to be brought into the county to develop new product lines or even entirely new undertakings. It acted as local market analyst, expert adviser, and all-purpose facilitator for factories and other enterprises within the county, as well as representative and promoter of Shulu products to potential buyers outside it.

One good example of the mixed vertical/horizontal orientation of the county government's commercial apparatus at that time can be found in the Shulu Foodstuffs Company, a major unit operating under Commerce Bureau guidance and control. The Shulu company was, in fact, a subsidiary of the larger, vertically organized Foodstuffs Company emanating from the prefecture and above. It obtained 80 to 85 percent of the goods it sold either directly from producers in Shulu or from prefecture-level company warehouses. In its commercial operations it attempted to avoid some of the constraints commonly associated with centralized bureaucracies that led to inflexibility and inefficiency. The Shulu company negotiated directly with suppliers outside the county to procure for sale especially popular or scarce items. It also frequently traded surplus inventory clogging its own warehouses and shelves with other branches of the company outside Shulu that had a market for them and could provide items the Shulu branch wanted in exchange. Neither of these types of transactions had to be arranged through or approved by the parent company at the prefecture level. Thus, while it is sometimes supposed that buying agents, sales reps, and commercial expediters have emerged to hit the road in rural China only under the reforms, in fact, in 1979—well before the reforms took hold in Shulu—some eighty employees of the local Commerce Bureau were reportedly making regular barter and trade trips to help the company move surplus items or to find sources of commodities lacking in the county. The company also frequently traded surplus stock with the rural supply and marketing co-ops, to better match supply with demand across the county.[3]

The Shulu Department Store, another company then operating under the Commerce Bureau, presented a less balanced set of horizontal and vertical roles. Before 1958 this company had the autonomy to buy directly from a variety of different suppliers in Dezhou, Shanghai, Tianjin, and Beijing. At that time, some 70 percent of its purchases were in fact made from factories and agencies outside Hebei province. But by 1979, 80 percent of the products purchased by the company for sale in Shulu were made within Hebei. Officials cheerfully attributed this to the multifaceted development of the provincial economy in the intervening years. But Maoist policies of the 1960's and 1970's, mandating local and regional self-reliance and limiting horizontal and regional commercial exchange, must have played an important part in this trend as well.

The Commerce Bureau was thus the chief enforcer of the rules of state-dominated trade in Shulu. It responded primarily to orders generated through the plan and to commands coming down from higher levels of its vertical system. Within the hierarchy and the guidelines thus imposed, however, its cadres and workers spent much time and effort on promoting local products for sale, on finding ways to meet local consumer needs and demands, and on rectifying some of the local manifestations of market imbalance attributable to central planning

STATE REGULATION OF PRIVATE COMMERCE

During the Mao period, rural private marketing, or free trade at rural market fairs, was strictly regulated by the local state apparatus. In principle, farmers were permitted to sell in their local "free" marketplaces most of what they produced on their private plots and did not themselves consume. In reality, commodities were closely scrutinized, prices were tightly regulated, and volume of trade on these markets was kept to a minimum.

In 1979, a moment between the Mao-period attack on private marketing and its spirited return during the Deng period, there were still only ten approved free marketplaces in rural Shulu. (This was even less than the sixteen marketplaces that had operated there in late Qing times! One such market, in downtown Xinji, is shown in the photo section.) Private market trade volume in 1978 was reported to stand at a very low ¥2,031,000—only about ¥4 per capita. These rural markets were regulated by the Industry and Commerce Management Bureau (Gongshang guanli ju).[4] Following provincial policy, Shulu markets were permitted to meet only every sixth day of the lunar calendar, which effectively prevented the development of an integrated, rotating periodic market network, and which made state regulation easier.

To carry out its regulatory tasks, the county government bureau maintained offices in the seven local administrative centers that dotted the countryside.[5] Each of these was staffed by four to eleven full-time bureau officials (depending on the size of the market), as well as fifteen to twenty-five so-called "market mediators" (jiao yi yuan) hired to work on market days only. This small army of trade officials divided each marketplace into separate spaces for different commodities so as better to supervise transactions. Even in the late Mao period, they also served sometimes as go-betweens to help negotiate the prices of major items, such as pigs, grain, bicycles, sheep, and draft animals. The mediators did not concern themselves with sales of handicrafts products, small kitchen utensils, or vegetables. But they recorded the prices paid for all regulated items, and reported these to higher levels of the bureau.[6]

These bureau officials and market mediators were also charged with discovering and punishing market infractions, which consisted of hoarding (especially grain), tax evasion, doing business in localities for which one was not licensed,[7] and "speculation" (selling at prices above the permitted range).[8] In 1978, some 2,724 separate violations were discovered in

Shulu, most involving grain. Bureau officials evinced no special concern at this level of illegal trade. They had a variety of measures at their disposal to deal with them, graded by severity as befit the infraction. In 1,140 (42 percent) of the 1978 cases, for example, the grain was purchased from the offender at the state price, and that was the end of the matter. In 259 cases (9.5 percent), the commodity in question was purchased at the best current price, just to prevent speculation. In 139 cases (5 percent), the grain was confiscated and the offender released. Some 931 offenders (34 percent) were compelled to take a course of reeducation before they were released, and 97 others (4 percent) were required only to pay the small tax that they had been trying to evade on grain traded at rural free markets. An additional 3 offenders were fined, 5 were handed over for prosecution to the Shulu people's court, and 150 were extradited to other counties because they came from outside Shulu.

Up to the summer of 1979, the bureau had been keeping only quarterly records of private market prices and sales. To cope with the increased volume of free trade that Shulu officials were expecting in the wake of national policy changes encouraging sideline production and private commerce, they were then just making plans to start keeping monthly records. Thus in Shulu the (local) state was increasingly committed to monitoring private trade even as (central) state policy gave the green light to free market expansion.

FOREIGN TRADE

Shulu was an export leader in Shijiazhuang prefecture, from 1974 to 1978 contributing an average of 46.8 percent to total prefecture export sales, mainly in the form of chemicals, fur and leather products, and textiles from its state-run factories. The Shulu county government, through its Foreign Trade Bureau, regulated and promoted export trade. Established only in 1974, by 1979 this bureau employed some 80 staff members, over one-eighth the total for the county government then. In 1979 the bureau was contracting for purchases from eight different county factories (including the prefecture-run chemical plant) and from five commune-run and even five brigade-run plants. It also purchased fruit from several rural production teams specializing in orchards, mink pelts from three brigades, and chickens and rabbits from seven teams with better-developed animal husbandry sideline operations. Total Foreign Trade Bureau purchases in Shulu rose gradually but steadily from ¥18.5 million in 1974 to ¥22.5 million in 1978 (Table 22).

The bureau at the county level was enmeshed in a tightly controlled vertical bureaucratic system (xitong). It received from its system superiors at Shijiazhuang prefecture and Hebei province strict quotas and budgets for purchases and precise regulations for quality standards.[9] All profits were to be remitted upward, while shortfalls or losses were covered out of higher-level budgets as well. The operations of the foreign trade xitong

TABLE 22

Shulu County Foreign Trade Bureau Export Purchases, 1974–89

(in thousands of yuan)

Year	Foodstuffs	Clothing and textiles	Native products	Animal by-products	Light industrial products	Handicrafts	Metallurgical products	Chemicals	Machinery	Total export purchases[a]
1974	793	5,291	190	2,500		208		9,463	90	18,536
1975	1,413	4,660	241	3,533		163		10,118	140	20,269
1976	1,539	5,687	196	4,007		160		9,462	90	21,211
1977	1,440	5,931	192	4,132	70	169		10,409	255	22,543
1978	2,539	3,828	204	4,261	14	192		9,777	141	22,456
1979	2,004	5,486	905	4,147	1,514	289	26	11,314	537	28,729
1980	2,208	6,862	1,978	2,324	4,022	833	396	11,331	820	33,618
1981	3,845	7,381	2,036	3,420	6,865	770	461	11,855	884	32,277
1982	2,540	6,580	2,084	2,511	1,626	756	391	12,444	1,245	30,227
1983	2,572	3,782	3,129	1,259	1,675	426	488	11,638	928	25,663
1984	1,925	11,971	973	195	1,440	147	529	10,699	235	27,926
1985	3,243	4,576	3,388	1,393	1,251	535	524	13,939	697	31,984
1986	5,892	15,564	4,472	1,633	3,690	377	1,242	14,886	1,290	49,479
1987	4,338	8,798	4,806	1,432	4,123	513	1,070	15,417	1,729	43,123
1988	6,911	6,617	2,720	3,350	5,021	1,222	5,451	35,173	2,702	76,371
1989	10,763	4,706	1,084	2,524	12,225	741	11,825	19,818	2,918	62,300
					7,922					

[a] Totals here may not be congruent with row totals because of rounding.

were highly self-contained. The bureau even possessed its own fleet of trucks to transport goods it purchased to its own warehouses.

Yet, like the Commerce Bureau, this did not prevent the Foreign Trade Bureau from engaging in certain activities designed to help develop the local economy by promoting export production. It received funds for its operations from the Shijiazhuang prefecture Foreign Trade Bureau in proportion to the volume of export trade it handled.[10] These monies were used to finance small incentives or concessions to producers that were often written into purchase contracts. For example, the bureau supplied brigades raising chickens for freezing and export with high-grade chicken feed and fish-powder-nutrient feed additives. It also paid Shulu producers slightly more than the state-set price for the birds. To give another example, with the assistance of the Native Products Company of the Foreign Trade Ministry, the county Foreign Trade Bureau also provided residents of Shulu's Ninth Street Brigade (of Xinji commune) with scarce lumber and wire to build cages for minks they were attempting to learn to raise for export.

The county bureau also provided interest-free loans to producing units signing contracts with it, using funds specially allocated for this purpose through the Foreign Trade Ministry system.[11] But the uses to which these loans could be put were tightly circumscribed, and decisions about them centralized. This was thought to be necessary partly because few Shulu enterprises produced solely for export, and the state wished to make certain that monies provided to a given enterprise to aid export development would not find their way into other enterprise needs more directly related to domestic production. Thus, if the Shulu Foreign Trade Bureau wished to loan money to a factory for the expansion of its fixed capital in export production, the bureau had to make application to higher levels of the foreign trade system, and approval had to be obtained from the central ministry offices in Beijing. The county Foreign Trade Bureau was also not permitted to use any of its operating funds to help its suppliers finance production. In short, it had little financial autonomy.

But it did have important administrative functions. It acted as a buying and transport agent. It purchased products for export from factories at prices fixed on the principle of cost plus 8 to 10 percent. It then warehoused and ultimately transported these goods to their next destination, as arranged by the prefecture bureau. Finally, the county bureau was responsible for specifying product standards and assuring that factories met quality control specifications.

It also possessed some discretion over the distribution of valued export contracts within the county. Producing for export had a number of advantages from an enterprise's point of view: preferential credit availability, assured profits, assistance in procuring special inputs, plus the intangible but unmistakable pride and stature enterprise managers and workers derived from being connected with this elite sector of the economy. (Such benefits were to become more tangible in the Deng years, when these firms found that they could build on their reputations to land lucrative contracts.) Most of the power to include or exclude a factory from the export group lay with the agencies of the Foreign Trade Ministry system. It was they—particularly their county and provincial offices—who decided if a Shulu factory could meet the quality and consistency standards China set for its foreign trade. It was also they who provided introductions and acted as intermediaries between foreign buyers and producers.

Commerce in the Deng Period

The first decade of the Deng period saw several major developments in Shulu commerce. For international trade policy and central fiscal control reasons, the tight foreign trade systems and procedures prevailing in non-coastal areas like Shulu proved the most difficult to loosen and reform. But in virtually all aspects of domestic trade—state-run, collective, and private—the changes wrought under the reforms have been nothing short of spectacular. In Shulu, as in many other rural areas, the most obvious (and usually the most welcome) of these changes came in the form of a private petty trade renaissance. By the end of the 1980's, peddlers were plying their wares, and farmers setting out their fruits, vegetables, and handicrafts, for sale all over Shulu. Although more "free" trade had clearly meant more headaches and more challenging regulatory responsibilities for the county cadre force, the positive impact on the daily life of ordinary citizens derived from this return of an articulated structure of specialized and periodic markets could hardly be measured. Presently we shall return to evaluate the complex role of the Shulu county government in both promoting and regulating this newly energized private trade sector. But first, let us consider the less visible but also significant changes that have come with reform in Shulu's state-run and collective trade sectors.

STATE-RUN AND COLLECTIVE COMMERCE

Probably the most significant single reform step to be taken in this sphere was the redetachment, effective January 1, 1984, of state-run commerce from commerce conducted by and through the network of rural supply and marketing co-ops (*gongxiaoshe* [GXS]). Central policymakers had concluded that the de facto merger of state and collective commerce during the late Mao era had constituted an unwarranted infringement on the semi-independence of the rural collectives. Subjected as they were to excessive "influence" emanating from state Commerce Bureau leadership, the "liveliness" of supply and marketing co-op trade had suffered badly, according to the new assessment, and only a decisive redetachment of the two would restore the necessary distance and difference between them.[12] The division of assets and responsibilities was evidently laced with some controversy and considerable bureaucratic strain was experienced by all concerned. But the required separation was gradually phased in, so as to avoid unnecessary shocks to either system. And postpartum growth, while certainly not sensational, was judged by local commerce officials to be proceeding satisfactorily for both networks in Shulu.[13]

The born-again *gongxiaoshe* in Shulu had developed to impressive proportions by 1990. It was made up of 46 independent accounting units, including 6 factories and 12 different companies.[14] Counted among the 12 companies were two large stores located in downtown Xinji, a fur and leather trade center, a fruit company, a hardware company, a firm dealing in animal products, another selling clay pipes and vats, and also a large construction materials company. In addition to these units, the GXS included 29 branch co-ops located in the various townships and towns (*xiang* and *zhen*) of Shulu. The entire GXS network employed 5,293 people in 1989, among which 171 were classified as "leading cadres." About half of these cadres and employees worked in the urban center of Xinji. The other half were posted at lower levels: around 1,500 of them staffing the 29 branch co-ops in the townships, and about 900 working in GXS factories.

The GXS in 1990 defined its main functions as of old: supplying producers' and consumers' goods to the rural areas, and purchasing agricultural products from farmers.[15] County GXS leaders pointed out that they were hoping, in the future, to expand the kinds of services they had to offer farmers, citing a desire to provide a refrigeration service for egg producers as an example. They also expressed interest in studying and adapting what they could from the very full-service model of the Japanese agricultural co-op system. But there was a noticeable lack of specificity about the plans for such study, as there was about the plans for the refrigerator facility.

In its separation from the Commerce Bureau, the GXS had reportedly restored its old, "more democratic" management system and style. The old collective-share system was reinstated during the transition. Local co-op branches that were relatively well run succeeded in attracting some farmer investment in the form of share purchases. But the poorly managed branches could not tempt farmers to part with their cash. To help rectify this situation, a three-year election term for branch co-op managers was introduced. Branch managers, once elected by the membership, appointed their own team of leading cadres to run the entire branch. The manager's election was subject to ratification by the GXS leadership at the county level, however, and individual managers could be terminated by county GXS officials as well in cases of malfeasance.

The new GXS no longer received obligatory state targets for purchases or sales, nor did it turn its profits directly over to state superiors. Its transactions were carried out on a contract basis, and it paid taxes on its profits, like any enterprise. Its business was liable for some seventeen different types of taxes in 1990, of which a business tax, a commodity tax, an income tax, and the local energy and construction special levy made up the heaviest burdens. As of 1990, the GXS was putting 70 percent of after-tax profits into expanding production (42 percent was used to supplement

TABLE 23
Development of Shulu Collective Trade, 1979–89
(in thousands of yuan)

Year	Purchases[a]	Sales[b]	Profits[c]	Fixed capital	Working capital	Bank loans
1979	46,450	68,210				
1980	73,360	73,840				
1981	69,790	79,190				
1982	84,340	77,420				
1983	133,680	75,760				
1984	140,740	81,470				
1985	123,350	111,610				
1986	137,640	167,720	6,520	23	17	90
1987	169,110	170,450	8,040	26	19	78
1988	136,280	148,220	8,800	30	21	111
1989	179,620	151,510	7,500	42	18	98

NOTE: Collective trade refers to trade conducted by the Supply and Marketing Co-op (gongxiaoshe [GXS]).
[a] Net purchases from units outside the GXS network.
[b] Net sales to outside units and individuals.
[c] Net (after-tax) profits.

working capital, 21 percent to fund construction of facilities, and 7 percent to fund scientific education). The remaining 30 percent of profits was devoted to current expenditures (21 percent to collective welfare expenditures and 9 percent to bonuses and dividends).

As Table 23 reveals, the total volume of trade handled by the GXS network rose steadily between 1979 and 1989. Although the amount invested in fixed capital in the network remained at an astonishingly low level through the 1980's, and although bank loans made available for the conduct of GXS business were also on the low side, the system was nevertheless consistently recording a modest annual profit in the years following its separation from Commerce Bureau leadership. The only potentially serious problem county GXS leaders had encountered in the 1980's, apparently, was the threat of heavy competition that had come with the expansion of petty private trade in Shulu. From the point of view of the GXS, the problem reached acute proportions in 1987 when private businesspeople (geti hu) were being permitted to buy inventory directly from factories and other primary producers. In this way, they had begun to encroach on wholesale trade in certain important commodities and products (such as salt, sugar, coal, wine, oil, and chemical fertilizer) that were the specialty of the GXS network. Restrictions on the scale of geti hu operations were introduced after the 1987 scare. "We want the geti hu sector to develop," insisted GXS vice director Zhao in 1990, "but they can't be allowed to become wholesalers."[16] The intention, obviously, was that private trade remain petty trade in Shulu; and that was one design, not surprisingly, that received the ringing endorsement of officials charged with responsibility for the development of Shulu's collective trade sector.

A summary of other interesting developments in the Shulu small private trade sector follows. But before we can leave this review of state-run and collective trade in the reform era, it is necessary to consider the evolving activities of the county Commerce Bureau, which throughout the 1980's, despite losing direct control over GXS collective commercial activity, did continue to handle the significant and still-growing volume of trade carried on by state-run enterprises.

The Commerce Bureau, in contrast to the GXS which served rural Shulu, catered primarily to urban-area producers and consumers. In 1990, this bureau reported a reduced total staff of just 1,429: 161 cadres and 1,268 other workers. With its loss of control over the GXS network, and with some additional losses of leadership responsibility over important enterprises—an oil company became independent of the Commerce Bureau in 1984, a coal company in 1983, and a pharmaceuticals company in 1980—the number of personnel on the bureau's own payroll had naturally fallen. By the end of the decade, however, the bureau retained administrative responsibility for eight companies, including a department store, a textile company, a hardware company, a candies and spirits company, and a restaurant supplies and service company. It also supervised four other factories or producing enterprises: a candied fruit factory, a vinegar and condiments factory, a freezing facility, and a bakery. All in all, in 1990 the Commerce Bureau had responsibility for some 71 different units scattered around Shulu, including wholesale and retail purchase and sales stations, commodity consignment stations, and service and repair stations. Even with the various losses the bureau had sustained, the volume of trade conducted under its leadership had generally been on the rise through the 1980s, though the rise was sluggish during the middle of the decade, as illustrated in Table 24. The GXS consistently handled much more in terms

TABLE 24
Development of Shulu Trade Under the Commerce Bureau, 1979–89
(in thousands of yuan)

Year	Purchases[a]	Sales[b]	Profits[c]	Fixed capital	Working capital on hand	Bank loans
1979	6,030	35,450	2,040	2,490	1,260	9,480
1980	7,780	35,270	1,800	1,180	560	5,560
1981	8,470	34,190	2,240	1,380	1,110	7,990
1982	8,310	35,210	1,780	4,050	1,280	9,470
1983	10,220	33,210	1,820	4,130	1,260	8,950
1984	13,780	32,210	1,550	4,840	1,310	8,750
1985	17,360	35,320	1,300	5,640	1,340	9,600
1986	20,310	37,340	1,620	6,510	1,560	9,980
1987	26,370	47,090	1,830	6,310	2,220	14,860
1988	40,100	62,990	3,010	6,200	2,300	18,060
1989	37,830	64,610	2,300	7,460	2,060	13,950

[a] Net purchases from units outside the Commerce Bureau *xitong*.
[b] Sales to units outside the Commerce Bureau *xitong*.
[c] Net (after-tax) profits.

of total volume of trade through this period than did the Commerce Bureau constellation of enterprises. But the Commerce Bureau, in the late 1980's, was gaining a little on the GXS: its total volume of trade rose from something under 20 percent of GXS trade volume in mid-decade to over 30 percent in 1988 and 1989.

A number of major reforms had been introduced over this period, intended to enliven state-run commerce around the country and in Shulu. Enterprises under the Commerce Bureau no longer received absolute state targets and no longer turned all their profits directly back to the state. They received "guideline plans" for production and trade instead, and paid taxes on the profits they earned. A contract responsibility system had been introduced for enterprises under the Shulu Commerce Bureau as well, and county cadres reported that the incentives entailed in these contracts had indeed served to enliven performance, efficiency and productivity in Commerce Bureau enterprises. The reform of the *xitong*'s finance arrangements had resulted in considerably greater profits being left with individual enterprises. Much of this, county cadres explained while pointing to the significant rise in fixed capital recorded in Table 24, had been used to expand business, inventory, warehousing capacity, and so on. No fewer than nine big stores in downtown Xinji had been built primarily out of these profits. Warehouse space had been enlarged by over 3,000 square meters, and bureau enterprises, by the end of the decade, operated with a fleet of more than twenty of their own trucks and other vehicles. Overall, therefore, Shulu could hardly have been said to present a picture of stagnating state-run commerce.

Part of the reason for this, of course, may lie in the fact that Commerce Bureau enterprises clearly had been showered with loans from local banks over the decade since 1979. About 90 percent of their working capital, in fact, came in the form of loans. County Commerce Bureau cadres did not fail to note, however, that the interest they paid on those loans was enough to make them want, in the future, to find ways to divert more of their enterprise profits directly into working capital funds.

An even more important set of reforms, perhaps, had been those that tended to change the basic networks and ground rules of commodity circulation in the state-run sector. During the late Mao period, Shulu Commerce Bureau enterprises were permitted to turn to only one or two state supply stations to secure the producers' and consumers' goods they required. Under the reforms, they were able to go directly to the producers of most products for supply, cutting out the higher-level bureaucratic middleman and thereby considerably shortening the distance between producer and end user. By 1990, the Shulu Commerce Bureau had established direct business relations with some 230 different companies and enterprises, including enterprises in provinces as far away as Tibet, Qinghai, Ningxia, and even Taiwan. In 1989 55 percent (by value) of all purchases made by Shulu Commerce Bureau units were made directly from producers. And about 40 percent of Commerce Bureau total sales were being made to units outside Shulu. This emerging pattern of direct (horizontal) commercial exchange had done a great deal to improve both production efficiency and customer satisfaction in the county. It was still far from adequately developed, however, according to Commerce Bureau cadres. They were striving, they said, to open up direct trade relations with many more units around the nation to, as they put it, "satisfy the ever-growing local appetite" for new and better products.[17]

In their effort to expand operations and make them more efficient, Commerce Bureau leaders reported that the biggest problems they faced in 1990 were tied to the poor educational background and business training of much of their staff. More than half of bureau personnel—63 percent—had only a lower-middle-school education or less. Most of the senior staff members fell into this category, while most of the younger recruits with better formal educations nevertheless lacked practical experience in business. In an effort to deal with the first problem, the bureau was making plans to set up its own small middle school to help employees earn their equivalency certificates.[18] There were no apparent plans afoot to give employees more practical business experience, however. And Commerce Bureau cadres readily admitted that many staff members still labored under the influence of management methods and business habits of the past. Changing the mentality of state sector managers from plan fulfillment to profit-making was still very much an ongoing process in Shulu in 1990.

DEVELOPING PRIVATE COMMERCE: THE HEBEI YIJI MARKET

The reforms in the sphere of commerce led, in Shulu as everywhere else in China, to a sudden renaissance of petty private trade. The gratifyingly lively consequences for Shulu consumers were visible everywhere on the streets in the middle and late 1980's. Street peddlers there ran the gamut from retired grandparents who daily minded their tiny tables of already rusty homemade knives and cleavers for sale, to ambitious young entrepreneurs working far-flung private networks to bring in exotic luxury items, like bamboo from Sichuan, or cheap thrills, like luscious fresh chewing sugarcane from steamy Guangdong, to tempt shoppers strolling the dry and gritty streets of Shulu. Perhaps the most spectacular and certainly the most ubiquitous, in season, were the watermelon peddlers, who hauled cartloads of fruit with them into the towns, dumping the melons in enormous piles on roadsides and sidewalks, and setting out an assortment of low rough wooden benches and tables on which to serve their potential customers. These peddlers—young farm men and women usually, but sometimes whole families—lay on the chill sidewalks in the open air under their greasy quilts night after night, guarding their fruit piles until they were sold out, and struggling for some rest against the jarring street clatter of motorbikes, car horns, bicycle bells, and donkey carts that commenced every day before dawn. Experienced pedestrians instinctively watched their step as they skirted the little street domains of the watermelon peddlers, taking care to avoid the slippery land mines of discarded rinds and seeds lying all about on the sidewalks and in the gutters.

Some paradigms of political economy posit a basic opposition between the exercise of state authority and the development of the private market in the contemporary Chinese context. In contrast to the assumptions of such paradigms, in Shulu the county government had plainly been extremely active in the development of private commerce during the 1980's. Nowhere was this local state involvement more evident, perhaps, than in the rise of the Hebei Yiji Market. The Hebei Yiji Market is the present-day namesake of a large market that had flourished in Xinji for centuries before the Japanese occupation. And as they contributed to building this market anew, Shulu county government officials explicitly understood it as a continuation of that long and strong local tradition: "Historically our county was a major commercial and industrial center, widely praised as 'the number-one market of Zhili [*zhi li yi ji*].' In Ming times [it was written that] 'this market has rows upon rows of dwellings, scattered all over the place. Among the goods it receives are cassia wood boats and orchid oars. There can be found merchants selling rarities.'"[19]

But if history provided the inspiration and even the nomenclature, the reasons the Shulu government undertook to build the new marketplace in the mid-1980's were far more immediate. The expectation of Shulu officials in 1979 that private trade would be expanding proved correct—probably beyond their dreams. By 1983, commercial traffic congestion in Xinji had become unbearable. With the relaxation of controls on travel and migration, farmers and traders who were flocking into the county seat to engage in trade or to look for work were quite simply clogging city streets, sidewalks, and alleys.[20] And in the general crush, the county government's Industry and Commerce Management Bureau found itself facing growing difficulty in regulating and taxing the private markets. In the fall of 1984, this bureau made a suggestion to the county leadership about constructing a marketplace to accommodate the throng. Though Shulu officials did not say so, this concept of constructing a central marketplace for petty private trade probably did not leap full-blown from the imaginations of local planners; several such projects had already been built and publicized in Hebei.[21] Shulu government leaders, apparently intrigued by the idea of going neighboring localities one better—or at least one bigger—commissioned the Urban Construction and Environmental Protection Commission, in consultation with the Industry and Commerce Management Bureau, to draw up some preliminary plans for what would prove to be the largest such marketplace in Hebei.[22] On the basis of these plans, the county government then sought and secured the various approvals it required from the Shijiazhuang prefecture Urban Construction Bureau for the siting and scale of the construction project, and for the necessary conversion of a large piece of agricultural land to nonagricultural use. The elaborate scheme drawn up for the Hebei Yiji Market revealed also that it was intended to become the nexus of an overall redevelopment plan for the western part of downtown Xinji, a plan that included a multipurpose park, a cultural center (gongren wenhua gong) and several new roadways. Indeed, once built, the mammoth marketplace would actually create a new center of gravity for Xinji lying north and west of the old downtown hub.[23]

The marketplace, once constructed, consisted of three main types of spaces spread out over nearly thirty hectares. Its most prominent feature was an imposing, block-long building in traditional Chinese style, with sections rising stepwise to three, four, five, and six stories. It fronted on a four-lane boulevard specially widened in connection with the project. This front building contained the larger office spaces, workshops, and retail spaces that would be sold or leased to state and collective enterprises wishing to set up trading operations in the new marketplace. The important state-run Shulu Fur and Leather Tanning Factory maintained a large retail outlet and sales office there, for example. A second area of the marketplace consisted of a series of 351 two-story combined residential/commercial units arrayed in 8 rows running behind (and perpendicular to) the main building. These units were sold as condominiums to individual households of petty traders and producers (geti hu) as places both to live and to do business.[24] The third area was made up of rows of covered market stalls, sufficient space to accommodate one thousand merchants, also running perpendicular to the main building in the open-air spaces between the rows of condominiums. These stalls were designed to be rented to private merchants by the Industry and Commerce Management Bureau. (For photos of Hebei Yiji, see the photo section.)

With the necessary zoning and land-use permits in hand, the county government proceeded to make its financing arrangements. It summed these up with the slogan "The people's city is built by the people [Renmin chengshi, renmin jian]," high-sounding words for raising the necessary capital directly through advance payments made by those enterprises and individuals wanting to buy space in the new marketplace. The condominiums in the complex were offered to individual investors through prospectuses sent to county-level industry and commerce management bureaus in Hebei and contiguous provinces, and to provincial-level bureaus elsewhere. These fraternal bureaus were asked only to promulgate the prospectuses, not to promote the venture themselves. Within a month, any fears that the project might not draw the desired investor response were put to rest; six hundred offers were received, and all the units—as yet unbuilt—were contracted for on a first-come, first-served basis. The price was ¥4,800 each.[25] Industry and Commerce Management Bureau director Heng was later to congratulate the owners on their shrewd investment. "You can't get a home that inexpensively elsewhere, and now [late 1986] they're worth at least ¥10,000."[26]

The county government's own investment in this ¥7 million project was a modest ¥600,000: ¥200,000 put up by the Industry and Commerce Management Bureau for the cost of the open-air covered market stalls—a sum it planned to recoup from rental revenues within two years—and ¥400,000 advanced by the Finance Bureau to pay for public spaces such as roadways and sidewalks.[27]

By 1986, the market was thriving. Official figures on annual trade volume in Hebei Yiji's private-sector shops were between ¥25 and ¥27 million for every year between 1986 and 1989. But Director Heng was candid in saying that this figure was unreliably low. He knew that merchants underestimated their turnover to reduce their tax payments, a phenomenon that he regarded with more resignation than rancor. Moreover, occasional very large deals concluded by Hebei Yiji merchants would tend to skew any given set of figures. For example, the Shulu Fur and Leather Tanning Factory occasionally made contracts in the range of ¥5 million from its sales office in the marketplace, and during special three-day trade expositions staged there, total turnover might reach as high as ¥30 million. The marketplace attracted merchants from as far away as Sichuan who had heard about the Hebei Yiji Market by word of mouth and decided to buy in as residents. And it became the base of operations for local businesspeople engaged in long-distance commerce. The splendid new marketplace was enough of a success that the directors of twelve provincial-level industry and commerce management bureaus, as well as the director of the market office of the national Industry and Commerce Management Bureau, all made pilgrimages to the site to study and laud it.

The planning and execution of the building of Hebei Yiji provide an excellent example of the Shulu county government acting in the mode of a developmentally oriented state.[28] In orchestrating this massive project, the county government could be seen carrying out many of the same kinds of vertical and horizontal coordination that had been evident in its local developmental role in the late Mao period. Looking upward, it worked with prefectural, provincial, and even central-level offices of the Industry and Commerce Management Ministry and the Ministry of Urban Construction and Environmental Protection. Looking downward, it rented and sold space to rural collective enterprises and to individuals. Horizontally, it coordinated the activities of its own bureaus of urban construction and environmental protection and of industry and commerce management in planning and then overseeing the construction of the huge market. It also worked with county-level enterprises (and their superior bureaus), which took space in the new buildings.

Moreover, the county government undertook this activity as a government and not as an entrepreneur. The tendency of some local governments to assume the role of entrepreneur in the climate of the recent reforms contributes to serious developmental and distribution problems: official corruption; inflation; and uneven, imbalanced, and overheated patterns of local economic growth. The Shulu county government, it should be noted, undertook the entire Hebei Yiji project on a nonprofit basis. Its stated goals were to resolve the problems of urban congestion and to facilitate both free trade and the lawful regulation of free trade. It did not use the project to make money for the local government as such. It left profit-making to the enterprises and the shopkeepers to whom it sold parts of its real estate development.

Further, the county government did this in ways that did not particularly favor its own county-level enterprises. In the aisles of the Hebei Yiji Market, farmer-peddlers and small collective enterprises were brought together for head-to-head competition with sales representatives of some of Shulu's largest state factories. The director of the state-owned Shulu Fur and Leather Tanning Factory, the biggest local manufacturer of the county's traditional specialty, leather goods, complained in 1986 about the stiff competition he was encountering from small village-based collective fur and leather workshops. He had reason to be concerned. His factory's retail outlet at Hebei Yiji was definitely sleepier than the stalls of his small competitors right outside his back door. Meanwhile, the Industry and Commerce Management Bureau was taking positive steps to encourage just this kind of competition by helping to strengthen the economic position of the independent merchants in Hebei Yiji. Specifically, it granted them a one-year holiday on the market's management fee, and after the first year it set the fee at what it deliberately estimated would be a very low rate—.05 percent of gross sales.[29]

This example of the Hebei Yiji Market suggests a complex concept of the county government as a component of the Chinese state. In one optic it appears to be a variegated set of institutions with different and potentially conflicting interests: for example, the state-run factories, with their interest in maintaining a monopoly, versus the Industry and Commerce Management Bureau's role in fostering private trade and vigorous competition. But with another lens it presents itself more holistically as an agency of the larger state, possessing some autonomy from its component institutions. The local state could, for example, act to give private traders—toward whom, it must be said, it otherwise tended to maintain an attitude of guarded suspicion—a competitive edge in the marketplace against the very same state-owned factories for which its industrial bureaus were responsible, while at the same time keeping revenues collected by its Industry and Commerce Management Bureau from the private businesspeople lower than they might have been. What is notable about the case of Shulu is not just the complexity or the relative autonomy of the local state apparatus, but the tendency of the Shulu county government, even after the introduction of the reforms, to exercise its autonomy in pursuit of all-around local economic development, not only in the service of its own bureaucratic and financial self-interest.[30]

The example of the Hebei Yiji Market illustrates how, in the first decade of the Deng period, the relationship of state and market in China did not necessarily constitute an antinomy. Hebei Yiji was conceived by the Shulu county government to solve public problems of traffic control, urban overcrowding, and commercial regulation. It was designed by government bureaus as part of a wider urban development scheme that included nonmarket elements such as roadways, a cultural center, and a park. It brought together, in convenient and open competition, state enterprises subject to state planning, collective enterprises, and private firms. It served as a place in which the state could more efficiently and effectively regulate private trade to prevent abuses such as price gouging, tax evasion, and black marketeering. It was a place in which the county government, for all its heavy involvement, was after no direct profit for itself, but sought rather to create the opportunity for other institutions—institutions in the state, the collective, and the private sectors—to conduct their business and strive for profit in an atmosphere of free competition and fair trade. In every sense of the term, Hebei Yiji was a *planned market*.

REGULATING AND RATIONALIZING PRIVATE COMMERCE

Beyond Hebei Yiji too, petty private commerce was thriving in Xinji and the smaller towns and villages of Shulu county through the 1980's (see Table 25). The volume of trade in this sector, rising from a mere ¥3.5 million in 1979 to nearly ¥64 million in 1989, had grown by nearly eighteen times over the decade, as compared to just a doubling or tripling of total volume in the state and collective sectors. This sudden expansion of free trade in the county might be seen in many ways as the most significant aspect of commerce reform during the Deng period. But again, the pattern of development of "free" trade in Shulu was hardly free of control or direction by the county government. The Industry and Commerce Management Bureau had clearly applied a heavy hand in guiding private market growth, playing several key roles at nearly every step of the way. The bureau acted as both market organizer and market rationalizer. In certain

TABLE 25
Volume of Private Trade, Shulu County, 1979–89
(in thousands of yuan)

Year	Urban	Rural	Total
1979	700	2,867	3,567
1980	1,824	2,631	4,455
1981	2,407	3,814	6,221
1982	1,939	3,929	5,868
1983	7,473	7,852	15,325
1984	6,646	10,627	17,273
1985	10,481	27,069	37,550
1986	34,650	22,479	57,129
1987	37,340	22,799	60,139
1988	35,801	25,734	61,535
1989	37,201	26,559	63,760

cases, on a small scale anyway, it coordinated "r & d" for merchants and played the role of a local products promoter as well.

Both in Hebei Yiji and outside it, the bureau granted licenses for specific shop locations, so as to help create or reinforce a deliberate pattern in the geographical distribution of specialized markets. In 1990 there were various such specialized markets in operation: three for fur and leather products (one a restoration of the traditional marketplace), six for vegetables, and others for traditional products, small commodities, industrial products, and textiles and miscellaneous goods.[31] Working again in conjunction with the urban development plan formulated by the Urban Construction and Environmental Protection Commission,[32] the Commerce Management Bureau was planning to bring the textile and miscellaneous goods market, which had been located at the northern end of the urban center, and the farmers' market, which had been at the southern end, into closer proximity, to reduce traffic congestion caused by shoppers moving between them, to make shopping more convenient, and to increase the flow of customers at both markets. The Bureau also was making sure that fresh vegetable markets were distributed throughout the downtown area, according to a design intended to maximize shopping convenience and reduce traffic.

As for the layout and internal organization of these private markets, the bureau (once again) had a hand in the design. It had built, for example, fixed and temporary canopied market stalls to accommodate two hundred traders in the farmers' small commodity and traditional products markets. It charged fees for their use that were graded by the attractiveness of their location. In 1986 the bureau discussed plans to introduce electronic scales and other modern retail equipment into Shulu markets, though by 1990 it had not yet accomplished this. But by 1990 bureau officials had still newer ideas to discuss: more counter space, to reduce the clutter of goods laid out for sale on the ground; walkie-talkies to make life easier for the bureau's busy market managers; and even video monitors to be put up in Hebei Yiji not so much to guard against theft (as perhaps the merchants might have wished) as to keep track of trade volume, the better, no doubt, to assess the tax liability of petty merchants doing business there.

The bureau also directly regulated commerce in various ways, some of them genuinely helpful in encouraging the proper functioning of a market, and some of them more interfering. On the helpful side, it required, for example, that all merchants be licensed, and it issued the licenses. It also made sure that food merchants kept their health certificates up to date. On the other side, it vigilantly also engaged in comprehensive price regulation, requiring that (maximum) prices be publicly displayed, to facilitate its own regulatory work and to protect customers against what it defined as price gouging.[33] With a total staff of 140 in 1990—up from a mere 15 or so before 1979—and with offices in every township, the bureau deployed a large army of smartly uniformed market monitors (or market police) who circulated through Shulu's various marketplaces on trading days, checking licenses, monitoring prices, looking for signs of fraud or sharp trade practices, and resolving disputes.

The bureau's staff had grown so dramatically after 1979, according to its director, because "the state was putting more emphasis on commercial regulation in these years."[34] But of course such a ballooning in staff size was more a reflection of the sheer expansion of market activity itself, coupled with the local state's determination, in Shulu, to stay on top of the situation. To some observers, who apparently expected a veritable bureaucratic retreat in the wake of the reforms, it may seem ironic to observe that a move away from state planning has not automatically yielded a smaller state or, at the very least, a lowered profile for the state in the economy of a place like Shulu county. But this pattern of local state expansion, as shown in Chapter 3, was apparent not only in commercial affairs but in many other aspects of the county government's work during the 1980's. Moving away from central planning may indeed signify a decline in resources and, in the final analysis, a decline in the power of the central state. But insofar as the transition generates new regulatory and administrative tasks to be managed at lower levels, the move from a planned to a market economy may serve, in certain ways, to empower and to enhance the profile of the local state in local affairs.[35]

At any rate, with all the new staff at their disposal, Industry and Commerce Management Bureau officials' claims to have been successful at eliminating black markets in Shulu seemed largely plausible. They reported no serious instances of attempted trade in illegal commodities such as narcotics, stolen or illicitly imported goods, endangered species of plants or animals, or human beings. They had found little more in the way of such trade violations in Shulu than some materials classified as "pornographic," and some illegally felled lumber in transit. This success they attributed primarily to their own vigilance, but also to local government efforts to educate the population about relevant laws and punishments, and to the generally flush condition in most markets. Moreover, in addition to the Industry and Commerce Management Bureau itself, a number of other county government agencies also had a hand in keeping out black market trade and in commercial regulation more generally. Vehicles engaged in intercounty transport were required to have permits from the transportation management office of the Transportation Bureau, for example, to help prevent shipment of illegal goods.[36] The transportation management office also regulated freight charges and printed tickets sold by private bus companies as a way of regulating their fares. The Price Bureau too, although little involved in private market price regulation, occasionally would be called in to enforce upper limits called "reference prices" (cankao jia), such as for pork at Spring Festival time when demand always skyrockets. Commercial tax collection, of course, came under the jurisdiction of the Finance and Tax Bureau, and private merchants and peddlers were accordingly required to report to that bureau on their business circuits, to keep account books (including information on sources of supply), and to permit these to be inspected on demand by tax authorities.

In addition to all this, the Shulu county government also had a political strategy for controlling and perhaps co-opting private traders. In September 1986, the Industry and Commerce Management Bureau had established the Individual Household Laborers' Association (Geti Laodongzhe Xiehui)—a local branch of a nationwide organization for private traders. By 1990 the bureau reported that *every* private merchant in Shulu had joined, casting doubt on the supposed "voluntary" character of membership in the organization, but bringing the rolls to almost 19,000 petty traders in the county. This organization's functions included publicizing market information—also a task of the bureau—on bulletin boards, at meetings, and in occasional digests of information from *Market News* (*Shichang bao*), published by provincial-level bureau offices throughout China. It also facilitated the flow of information to help private enterprises upgrade their operations, by inviting technicians for visits or arranging field trips by local businesspeople. It also served—and this did seem to be its primary function—to explain and clarify bureau policies and regulations to the merchants. It was supposed to represent the views and interests of Shulu's private merchants to the bureau as well. But the facts that it shared offices with the bureau, that it was described by bureau officials as "a mass organization under the leadership of the Party and the government," and that it was part of a national association in which the "upper levels give direction to the lower levels" gave pause about both its democratic and its representative character.[37]

All this paternalistic organizing, policing, and regulating did not seem to have deterred the overall development of private commerce locally. Traditional rural periodic markets continued to proliferate through the reform decade. At the end of the Qing Dynasty, in 1906, there had been sixteen periodic markets operating in Shulu county, comprising three clearly discernible circuits (see Map 8). By 1986, there were over forty periodic markets (see Map 9). They were so thickly developed that their circuits are not clearly discernible. Of the ten markets that existed in both 1906 and 1986, nine met on the same market days in 1986 as they had in 1906. This is interesting as an example of historical continuity; it also suggests either that the process by which the markets were restored involved little political interference or that, to the extent that Shulu authorities did oversee the resuscitation of periodic markets, they did so in ways that conformed with the tenacious impulses of society, which the Chinese state had attempted to break in earlier periods.[38]

The bureau had also been active in promoting the development of a belt of ten specialized seasonal and year-round wholesale markets dealing in vegetables, vegetable seedlings, melons, fruits, and saplings of the famous Chinese toon (cedar) tree native to Caiyuan village near Jiucheng.

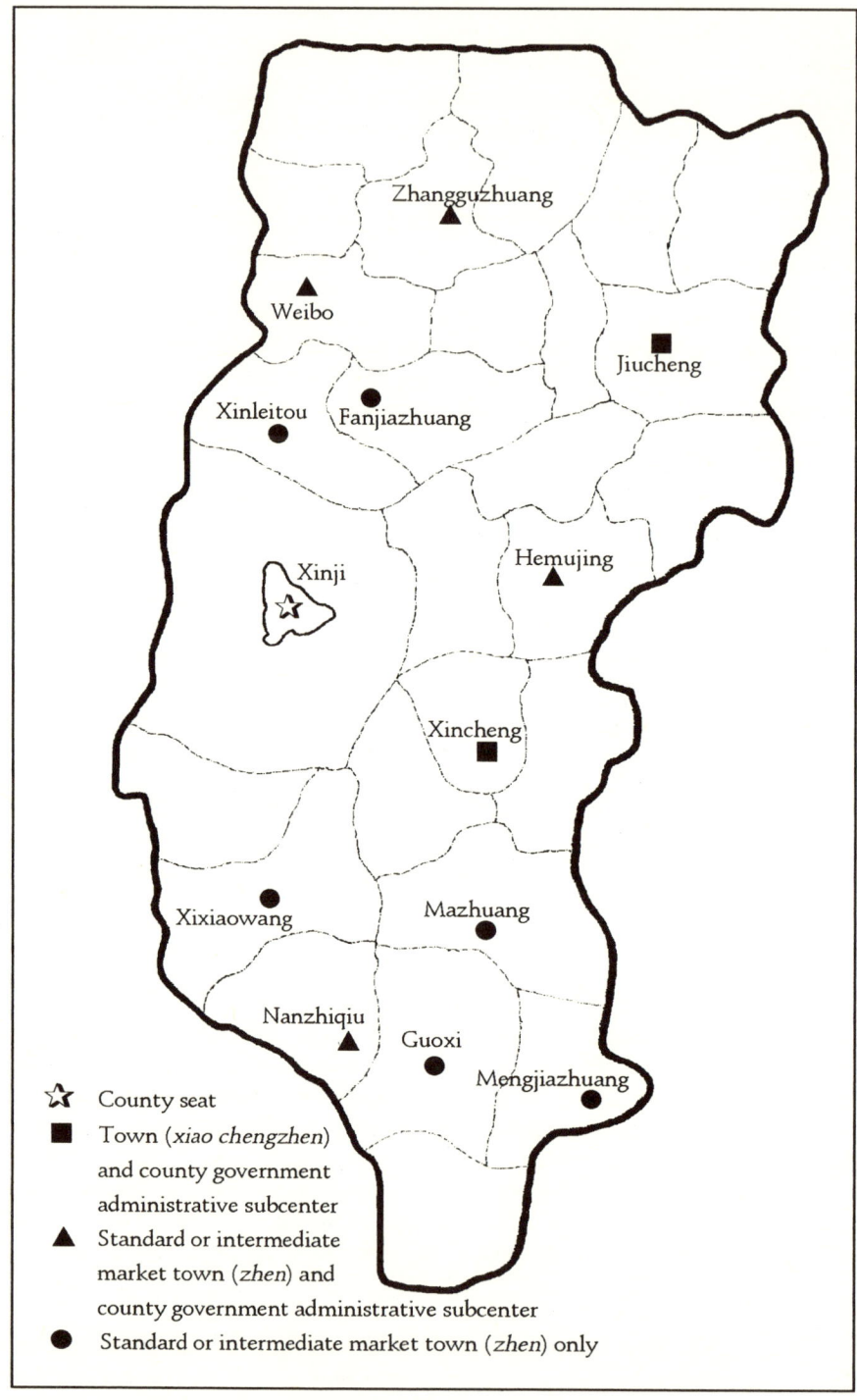

Map 8. Markets and administrative centers, Shulu county, 1906
SOURCE: Information from *Shulu xiangtu zhi*, superimposed on a modern map of Shulu.

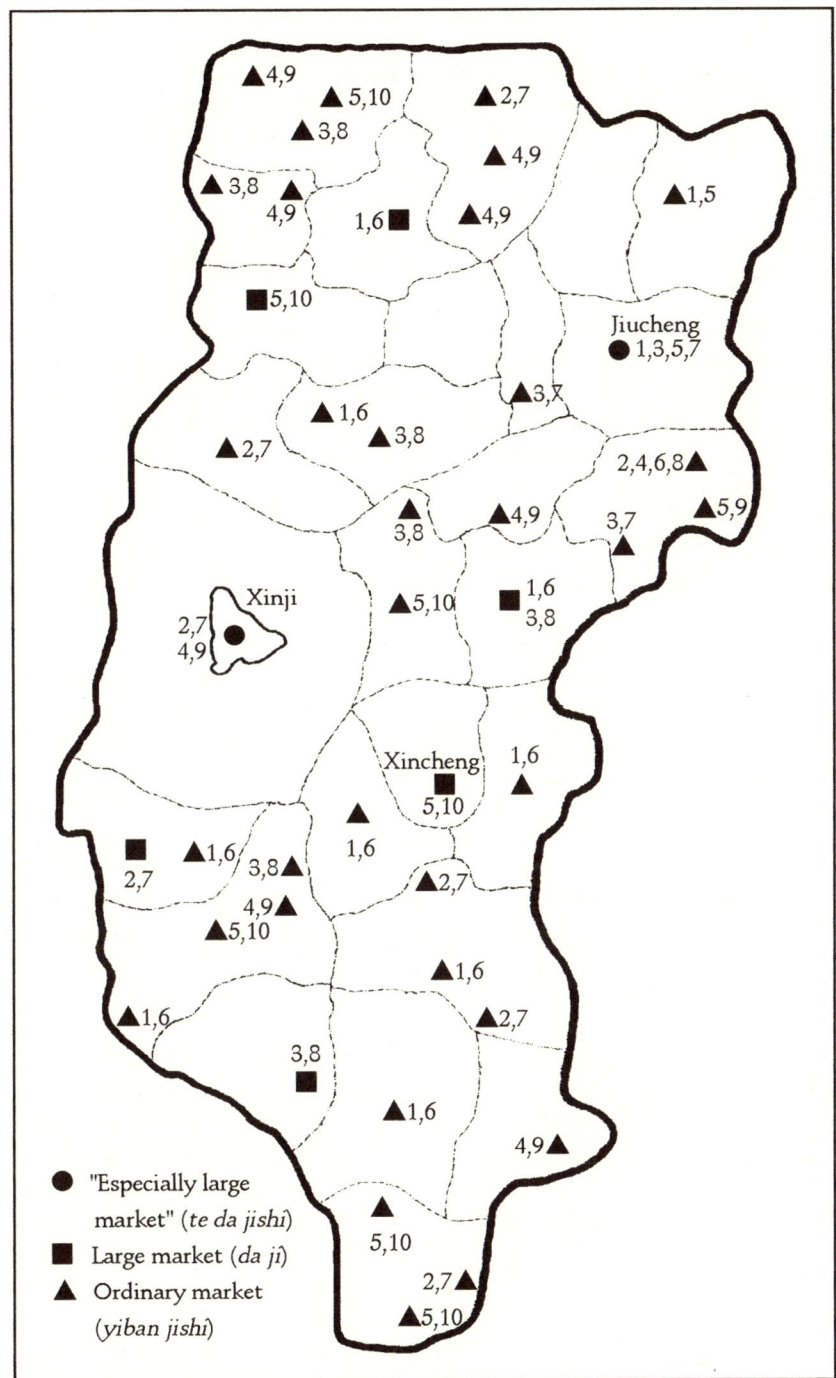

Map 9. Periodic markets, Shulu county, 1986
SOURCE: Based on a table prepared by Shulu County Industry and Commerce Management Bureau.

All but one of these were located along the Cangzhou-Shijiazhuang highway bisecting Shulu, and were under the administration of the bureau's office in Jiucheng.[39] There they could attract traders from major cities in the greater Hebei-Shandong region (including Beijing, Tianjin, Shijiazhuang, Dezhou, Jinan, Xingtai, and Handan). One of these, for example, was the thriving chive market in Junqi which, in the busy month of March, might turn over as much as 300,000 *jin* (150,000 kilos) of chives in a day, and where the roads and local roadhouses were often clogged with truckers who stayed only long enough to make their pickups and then headed out, their rigs piled high with Junqi chives, to markets as far away as Shenyang and Inner Mongolia. Some of these specialized markets the bureau organized and operated itself in connection with governments of towns, townships, and villages, as well as with private businesspeople. Others were run by associations of private traders but received bureau assistance in the form of market information and publicity. All were subject to its regulation and served as sites for the bureau to collect information.

From an office in Hebei Yiji, the Industry and Commerce Management Bureau published a daily newsletter listing up-to-date prices on key products and alerting both local merchants and, through contacts with industry and commerce management bureaus elsewhere, traders in distant places to good opportunities for trade in particular commodities. The bureau was also involved in product development and promotion. It was planning to organize a seedling market as part of a move to expand vegetable production in the county.[40] It was attempting to resuscitate a traditional method for roasting donkey meat, which had once been a local specialty. The recipe and technique had been lost as the old-timers who knew the art had died out. In 1986 the bureau was conducting culinary research, and was also working to identify relatives and apprentices of the former artisans, many of whom had moved far away from Shulu. It was planning to validate its efforts by holding a competition to be judged by some former expert chefs and local gourmets. The tasty products of early efforts to retrieve this lost delicacy were on sale at the Hebei Yiji Market and other stalls around the county. The bureau was making similar efforts to reclaim the skilled techniques in fur and leather craft for which Shulu had been famous as far back as the Ming dynasty, but progress on this score was less in evidence.[41] Although Shulu leather goods continued to enjoy a solid reputation on the domestic market, quality and product types remained too lackluster to command interest in the faster-paced top-quality and luxury leather goods segments of the international high-fashion clothing markets.

Considered all in all, the county government had certainly become more and more deeply involved in both the regulation and the promotion of local private trade through the 1980's. And the Industry and Commerce Management Bureau, with chief responsibility in this realm, had certainly risen to become one of the most visible of local government units, interacting with ordinary citizens in one way or another virtually every hour of every day. Private trade in Shulu had clearly not developed at the expense of local state power or authority. The two had been rising together.

FOREIGN TRADE

Export production was ratcheted upward to a higher range with the advent of the Deng period. Shulu's foreign trade grew, and so did its Foreign Trade Bureau, which reported a total staff of 103 in 1990. But this pattern of development was not quite as spectacular as might have been expected. First, other counties in Shijiazhuang prefecture grew even faster.[42] And second, Shulu was not included among a group of counties and municipalities of eastern Hebei that were singled out by the state for special emphasis on and deregulation of foreign trade.[43] Moreover, Shulu's export volume was rather erratic through the 1980's, both in terms of total purchases made for export and in terms of the composition of those purchases. Real profit levels also journeyed unsteadily through the decade (see Tables 22 and 26).

The variations over the years recorded in Table 26 are difficult to account for specifically. But it is perhaps worth pointing out that they do not directly reflect shifting market forces. In Shulu throughout the 1980's foreign trade remained largely unaffected by attempts at economic reform. Early in the decade, it is true, the bureau had reorganized itself into a "corporation" (*gongsi*), and by 1990 it had spawned two constituent companies, an Industrial Products Company and an Agricultural Products Company.[44] This quasi-corporate reorganization, plus the introduction of a contract responsibility system for bureau cadres and workers, had apparently helped in creating some incentives for internal administrative efficiency. But, as bureau vice director Zhang said of the bureau-*cum*-

TABLE 26
Shulu County Foreign Trade Bureau Financial Breakdown, 1979–89
(in thousands of yuan)

Year	Export earnings	Domestic sales earnings	Other income	Other expenditures	Property losses	Taxes	Business expenses	Profits
1979	450	73	63	1	31		179	375
1980	584	18	340	3	2		456	481
1981	789	22	316	3	22	11	376	715
1982	490	(8)	247	2	1	9	390	327
1983	330	62	170	8	3	1	350	200
1984	331	33	100	27	23	9	327	78
1985	418	27	62	28		6	299	174
1986	755	40	80	35	1	11	739	89
1987	735	2	98	16		28	622	169
1988	740	298	152	36		61	839	254
1989	814	403	168	66	3	62	1,144	110

NOTE: Parentheses indicate negative number.

corporation in 1986, "We have two names but only one office. Foreign trade is a system [*xitong*], with unified income and expenditure [*tong shou tong zhi*]. . . . Our bureau is just a branch of the provincial and prefectural foreign trade bureaus, for whom our main function is doing purchasing. . . . Our personnel and finances are administered vertically."[45] And three and a half years later, in 1990, Zhang was still at pains to point out that his bureau of the county government constituted "the lowest level in a vertical *xitong*. What we primarily do is make purchases according to directives. We do not have responsibility for business decisions."[46]

Some reforms of the foreign trade *xitong*, intended to give greater independence and discretion to the provinces, had been tried around 1984. But this had resulted in provinces attempting to undercut each other's prices and in long-term relationships between export suppliers and foreign buyers being disrupted, all of which hurt foreign exchange earnings. The decentralizing reforms were thus largely abandoned. By the end of the decade, foreign trade corporations in fourteen large coastal cities retained the right to engage in direct export agreements with overseas buyers. But export-producing enterprises and foreign trade bureaus in small localities in the interior such as Shulu remained encapsulated in a highly centralized vertical bureaucratic system.

The style of bureaucratic behavior practiced in the foreign trade *xitong* remained reminiscent of the Mao period, in fact. The instinctive reaction of the bureau to rising purchase targets (as to quotas in the past) was less to build horizontal bridges to other units operating in Shulu than to cement its relations with units already producing for it and to strengthen production actually carried out within the system itself. For example, the Shulu Foreign Trade Bureau (with loan money allocated at a special low interest rate by higher levels of the system) invested in building its own shirt factory in 1988. The Japanese equipment installed in the factory was both modern and reliable. But the main motive for investment was less to raise the local quality or quantity of shirt production or to make profits than to maximize local bureau control over its ability to meet its purchase targets. Zhang Zhenxiu explained, "Running our own factory helps make it easy to get the purchases we need to make. This way we don't have to rely on factories and individuals just being willing to sell to us."[47]

Clearly, for many commodities and products the Foreign Trade Bureau wanted to purchase, competition from domestic markets was stiff and likely to get stiffer. Many Shulu producers who had signed agreements to sell to the bureau were tempted to renege when other (domestic market) buyers came into the county offering higher prices. In 1988, in fact, the Shulu government had to promulgate an order prohibiting this kind of trade. Purchasing agents coming into the county to buy up products that were supposed to be sold to the Foreign Trade Bureau would pay a heavy fine if caught. And Shulu enterprises producing for export, according to the new order, had to guarantee that they would meet their targets. Foreign trade was one commercial sector, at least, in which the basic concepts and the methods of doing business had not changed much from the prereform past.

NEW COUNTY COMMERCIAL INITIATIVES

Even to a small locality in the interior like Shulu county, the reforms have clearly brought a welcome expansion of commercial activity of all kinds. New commercial opportunities have in turn helped to enliven virtually the entire local economic picture. Agricultural and sideline production for the market are up; prices paid to farmers have risen; enterprise efficiency has improved somewhat; enterprise profits generally have been on the rise; tax receipts are up too; and, most important perhaps, consumer demand is now much better satisfied than before. Still, the situation in China's partly state-planned and partly supply-and-demand-driven commercial system at the end of the 1980's remained one in which exchange markets and relations were still very far from fully rationalized and very far from smoothly coordinated. Despite the reforms, and of course also because of the reforms, many problems remained to inhibit both domestic and foreign trade. And insofar as such problems were having a detrimental effect on the Shulu economy, it fell, not surprisingly, to the county government to attempt to address them as best it could, through its own combinations of political-administrative and marketlike measures. We can explore some aspects of the county government's efforts in this regard by considering the activities of two offices of the local government newly set up in the 1980's. These two are the Shulu County Border Region Trade Company and the Shulu Office of Economic Cooperation.

The Shulu County Border Region Trade Company

The Shulu Border Region Trade Company was established in 1988. It was created in order to promote and expedite certain kinds of barter trade deals with counterparts in what was then the Soviet Union and other countries "bordering" China. Given the oversupply and undersupply of various commodities and products in both China and the USSR, the possibilities for cross-border trade were great and growing. But because of nonconvertible currency problems, and because small local enterprises and local government offices like those in Shulu county had little if any access to foreign exchange certificates (FECs, until recently China's foreign trade currency) or convertible *yuan*, only barter trade was feasible and lawful—and this only under certain administrative auspices. In China this type of trade is generally handled by official provincial-level trading corporations established by and located in provinces actually bordering on the USSR and other states. Shulu county, located in Hebei province and dead in the middle of the north China plain, cannot by any stretch of the geographic imagination be supposed to qualify as a border region. Still, Shulu did have some commodities to offer that evidently could not be found in border provinces and that very much interested some potential Soviet trading partners. Shulu fur and leather products and its pears were specifically cited. Furthermore, Shulu county leaders clearly thought they might have a use for various products the Russians were apparently hoping to unload. Therefore, by a stretch of the administrative imagination that defies recapitulation, Shulu's Border Region Trade Company was set up both as a branch office of the Heilongjiang Province International Commerce Corporation[48] and as a subordinate office of the Heilongjiang Province Commercial Products Quality Control Bureau.[49] This meant that the Shulu Border Region Trade Company was *both* an office of the local county government *and* a branch of a corporation *belonging to another province*. The Shulu company, as of 1990, was the only branch of the Heilongjiang corporation permitted to operate outside Heilongjiang province. And on the governmental side of things, as the company director, Lin, explained, since his office was a subordinate of a Heilongjiang province bureau but not a Hebei province bureau, he didn't report to any office of any bureau in the Shulu government. He reported instead directly to the mayor, which, as he noted, gave him a considerable advantage in getting things done.[50]

To cap the organizational and conceptual confusion here, it should also be noted that the Shulu Border Region Trade Company was collectively owned: collectively owned, that is, by the county government itself. When asked what, concretely, this collective ownership implied, Lin replied that it meant his company was not in the budget (*yusuanwai*). Just as with the old (prereform) extrabudgetary enterprises, this company was receiving official and financial support from the county government, but it received no appropriations through the official state budget process. And the portion of the company's profits that was routinely remitted to the county government stayed with the county; it was not sent upward to higher levels of government as it would have been were the company classified as state-owned.

The company made its profits by selling, both within and beyond Shulu, the Soviet products it procured through barter. But profits as of 1990 were not impressive. The initial investment to set up the company (with a total staff of nineteen persons) came in the form of a loan from the local branch of the Industrial and Commercial Bank. With this loan an office building was built and a car was purchased; what early profits there were went mostly to pay the interest on the loan. Things looked quite bleak in 1989, apparently, when the central government's "austerity program" threatened possibly to abolish provincial trading outfits like the Heilongjiang home company. But business picked up again after Li Peng made a special visit to Heilongjiang to look the company over and agreed, while he was there, to allow it to continue operations. There was talk in the summer of 1990 of the Shulu company netting perhaps ¥1 million in profits during the second half of the year.

By 1990, Russian buyers were making regular trips to Shulu to look over available products and discuss potential deals. But doing business with the Russians was not always easy. Shulu company executives hoped to make deals that would bring Soviet lumber, cement, steel, or chemical fertilizer into the county. Yet often what their Soviet counterparts had to offer in exchange—tractors and train cars, for example—were neither usable in Shulu nor salable elsewhere in China. On the other hand, barter trade can create opportunities for certain kinds of deals that would be most unlikely in cash markets. Shulu company executives discovered, for example, that some of their counterparts in the Soviet Union had a surfeit of deerskins on hand which, apparently, they were not able to find a way to have processed to meet high quality standards. Since, as it happens, Shulu county leather tanning skills are legendary, the Soviets agreed to turn a large quantity of raw skins over to the Shulu company, which undertook to have them processed locally, and which then repaid the Soviets with processed deerskins. About half the number of raw skins brought into Shulu were returned, fully tanned, to the Soviet side. The other tanned skins remained in Shulu for further processing or sale in China.[51]

China's domestic market for fur and leather goods suffered a major collapse in 1989, after a period of rapidly surging prices and demand. The Shulu fur and leather industry was hit hard, with several smaller enterprises going bankrupt. Company director Lin felt certain in 1990 that he would be able to move a significant quantity of Shulu's surplus leather products in barter deals with the Soviets that year, deals that he thought might just be sufficient to keep a couple of other sinking Shulu factories afloat for at least a while longer. Primitive and sometimes low-profit as these barter deals might seem, therefore, they were plainly capable of making contributions to the short-term health of the local Shulu economy.

Even so, the possibilities for expanding barter trade with the Russians did not appear to be endless. Pears, for example, were still subject to state controls that kept fruit prices artificially low inside the USSR and, therefore, in at least some deals (such as one in which company officials took Russian calculators in exchange for second-quality Shulu pears), the Chinese side still reckoned the bargain to have been a bad one. Partly as a result of this, Shulu county government leaders were actively urging their local company to branch out and explore barter possibilities in and through Inner Mongolia, Xinjiang, and North Korea. Company officials were proceeding cautiously, however, especially with the North Koreans, who they said they had reason to believe might not always keep their agreements. Director Lin sounded a somewhat more upbeat note, however, in discussing a "border" trade barter contract Shulu had recently signed for some Romanian chemical fertilizer. The contact with the Romanians had been made in Shenzhen, through a branch office opened there by the Heilongjiang parent company.

The opening of this Shenzhen office by the Heilongjiang corporate executives promised to lead to more opportunities for barter trade agreements involving Shulu with still other countries of the former socialist bloc. But all things considered, the Shulu county government was reportedly anxious to "disentangle" its Border Region Trade Company from the Heilongjiang parent organizations, if it could. The Heilongjiang offices ended up with too large a portion of their profits, they complained. And then too, Heilongjiang provincial regulations prohibiting exports (from the province) of scarce products such as chemical fertilizer were also perceived as disadvantageous to the Shulu branch company. Reconfiguration of the Shulu company under a Hebei province parent organization was apparently a possibility under active discussion in 1990. In fact, Director Lin noted with dismay, provincial authorities were then encouraging every Hebei county to get into the barter trade arena if possible. Needless to say, the prospect of so much suddenly added local competition was a hard one for the pioneers of the Shulu company to swallow. On the pros and cons of these and other complex considerations, Shulu's barter trade specialists were making their calculations every bit as much in response to the changing market and the changing state policy environment as were the more conventional cash-market merchants and traders operating in the county.

The Shulu Office of Economic Cooperation

The work of the Shulu Office of Economic Cooperation provides another glimpse of local government efforts to cope as effectively as possible with the only partially modern and depoliticized bureaucratic system and the only partially commercialized local and national economic system which were the products of the reform era of the 1980's. The Shulu office was established in May 1985, its mission being to help in "breaking up the old vertical and horizontal [*tiao/kuai*] administrative divisions so as to enhance mutual exchange relations between various units and localities."[52] This office, with a total staff of seven cadres and one worker, also reported directly to the very top leadership of the county. It was conceived as primarily a service organization, coordinating and facilitating a great variety of specialized technical, labor, equipment and other exchanges involving Shulu units with outside units, as well as acting in an intermediary capacity in certain investment and trade deals.[53] The office operated as a clearinghouse for information about possible exchanges, and it also frequently did background and feasibility studies on particular proposals for investment or exchange, sending its reports to the county leadership for final consideration.[54] The office spent its annual budget of about ¥80,000 mostly on getting and sending out information about possible exchanges, and paying for business trips in and out of Shulu.

The office also reportedly attempted to put emphasis on Shulu's best products, to enhance Shulu's business reputation, and to strengthen further its areas of comparative advantage. By mid-1990 the office, which saw itself acting only as a "bridge" in most cases, claimed to have been of assistance in a total of 1,232 different projects: 947 involving investments, and 285 involving technical cooperation only. Its contributions had ranged from making the initial connections and introductions of interested parties, to working out special living arrangements for visiting technicians, to mediating disputes between cooperating units. The office had a hand in the negotiations for the new (and so far profitable) Shulu clothing factory joint venture with investors from Hong Kong. It had assisted a local television-tube factory to make contact with a larger and more modern factory in Shijiazhuang, which had contributed to achieving and maintaining better product quality at the local factory. The office had also helped a small steel grinding ball plant located in Shulu's Nanzhiqiu township to enter into an exciting cooperative agreement with both a scientific institute in Shenyang and a technical college in Hebei. Under this agreement, the Nanzhiqiu plant had begun carrying out experiments and trial production of a new type of low-alloy steel ball never before produced in China.

One of its more spectacular success stories concerned the office's contribution to securing, in 1989, an investment of some ¥15 million in the Shulu No. 8 Chemical Factory. The ¥15 million came, interestingly enough, from the Hebei provincial government Public Security Department (or Gonganting), which, it seems, had accumulated earnings from the productive labor of its labor camp inmates that it wished to invest. It was looking for something "with a better market future," Shulu officials explained. The Public Security Department had not been disappointed, at least in the short term. Its Shulu chemical plant investment had reportedly yielded it a 50 percent profit return in just one year! Shulu county counted this factory opening a valuable asset as well. It provided over 300 jobs for Shulu people, more than 70 percent of which were new positions.

One of the most useful activities of the Shulu Office of Economic Cooperation was to establish and cultivate "friendly city" relations with other counties and with selected small cities around the country. Shulu had "friendly relations" arrangements in place with about twenty different localities by 1990, and these were set up with much more in mind than mere expressions of mutual good will. A declaration of friendly relations was expected to serve as the basis for the growth of more direct and comprehensive trade and other economic relations between the governments and among the various enterprises of the two localities. Such relations were established with the potential complementarities of the two local economies very much in mind. Shulu, for example, regularly tends to run short of coal in the winter. It set up friendly relations with a small city in Shanxi producing a surplus of coal precisely with this deficit in mind. In exchange for good terms on direct purchases of Shulu wheat and vegetables, the Shanxi city's coal authorities diverted 180,000 tons to Shulu in 1989. A similar complementarity was found with a small city in Heilongjiang. On the basis of friendly relations between the two localities,

Shulu was able to purchase some much-needed lumber (hard to get on the north China plain, but in abundant supply in Heilongjiang) in exchange for sending some Shulu fur and leather tanning specialists to the Heilongjiang locality to teach people there the skills they needed to process locally available animal skins.

The original idea or initiative for exploring mutually beneficial direct trade possibilities such as these apparently often came through personal relations, or through the grapevine of market information about sources of locally scarce commodities and materials. But it was up to the county government's Office of Economic Cooperation to follow up on these personal contacts and scraps of information with investigations and exploratory meetings, until finally "friendly city" agreements, useful in plugging some of Shulu's persistent trade gaps, could be formally negotiated and consummated. In this as in so many other ways explored in this chapter, the range of local government responsibility and authority had been elaborated and enlarged in tandem with the rapid development of local commerce after Mao.

Writing in 1989 about the activities of offices of economic and technical cooperation like this one in Shulu, one leading Western expert on Chinese commercial policy and practice summed up the situation this way:

> The Chinese approach to economic reform has a strong statist, organizational component. In the leadership's effort to keep a grip on unplanned transactions, it is relying on old organs whose cadres know the market, and it is designing new offices that often emerge without significant metamorphosis from the units that made up the original state-run bureaucracy and that directed the planned economy. In the process, they are further empowering the public side of business, rather than as they proclaim to wish to do, "separating the government from the enterprise."[55]

This assessment captures well not only what we were able to observe about the operations of the Shulu Office of Economic Cooperation, but much else that was happening under the heading of commercial reform in the county.

CHAPTER 7

The County Government in Urban Development

An important and distinctive feature of Chinese development policy and practice both in the Mao and Deng periods has been the emphasis placed on the development of small and medium-sized towns and cities. Economic planners have stressed the capacity of such smaller urban centers both to absorb large amounts of labor released from agriculture and to serve as loci for the development of more flexible and efficient collective and private-sector industries. Yet a small-scale urbanization strategy has also had its detractors. Some have pointed to the difficulty these cities will have attracting population, given their poorly developed residential, commercial, and cultural infrastructures. Others argue that small cities simply cannot adequately plan for and administer a growing population. Still others have pointed to the financial constraints facing small towns. Despite these reservations, though, small-scale urbanization continues to be an important phenomenon in China.[1]

Xinji, the urban center of Shulu county, provides an example of this type of urban development, and it provides an opportunity to analyze the role of local governments in fostering and regulating small-scale urbanization within a rural setting. It has succeeded precisely because the central state and the local state have been able to resolve the major problems to which critics of small-scale urbanization have pointed. As we shall see, the Shulu county government has undertaken comprehensive planning to make Xinji a reasonably attractive place to live. This has often entailed intrusive local state regulation of the burgeoning economy, which in turn has demanded, as we have seen in Chapter 3, an ever larger, more complex, and professionally trained local bureaucracy. It has also called for greater budgetary resources to be devoted to urban development, from both local and provincial coffers.

As explained in Chapter 2, Shulu has had three different county seats in its history—Jiucheng, Xincheng, and Xinji—all of which remain sizable settlements today. By the early part of this century, county settlement patterns evinced a fairly well-developed urban structure with an intricate interweaving of administrative and economic hierarchies. This early history of urbanism left discernible residues even in the Mao years, when Shulu's administrative structure was more diverse and displayed greater continuity with earlier patterns of local economy and geography than would be expected on the basis of analyses that emphasize the power of Maoist transformation toward social uniformity. By the beginning of the reform period, Shulu's urban structure had become only more elaborated and complex. And by 1990, Xinji was once again a thriving little metropolis, and some of Shulu's smaller towns appeared larger and more fully developed than the seats of neighboring counties.[2]

The growth of Shulu's urban areas posed a variety of challenges and opportunities to its county and town governments. Burgeoning commerce had produced serious overcrowding in Xinji, which made commercial regulation and traffic control difficult but which in turn provided the impetus for designing and establishing the remarkable market, Hebei Yiji.[3] Industrial development created increasing demand for labor, which was constrained by policies to limit cityward migration. This led in turn to the extensive use of rural contract labor.[4] Xinji's relatively rapid growth, in both economy and population, occasioned the elevation of the entire county to the administrative status of a municipality (shi). While this naturally raised Shulu's profile within the regional political economy, it also involved significant internal reorganizations—such as the conversion of the townships around Xinji into new institutional formations known as "administrative districts" (banshichu), and their incorporation into the city government.[5]

In this chapter, we explore several other urbanization-related policy arenas in which the county government was active: environmental protection, urban planning, land-use control, and housing regulation.

Environmental Protection

The rapid growth of urban centers and of industrial production in the Chinese countryside has posed new and serious environmental problems. These tend to present themselves to local governments, including county governments, at the levels of both politics and policy. County governments are called upon to resolve disputes between local factories and farms, between local units and units operating beyond their borders, and between themselves and higher authorities at prefecture and province governments which oversee neighboring counties and are necessarily drawn into their disputes and negotiations. When quarrels over environmental questions take place within the county, the Shulu government is cast as a mediator. But disputes with units beyond its borders place it in the role of advocate for local interests. As for policy, environmental issues pose problems that demand careful long-range planning to prevent the burgeoning new urban areas from becoming unlivable in themselves and, by spreading pollution, from damaging the surrounding countryside as well. The implementation of such plans may in turn involve some complex politics.

POLLUTION, MEDIATION, AND REPRESENTATION:
A CASE FROM THE MAO PERIOD

One example of the role of the county government in pollution politics concerns violations by the Shulu Fur and Leather Tanning Factory. During much of the 1970's over eight hundred tons of waste water containing arsenic were flowing from this large tannery every day. Most of it ran into the fields of farmers in Ji county to the southeast, which, to complicate matters further, was administered as part of Hengshui prefecture. The Shulu tannery was in violation of a 1974 national industrial effluent toxicity standard of 0.5 mg./liter for arsenic and its inorganic compounds. But no attention was given the matter until 1977, when new environmental protection laws mandating investigations, fines, and even plant closings for violators came into effect. In Hebei, environmental protection departments were established at the province and prefecture levels under the Public Health Bureau. They were conducting routine tests of the water in Shulu and Ji counties in early 1977 when the contamination came to light. Worried Ji county farmers went to their county government and also lodged complaints directly with the tannery and the Shulu government. The tannery responded with a plan to clean up its effluent, but it did not put the plan into effect quickly enough to suit the people in Ji county. Prefecture and province officials were called in to mediate the dispute. The two counties were represented in the meetings by members of their respective planning committees.[6] The Shulu factory was fined on three separate occasions—evidence of ongoing disputes and attendant politics. The monies, totaling ¥44,000, were used to compensate Ji county farmers for the damage. The funds were paid out by the Shulu Planning Committee, but were in turn deducted from the factory's own operating funds. Some ¥600,000 was also invested in a new wastewater treatment system, at least part of which was financed through the state budget. By 1986, the problem of arsenic effluence had been solved, though the plant still emitted an obnoxious smell that slated it to be moved out of the residential quarter where it was located and into a new industrial zone.[7]

In this case the Shulu government had to represent its constituent units and their interests to outsiders, and had to take responsibility for their mistakes, make amends, and work with its own units and those above—that is, horizontally and vertically—to take measures to correct them. It also had to mediate disputes between its own farmers, whose irrigation water was also polluted, and the tannery. In short, the county government found itself in the politically delicate position of acting simultaneously as advocate and as mediator in related and protracted issues involving the same units.

ENVIRONMENTAL PROTECTION IN THE REFORM PERIOD

The onset of the reforms increased the pace of urban development in Shulu. Government officials date the actual speedup from 1983, which occurred at least partly because the decollectivization of agriculture in 1982–83 released much surplus labor from the land and allowed rural migrants to enter Xinji to work. As early as 1979, the county government had foreseen and made some provision for Xinji's urbanization under the reforms by establishing the Urban Construction Bureau (Chengshi Jianshe Ju). This office moved expeditiously to deal with the environmental effects of quickening urbanization starting in 1983, establishing the Environmental Protection Office within the Urban Construction Bureau in that year. During the rest of the decade, the Shulu government gave heavy and growing emphasis to environmental protection. In 1986, both the bureau itself and the Environmental Protection Office within it were given higher profiles with the bureau's transformation into an Urban Construction and Environmental Protection Commission (Chengshi Jianshe Huanjing Baohu Weiyuanhui). Spending on environmental work more than doubled from 1986 to 1989, increasing 23 percent faster than total budgetary expenditures. Environmental protection and urban planning was the third largest line item (of fifteen major lines) on the expenditure side of the budget in 1988, and fifth largest in 1989.[8] One of Shulu's vice mayors was specifically charged with overseeing environmental protection work; and this had also been a particular concern of Mayor Liu Baolu, who led Shulu through much of the 1980's. The Urban Construction and Environmental Protection Commission had a well-educated staff in its Xinji headquarters. Many were graduates of the national keypoint Xinji Middle School. It also had posted personnel in every township in Shulu.

The commission approached the task of protecting the Shulu environment by several means, including planning, regulation, exercise of administrative authority, and education. In 1986 it had set forth an environmental protection plan through the year 2000. This included not only targets—Shulu's industry was to meet national environmental quality standards by 1990, and higher local standards by the year 2000[9]—but also specific projects such as construction of a ¥30 million sewage treatment plant. Plans for new plants in Xinji had to be vetted for environmental safety by the commission, which, among other things, forbade the construction of new factories emitting lead, mercury, chrome, and phosphates. The commission regularly monitored the quality of subterranean water, air, and the liquid, gaseous, and solid waste of every factory in Xinji. Any factory exceeding pollution standards was required to formulate a remedial plan and to pay a fine, 80 percent of which was then reallocated to the plant to help meet the costs of the cleanup.[10] Enforcing and collecting fines, it was claimed, posed no particular problems. Commission officials averred that "since we are backed by state policy, there isn't a lot of complaining" by factory managers.[11] Indeed, they proudly proclaimed themselves to be the toughest finers in the prefecture, a distinction attributable both to the existence in Shulu of some of the prefecture's major polluting industries (especially chemical factories) and to the political emphasis given environmental work by county authorities. Commission cadres hastened to illustrate the effectiveness of their enforcement measures by reporting the decline in density of particulate matter in the Xinji air from 1,000 to 700 mg. per cubic meter over the latter half of the 1980's.

The commission also operated a mobile testing unit to monitor air and water pollution around Shulu. But staff members admitted, and lamented the fact, that they could not keep up with the pollution caused by the swiftly proliferating rural industries. Commission staff also coordinated local efforts to enforce national legislation on noise pollution with the broadcasting and public security bureaus. The commission was involved in educational work as well. It sponsored not one but two "Earth Days" each year, conducted programs in the county's primary and secondary schools, and arranged for 160 factory managers to receive subscriptions to *China Environmental News*.

One major approach to pollution control in Xinji was integrated with the urban planning duties of the commission. Factories with noxious effluents or emissions, and those handling explosive materials, were being moved to the southern and eastern part of the city, downwind from the residential, commercial, and administrative districts and, conveniently, near the railway (Map 10). Xinji's chemical plants, the anchors of its state-owned industry and the smelly sources of some of its most serious environmental dangers, were already there; and their most hazardous operations had already been moved away from the nearby grain mill, with the rest slated for relocation later under an incremental long-range plan. New chemical factories were being sited in the extreme southeast of the new industrial zone, so that the summer's prevailing winds would carry their emissions away from the city center. Also being moved to southern Xinji were cement, leather tanning, and asphalt plants, a coal depot, gas storage tanks, and a cotton warehouse. These relocations protected not only nearby residents but also the products of other factories that were especially subject to damage from air pollution, such as grain being processed in the grain mill. Food processing and textile plants were already being concentrated in the western part of the city, away from the emissions of the heavy industrial plants, and future facilities related to these industries

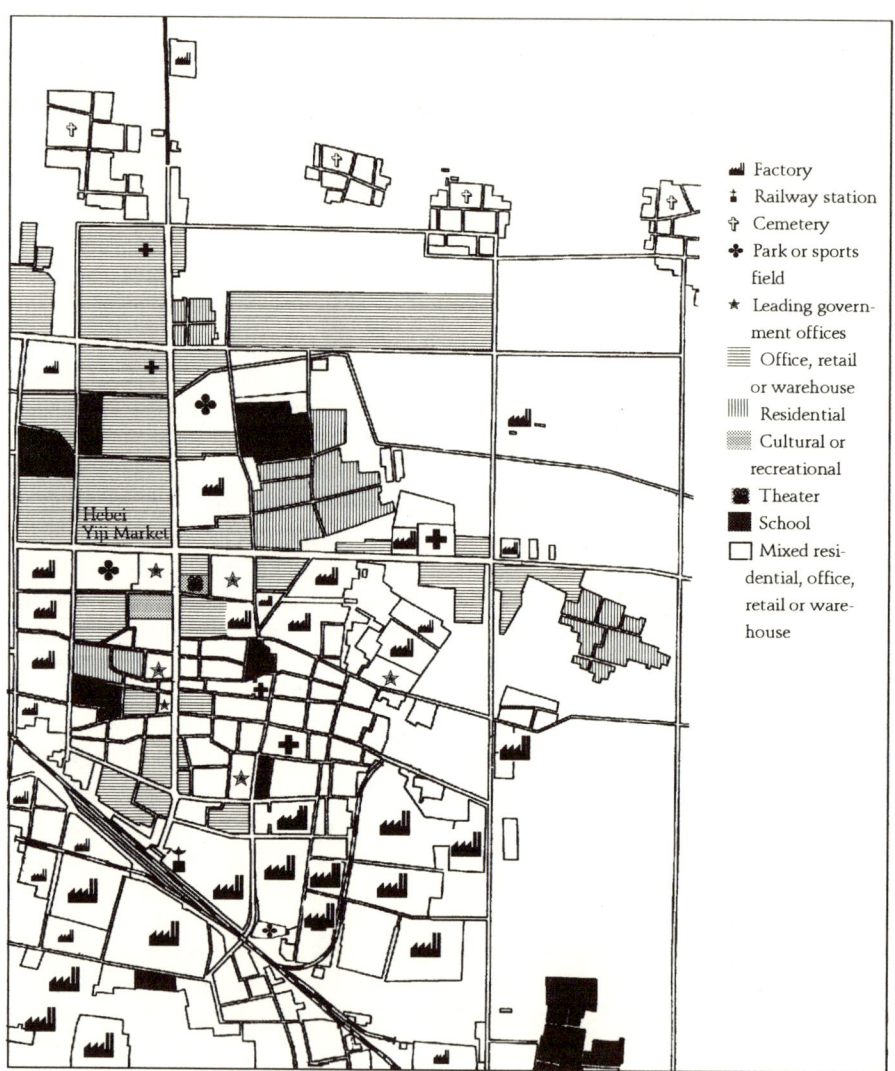

Map 10. Xinji city

were to be located there. Finally, a warehouse district was to be sited in the southwest corner of the city, a location near the railway station and thick with roadways. In short, Xinji's industrial relocation plan was broad in scope, ambitious, and complex.

Implementing it when, for example, a factory had to be moved, would require that considerable resources and political clout be brought to bear. Since the plan bore the imprimatur not only of the county government and Party authorities but also of the relevant authorities at the prefecture and the province, Shulu officials portrayed it as carrying great force. In reality, a characteristic combination of carrot and stick was being used to carry out this comprehensive plan.[12] On the one hand, the state provided subsidies through the ministerial systems (*xitong*) to enterprises slated to be moved. On the other hand, enterprises with sufficient resources to afford a move (after the subsidy) were given no alternative but to do so, though on occasion, it was admitted, pressure from the Public Security Bureau and its police force had to be brought to bear. Yet in the context of the problem of late-1980's declining profitability in Shulu's state industry,[13] even planned subsidy carrots just did not make relocation affordable for many factories. In these cases, Public Security Bureau sticks were being held in abeyance.

Another major physical infrastructure approach to improving and protecting the Shulu environment was the construction of a greenbelt around the city. Greenbelts not only provide beauty and refresh the air, they also define a physical border that limits industrial expansion and helps protect surrounding countryside from the ravages of nearby industry. In Shulu, greenbelts were built in the late 1980's around the downtown park, the Xinji Middle School, and, most ambitiously, in a thirty-meter-wide swathe along the eastern ring road of the city, a planting that would also serve as a tree farm. The commission had worked with the county and provincial governments to acquire the land from the townships to which it belonged through exercise of the state's right of eminent domain; the townships were to be compensated with the proceeds of the sale of the trees.

Urban Planning

Urban planning for Xinji began immediately with the onset of the reforms. In 1979, the newly created Urban Construction Bureau prepared its first plan for 1980–85. By 1983, under the pressure of rapid urbanization beginning that year, the bureau, now outfitted with its Environmental Protection Office, produced its first long-term plans through 1990 and 2000, integrating within them urban planning and environmental protection. It was these plans that began to chart the industrial relocations that have already begun to ameliorate certain forms of environmental pollution in Xinji.

The uprooting of factories was conceived and implemented not just for environmental protection but also as part of an ambitious plan to rationalize Xinji's urban space by dividing it into functional districts. The layout of the city as it emerged from the Mao era was "fairly reasonable," according to Shulu officials.[14] Industry had grown up mostly in the southern part of the city, naturally enough near the railway. This quarter, though, was regarded as needing internal reorganization. Apartment buildings and other dwellings, constructed and owned by industrial enterprises, stood amid factories. Food-handling factories were jumbled together with heavy industrial plants. Factories with dangerous or just pungent gaseous emissions were located where prevailing winds would carry their discharge into the city. Chemical enterprises and warehouses with a substantial danger of explosion were sandwiched together with other buildings, and were located north of the railway, too close to downtown. Thus the new plans were designed to rationalize and reorganize the city's layout. The southeast quarter would become the center for industrial production. The southwest was slated to become a warehouse district. It would be convenient to another new district, in west-central Xinji, to be devoted to administrative offices of industrial and commercial organs such as the Foreign Trade Bureau. The southeast industrial zone was also determined to have pressing infrastructure needs; in particular, additional roadways and bridges were required to traverse the railway. (Two of these were already in service by 1986.) The Urban Construction Commission took all these and many other factors into account in formulating its plans to leave southern Xinji as an industrial zone but to reorganize and develop it.[15]

The rest of Xinji's urban development was planned northward. The heart of downtown was to become a commercial district, the center of which would be the giant market, Hebei Yiji. The east of downtown was slated for residential redevelopment, including housing and hotels. Further out on the eastern periphery, just on the urban side of the greenbelt, were new commercial and light industrial buildings, housing the headquarters and plant works of international businesses such as a Bank of China branch and a textile factory that was Shulu's only joint venture in 1990. To the west of downtown were being sited yet other new offices and a hotel, as well as some light industrial facilities. Construction of these new streets and buildings was fairly advanced by 1990. The Xinji urban plan was worked out at a high level of detail; for example, it included precise figures on land use for various purposes: 23 square meters per capita of residential space, 5.5 square meters of public green spaces, 9 square meters of public buildings, 8.1 square meters of roadways and plazas, and so forth.

These plans were formulated to deal with Xinji's tremendous population density. As mentioned in Chapter 2, its built-up area contained almost half as many people per square kilometer as downtown Shanghai. Xinji's main arteries still do not possess anything approaching the human wave of Nanjing Road, though. One reason is that, with so many Xinji people living on the grounds of their factories, there are proportionately fewer commuters. Nevertheless, with almost 10,000 people per square kilometer, crowding is an extremely serious problem in Xinji that had already begun to make itself felt and would do so again. The streets had become clogged with private merchants in the early 1980's, a problem solved only by constructing the massive Hebei Yiji Market to which we shall turn directly. And as Xinji urban planners' vision of an urban space with distinct residential and industrial districts continues to make its way from the drawing boards to bricks and mortar, Shulu's newly widened main drag, the Andong highway, may indeed start to look and feel more like Shanghai's Nanjing Road. All too well aware of present and potential problems, Xinji urban planners had in mind the fourfold expansion of the built-up area to around 25 square kilometers by the year 2000. This would reduce downtown population density even as population expanded. But it would also involve the conversion of much periurban farmland, which was supposed to be a carefully planned and regulated process, as we shall see below.

As already mentioned, the centerpiece of the first urban plan was Hebei Yiji, which the Urban Construction Commission conceived and planned in conjunction with the Industry and Commerce Management Bureau. As discussed in Chapter 6, this project combined commercial development and regulation with specific urban planning concerns about human and vehicular traffic congestion. The big central market was intended to provide a rationalized place of business for the thousands of merchants and shoppers who were clogging Xinji's major thoroughfares and small byways. Meanwhile, other urban planning elements were built into the project as well. A broad landscaped and lighted boulevard was built fronting the new market, on land where no roadway had existed before (see photographs). The market was sited just half a block from the Andong highway, which formed the city's north-south axis, while on its other flank was built the new ring road that was designed to serve as a bypass as well as a delivery artery. And the striking architectural design of the market, combining traditional Chinese motifs, functional convenience, and modern features such as a clock tower and broadcast antennae, was produced by the Urban Construction Commission.

To make the area around the market pleasant, diversify its use, and help reduce congestion over the long run, a public park as large as the market itself was planned and built directly across the boulevard. It contained an artificial lake and hill, fishponds, gardens, amusement rides, and even a small zoo. The latter featured a monkey island, a relatively new concept in housing and displaying primates that commission officials planned based on their study of international zoo designs. Around the corner from the park but adjacent to it, a new cultural center was sited on a plot of some

3,000 square meters.[16] And just down the street from the cultural center was erected a new 1,800-seat public theater (see photographs).[17]

The first urban plan also included several other elements that had already been put into place by 1990, changing the visage of downtown Xinji. The part of the Andong highway which formed the city's "Main Street," on which the cultural center and the theater were located, had been widened and thoroughly redeveloped. This major undertaking involved several related projects and complex coordination among them as well as among affected units in the county and above—once again, horizontally and vertically. Enterprises and offices lining the highway had been encouraged to demolish the walls that fronted their lots, to make way for a widened roadbed and new sidewalks and curbs. Lots along the road were made available to enterprises and bureaus for new construction on the condition that they abide by regulations stipulating that the ground floor be used for commercial purposes only. Sewer lines were laid under the newly built sidewalks. The highway was repaved; since it was a state artery (*guojia ganxianlu*), the county government became involved in obtaining finances through its Transportation Bureau from prefectural and provincial superiors. The highway redevelopment also included new lighting and wired broadcast network speakers, the latter task requiring coordination with the county's Broadcasting Bureau. The commission also undertook efforts to beautify Xinji. It did some landscaping around town, occasionally accompanying its planting with iron fences fashioned in a pattern that included a deer, the county emblem. The most extraordinary example of this work was the erection at the city's main intersection of an enormous metal statue, in the heroic style, of a deer with antlered head thrust back rearing itself on its hind legs (see photographs).

Urban planning in Xinji needed to take account of the relations of the city to the countryside that surrounded it. After all, the movement of rural people into the city was a major stimulus to undertake the planning in the first place. In the Mao period, the state had pursued policy measures to prevent farmers and their families from coming to towns and cities.[18] Now that they were coming in numbers large enough to clog traffic, complicate commercial regulation, and occasion major urban planning efforts, one might have expected the Shulu authorities to fall back on historical practice by trying to shut them out again. Modern urban planning even in capitalist societies can be deployed in the service of such social control.[19] But a key principle of the physical plan for Xinji was to permit convenient access to the city by rural dwellers, an indicator of the breadth of change in the attitude of the state, and in particular the Shulu county leadership, about urban-rural flows. Thus, for example, six parking lots were included in the downtown redevelopment plan. These were needed partly because, in coordination with the Agriculture Bureau, the Xinji plan called for encouraging nearby townships to specialize in production of vegetables that farmers would bring to town and sell in proliferating vegetable markets.

And in terms of a rather different sort of urban-rural flow, industrial siting also took into account the need for clean wastewater to flow into the rural irrigation system.

Land Use Regulation

The Shulu county government's mission of protecting farmland meant that it devoted a great deal of time, energy, and resources to regulating land use in the countryside, where it dealt with farmers seeking to build private homes and with entrepreneurs and villages wishing to construct industrial and commercial buildings.[20] The bureau was active in Xinji too. No land in the city could be taken out of cultivation without the approval of the Land Management Bureau. And the Urban Construction and Environmental Protection Commission also regulated land conversions in two ways. First, it had to approve the purposes to which the land was being put, to assure its conformity with the overall urban plan. And second, it had to assure that the new buildings met its construction codes. All these requirements applied even to enterprises under the direct ownership of the central government, such as the North China Petroleum Company, which operated some wells and a refinery on the northeastern outskirts of Xinji. In all cases of land conversion, a compensation fee (*buchang fei*) of ten to twenty times the average annual value of the crops from the land in question had to be paid to the Land Management Bureau, which passed it along to the street or village committee that formally (and collectively) owned the parcel.[21] This was not a purchase, but a grant of use right for a specific period. During the bureau's first three years in operation, it granted permits for conversions of 167 hectares, which was only 1.4 percent of the agricultural land in Xinji (where most of the conversions took place). It fined offenders, including those who made deals with street- or village-level officials but did not clear them with the appropriate county bureaus.[22] It could—and occasionally did—confiscate or demolish unapproved structures. Cadres at the levels of the village or street committee and township or administrative district were prone to be more lax or flexible about land regulation in the face of potential profits from land diversions.[23] By contrast, and perhaps partly as a result, the county-level bureau was taking very seriously indeed its responsibility for regulating farmland conversion. Even Hebei Yiji, the flagship project of Xinji's urban development in the reform period, was unable to consider expansion partly because of restrictions on further conversion of farmland.

The Shulu government, through the Land Management Bureau, also tightly regulated the appropriation of farmland for housing construction in Xinji.[24] It did so by restricting private construction by individual households, and also by directly undertaking the construction of new housing. As an example of the former type of regulation, in the Ninth Street Residents' Committee, as of 1990 only eight households—2 percent of the total—were permitted to undertake improvements on their houses each year, even though many more in this wealthy community had the financial wherewithal to do so. Ninth Street families wishing to build and to make additions first had to apply to their residents' committee, but those selected by the committee still had to gain the approval of the county-level Land Management Bureau. The committee set a high "compensation fee" for land in the Ninth Street neighborhood—¥1,000 for a .013-hectare lot—because of the high value of the crops the land there could yield, the intense demand for land in this neighborhood, and no doubt also because the proceeds of all land transactions largely came back to the committee itself. For this reason, many of the Ninth Street residents lucky enough to gain permission to build were expanding their homes vertically.

The Shulu government also directly controlled housing construction in Xinji through its Real Estate Management Bureau (Fangdi Chan Guanli Ju), which had a monopoly on building done by anyone other than the occupants themselves (including enterprises). This, clearly, was a means also of preventing any possible emergence of any significant private speculation in real estate. An indicator of the expansion of housing construction activity in the reform period is that in 1985 a Housing Construction Group (Fang Jian Zu) was established to specialize in this work. It in turn was redesignated a "Real Estate Construction Company" (Fangdi Chan Kaifang Gongsi) in 1986, though this did not signify its transformation into a more commercial operation. It contracted with individuals and enterprises in Xinji to put up residential buildings.[25] It assumed the responsibility for arranging appropriate permits and coordinating work with the Planning Department (Guihua Bumen) and the Design Department (Sheji Bumen) of the Urban Construction and Environmental Protection Commission, as well as with the water, sewer, and electrical authorities. Sometimes it even helped individual buyers secure bank financing, or it loaned them money from its own accounts.[26] The company could build for any household that resided in Xinji, including those with rural household registrations—which included most of the residents of the four administrative districts and even many residents of Xinji—and even including in-migrants (liudong ren) who had only temporary permits to live in Xinji. But after several years in operation the total volume of new housing constructed by the company was still rather small: it planned to put up 30,000 square meters from 1990 to 1992, which would only increase Xinji's housing stock by 3.5 percent. This is further evidence of the tight control the county government was exercising over conversion of farmland to nonfarm purposes. Xinji was still booming in 1990, but in a closely regulated way.

Housing Market Regulation

In 1990, the greater part of housing in Xinji—500,000 square meters out of 850,000 square meters—was privately owned. This was not the result of any extensive privatization. Rather, if this figure seems high by comparison with other Chinese cities, the reason is that most of the Xinji population were formally classified as rural householders because they had been residents of Xinji People's Commune or one of the four communes on the city's periphery that had been incorporated into it as administrative districts in 1986. Like farmers throughout China, most of these people owned their own houses. Another 300,000 square meters of housing belonged to enterprises, which allocated it to their employees. Thus the county government, through its Real Estate Management Bureau, controlled only 50,000 square meters—5.9 percent of Xinji's housing. Much of this was inhabited by employees of the county government. It set the rents according to strict national guidelines that afforded only the slightest administrative discretion to the bureau.

But the county government involved itself in regulating aspects of the "markets" for housing owned by enterprises and individuals. It set binding prices for sales of enterprise housing to individuals or to other enterprises, again according to national regulations concerning the size and condition of the buildings. Sales to individuals had begun in 1987; though demand was high (since the prices were low), state regulation still kept the volume of sales small.

A more lively realm for its regulatory activities was the burgeoning private market for housing of migrants: people who came to Xinji for short- or long-term stays to engage in business or find employment in the burgeoning collective and private commercial and industrial sectors. These people needed places to live. The Real Estate Management Bureau had some space to rent them, on which it turned a modest profit. But many migrants rented space from Xinji residents, creating a market that the bureau, together with several other county government agencies, was involved in regulating. Individuals who wished to rent space in their homes to migrants had to get the bureau's approval, for which they also had to pay a small fee. The bureau regulated the rental prices in this inflating market. Enforcement was coordinated with the Industry and Commerce Management Bureau and the Public Security Bureau. To get a permit to reside and work in Xinji, migrants needed the approval of these two agencies, which in turn required them to report where they were living. This information was passed along to the Real Estate Management Bureau for its use in regulating the rents and collecting the fees.

Shulu Government in Urban Development: Roles and Relationships

In fostering the rapid development of Xinji into the premier urban center of Shijiazhuang prefecture, the Shulu county government played several roles and entered into a variety of relationships with governmental organs below and above it. As indicated in the discussion above, the county government played the role of developmentally oriented state in a number of ways. It created comprehensive plans for the urban area. It built the major public works and infrastructure projects that were envisioned in those plans, such as the Xinji ring road, the railroad underpasses, parking lots, and the greenbelt. It undertook esthetic projects such as the downtown park and the sculpture of the city's emblematic deer that, in turn, promoted urban development by making the city more commodious and prominent. Yet, as also indicated in the preceding sections, the county government simultaneously played the part of a state with a vigorous regulatory orientation in its extensive and complex work on environmental protection, land use control, and housing regulation.

In the urban development sphere, the county government's relations with its constituent units also ran a similar gamut. In disputes with authorities outside Shulu, such as the conflict with Ji county over the tannery effluents, it served as their representative. In conflicts among local governments within Shulu, such as the grievances of peasants against urban polluters, it worked as mediator. And as we have seen, it also was an avid regulator over a range of local activities, in connection with which it had to cajole (for instance, factories that had to move), coordinate (for example, among agencies keeping tabs on urban migrants), administer (for instance, rents and land use regulations), and coerce (for example, by fining and even demolishing the work of illegal builders).

All this was driven, also, by a variety of relationships between the county government and a host of higher state authorities. Hebei province and Shijiazhuang prefecture authorities had decided by the early and middle 1980's that Xinji ought to grow significantly into a center of industry and commerce—not for Shulu county alone but also for a wider region. Evidence for this comes in the plans they encouraged Shulu to make, the approval and support they gave to it to construct the Hebei Yiji Market and associated projects, the fact that they elevated the county to the status of a municipality in 1986, and the increased level of financial support for urban development that followed.[27]

Often the Shulu government found itself working on behalf of the higher levels of the state—to enforce national policies and legislation on environmental control or land use regulation, for example. Yet in most of these instances, the Shulu government acted for reasons and interests that it shared with central state authorities. And it sometimes even went beyond the expectations of its superiors. It is significant, for example, that the county government planned to exceed provincial and national guidelines in the targets it set for environmental quality.[28] Indeed, in going beyond what the center required of it, the Shulu county government showed again how some of its most creative and efficacious work in urban development was, in important ways, locally driven. The Shulu county government did not create and execute its complex program of infrastructure development, zoning, relocation of enterprises and facilities, and beautification simply or mainly as its response to higher-level directives to develop small cities. Had it been concerned mainly with having something to show the provincial or national urban development authorities, it would have committed far fewer of its own resources and been much less creative and assiduous in using them and the resources supplied from above. In this respect, then, Shulu's work shows how a county government in China can seize the initiative and how it can mobilize and allocate its resources for projects of its own conception to meet at least some needs and interests that it defines for itself. To be sure, the decision of the province and prefecture to promote urban development in Xinji was a necessary condition for all this, but it was not a sufficient one.

CHAPTER 8

The County Government in Rural Development

Having focused for the past five chapters on government, finance, industry, commerce, and urban development, it is important to recall that Shulu county has always been primarily rural, and that it remains so today and for the foreseeable future. Shulu agriculture is about average for the north China plain, as we have seen.[1] Just a few minutes of jogging or pedaling from the center of Xinji carries one into farm country. The towns and villages there are modest and indistinguishable from those in north China counties nearby whose central towns are far less industrialized than Xinji. Except for the occasional bare light bulb or television antenna, much of what is in view in rural Shulu is still distinctly premodern, including animal-drawn carts, low mud-brick dwellings without running water, and deeply rutted dirt roads and walkways. Specific urban plans call for over two-thirds of the county's population to continue to live and work in rural towns and townships such as these by the year 2000. Moreover, seven of the major Shulu government bureaus continue to be concerned exclusively with rural development. And, as we shall see, some of the most controversial and intractable problems facing the county and its government remain rural ones.

It is a commonplace conclusion, in both Chinese and Western analyses, that China's agriculture was stifled during the Mao period, and that subsequent rural reforms in the direction of the market and (semi-) privatization have led to vastly improved resource allocation, much-needed crop diversification, increased efficiency, and enlarged output. Shulu's experience conforms with much of this general assessment. Farm output and crop yields have gone up significantly since the reforms, and great progress has been made in crop diversification. Between 1978 and 1989 grain output increased 37 percent and yields grew 50 percent, for example. Cotton production increased 225 percent and yields 275 percent. Fruit production rose 70 percent and yields tripled from 1978 to 1986, and oil-bearing crop production rose thirteenfold from 1978 to 1989.

But the reason for this pattern of development in Shulu is not simply that the state has retreated, in recent years, from its former domineering stance vis-à-vis agriculture. The state in Shulu, most notably the local state in the form of the county government, undertook sizable infrastructure projects in the Mao years. In particular, in the last winter of that wintry era, it initiated and supervised the building of a massive water conservancy project that resolved very serious long-standing soil salinity problems in the southern third of Shulu, resulting in sharply increased crop yields. In the 1970's it also built an extensive network of roads that was a boon to agriculture as well as to industry, commerce, and social life. The Maoist state and its prograin, antimarket policies may have been more singularly dysfunctional for agricultural development in southern China, where, in the context of a rural (especially, rice paddy) infrastructure that had been painstakingly erected and maintained by farmers over centuries, it had less of a contribution to make at the margin through its massive mobilizations of labor power to carry out basic farmland construction drives and projects (*nongtian jiben jianshe*). But the fact that so many Western studies of rural China under the reforms have happened to focus on the south may inadvertently have caused us to underestimate the contribution that was actually made by "basic farmland construction" in the Mao period in other parts of the country, specifically in northern and inland dry-land farm areas like Shulu.

The role of the Shulu county government in rural development has varied tremendously—both quantitatively and qualitatively—over time. The most concrete indicator of quantitative variations, perhaps, would be the local state's official budgetary expenditures on agriculture (Figure 8). In the early and middle 1950's—years of land reform and cooperativization—the county government spent almost nothing on this sector of the local economy. This, however, was followed by a massive increase in allocations of county government expenditures to agriculture during the Great Leap Forward, the bulk of which almost certainly went to relief efforts. The next decade, which included a period of economic recovery and then the early political radicalism of the Cultural Revolution, found the county government spending a good deal more of its resources on agriculture than it had in the 1950's, reflecting the post-Leap readjustment of national economic development priorities away from single-minded industrialization. Even so, these appropriations to agriculture still did not amount to very much in the overall scheme of county finance. This general picture suddenly changed again between 1973 and 1979, when bud-

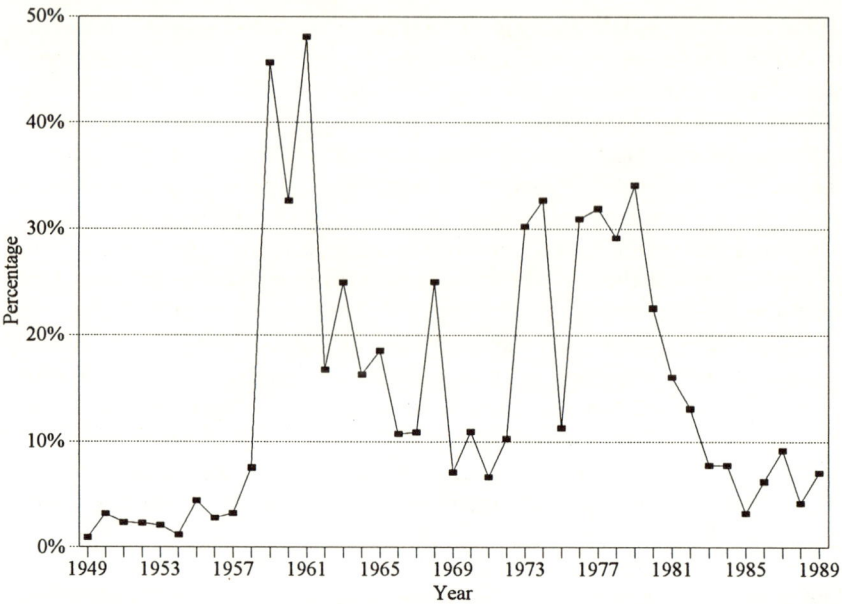

Fig. 8. Support for agriculture as percentage of budgetary expenditures, 1949–89

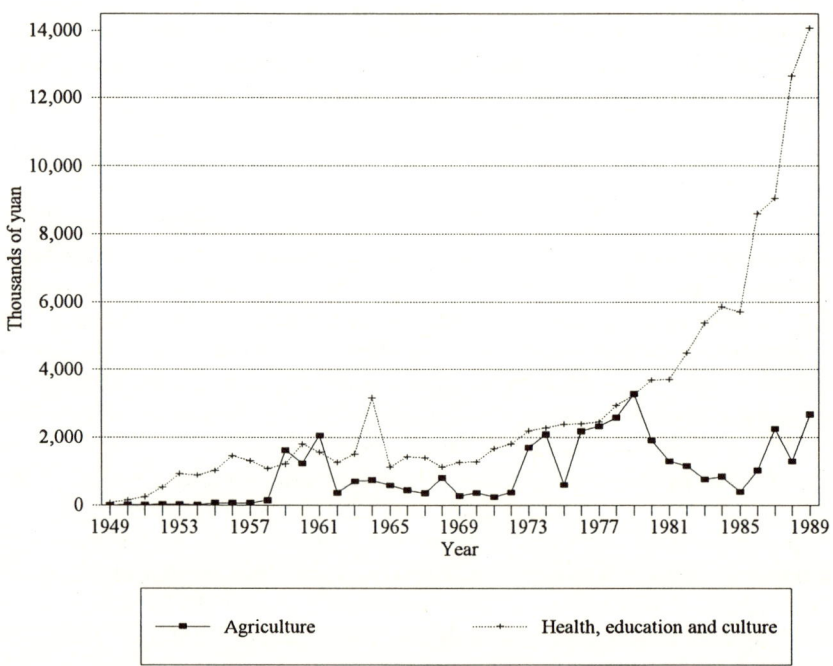

Fig. 9. Budgetary expenditures on agriculture and social welfare, 1949–89

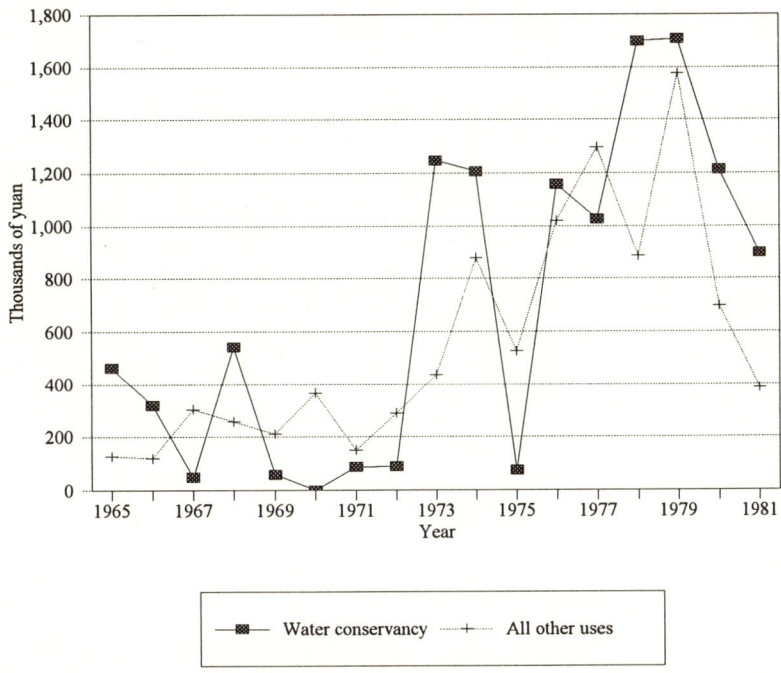

Fig. 10. Breakdown of budgetary expenditures on agriculture, 1965–81

getary expenditures for agriculture began to rival those for social welfare (that is, health, education, and culture), historically the largest spending category in the Shulu county budget (Figure 9). The bulk of these monies went to water conservancy work (Figure 10). The year 1980 ushered in yet another new period of reduced county government allocation of expenditure to agriculture. Local state appropriations in some years during the early 1980's actually returned to lows not seen since the 1960's, and to percentages of budgetary outlays not seen since the 1950's. In quantitative terms, then, these data demonstrate the marked temporal variation of the state's investment in and aid to agriculture in Shulu during the Mao period. They also illustrate the sharp drop in state spending on agriculture during the reform years, at least compared with the late Mao period. In the county government's 1986 long-term blueprint for local economic development, agriculture came last on the list of sectoral priorities, trailing both urban and rural industry.[2]

In qualitative terms, the role of the Shulu county government in economic development is both more complex and less sharply variable than this. In both the Mao and Deng periods, the local state has provided agriculture with infrastructure, offered development assistance, engaged in regulation, and carried out policy adjustment.

Infrastructure Development

During the late Mao era, the years of the county government's most active role in rural development, water conservancy took the lion's share of the budgetary expenditures for agriculture (Figure 10). Spending on water conservancy reached its all-time apex in 1978 and 1979. In the winter of 1977–78, the Shulu county government undertook its most ambitious and efficacious water conservancy project. This undertaking provides a model case study of the coordinating and developmental capabilities of a county government at the end of the Mao period. It also shows how the Shulu leadership conceptualized its developmental horizons and how the relationship of redistribution (between town and countryside as well as between rich and poor) was understood to be connected to the process of development.

THE LATE MAO ERA: THE 1978 WATER CONSERVANCY PROJECT

A large portion—42 percent—of Shulu's cultivated land lies in a historically disaster-prone region known as the Heilonggang.[3] Farmland in this region has always had lower-than-average yields. The land there is low-lying and subject to waterlogging and alkalinity. In 1976, for example, ten of the most heavily affected communes averaged grain production of 3.98 tons per hectare, while the rest of the county averaged 5.72. In 1977, the entire area of ten communes in this zone was flooded in heavy rains. There was no autumn harvest of grain or cotton whatsoever on 21,300 hectares. On the 12,700 hectares that did produce, wheat yields were down to 1.64 tons per hectare. The effect on the county's overall agricultural output was disastrous.

In the face of the crisis, in 1977 the Shulu County Revolutionary Committee took the initiative to organize a survey team to ascertain what system of canals, ditches, and other waterworks would be needed to assure adequate drainage as well as better irrigation of the area. At the same time, it held a series of conferences with representatives from the affected communes, to solicit their opinions and formulate a plan of work. It was decided to organize a very large force of workers to attack the project all at once, and to finish it in one season. In September, a delegation of fifteen cadres from the Revolutionary Committee, headed by the vice chair himself, set up headquarters in the southeastern part of the county to complete the actual planning. It was necessary for several communes to agree to straighten their boundaries so that the canals could be put through. There were some protracted negotiations between communes and brigades, mediated by county officials, over boundary changes and fair exchanges of land.

One hundred thousand people—44 percent of the county's total labor force—were mobilized to work on the project. They worked all through the winter and spring of 1977–78 to finish it.[4] The digging was done almost entirely by hand. Seventy thousand of the workers on the project came from the ten communes that would benefit directly from it. This included a total mobilization of their regular labor forces as well as approximately ten thousand people from the ten directly affected communes who were not normally part of the labor force—retirees, housewives, schoolchildren, or state employees who were not even considered formally as part of the rural population because they held urban household registrations. An additional thirty thousand workers from other communes—around one-fifth of their combined labor force—were also organized to participate on the promise that when their communes undertook capital construction work sometime in the future, the ten communes would reciprocate by sending thirty thousand of their own workers for commensurate periods of time.

The county government made a very large financial contribution to the costs of the project, including that of the labor. It paid each commune a subsidy of ¥.45 per worker per day toward the work points they were paying their members for working on this project, an amount that came to three-fourths of the value of their income. It paid for the food they consumed on the job. The county government also arranged for an exemption from Shulu's annual obligation to contribute labor to the maintenance of the Hai River project so that it could concentrate on its own water control work.

The cost of the whole project was roughly ¥5 million, which the county government put together from several sources. It in effect received ¥1.5 million on credit from various county bureaus (for transportation, machinery repairs, and so on) and from the ten southern communes (for food and food preparation). These debts had been almost completely repaid by the summer of 1979. Another ¥1 million came from higher organs of the state, presumably through the Water Conservancy Bureau. The remaining ¥2.5 million was drawn from the county's own extrabudgetary fund, making the county government itself the largest single contributor.

The canals were not lined with cement and the sluice gates were most simply constructed (see photographs). Nevertheless, the project did succeed in lowering the underground water table, and in bringing 12,700 hectares newly under irrigation while improving water control on another 18,000 hectares. Maintenance and desilting of the canals was to be carried out by the teams and brigades that bordered them, keeping down future costs for the county government.

Results were already evident as early as 1978, when grain yields on the 12,700 hectares of newly irrigated land rose to 3.73 tons per hectare (from 1.64 in 1977). By 1986 Shulu officials declared the Heilonggang problem solved. If Wangkou, Shulu's southernmost town, is any indication, they were right: its grain yields increased from 4.57 tons per hectare (70 percent of the county average) in 1978 to 7.54 (84 percent of the average) in 1986.

The project's success illustrates three important features of the developmental role the county government could play at the end of the Mao era. First, it could coordinate and finance a key local undertaking that individual bureaus or communes alone did not have the means to carry out. In this instance, it worked horizontally as well as in both vertical directions. Horizontally, it mustered contributions of ¥4,000,000 from bureaus and enterprises at the county level. Looking upward, it mobilized financial resources from one higher-level state agency and received dispensations from the county's normal obligations to another. And from the communes below it drew, organized, and subsidized the enormous phalanx of laborers who actually constructed the vast project.

Second, in undertaking this project it took the county as a whole, not just the affected area, as a field for accumulation of the needed resources, for planning and coordination of the construction, and even for assessing the benefit from it. Of course the ten flooded communes clearly did not possess sufficient resources on their own to finance such a comprehensive network of canals. Objectively, then, the decision to undertake this project was a decision to redistribute wealth generated primarily in some parts of the county economy to others. Yet county planners conceptualized the project, built in the southernmost third of its territory, in countywide terms. The initial motivation for the project, as county officials explained it, was to raise and stabilize the county's overall agricultural production. Liu Baolu, in 1979 still vice director and chief technical expert of the Shulu County Communist Party Office of Agricultural Production (but a man destined within a few years to become head of the county government), spoke of the southern region not merely as an area of poverty, but as a "drag on the rest of the county economy"—an area that did not generate its share of revenues and into which subsidies had to be sent. Thus it was not only this poor region but the county as a whole that was, in his view, a beneficiary of the project. The 1978 water conservancy project would, he predicted then, "change the face of the county."[5]

Third, mobilizing countywide resources for this project involved not only a broad geographic scope, but also a sectoral one. The county government invested sizable sums of money derived from Shulu's industry in this project. As we have seen above, half of the budgeted cost—¥2,500,000—came from the county's extrabudgetary fund, which was made up in large part of profits earned by county-run industries.[6] In addition, the county government arranged for the project to receive short-term credits from various urban enterprises for matériel and services. This is an example of how the county, as a unit of territory and governance combining sizable urban industry with agriculture, was well positioned in the Chinese administrative hierarchy to undertake such urban-to-rural transfers.

THE DENG PERIOD

The Water Conservancy Bureau's role changed with the reforms. First, it became more indirect—or, to put the matter slightly differently, its indirect activities became a proportionately larger part of its work. In 1986, it was spending some of its diminished budget on subsidizing the interest farmers were paying on loans they took from the Agriculture Bank for water conservancy investments. Second, it became more commercialized. By 1986, its well- and channel-digging teams were hiring themselves out to farmers and village committees (former production brigades) for fees high enough to turn a profit (which was used to subsidize the bureau's work). It had also founded its own (state-run, tax-exempt) fur and leather factory in April 1986; no small workshop, this enterprise employed 150 people and by the end of 1986 had turned a profit of ¥100,000 on output value of ¥1 million.

In the 1980's Shulu was facing four fundamental kinds of water conservancy problems. The first—a ubiquitous one in early reform China—was neglect of routine water conservancy activity after decollectivization. Here the solution was partial privatization: two-thirds of Shulu's wells—mainly the smaller ones—were transferred to households (usually to groups of households). In effect this was a way of shifting the burden of well maintenance and operation from the state and the collective to the farmers themselves. That probably explains much of the difficulty that accompanied the privatization of the wells.[7] Second, decollectivization also resulted in sabotage of and theft from water conservancy infrastructure. Some people were stealing stones and soil from dams. Others were stealing water by breaking through canal bunds to irrigate their own land. These problems were serious enough throughout China that a national Water Conservancy Law had to be passed in 1988 to deal with them.

Third, the costs of water conservancy were rising. Shulu derives most of its water from wells. The water table in the county as a whole was dropping, however, at a rate of about one meter per year through the late 1970's and early 1980's. This was the result of much heavier demand due to local industrialization and agricultural intensification and diversification (especially the rise of vegetable and fruit production, to which we shall turn directly). The water table had reached depths of 100 to 150 meters in northern Shulu by 1986. In 1985, expenditures on water conservancy had to rise by one-third over the previous year in order to pay for new pumps needed to pull water up from greater depths, and to advance the conservation and use of surface water in the county. By 1986 Shulu Water Conservancy Bureau officials were beginning to anticipate the day when their subterranean water—their main source—would be used up. In fact, they saw no way to increase the supply of water absent some massive state intervention such as the renewal of the abortive and environmentally risky national plan to channel water from southern China northward. Shulu officials hoped for such a project, but recognized the political, financial, and environmental obstacles to it. They also felt powerless to influence such a large decision.[8]

The only short-term solution available in Shulu was to reduce water usage, which was to be accomplished in several ways. The cost of water was going up for Shulu farmers in the 1980's, primarily because the price of oil to run the pumps and vehicles needed to carry water was rising quickly. By 1990 it cost around ¥1,000 to cultivate one hectare of wheat. Irrigation alone accounted for ¥150–300 of this cost. As a result, Shulu farmers had already come to irrigate only three to five times per crop, not seven as before. Furthermore, farmers were being encouraged by the bureau to irrigate at night, when losses due to evaporation are lower. Another approach to conservation was to expand the network of underground pipes, which also cuts down on evaporation loss. In 1986 there were 30,000 meters, and by 1990 200,000 meters, of underground irrigation pipes installed. Moreover, Shulu Water Conservancy Bureau officials placed at the top of their wish list—codified in their Eighth Five-Year Plan—the further expansion of this network to 300,000 meters. But this is a very expensive investment: in 1990 cement pipe alone cost ¥8 per meter, and plastic ¥10. In the 1980's, the state had picked up 60 to 70 percent of the cost of the pipe, with farmers paying for the rest with help in the form of loans from the Agriculture Bank.

A related effort contemplated in 1986 was the development of underground drip irrigation. The Shulu Water Conservancy Bureau officials were attracted by one type of technology developed in Israel. The system uses a series of progressively smaller pumps to place water very precisely and in very small quantities directly under the crops. The 1986 plans called for placing this system under 4,000 hectares of orchards by 1990. A 1987 experiment on 20 hectares proved it effective. But in the end the cost of ¥2,250 per hectare was prohibitive; as Shulu's Water Conservancy Bureau director Li Yunhuai said, "With the responsibility system, farmers don't want to invest this kind of money."[9] And even if they had, the credit squeeze of the late 1980's placed a major obstacle in their path.

Finally, water conservation was being pursued through restrictions on new well digging. The 1988 Water Conservancy Law stipulated that government approval had to be obtained to sink a well. The problem seemed to be a serious one locally, even though Water Conservancy officials tended to downplay it. In the first year the law was in effect, one well in seven dug by Shulu farmers was illegal. But the bureau claimed that it was powerless to enforce the new legislation in any case, because necessary local regulations had not yet been drawn up.

Shulu's fourth water conservancy problem was the new demand being placed on water supplies by rising fruit production. Orchard area had doubled between 1982 and 1990. Most of the expansion resulted from reclamation of dried-up riverbeds, whose sandy soil was well suited to the cultivation of fruit trees; the irrigation requirements of these new orchards were not offset, then, by reductions from displacement of other crops. Because fruit crops are especially high in water content and are often planted on sandy soil, they require up to twice as much water per irrigation as other crops.¹⁰ Interestingly, Shulu Orchard and Forestry Bureau officials had a much more optimistic view of Shulu's potential water supplies than did their colleagues in the Water Conservancy Bureau. Thus they had put forward only a modest proposal—to line some surface channels with cement—for dealing with the constraints that water supplies might place on their plans for doubling orchard area yet again in the near future. Orchard and Forestry Bureau officials simply argued for taking more water from under the ground in order to support the expansion of fruit growing. But the fact that only half of a 1982 plan to increase orchard land to 200,000 *mu* (13,300 hectares) could be completed by 1990 suggests that there were in fact serious local conflicts over the water supply issue and definite constraints on this very lucrative form of agricultural diversification.¹¹ Meanwhile, the rather gloomier officials at the Water Conservancy Bureau had no immediate solution to offer either. They expressed the view that the matter would have to be dealt with by economic rather than administrative means—that is, by raising the price of water or lowering the incentive to produce fruit. One example of a policy that fit this approach was the 1989 intervention by the central state in raising the forest and orchard special products tax (*lin techan shui*) rate by 300 percent. But the revenues from this levy were not specially earmarked for water conservancy; rather, in the spirit of the economic retrenchment and antimarket reversals of the day, this tax approached the problem by apparently trying to discourage orchard production in favor of grain and cotton. Still, the domestic and international markets for fruit are not likely to evaporate as quickly as the water; in June and July of 1990, despite the new tax, Shulu streets remained choked with watermelon vendors.

The conflict between diminishing water supply and expanding fruit production will, then, very likely continue. And in 1990 state agencies and leaders—in Beijing and Shulu—evinced little in the way of a constructive approach to the problem; they were contenting themselves merely with regulatory efforts. Insofar as water supply involves significant state planning, regulation, and investment, while the demand for water is subject mainly to ever-increasing pulls from the market, water conservancy problems in Shulu, as in so many other parts of the world, are likely to remain chronic. In the Deng period the Shulu county government approached the water situation as a constraint to be coped with, not, as it might have in the Mao period, as a contradiction to be tilted against and resolved.

ROADWAY CONSTRUCTION

Roads have multiple functions and significance. They are, of course, a necessary condition for economic development, a fact plainly recognized in China as elsewhere.¹² Roads also facilitate and convey power. They are often a political good that is much sought after by leaders wishing to exert control as well as by citizens wishing to expand their own economic, social, and even political horizons. Officials of the Shulu Transportation Bureau said that "farmers really began to demand roads in 1984, after the responsibility system was implemented." Indeed, one of the first public expenditures made by Wangkou, Shulu's exemplar of economic success under the reforms, as soon as it became prosperous was to invest in a network of roads connecting every one of its villages to its central town.[13] Rural people throughout the county were envious of this investment because of the opportunities it opened up for village-level enterprise development, according to Shulu officials who had to deal with their demands. Yet roads can also pose a threat to local communities because they can disrupt the economic status quo, as we shall see in Shulu's attempt to extend its highway connections to its neighbors.

As of 1970, Shulu county had only two paved roads, both of which were segments of the wider regional highway network, totaling 72 kilometers.[14] Only one ran through Xinji, and together they passed through or near only 11 of Shulu's 31 communes.[15] All the other communes were served by fair-weather roads only. Befitting the centralized-cum-self-reliant nature of the Maoist political economy, Shulu lacked connections among its rural towns. For example, there was still no road connecting Jiucheng and Xincheng, the second- and third-largest towns in Shulu (and both former capitals); traffic between them had to take a circuitous route through Xinji. It was between 1970 and 1978 that the bulk of Shulu highway construction was completed. Paved road mileage tripled to 216 kilometers. By 1980, paved roads reached into all but three communes and improved connections among them (including the key Jiucheng-Xincheng gap). Many routes were rationalized and straightened (a development probably related to the rationalization and squaring-off of fields over the 1970's). As of 1980, however, there were still 8 commune seats that could not be reached by paved roads.[16] Between 1979 and 1986, another 71 kilometers were completed. This put paved roads through at last to all township (that is, former commune) seats, while also elaborating connections between them and even among villages within them. Yet this phase of the work mainly involved completing the construction of major roadways in Shulu, a task mostly accomplished in the late Mao period.[17]

There were five types of roads in Shulu: 1) main arteries (*gan xian lu*); 2) intercounty roads; 3) oilfield connectors;[18] 4) roads to communes/townships; and 5) roads to villages. In terms of finance, the state paid in full for the main arteries and the intercounty roads, the petroleum ministry system for the oilfield connectors. Expenses to build roads to communes/townships were shared, with the higher levels of the state supplying the materials and the county and the communes/townships the labor necessary to build up the roadbed. Roads to villages were paid for by the villages themselves with, in some cases, only the most paltry of subsidies from the county government.

These conventions for financing road building had two interesting implications. First, the eight communes whose seats were not connected to the paved road network in 1978 tended to be among the poorer ones in the county; average per capita collective distributed income was ¥83.40, compared with ¥87.80 countywide. This serves as a good reminder that, despite the Mao period's vigorously redistributive thrust in theory and sometimes in practice, the importance of the self-reliance principle—which in this kind of situation dictated that the costs of infrastructure investment should be borne by the units benefiting from the improvements—often kept it from being utterly egalitarian in outcomes.

A second implication of the highway finance structure is that, with the completion of the main state roadways (nos. 1–4 above) in the Mao period, the burden of further roadway construction shifted downward in the Deng period. From 1979 to 1986, 41 of the 71 kilometers of construction were for roads to villages, which were financed almost fully by the villages themselves. The other 30 kilometers were commune/township roads, for which the state provided only partial financing by supplying materials.

In both the Mao and Deng periods, though, the county government, in particular its Transportation Bureau, played a pivotal role in planning, coordinating, and undertaking all this development. With respect to the main arteries and oil-field connectors, county bureau officials were limited to implementing plans made by higher-level authorities. And, as just explained, planning of roads to villages was left largely up to the communes/townships, who paid for their internal roads, with the county bureau supplying only very small subsidies and, for fees, supplying also the necessary construction equipment, technical assistance, and skilled workers. It was, however, over roads being built to link up with other counties and to link up its own communes/townships—that is, interestingly, in cases where they were spending monies supplied by higher levels of the state—that the Shulu authorities had some real discretion and where they also tended to become involved in some politics.

Intercounty highway planning brought Shulu county officials into direct political conflict with officials of neighboring counties and even prefectures. More than anything else, the elevation of Shulu county to the status of a municipality in 1986 signified that it was expected to become the economic center for the surrounding counties—the major central place between Shijiazhuang and Hengshui on the east-west axis and between Baoding and the Hebei provincial border to the south. Shulu economic planners regarded an expanded network of intercounty roads as one of the keys to this kind of development.[19] There were preliminary plans already drawn up that would better link Xinji into the regional road network. But Shulu officials were clearly not getting the cooperation they were going to need from adjacent counties and prefectures to proceed with these plans. By 1986, Shulu Transportation Bureau officials had approached those in five neighboring counties with their plans to build new roads that would connect with them, and they had found those local officials "unenthusiastic" about their proposals. They said, "Our first contacts suggest that the other counties don't want to build roads connecting with us, because their own central towns are far from their peripheral areas. They have their own plans. They haven't yet finished their internal roads, and they are tight for funds." Leaders of neighboring counties may also have feared that their own peripheries would be drawn into Shulu's economic orbit. The entire matter was made more complex by the fact that Shulu's plans put it into conflict with counties under the jurisdiction of other prefectures. This had the effect of raising the administrative level at which it would be necessary to attempt to iron out the apparent perceived conflict of interest that from the Shulu point of view was slowing the progress of road building in the region. These sorts of spats are the natural product of uneven development, and are becoming increasingly common in China. By 1988, none of these proposed roads had been built, even though in several cases they would have required only very small commitments by neighboring authorities to provide small connector roads of one or two kilometers linking their existing paved roadway networks with those in Shulu. Clearly, Shulu's burgeoning economic power and elevated administrative status could not yet overcome all aspects of the residual political power of its slow-lane neighbors.

Plans for the construction of internal roads to or between Shulu's communes/townships originated with the county Transportation Bureau. They required approval by the county government and then by the prefectural Transportation Bureau concerning allocation of necessary finances and materials. This is another example of the coordination of horizontal and vertical flows of authority and resources that needs to take place to make things happen at the county level. The county government undoubtedly took on several different political roles here: balancing and mediating the demands of its constituent communes/townships for roads, while also playing advocate for county interests in the prefectural competition for roadway funds and the scarce trained teams of surveyors, heavy machinery, and other inputs needed for construction. Bureau officials too played the political game: they said quite bluntly that they used their periodic reports to their own prefecture-level superiors to build cases for upcoming requests for funds and materials.

Two themes emerge from this part of the discussion, then. First, highway construction involved Shulu county government in a variegated set of political and administrative relationships both vertical and horizontal, internal and external. Its Transportation Bureau served as instrument and local coordinator in a vertical bureaucratic system when it carried out prefectural and provincial authorities' regional projects in Shulu. Yet it also had horizontal external relationships that cast it as an advocate in direct negotiations with other counties. And on local projects it acted as advocate (to gain resources from higher-level authorities) and as planner, mediator, and arbitrator (among competing requests from its communes/townships). Moreover, it often had to coordinate work and funding from diverse sources, including the Ministry of Petroleum Production, higher levels of the Transportation Ministry, and local authorities in communes/townships and villages.

Second, as with water conservancy, the late Mao period was a time when the state, including the Shulu county government, expended considerable resources to develop infrastructure that made rapid commerce-based economic growth in the reform period possible. This work was largely complete by 1978. Over the following decade, the missing pieces of the local transportation network laid down previously were put into place. Some attention was also turned to the filigree work of expanding village-level road building, though with an intensity of activity that pales by comparison with that of the 1970's. Moreover, these newer local webs were paid for locally, not by the state. Thus, in just one example, when county government leaders point to Wangkou as the greatest success story of the 1980's, and when they as well as local people cite completion of the paved road to this remotest of Shulu towns as a necessary and important condition of the local economic miracle, they are really saying that in the most literal sense the spadework of the 1980's was done in the 1970's.

Rural Industrialization

Rural industry was a very significant part of Shulu's economy by the late Mao years. In 1978, 1,261 commune- and brigade-run enterprises turned out 28 percent of the county's GVIO and an astonishing 81 percent of the total output value of the communes and brigades.[20] Table 27 documents aspects of its even more extraordinary growth in the reform period.

TABLE 27
Development of Town and Township Industries, 1980–89

Year	Enterprises	Employees	Gross receipts (thousands of yuan)	Taxes paid (thousands of yuan)
1980	854	17,650	49,600	
1981	819	16,475	51,140	
1982	730	16,533	54,380	
1983	612	16,506	61,660	3,570
1984	6,265	32,478	128,000	8,090
1985	6,076	42,133	202,380	12,350
1986	6,532	45,464	286,810	13,460
1987	7,671	52,273	434,760	15,470
1988	8,505	54,810	620,920	15,890
1989	8,744	56,067	726,820	13,750

TABLE 28
Gross Value of Output (GVO), Profits, and Profit Rate
of County and Rural Industry, 1979–89

Year	GVO (thousands of yuan)		Profits (thousands of yuan)		Profit rate (profits/GVO)	
	County industry	Rural industry	County industry	Rural industry	County industry	Rural industry
1979	136,441	51,040	21,361	25,050	15.7%	49.1%
1980	146,225	53,080	19,979		13.7	
1981	139,335	53,480	16,925		12.1	
1982	144,022	56,820	14,665		10.2	
1983	146,740	60,950	14,526	15,990	9.9	26.2
1984	158,548	144,600	15,865	36,610	10.0	25.3
1985	168,296	242,100	19,430	51,000	11.5	21.1
1986	217,340	353,080	21,586	64,670	9.9	18.3
1987	255,450	509,390	23,956	65,370	9.4	12.8
1988	329,980	720,700	32,298	49,320	9.8	6.8
1989	352,790	800,250	33,281	84,610	9.4	10.6

By 1985, rural industry surpassed county-run industry in gross value of output, and it has never looked back. As Table 28 shows, it earned more profits in every year since 1979 for which we have data, and its profit rate (profits/GVO) has been higher—sometimes dramatically so—in every year but one.

As elsewhere in China, in Shulu the county government cannot claim a great deal of direct credit for this achievement. Much of this impressive record in both the Mao and Deng periods is the result of centuries-old traditions of handicrafts, sideline production, and entrepreneurship, a favorable location along major transport arteries and within reasonable proximity to major urban centers, and the effort and imagination of local working people and managers.[21] Still, the state did play valuable roles both directly and indirectly. The network of roadways and the large market, Hebei Yiji,[22] it constructed are examples of the latter, as we have seen. Meanwhile, the local state did also make some direct efforts to promote rural industry.

The Township Industries Bureau was the county government agency concerned exclusively with rural industry. The bureau's activities ranged widely, and specifically included promotion, organizational development, ownership restructuring, economic planning, training, auditing, regulation, and information gathering. It helped townships to establish for-profit companies to rationalize and professionalize their purchasing operations, a practice that it had learned from its study of rural industry in Wenzhou and Suzhou, which have been national centers of rural industrial development. It also operated eight enterprises of its own.[23]

The most impressive venture of the Township Industries Bureau was its work in 1989 with the Eighth Street Residents' Committee in Xinji to create a "collective" barium salts factory that would go into direct competition with the flagship Xinji Chemical Factory. The county government had sought to expand barium salts production at Xinji Chemical. But, according to Qi Fachuan, the Township Industries Bureau director, "since the factory is state-run [*guoying*], the management was too timid."[24] So he and the Eighth Street leadership decided to jump into the breach. The bureau put together the financing from as variegated a set of institutions as the Shulu Agriculture Bank (formally responsible for credit to collective industry, which was generally rural, though not in this case), the Hebei Foreign Trade Bureau (which would handle the exports), the Hebei Electrical Power Bureau and the Bohai Petroleum Company (both in all likelihood providers of key inputs), and the Shulu Township Industries Bureau and the Eighth Street people themselves. Retired Xinji Chemical workers who had taken jobs in barium salts plants in Hubei and Hunan were found and lured back home by higher wages. The Eighth Street plant was so profitable that it was projected in its second year of operation to make back almost three-fourths of its investment by year's end. Xinji Chemical sent up howls of protest to the Hebei Chemical Industry Bureau, questioning the quality of Eighth Street's barium salts. But the bureau's inspection team found no problem at Eighth Street, and closed the matter with a public statement calling for collaboration between the competitors. Bureaucratic and political obstacles, including the hurt pride of Xinji Chemical's director, prevented this. But the big factory did respond to Eighth Street's challenge by increasing its productive capacity 25 percent, which could make it soon the world's largest producer. For his part, Director Qi was happy about this outcome: the new firm he had helped to form was highly profitable, yet he could still point to the salutary effects on Xinji Chemical and on the Shulu labor force (which got back skilled workers) in order to protect himself from criticism, common in China in 1990, that collective industries were harming the state-owned industrial core.

In the sphere of planning, the Township Industries Bureau identified communities with the strongest potential for rural industrial development, which in turn qualified them to receive certain material benefits. It also chose eight townships to become industrial development districts,[25] using several criteria for selection: a record of "rational and concentrated [*jizhong*]" industrial development, sufficient supply of water and electricity, and good access to transportation routes.[26] It also was committed to the goal of locating these districts fairly evenly over various parts of the county.[27] Selected communities and units received preference in the distribution of electricity in times of shortage, consideration for foreign investment, expedited conversion of land to industrial purposes, and priority in bank credit. The bureau was consulted by the Agriculture Bank when the latter was reviewing loan applications from rural industries, so the bureau's priorities were important. Choosing to emphasize or deemphasize particular productive sectors—an activity often referred to in Western discussions of developmental state activity as "picking winners and losers"—

was another way for the Township Industries Bureau to influence the fates of rural industries.

It had at its disposal various means to encourage would-be winners or discourage those it thought to be losers. Any enterprise wishing to make an investment in excess of ¥500,000 needed the approval of the bureau and the Rural Industry Leadership Task Force,[28] based on a feasibility study conducted by the bureau concerning the economic efficacy of the proposed investment.[29] It had been instrumental in arranging to have the Wangkou Appliance Factory selected by the provincial government for "raising the level of management [*tiji guanli*]," for example.[30] The bureau had been of assistance in arranging loans totaling some ¥20 million to help selected rural enterprises acquire energy and raw materials between 1984 and 1986. It was also in a position to discourage banks and input suppliers from cooperating with particular firms, which had already resulted in the closure of between forty and fifty firms in difficulty during the late 1980's. So the Township Industries Bureau could indeed wield the power of life and death over rural firms.

In making its choices of communities or sectors, it sometimes applied national criteria on sectoral development of rural industry. In 1990 the center was calling for the discouragement of sectors experiencing economic or operating difficulties. The Shulu bureau obliged by deemphasizing spinning factories, which were experiencing shortages of raw materials as Shulu farmers cut back on cotton production (discussed below), and oil refineries (whose products were of substandard quality). But the Township Industries Bureau could also use its own priorities even if they contravened central ones. For example, in 1990, a period of nationwide economic austerity and consolidation of rural industry, the Bureau was emphasizing its support for firms engaged in the production of chemicals, on the basis of Shulu's historical development and continuing comparative advantage, even though this sector was not to be given priority according to higher levels. In other cases it found ways to stretch central policies and priorities to fit its own goals. For instance, in 1990 it was able to support the stumbling fur and leather industry locally by stretching a definition, interpreting this industry as falling under the center's emphasis on foodstuffs.

The bureau also had developed some ideas for the structural reform of Shulu's rural industry. It had attempted to help rural industrial enterprises convert to share ownership, which complemented its efforts to help those enterprises procure financing. This was a complex affair that involved the bureau in the tasks of asset valuation, issuance and distribution of shares (by sale, to workers, and transfer, to township governments), establishment of shareholders' committees, and establishment of regulations on profit distribution. Its ambitious 1986 plan to convert one-third of Shulu's rural enterprises to share ownership had run aground by 1990, mainly because the county government ultimately decided that the shift in ownership was too dramatic and nettlesome for it to confront.[31] Before the retrenchment of 1989, however, the bureau had certainly been thinking big.

These grand (and, in Shulu, abortive) projects aside, the Township Industries Bureau also busied itself with a host of more humdrum but nonetheless potentially significant activities. It collected statistics on and audited the books of rural enterprises, to be used in overall planning and in identifying the moving target of leading and losing sectors. It became involved in regulatory work, setting up a task force jointly with the Urban Construction and Environmental Protection Commission and the Statistics Bureau to investigate environmental problems caused by rural industries, which are widely known to be among China's worst polluters. It also ran a network of training centers at the county and township levels. There rural industrial managers could study accounting, statistics, management, and quality control, free of charge. This bureau, then, had its hand in just about all activities related to the ongoing development of rural industries in Shulu.

Three main points about its activities deserve to be emphasized. First, like many other organs of the county government, the Shulu Township Industries Bureau worked a complex nexus of vertical and horizontal relationships. Horizontally, it advised the Agriculture Bank on loan decisions, and worked closely with the rural industry task force and other specialized governmental task forces (such as the one investigating pollution by rural industries). Vertically, looking upward, it was an advocate for Shulu industry with the provincial authorities. And looking downward, it had a close working relationship with township governments, vetting applications for new investments and paying the salaries of township government rural industry officials.

Second, this county bureau played a variety of substantive roles, running the gamut from attempting to improve the liveliness of local business, to dealing with the challenges of organizational and economic restructuring and planning, to managing the political complexities and maneuvering involved in administrative coordination and bureaucratic advocacy, to taking responsibility for the important routines of regulation, training, and financial and statistical investigation and record keeping.

Third, the Township Industries Bureau clearly balanced its many local responsibilities with a definite measure of political caution and orientation to the policies of the central state. Bureau Director Qi described and justified his efforts in helping the Eighth Street Barium Salts Plant get off the ground in other terms than would have fit the kind of voracious entrepreneurship that sometimes characterizes officials in other, more economically freewheeling counties.[32] He spoke of the beneficial effects that competition with the new plant had on Shulu's flagship state-run chemical plant, forcing it both to expand and to become more efficient. In 1990 he was full of talk of the need for rural industry to consolidate, prune back, and increase production quality—all major themes in national economic policy of the day. He eagerly pushed upon us copies of recent state council regulations on rural industry, and (unlike most of his colleagues working in the Shulu county government) even showed an amazing facility in iterating for us sloganlike catchphrases pertaining to rural industry, such as "Since 1989, there is an 8-character directive: *tiaozheng, zhengdun, gaizao, tigao* [adjust, consolidate, transform, lift up]."[33] Director Qi was able to explain in mind-numbing specificity just how this new policy slogan would be put into effect in Shulu. For this reason, he and the bureau he directed provided good illustrations of the ways in which Shulu county government leaders managed the sometimes difficult task of combining close attention to state priorities with their own developmental impulses.

Orchard and Forestry Development

Fruit production is Shulu's most important form of agricultural diversification. Tianjin pears cultivated in the county have received national awards from the Ministry of Agriculture, and were the first to be exported from China. Shulu also produces peaches (historically of such quality as to have been judged suitable for sending as tribute to the Empress Dowager), apples, dates, apricots, grapes, and plums. Fruit production has also, therefore, grown into a very significant part of Shulu agriculture in recent years, producing ¥30 million in gross output value—9 percent of total GVAO—in 1989. What has the role of the county government been in this area of development?

The county's record defies the commonplace generalization that agricultural policy during the late Mao period universally deemphasized and led to a decline of nongrain production. Figure 11 shows that fruit production roughly doubled over the decade starting 1970, and also that this occurred with no significant increase in orchard area. This pattern of growth based on rising yields (Figure 12)—which, interestingly, also was the way that grain production registered its increases in this same period—undoubtedly involved the application of new technical inputs and training for farmers.[34] Both of these could in those days only have been provided by the state through the county government, though the historical record runs too thin to permit discussion of the specifics.

Under the reforms, fruit production grew at double the rate that it had in the previous decade (see Figure 11). But this was due as much to extensive growth (in orchard area) as to crop intensification: since the late 1970's fruit yields per unit of land increased at about the same rate that they had in the preceding ten years (see Figure 12). The extension of orchard area was the result of specific policies undertaken by the Shulu county government. In 1982 and 1983, under the leadership of county head Qian Anle, it set a goal of .4 hectares of orchard for every twelve Shulu residents. The policy also stipulated that this increase was to be

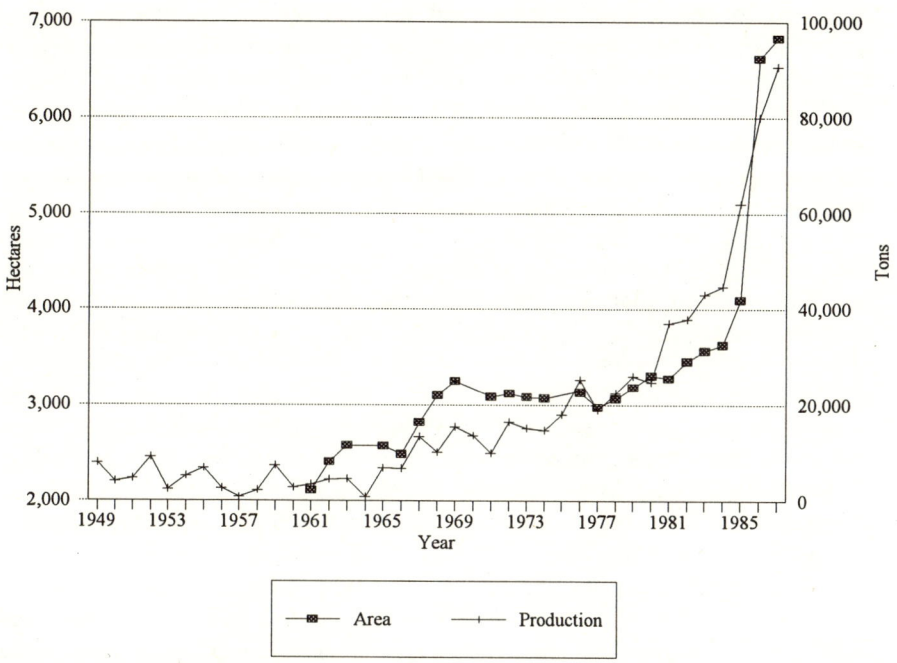

Fig. 11. Fruit area and production, 1949–87

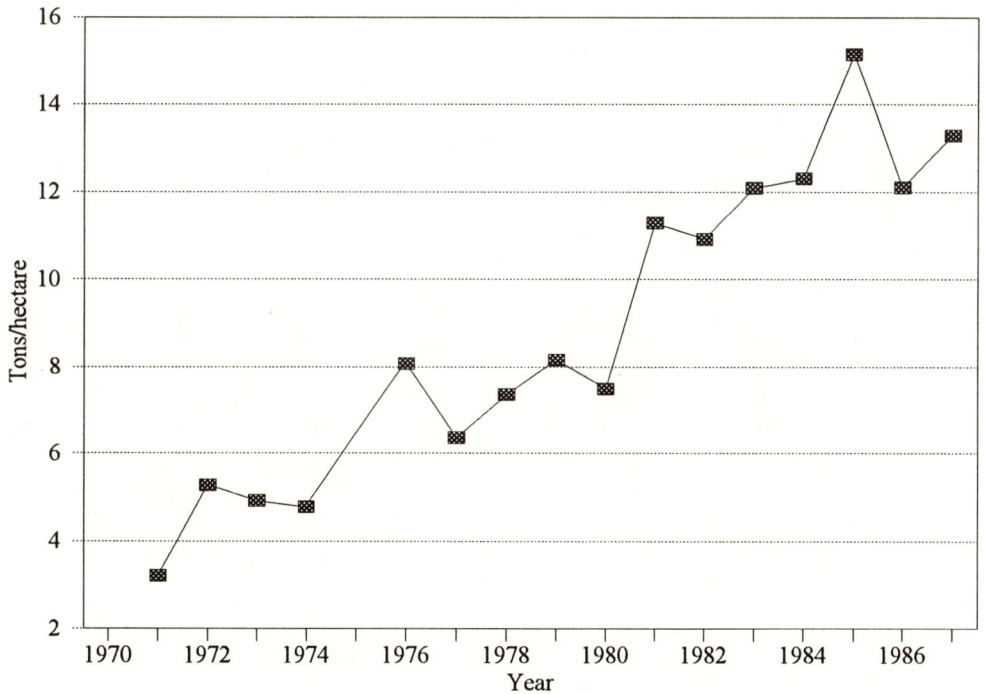

Fig. 12. Fruit yields, 1970–87

achieved by reclaiming unused land such as former beds of rivers that had changed course, where the sandy soil is well suited to growing fruit. It was specifically forbidden to displace existing crops with fruit. This, in the event, appears to have made it impossible to realize the goal for orchard expansion, only half of which had been achieved by 1990. Even so, the increase in lucrative fruit production and agricultural diversification achieved by this county government policy remained impressive.

Like the Township Industries Bureau, the Shulu Forestry Bureau, which had responsibility for orchard production and development, engaged in strategic planning by concentrating its efforts on specific localities. Its criteria in the 1980's were: availability of land that could be reclaimed for fruit production; the relative skill level of the local people in fruit raising; and the existence of sandy soil and sufficient water. Of the seven areas that it chose, only two were also selected by the Township Industries Bureau as centers of rural industrial development.[35] According to Township Industries Bureau officials, this was no accident; they claimed that lucrative fruit production possibilities tend to undercut the incentive for farmers to develop rural industries. And unlike the selection of the industrial centers, these could not be chosen with geographic distribution as a leading criterion. Rather, because of the natural and geologic requirements, the seven sites selected formed contiguous tracts in two zones: one in east central Shulu, and the other toward the southwest. The Forestry Bureau gave these selected localities preferential distribution and pricing of fertilizers, pesticides, and equipment needed in fruit production.

But the Bureau also serviced other towns and townships that were not specializing in fruit. In the late 1980's it was allocated ¥90,000 per year through the county budget for expenditure on technical extension work related to fruit. It also occasionally received special allocations from the provincial or central levels of the Forestry Ministry for renovation of underperforming orchards. It was the specific policy of the Forestry Bureau to help places that were lagging in their fruit production. It also permanently stationed technical specialists from its own staff in twelve towns and townships, only three of which were fruit production keypoints.[36]

Yet there were limits to the bureau's work. Though officials crowed about the selection of their Tianjin pears as the premier export of this variety, and though in the bureau's technical work it was emphasizing the expansion of export-quality production, its leading officials did not make any efforts to persuade the Foreign Trade Bureau to purchase more fruit. They said, rather, that this was the responsibility of the farmers. Their reticence may also have reflected the realization that the Shulu Foreign Trade Bureau was tightly constrained, in terms both of the quantities it might purchase and the prices it might offer, by the centralized character of the foreign trade system (*xitong*). In fact, there can be little doubt that production for the growing, sometimes superheated, and less quality-conscious domestic market suited both the Forestry Bureau and individual fruit growers better than the deals that could be offered by the Foreign Trade Bureau cadres. Interestingly, however, in 1990 the bureau had no clear plans for the future development of fruit production; bureau officials tended to speak instead of incremental growth at most. This, in all likelihood, was the result of their having been stung by the overly ambitious 1982–83 plan, and of the material limitations in expanding fruit production in their land-short, water-short county. It was probably also a consequence of the politically influenced economic priorities of 1990, which called for reemphasis on production of basic grain crops and cotton.[37]

The Responsibility System

The uniform timing of the adoption of the household responsibility system in the winter of 1982–83 by every Shulu commune, and the fact that as of 1990 two rather different communes (Jiucheng and Wangkou) where we talked with officials had complex but identical contracting systems, suggests the operation of strong central political pressure on and through the county government in the process of decollectivizing agriculture. Yet even here the Shulu authorities had some room for maneuver in bringing this reformist policy from the drawing boards to reality. They used this latitude in order to make necessary adjustments and emendations to the policy in the context of shifting political and economic situations.

When farmland was first contracted out to households in the winter of 1982–83, concern by commune officials and farmers that the land be divided equally resulted in each household signing contracts for multiple and often widely separated pieces of land—on average, as many as seven or eight.[38] This not only wasted farmers' time and energy but also complicated the contracting and the record keeping associated with it, since a contract was made up for each parcel. Resolution of this problem called for action by the Communist Party's Rural Work Department. It organized the establishment of a land readjustment small group (tiaozheng tudi xiaozu) in each village. Each of these assessed the quality of various household-sized parcels of the village's land, and set the procurement quotas accordingly. Then these assessments were submitted to the farmers for their approval. The final step was the assignment of the parcels to households by lottery. The Shulu Communist Party Rural Work Department claimed the credit for formulating this method, though it had submitted the plan to the county Party Committee for final approval before implementing it at the grass roots.

Another example concerned orchard contracts. When orchards were first contracted in Shulu, there was relatively little interest in them because fruit prices were low. Thus the contract fees were also set low. But soon fruit prices rose, and those who had signed contracts for orchards for the low fees were receiving a windfall of sorts. Protests began to be heard from other farmers. Here too the Party Rural Work Department took the lead in working out a revised contracting system, coordinating closely with the Forestry Bureau, on whom it relied for much of the substantive detail involved.

A new triple-tiered structure of contracting was worked out. First, 60 to 70 percent of Shulu's orchards were contracted out to individual households (*fenhu chengbao*) for ten-year terms. The terms were so lengthy partly because the farmers had confidence in the long-term strength of fruit prices, and partly because annual rewriting of so many contracts—most households took some orchard land—would have been too burdensome. The second form—contracting to specialized teams (*zhuanyedui chengbao*)—was tailored to 5 percent of orchards located in villages that were relatively prosperous, where fruit growing was not the most significant or lucrative economic activity, where population density on land was relatively high, and where per-capita fruit area was low.[39] In these places, there was not enough orchard to go around; if distributed under *fenhu chengbao* each household would get too little. Moreover, there were some other attractive economic opportunities in these places. So the farmers there were relatively content to have specialized teams work the orchards. These contracts ran for only one year, because the contractors, who specialized completely in fruit production, did want to minimize their risk in case of fruit crop failure due, for example, to insect infestations or hail. Third, the remaining 25 to 35 percent of Shulu's orchards was let out to groups of associated households (*lianhu chengbao*). Because these contractors were also engaged in other agricultural pursuits, they were willing to take longer contracts of four to five years. The contracts were let out through competitive bidding.

Officials of the Forestry Bureau and the Party Rural Work Department claimed that this contracting system was popular and successful. They attributed to it the absence of any sabotage to contracted orchards, as has occurred elsewhere in China when disgruntled farmers took revenge against neighbors who managed to gain unfair advantage in winning contracts to cultivate, for private gain, orchard land that had been developed through collective labor over many years. While we cannot be sure how Shulu farmers feel about the contracting system, the economic indicators of rapidly expanding fruit production are certainly consistent with the county government and Party leaders' assertions. But even if for some reason those claims are fatuous or misleading, what emerges from this case is a clear illustration of the complex role the county-level leadership had to play, and the room for maneuver it had to have, in putting into place general policies of the state.

The land contracting systems in use in the various towns and townships around Shulu have actually been through many changes since contracting began there in the winter of 1982–83. In Wangkou *zhen*, for example, all farmland was re-collected by some *cun* (villages) and then redistributed again to households. The criteria for redistribution varied somewhat from *cun* to *cun*. But the point of this elaborate exercise was to make adjustments in allotments in accord with changes in household size and labor patterns that had occurred in the intervening years. This referred not only to births, deaths, and physical infirmities, but to the fact that many more Wangkou people were beginning to work full-time in local industries, and they either could not or did not wish to give as much time as before to farming the land. In Jiucheng *zhen*, a different method had been devised to deal with a similar situation requiring frequent readjustments in land allotments to families. A way was found to have *both* fifteen-year fixed responsibility contracts to households *and* a *cun*-by-*cun* flexible land reallotment every three years. Each household was guaranteed a certain plot of land that would remain assigned to it for fifteen years. But each *cun* also maintained a number of "movable plots" (*jidong tian*) that it could assign as needed on the basis of a regular triennial review of land allotments in the *cun*. If a household's size increased over the three-year period, it kept its original parcel and was assigned more land from the *cun*'s "movable plots." If household size went down, it kept its original assigned parcel of land but was required to sell more grain to the state. The county government plainly had approved quite a variety of flexible farmland contracting systems over the years to take account of highly specific and variable conditions in the Shulu countryside.

Contracting to households had become the norm in the 1980's. But not even this was held to be sacred. "Because farmers could see that contracting to households was not rational where mechanization was advanced," contracting to groups (*zu*) was also common in the county.[40] The Shulu county government even had the capacity to permit (or at least tolerate) failure to implement the household responsibility system altogether. In 1979, the relatively industrialized Ninth Street Production Brigade, part of the Xinji Commune, was practicing brigade-level accounting. In this first year of the reform effort, they could still say:

> We answered the call of Zhou Enlai and Chairman Mao to learn from Dazhai. We met all six criteria set down for moving to brigade-level accounting. We will never retreat from it. Yes, we did have a mass discussion of the Xiangxiang and Suzhou experiences [of rural reform]. But the masses didn't agree to move backward. The experience of these places is not suitable to all brigades.[41]

In the event, brigade accounting was no longer an issue after the 1984 conversion of communes into *xiang*. But as of 1990, that former brigade had not divided up and contracted out its land to households because, its leaders asserted, "with about 27 *ha*. and 400 households," doing so would have made it impossible to use Ninth Street's valuable stock of agricultural machinery.[42] Nonetheless, in a move that would have caused Dazhai leader and brigade-accounting advocate Chen Yonggui to roll over in his grave, sowing and harvesting had been contracted out to groups of households, some from within Ninth Street but some also from Linzili village in the neighboring Chengdong urban administrative district. These groups provided labor and farm management, and Ninth Street the machinery. By that time, Ninth Street residents themselves were primarily employed in small industry and in commerce, and would not have found it easy to take off time to do the sowing and the reaping of their residential unit's crops. The Shulu government had played no apparent active role in promoting or preserving this unusual contracting system, but the phenomenon is worth noting because it shows that, at a minimum, county authorities had the latitude to permit this unorthodoxy to persist through a decade of the reformist juggernaut.

Regulation of the Political Economy

The rapidly expanding Shulu economy placed great pressure on scarce natural resources, threatened to derail some wider economic priorities of the state, and created new social problems. Much of the energy of the Shulu county government in its countryside was taken up with regulation of political and economic activity to deal with these matters.

LAND USE

One arena of profound concern in Shulu's development was the issue of land use.[43] In 1990 rural courtyard and village walls all over the county were covered with red-lettered exhortations to protect scarce, precious farmland from encroachment by commercial and residential development. The county government did far more than paint slogans, though. In March 1987, two months after the promulgation of a national land law, it established a Land Management Bureau, by joining the land sections (*tudi gu*) of the Agriculture Bureau and the Urban Construction and Environmental Protection Commission and then almost doubling the size of their combined personnel (from twelve to twenty-two people). Among this new county government bureau's first tasks was the completion of a comprehensive survey of land use in Shulu.

When this was completed, it established detailed procedures to regulate residential conversion of farmland. Farmers wishing to construct new housing needed to apply to their villagers' committee (*cunmin weiyanhui*); after discussion there, the approval of the township government and then the county Land Management Bureau were required before the latter would issue a building permit. The bureau balanced the availability of land in the village in question against the age composition of the families applying to decide whether and how many could be approved at a given time; preference was given to families with two children over the age of sixteen and to those into which a bride had recently married. The bureau also decided whether to require that new housing be constructed on existing housing sites or on new ones. Finally, it enforced provincial guidelines concerning the allowable size of residential lots.[44] Fees for residential land conversion, set by the village-level organs (which retained formal ownership rights to the land) were generally low, but they were rising: in Xinji, people of the Ninth Street Residential Committee had to pay ¥1,000 for a 134-square-meter plot. Moreover, in 1987 the Finance Bureau had begun levying a land occupation tax (*gengdi zhanyong shui*) of ¥2.5 per square meter as a one-time lump sum.[45] The Land Management Bureau levied penalties against those involved in illegal land conversions, ranging in severity from fines of ¥500 to demolition of the unauthorized building. Bureau officials maintained that violations had been a serious problem until 1987, but that the passage of the national land law, the subsequent establishment of the bureau, and its regulatory vigilance had been effective in curbing offenses and abuses. They also admitted, however, that violations were continuing in 1990, with the most serious problems clustering in the more prosperous villages.

The Land Management Bureau also issued building permits for conversion of agricultural land to use by rural industries. Its consideration of the land-use implications of new rural enterprise construction was built into the process by which the Township Industries Bureau and the Economic Planning Commission evaluated the economic feasibility of the project, rather than constituting a separate bureaucratic step. Moreover, if the Land Management Bureau had any reservations about allocating land to an enterprise its fellow county government organs wished to approve, special meetings would be held, attended by representatives of these two bureaus as well as by representatives of the Economic Planning Commission, the Science Committee, and the relevant banks. The consultative nature of this process provides another example of the often complex horizontal coordination that routinely went on among agencies of the county government.

The Land Management Bureau brought to bear on its evaluation of applications for new or expanded enterprises the generally very tight constraints on converting farmland to nonagricultural uses that were embodied in the national land law and directly relevant to the land shortage that Shulu faced. Moreover, the Finance Bureau levied its land occupation tax on enterprises at double the residential rate: ¥5 per square meter. Village- and township-level firms had found a way around these constraints, by renting directly from farmers land contracted for agricultural production. The fees paid exceeded the taxes the farmer had to pay for the land plus the cost of purchasing on the market the commodities the farmer was responsible for turning over to the state as the quota for using the land. Township officials said that this system preempted the need for enterprises to gain the approval of the county government to expand. It also reduced the large outlay required if the enterprise were to purchase a piece of land and pay the land occupation tax; by simply renting the land on an annual basis, they could gain needed flexibility in China's fast-changing rural economy, while also reducing their start-up costs. That the township officials who described this were themselves Communist Party members, and that they did so in the presence of their county-level bureaucratic superiors, indicates that the Shulu county government and Communist Party did not, in 1990 anyway, view the practice as untoward. This violation of the spirit of the national land law in turn suggests a certain willingness on the part of county-level Party and state officials (at least where rural industry and local economic expansion were concerned) to be lax about even their own official responsibilities.

HOUSEHOLD REGISTRATION

Still in effect in 1990 was the household registration (*hukou*) system, according to which every Chinese was assigned a formal status as a rural or nonrural householder. In the Mao period, this classification scheme had been used to prevent farmers from moving to towns and cities, where they would put pressure on relatively scarce employment opportunities and even scarcer housing and other urban amenities. This system was effective in keeping rural people on the farms but, in industrializing localities like Shulu, it had put constraints on needed expansion of the urban labor force. In the Mao years the temporary contract labor system had provided a way out of this dilemma.[46] This system, predicated on the existence of rural collectives, however, became even more of an impediment to the processes of economic development that were hastened with the reforms. Farmers began to move to town in significant numbers. Even though they were still kept out of employment in county-run industry by specific state labor policies, the Shulu county government actually facilitated their movement into Xinji, while also working to find ways to cope with the influx, and while maintaining strict controls on the numbers of people permitted to change their *hukou* classification from rural to urban (*nong zhuan fei*).[47] The government orchestrated the construction of the Hebei Yiji Market, for example, in which at least some of these rural people could purchase properties in a planned residential/commercial community that reduced and organized their pressure on urban space and facilities. It also created a real estate exchange office within the Shulu Real Estate Management Bureau to assist in-migrants in finding housing space to rent.[48] According to provincially approved urban development plans for Xinji, large numbers of people with rural household registrations were going to continue to be permitted to move into Xinji in the years to come. Shulu government officials gave every evidence of being both institutionally well prepared and psychologically braced for the administrative and regulatory challenges that would be entailed. They were determined to keep a grip, through regulatory vigilance, on the social welfare, public security, and other potentially adverse consequences of urban migration.

CROPPING

Cropping policy—the control over what farmers plant—was one of the most tightly monitored and centralized areas of state policy in the Mao period. Communes all over the country were expected to conform to national policies of food grain "self-reliance" and "taking grain as the key link." In Shulu, the county government had little latitude over cropping patterns. It closely regulated farmers' behavior in order to fulfill the responsibilities with which the Hebei provincial government had charged the county, so that the province's own responsibilities to the center could be met. In doing so, the county government often issued similar instructions to all the communes under its purview. For example, the grain multiple cropping index in three rather different communes increased at an almost identical rate between 1965 and 1971, the years when "taking grain as the key link" was emphasized.[49] Moreover, in this period and the subsequent one of 1972–78 those three communes all achieved growth in the same way. Specifically, from 1965 to 1971 they all increased their grain production by increasing the sown area of grain. And in 1972–78, they all followed a uniform strategy once again, this time raising grain yields rather than grain sown area. This latter feat was accomplished largely through very similar rates of increase in the use of chemical fertilizer, a state-controlled input, a fact that suggests the operation of a uniform, perhaps rigid, yet probably quite evenhanded county government policy in distributing this scarce input.[50]

In the reform period, the county government was less involved than in preceding years in cropping policy. With the change to the responsibility system, the state's needs for a particular pattern of cropping were reflected and implemented through stipulations in land contracts. The county government simply divided up the quotas it received from Shijiazhuang prefecture and Hebei province among its constituent townships. They in turn built their crop delivery quotas into the contracts. The county did have some latitude over the distribution of its quota responsibilities among townships. For example, in 1990 grain production levels throughout the county, and particularly in the previously troubled south, had risen sufficiently to allow some central townships, with the county's blessing, to exploit somewhat their comparative advantage in vegetable production. Yet the county government's room for maneuver in responding to such economic forces was very limited. In 1990, for instance, when the state was feeling the pinch of farmers' evasion or nonfulfillment of contracts in the form of a cotton production target shortfall, the Shulu government was obliged by higher levels to impose mandatory *area* (not delivery) quotas on farmers in the course of signing local contracts. This was the first time sown area quotas had been imposed for any crop since the Mao years.

But if the Shulu county government used mainly political pressure (in the Mao period) and mainly administrative control (over contract-writing under the reforms) to achieve state cropping policy goals, it also had some material incentives at its disposal. Of course a county government is not in a position to manipulate prices and taxes. These are economic levers reserved primarily for the central government and, to a lesser extent, the provincial government. Lacking these powerful economic instruments, county governments could still offer economic inducements by selectively providing farm support services. These might include agricultural research and extension; and provision of seed, fertilizer, agrochemicals, diesel oil, irrigation, information, credit, machinery, and repair services. Strong and well-coordinated farm support services could result in substantial improvements in farm productivity. Conversely, weak and poorly coordinated services would have a negative impact on production.

In the reform period, the inability of households all over China to provide such services for themselves has raised the demand for them. This enhances the county government's ability to influence farmers' behavior by selectively supplying such services. For instance, by the late 1980's the shortage of chemical fertilizer had become the keenest concern of many farmers throughout the country. In 1987 there were over 10,000 incidents in which state warehouses of chemical fertilizer were looted.[51] In the same year, the national government instituted an incentive policy called "three linkages," in which advance sales of high-grade chemical fertilizer were a part of the rewards granted to those farmers who signed contracts to deliver selected crops to the state.[52] The linkage programs, however, were administered by local governments. Because the national government usually could not guarantee an adequate supply of chemical fertilizer, it asked local governments for supplements either through local production or through purchases from outside suppliers. Local governments were thus in a good position to manage linkage programs in a way most beneficial to local interests, rather than to the center. In Shulu, Communist Party Secretary Bai Runzhang and Mayor Liu Baolu, the latter a former chief agricultural official in the county, frankly acknowledged that the selective provision of farm supply service was a powerful weapon for implementing their plan: "To get farmers to go along with our cropping plans, we first rely upon propaganda. Then we offer them low-priced seeds, fertilizer, and so on, to make it in their own interest to go along with these plans."[53] The County Forestry Bureau, for instance, provided technical personnel assistance and material inputs to its selected keypoint townships for fruit production. In distributing such inputs as fertilizer, pesticides, and mechanical equipment, the bureau not only gave priority to those townships, but also charged concessionary prices. Likewise, the Water Conservancy Bureau could use differential prices of water, the banks and credit unions could give priority in loans for a particular kind of development, and so on. So local government's control of backward linkages of agricultural production remained a potentially effective means of regulation.

Even though the Shulu county government generally deployed the tools at its disposal in the service of the goals of higher levels of the state, it did have some room for maneuver to affect cropping patterns in accord with local interests as it defined them. By 1990 some townships in the central region of Shulu (such as Junqi) were replacing cotton with chives, a favorite vegetable in north China that brought very high prices because it was in demand not only in local markets but also as far away as Beijing, Tianjin, and even Heilongjiang. To compensate for the loss of cotton area, in 1990—the same year that mandatory cotton area targets were reimposed by the center—the county government reduced cotton area targets of chive-growing townships and imposed the differential on others in southern Shulu. It assured southern local leaders and farmers who were unhappy about growing this labor-intensive, risky, and unprofitable crop that it would make sure they got the supplies of fertilizer and pesticides they needed, on preferential terms, if necessary. In permitting, if not encouraging, a high-yield area to abandon some of its cotton fields and forcing lower-yield areas to make up the difference, the Shulu government could meet the letter of the center's new mandatory cropping policy while also pursuing local comparative advantage. And if cotton yields in the south were lower than in places like Junqi, which the county government had permitted to reduce their cotton area, the county economy would not suffer, since it did not have the same stake in cotton production as Beijing did. In short, the administrative flexibility the county government had at its disposal even at a time of very intrusive central leadership permitted it to undercut the central state's objectives while fulfilling the letter of its mandated policies.

Another Shulu case also points toward a politics in which the intermediate governments—in this case at the township level—were pursuing interests different from the central government's on cotton, even as they carried out directives from Beijing. In 1990, the county government increased cotton area quotas for many townships due to pressures from the center. Instead of displacing other crops, some townships decided to meet the higher quotas by intercropping cotton with wheat.[54] In Shulu, cotton is usually planted in April and harvested in October. To intercrop cotton with wheat, it has to be planted in late May or early June, and harvested before the wheat. The result was very low cotton yield and increased labor for both crops. But farmers were happy, because net income was much higher on a unit of land with wheat and cotton intercropped than with wheat alone or cotton alone.[55] And the county government was happy because it could report to the provincial government that it fulfilled its cotton sown-area targets, and also because the intercropping increased the amount of grain available to meet the needs of the burgeoning urban market in Xinji. But Beijing's express desire to increase cotton production was undermined.

Shulu Government in Rural Development: Roles and Relationships Before and After Reform

Several interesting observations about the Shulu county government emerge from this examination of its role in rural development. First, in both the Mao and Deng periods, it has not operated only as a mere arm of the higher state authorities. Of course, it has busied itself with extraction, regulation, and policy implementation. But in both periods it has also engaged in a wide and significant range of projects it initiated, involving significant developmental planning and administration. The 1977–78 water conservancy project, its road-building efforts, and its plans to expand fruit production are the major ones. To be sure, the orientation of these projects changed over time. In the late Mao years, the county government's major developmental efforts focused on basic infrastructure, while in the reform years they concentrated on production itself. Yet the Mao period's attention to the development of infrastructure was a necessary condition for and a significant contributor to the reform period's successes in raising production.

In both periods the county government has been closely involved in regulating and shaping the rural economy. Any theory that the Chinese rural economy has been less subject to the will of the state in the Deng period cannot find support in Shulu. It is true that the modalities of state intervention have been supplemented. Economic levers are now available to the county government, though, as we will explore more fully in a moment, they are more limited than is sometimes thought. And as we have just pointed out, new substantive goals (such as crop diversification and increased profitability) have appeared. But many of the Mao period priorities and developmental orientations persist as well. In 1990 the Shulu county government was once again enforcing quotas for cotton planting (not just production), a return to the cropping control methods of the Mao years. It was closely regulating the development of rural enterprises. And it was carefully guarding and restricting access to nonrural household registrations.

This combination of new policy activities and approaches with the persistence of older ones meant that the Shulu county government was engaged in a wide variety of tasks. The very multiplicity of its purposes inevitably produced disagreement and conflict among the various agencies involved in a particular project. For example, the Water Conservancy and Forestry bureaus disagreed over the key question of how serious Shulu's groundwater resource problem was at present and into the future. In many cases, the skilled leadership of county government managed to coordinate relatively smoothly the complexities it faced and the disagreements they generated. In others, undoubtedly, it did not.

This raises a final point, concerning one of the major obstacles facing the county government. If the reforms opened up new substantive issues and provided new levers with which to deal with them, they also provided new constraints and sharpened and brought into the open new contradictions. In particular, the county government found itself working right at the face of the many contradictions between state planning and market reform. Ambitious plans to expand fruit production were made in the early 1980's by a Shulu leadership seeking to respond to the new economic and developmental thrust of the Deng period that was dawning; but they soon had to be scaled back as they ran up against the continuing demands of the state for protecting and expanding grain and cotton production. The Forestry Bureau, with its eye on the lucrative fruit market, sought to draw far more water from the ground beneath Shulu than did the Water Conservancy Bureau, which was more oriented to the responsibility of the state to provide water and protect supplies over the long term. Problems like these will tax heavily even the most capable local leaderships.

CHAPTER 9

Conclusion: Moving Structures and Changing Demeanors of the Local State

Many of our good working theories of the contemporary Chinese state and of state-society relations in China since 1949 have been underpinned by the theorists' perceptions of a sharp polarity between the upper levels of government and the grass roots. On the one hand, much recent research in the West has focused on elites and institutions in Beijing and provincial capitals. On the other hand, a number of other fine studies of very low-level units—of rural villages and, to a lesser extent, of factories, neighborhoods, schools, enterprises, and other professional and work units—have also lately proliferated. Available theories of the state in China, therefore, have tended to reflect the long stretch between these very distant points. Most scholars and writers conceptualize a potent and commanding centralized Party-state busily dividing and organizing society into tiny communities and units, over which it is capable of ruling in multifarious ways.[1] Some analysts, by contrast, have chosen to focus more on the capacities of ordinary people and of their local leaders to find small but significant ways to resist, to constrain, and even to put pressure on the center.[2]

Much has been learned from these sorts of studies and from the theoretical debates they have sparked. Yet, while there may be great drama and potential heroism to be chronicled in the struggle between a Gulliver and the Lilliputians, there is also something ultimately quite limiting and dissatisfying about a general theory of the state that conceptualizes it as a behemoth with a head and feet but no body. And there is something confining also about a theory of economic development and of state-society relations that pits the very top against the very bottom. Can a satisfactory explanation for China's specific patterns of economic development and social change be fashioned only with knowledge about high-level policy and politics plus grass-roots activity?

Of course the nature of the Chinese state, of state-society relations, and of political life in China are all necessarily affected by what goes on in the vast middle ground between Beijing and the bottom. Most Chinese government leaders and officials serve in subcentral organs. Likewise, most ordinary Chinese citizens never confront the center or central authority directly; for them, the state is a township or county office, a factory or city agency, or simply an individual official. The rare occasions when center and citizens have met in recent Chinese history have primarily been moments of state crisis. The state center more routinely keeps society at several removes; the provincial party and state apparatuses and the county and municipal institutions below them form at least two thick layers of insulation. At the same time, the elaborated hierarchy of vertically structured government ministries and functional bureaus works in tandem with the horizontally delineated administrative jurisdictions to buffer interactions between citizens and local leaders on the one hand and central authorities on the other.

In the wider field of comparative politics, the best theoretical work on the state, its developmental roles, and its relations with society has been more textured. Researchers working on other polities have delved into the complex structural tensions within the state itself: tensions between localities and the center, tensions among different segments of the bureaucracy, and tensions between bureaucratic segments and politicians. They have explored the dynamics of political conflicts among leaders with different inclinations and ideologies, along with the mechanisms that have linked these politicians to their publics. There is a vast body of scholarship on the intricate intermediations between state and society, from the angles of political institutions (for example, pluralism, corporatism), political sociology (for example, class, race, gender), and cultural studies (for example, hegemony theory). Such conflicts within the state, and the intermediations between state and society, have certainly been more difficult to study in China than in many other countries. This difficulty flows from the opacity of the state system itself, as well as from the dearth of meaningful institutions of civil society in contemporary China. Nevertheless, in recent years scholars have taken up the challenge.

As it became clear that the reforms were transferring a good deal of political and economic power downward through the system, decentralization became a subject of much fruitful research. As a result, substantial progress has been made recently in filling in the blanks between the head and the feet on our sketches of the Chinese polity. Brisk bargaining and patterns of lively bureaucratic politics between central and provincial authorities, and between governments and enterprises, have been brought to light.³ Studies of bureaucratic politics in China have revealed some important limitations on the power of the central government and the party in carrying out routine business, not to mention reform. At the same time, as reformist thrusts in the direction of bureaucratic decentralization have been traced backward by scholars to their roots in China's earlier political history, it has forced a new appreciation of the Mao period's legacies and their salience for the present. Substantial continuities in the underlying givens of Mao- and Deng-period politics have been uncovered and widely acknowledged.⁴ The findings of such studies have also informed some ambitious new theories of the workings of China's reformist political economy, as well as some astute diagnoses of its shortcomings where efficiency and macroeconomic balance are concerned.⁵ Finally, some of this new work has begun to fathom the crisis of the Chinese state and to ruminate, sometimes darkly, about the future of the world's largest nation.⁶

Signaling its success as well as its limitations, this new scholarship has run up against two obstacles to further development. The units on which analysis has focused remain, for the most part, extremely lofty ones. Though the terms "local" and "decentralization" abound in this literature, the intended reference is most often to the provincial level. Provinces in China are not in fact localities at all, but administrative units of gargantuan size. Eight Chinese provinces have populations roughly as large as or larger than France. Provincial governments wield enormous power over the administrative units arrayed beneath them: the prefectures, municipalities, counties, towns, townships, and villages. Our fieldwork has taught us that officials working at the county level often do not make any distinction in ordinary speech between the province and the center, referring instead to an undifferentiated authority they call "the higher levels" (*shangji*). And they frequently use the term "the center" (*zhongyang*) when what they really mean is their provincial leadership. The county in China, historically, has been the strongest and most coherent subprovincial administrative unit. It is, further, the lowest level of unalloyed state organization, the foundation of China's national government. If a theory of the Chinese state and an understanding of Chinese political economy demand a grasp of the patterns of contestation and cooperation between the center and the provinces, all the more then do they require an appreciation of the likewise contention-prone yet often collaborative relationships between China's counties and the enterprises, townships, and villages below them, as well as a knowledge of the relationships of counties with the prefectures and the provinces above.

Thus a second and an analytically prior problem with the literature available to us at present is that the formal institutions, the routines, and the processes of government at the intermediate levels of the Chinese state remain basically unexplored through first-hand research and investigation. Even the burgeoning literature on center-province relations has proceeded in the absence of systematic study of Chinese provincial government. The only major work in English on county government was published thirty years ago, on the basis not of field research (which was almost impossible at the time) but of interviews in Hong Kong with just one informant.[7]

It is our hope to have made here a contribution to the development of a more suitably textured theory of the Chinese state, of state-society relations, and of political and economic development in China by refocusing analytical attention toward the most basic level of Chinese state organization, and by explicating the institutional and substantive terrain on which politics within the state and between state and society take place there. We have sought to do so in a dynamic rather than cross-sectional way. Our study spans the last decade of the Mao era as well as the first decade of the Deng period. Our work, therefore, has something to say about the development of the county government over a period of time in which Chinese political economy undertook a major change of course in its trajectory of development. We hope to have specified some of the many palpable and significant changes that took place then, as well as underlying similarities and continuities with the earlier period.

The Moving Structures of County Government

The Shulu county government grew considerably over the period under study, and especially after 1978, in terms of all the relevant absolute indicators: number of personnel on the state payroll, number of offices, size of administrative budget, and so on. There are several theories about Chinese political economy that would explain such a development: self-serving activity by government officials,[8] financial decentralization,[9] other sorts of administrative decentralization (for instance, over material allocation, or the proliferation of local "ownership"),[10] decollectivization,[11] and the general development of the local economy.[12] Our findings tend toward the last of these explanations. We have argued that the rapid growth of the local state in Shulu after 1978 was a fairly direct result of the reforms and of the attendant spiraling demands of administering, regulating, and planning a swiftly growing economy and a society that was increasingly on the move. The work of the county government was becoming more detailed, intense, specialized, and technically sophisticated and demanding. Yet the stimulus that this provided to growth in the size of the county government was not excessive. In Shulu, while the size of the local state apparatus about doubled over the period from 1978 to 1989, the local economy that apparatus was charged with administering was growing to somewhere between four and five times its original size.[13] Thus, while we do not wish to take issue with any of the possible explanations listed above for administrative growth under the Chinese reforms, it did appear to us that the one chalking up administrative growth to bureaucratic self-interest did not fit our evidence well. After all, a self-indulgent bureaucracy might well have been expected to expand itself at a rate more proportional to, or in fact faster than, economic growth. Moreover, as noted in Chapter 3, the Shulu county government showed none of the trappings of luxurious consumption that are seen in some other counties experiencing rapidly increasing prosperity.

In the decades on both sides of the 1978 divide, the county government had a complex structure of vertical and horizontal lines of organization and authority, reflecting the same kind of warp and woof that characterized the wider state in which the county government was enmeshed. Most of the agencies of the county government were oriented both vertically and horizontally, though in many cases one or the other of these orientations was predominant. This pattern of organization created formidable tasks of bureaucratic coordination, consultation, and authorization with which county officials perforce grappled on a daily basis. But such a crisscrossed pattern of local state organization also afforded county government leaders opportunities for financial, administrative and programmatic flexibility as well as for executive creativity. This was demonstrated in the cases of the 1977–78 water conservancy project, the building of Hebei Yiji, and the development of the larger urban plan of which the Hebei Yiji market was part. Whether a particular county government sinks under the weight of reconciling the vertical and horizontal lines of organization and authority that comprise its bailiwick, or rises to the challenge of energizing and utilizing them, depends on many factors. These include its financial resources and constraints, the institutional and political latitude afforded it by higher-level authorities, and the skill of its leadership.[14] In both the 1970's and 1980's, Shulu county possessed sufficient favorable conditions, especially the political ones, to make some creative use of its local concatenation of vertical and horizontal structures, pressures, and demands.

The complexity of the intersecting vertical and horizontal gridwork of county government should not be confused, then, with bureaucratic rigidity or gridlock. In fact, we were repeatedly struck with the flexibility, and even sometimes the utterly ad hoc manner, with which bureaucratic processes and procedures might be changed, either to conform to changing routines at higher levels of the state apparatus or to accommodate local needs and interests. We also noted many bureaucratic adaptations that evolved in order to cope with the strictures of the system in place, especially during the Mao period. These had tended, by 1979, to produce something of a maze of special administrative relationships and understandings within county administration. Most of the bureaucratic reforms of the 1980's aimed to install greater comprehensiveness and professionalism in the routines of local state administration, and to a certain extent these aims were being realized in Shulu. But the 1980's remained a period of markedly ad hoc maneuvering in state administrative affairs. Tough bargaining, special petitioning, stopgap measures, and flying by the seat of the pants were all plainly in evidence in the daily administrative affairs of the Shulu county government.

Equally intricate were the structures of socialist ownership and organization prevailing in Shulu. Critiques of state socialism often cite its tendency to be excessively monolithic on this score. Perhaps that is why we have considered it so important to stress here our general finding that Shulu industry was comprised of a dizzyingly variegated set of ownership, financial, and planning relationships. These relationships included some forms of organization that were centralized in the conventional state socialist way, but also some that were more decentralized and horizontally coordinated at the level of the county government.

The coexistence within Shulu's industrial structure of centralized and decentralized and vertical and horizontal forms of ownership, organization, and administration formed salutary conditions for certain kinds of developmental activity by the county government. It provided county government leaders with the administrative and financial capacity to undertake some key local development initiatives. It also provided the basis for the county government to assist in promoting the growth of new enterprises in both urban and rural areas, as well as in the county-run and rural collective sectors. It made it possible, furthermore, for county officials to collaborate with enterprise managers to rescue and expand existing operations undergoing the stresses or responding to the new opportunities that have each come with the recent economic reforms.

At the same time, the complex gridwork of responsibility in which county government offices themselves were enmeshed also provided the trellis of administration along which the county maintained its relationships with the political-administrative organs below and above it. As for subcounty institutions, the county government was called upon to serve at various times as their representative and advocate, their mediator, their regulator, and their development planner. In its relations with higher levels of the state, particularly with the province, the county government obviously most often found itself working locally on their behalf and constrained locally by the structural and policy parameters those higher levels had set. In many respects, constraints like these could potentially frustrate development in Shulu. The Mao period's strenuous emphasis on agricultural development and its unrelenting antipathy to commercial development could not but have hurt a county like Shulu, for example, whose historical comparative advantage—indeed, its modicum of celebrity and renown—lay precisely in its commerce and industry. The opportunity costs of pursuing the Maoist development model in Shulu must, in many ways, have been painful to pay. Yet even within such generally detrimental central policy parameters as those prevailing during the Mao period, the county's leadership did prove able to identify and build upon elements that suited or could be made to suit local conditions and that provided some benefits for local development. Thus Shulu government leaders found a way to make the overall Maoist priority on agriculture help the county's development by conceiving and undertaking a large and complex water conservancy project that eliminated a long-standing drag on the county economy. At a time when so many eyes are trained on China's commercially and industrially dynamic new south, it is also worth recalling that the Maoist approach to development, whose shortcomings are now quite generally known, could nevertheless have contained some elements that proved constructive in specific conditions. The benefits of basic farmland construction to agriculture in northern and eastern China could provide us with many such examples. But, as the Shulu case suggests, actually being able to generate such benefits locally during the Mao period may have required also that there be a local leadership capable of seeing and seizing opportunities within what was a generally unfavorable national political and policy environment.

Moreover, it was not only in the Mao period that Shulu leaders found central policies not completely to their liking. Shulu, after all, was a relatively high achiever under the rules of the old Mao-era game. The changes in those rules, which came so quickly in the 1980's, inevitably represented a potential threat to Shulu. The county was not so much hurt by reform as it was not positioned well to take maximum advantage quickly of the new opportunities and new structures it presented. Other areas and localities had more to gain more quickly than a place like Shulu. Therefore, while Shulu leaders definitely welcomed the economic growth that the return of private commerce brought to the county by reform, they were also plainly suspicious of its tendency to promote economic inequality, to disrupt urban orderliness, and to undermine the viability of county-level commercial enterprises. In the Hebei Yiji Market they found a tangible, even grandiose way to reconcile the center's goal of encouraging private commerce—a goal they partially shared—with their own interests in promoting urban planning, in closely regulating and taxing private merchants, and even in assuring orderly street traffic. Such mundane but important tasks of local governance were facilitated by the construction of an organized and easily monitored shopping center.

This sort of selective, sometimes creative adaptation aside, the Shulu county government frequently related to higher levels of the state in several other ways that revealed its penchant for regulation, local development, and local protection. It was, for example, capable of reinterpreting higher-level policies and instructions for purposes of its own: purposes that sometimes differed from the ones intended by those above.[15] Sometimes, as in the matter of pollution control standards, it found the expectations of higher levels not so much detrimental as inadequate to the challenges posed by its relatively advanced and environmentally threatening industrial base. In this case the local state proved capable of going beyond regulatory standards emanating from the center. At still other times it could undertake detailed regulatory actions that contravened the spirit of central policy but were not specifically forbidden by it.[16]

But the interests of local state leaders are not always inimical or hostile to central goals and guidelines, and the Shulu leadership did not always find higher-level policies and decisions distasteful or detrimental to the county's interests. Hebei provincial authorities, so it seemed, had long tended to look upon Shulu with some favor and with trust. (If this had not been the case, we surely would not have been permitted to begin our early research there in the summer of 1979.) In the 1980's, Hebei province officials specifically identified Shulu as a leader in its prefecture: a place slated to grow faster than its neighboring communities into a regional center of industry and commerce. Although never showered with the very mixed blessings of being selected as a political "model," Shulu county had clearly benefited over the years from a generally attentive and understanding attitude on the part of prefectural and provincial bureaucratic superiors. Even when it was not being singled out for special treatment, it might still be positioned to benefit from numerous and sundry higher state policies.

Demeanors of the Local State

The Shulu county government played a number of roles. One of the most noticeable and important of these, in both the late Mao and the Deng periods, was the one we have associated here with the theory of the developmental state. As used in the literature on East Asian capitalist development, this concept refers to a state that dynamically helps to create the political and infrastructural conditions for economic growth by, among other means, carrying out strategic planning, protecting and nurturing key sectors of the economy (and weeding out losing ones), facilitating accumulation and investment, coping with cyclical movements in the domestic and international economies, regulating markets (including in particular the labor market), coordinating relations among enterprises, and promoting both general education and technical research and development.[17] Though the theory of the developmental state is grounded firmly within the capitalist economy, and therefore cannot be applied without some serious caveats to the workings of state socialist systems, it nevertheless does display some strong resonances with the activities of the Shulu government's role vis-à-vis its local economy, both before and after 1978.[18] Many of the activities of the Shulu county government are, after all, similar to those in which capitalist developmental states engage. Moreover, implicit in our developmental state concept is the notion that the state itself does not seek to make profits, but rather to create the conditions for enterprises to do so.[19] This specification also conforms generally to what we were able to learn about the situation in Shulu after 1978, when the pursuit of profits reemerged for the first time since the 1940's as a major force in the Shulu political economy.

In reflecting on the county government's many developmental roles, we must never lose sight of the fact that Shulu's economy was and largely remains organized on the principles of state socialism. What we believe this study has shown, then, is that even in a state socialist economy, an intermediate level of government such as a county can adopt a certain posture of distance from the specific enterprises and administrative organs within its purview—that is, it can confine itself to creating the conditions for them to engage in the productive, the entrepreneurial, and, in the 1980's, the profit-seeking activities that actually create economic growth, rather than directly taking up productive, entrepreneurial, and profit-seeking activities itself.

In the 1970's, the Shulu county government was engaged in a range of activities to promote enterprises' development and thus the development of the local economy. It provided technical assistance to its constituent communes and acted as liaison between them and prefecture and province agencies, to help commune enterprises develop new product lines or expand existing ones and then to broaden their sales. The county government promoted export production, which often required significant product upgrading and subsequent quality-control regulation. It provided a staff of buying agents, sales representatives, and commercial expediters to help local industries acquire inputs and move output—activities that are sometimes erroneously thought to have disappeared entirely during the Mao period.[20] The Shulu government also found ways to expand the urban industrial labor force at a time when stringent central policies barring the movement of farmers to cities were in force. It helped operate the Xinji Middle School, where technical specialists received their initial training. Most prominently, the Shulu county government engaged in some massive, essential, and effective infrastructure development, including the construction of extensive road networks and water conservancy projects.

In the 1980's, it continued to engage in many of these activities while taking up new ones.[21] Liaison work between rural industries and provincial industrial and foreign-trade authorities was expanded. Highly detailed, carefully researched, and technically sophisticated urban development plans were made and began to be implemented. Related to this, a large-scale program of market development and rationalization was undertaken, including both the construction of a sizable shopping center and residential condominiums (Hebei Yiji) and the re-siting of several private markets into specialized shopping zones. The county government collected and published up-to-date market information. It regulated competition for export contracts with an eye toward solving the problem, newly presented by the marketizing reforms, of local firms' undercutting each other on price to the benefit of foreign buyers. It promoted barter trade with the USSR, and developed investment and commerce in the internationally oriented Shenzhen Special Economic Zone. It made plans that identified key sectors and localities for specific types of development, coordinating with the banks to secure necessary credit. It tried to promote local agricultural specialization even within the confines of renewed stringent central control over cropping patterns and ever-tighter farm input constraints. It even supported the resuscitation of traditional special products and local delicacies, the production and marketing of which had atrophied amid all the turmoil, distractions, regulations, and restructurings that had been visited upon the county in the twentieth century.

In doing all this, the Shulu county government had quite strictly resisted crossing the line from a state apparatus oriented mainly toward a developmental role to one oriented mainly toward an entrepreneurial role. The latter concept refers to government activity designed to make profits for itself—to what in another lexicon is called state capitalism.[22] The Shulu county government built Hebei Yiji entirely on a nonprofit basis, even though it could easily have done otherwise. We found no evidence of county government administrative agencies using their political position or their economic resources to establish enterprises mainly to make profits, as we did in Guanghan county (Sichuan) where we conducted similar research.[23] For example, by the mid-1980's the Guanghan Rural Credit Cooperative Association had formed a dummy company through which to funnel the investment of rural deposits (to which it had access by virtue of its administrative function) into a downtown convention center and hotel development venture. In Shulu we found nothing of this kind. Instead, in the mid-1980's, a period of national economic boom, the Shulu government was focusing its attention on public works rather than on the kinds of state entrepreneurialism that were leading to economic overheating in many parts of China. To be sure, we have noted how some of the county government's agencies did establish small, potentially profit-making workshops. But increasing profits per se was patently not a major goal of these workshops' productive activities. Rather, the motives, both characteristic of the Mao period, included a desire to employ retired workers or family members of workers, thereby reducing the drain on the agencies' own resources caused by their responsibility to support these people; or, as a result of the tight and poorly developed market conditions in the reform period, a need to produce inputs and consumption goods that were not otherwise readily or affordably available. In loyal accord with bureaucratic-administrative reforms being carried out across the country in the 1980's, Shulu county did, on the surface anyway, reorganize several of its administrative bureaus and offices into "companies" (gongsi); yet the profit-making activities that such a name change would imply were scarcely detectable in their work. These offices may have put new nameplates on their doors, but they by and large continued to behave as before, handling the public business of the county and not going into business for themselves.

Contrary, then, to one prevalent perspective that emphasizes the dazzling disjuncture in political and economic philosophy that took place in China around 1978, the developmental orientation of local state activity forms a major continuity in the economic role of the Shulu county government during the last decade of the Mao period and the first decade of reform. Moreover, in acting in a developmentally oriented way, and in eschewing state entrepreneurialism, the Shulu county government conformed to some key principles of socialist reform as it has been articulated, if not always observed, under Deng Xiaoping. Government in Shulu, at least as late as 1990, was still true to the demand of the reformist leadership that it stay out of actual production, and that it respect the law of value by allowing, even fostering, the development of markets. This developmental orientation of state activity, where the state stays above the competitive fray while working to keep that fray vibrant, fits comfortably within a paradigm of "market socialism" or "planned commodity economy," a model now thought by many observers of Eastern Europe to belong on the scrap heap of history. In Shulu, anyway, the developmentally oriented local state activity we observed in the reformist 1980's strongly resembled, and even seemed to have originated in, the kinds of planning and resource mobilization that the county government undertook in the Mao period.[24]

If there has been continuity in the general developmental orientation of the Shulu county government, there has also been, not unexpectedly, more discontinuity in the means it has deployed to promote development. The 1970's saw the Shulu county government engaged primarily in bureaucratic command planning. In the 1980's, this aspect of the county government's work diminished somewhat, as state material allocation and production planning became circumscribed and greater scope was accorded to contracts rather than commands and to markets rather than plans. But shrinkage in the county's command planning roles and functions was more than offset by expansion and elaboration of its regulatory work vis-à-vis the burgeoning economy. Thus, for example, the Industry and Commerce Management Bureau found itself in the business of monitoring price movements and making sure that growing numbers of private merchants did not charge more than the posted maximum prices. In another key move to regulate private commerce, small merchants were forbidden by the local state to engage in wholesale trade after their activities began competing with the business of the county's collectively organized supply and marketing co-ops. Not all regulatory initiatives in the commercial sphere were entirely effective. The challenge was often in the chase. Bureau leaders were well aware of the fact, for example, that private merchants tended chronically to underreport their volume of sales in order to reduce their taxes.

A more affluent rural economy had also involved the Shulu county government in the expanded and more complex arenas of regulating both land use and rural industries, in the service of which missions it deployed a host of levers such as licensing, inspection, taxation, and financial penalties. In like manner, the desire of Shulu farmers to cash in on rising market prices for fruits placed new demands on the regulatory powers of the county Water Conservancy Bureau, an agency that had previously busied itself mainly with planning and construction. Devising and enforcing regulations to maintain the county's commitment to environmental protection became more pressing, complex, and difficult. Even rent control had become an issue. The rapidly growing burden of local state regulation was reflected, as suggested earlier, in a significant expansion in the size of the county government bureaucracy during the 1980's.

The developmental plus regulatory orientation of state activity characteristic of the Shulu county government represents a pathway in contemporary China's changing political economy quite distinct from the entrepreneurial orientation of local state activities found widely in the southern and coastal regions during the reform period. At a time when Westerners and Chinese have, understandably, evinced so much fascination with the rapid growth and change in those hyperdynamic areas, our study reminds us that there may be large parts of the country still operating with rather dissimilar inclinations and horizons. The reasons for this differentiation cannot be established with much certainty in the absence of more information about the inner workings of the Shulu government than we could uncover even in a research project spanning some fifteen years; and a mapping of the possible contours of such a pattern elsewhere in China must await investigations of many other localities. But our study does begin to suggest possible explanations for the Shulu government's developmental orientation during the 1980's, explanations that can be tested against data from other local case studies.

One obvious factor is Shulu's location. On the one hand, being in China's north and off the coast, it has not been readily subject to the entrepreneurial lures and pressures of international capital. On the other hand, Shulu's location on trunk railway and road lines, and along important commercial pathways, has been favorable to economic development.[25]

Another ingredient is the strong legacy of the county government's developmentalism in the Mao period. There was considerable continuity in the ranks of Shulu's leadership between the 1970's and the 1980's. Liu Baolu, who was the liveliest and, to our minds, most knowledgeable, forthright, and capable official we met on our first visit to Shulu in 1979, and who had worked his way up through the ranks during the 1960's and 1970's, was elevated to head the county government soon afterward to lead it through the early reforms. This same continuity of leadership prevailed in many of the bureaus whose work we studied. Many of the men and women of the Shulu government of the 1980's were people who married enthusiastic support for rapid economic development through loosening the planning and control mechanisms of the Mao period with a residual concern about the dangers of unbridled marketization for quality of urban life, the environment, employment, and social and economic differentiation. Moreover, by contrast with leaders in other counties where we have done similar research they seemed decidedly to lack entrepreneurial inclinations of their own.[26]

A third element, and one rarely stressed in the literature on the political economy of Chinese local government, is the professionalism of the Shulu county government and its administration. As we have seen in Chapter 3, the county government has placed considerable emphasis on recruiting and maintaining a well-educated staff. In this effort, it had the benefit of the Xinji Middle School, which eventually became a national keypoint institution, and which had provided a large cohort of technical specialists who worked in the Shulu government even by the late 1970's. Not unlike their counterparts in the government organs of many other developing countries, they took pride in using their knowledge to promote local development and quality of life. To mention just a few examples, the director of the Township Industries Bureau took obvious delight in having helped develop the new Eighth Street Barium Salts Plant and in having saved a dying Xinji machinery factory; the staff of the Urban Construction and Environmental Protection Commission were seriously concerned about the effects of pollution, and enthusiastic about their plans to relocate and regulate the dirtiest industries, to develop urban green spaces, and the like; Forestry Bureau cadres, likewise, took seriously their aim of increasing Shulu fruit production, and displayed a good command of agronomy and hydrology in discussing their efforts to reach their goals. That technical specialists can play an extremely important role in setting both political tone and economic direction is widely understood in political science, and in China studies.[27] The literature on the East Asian NICs, especially Japan, has often stressed the political importance of technocrats.[28] Yet, in the literature on Chinese local government and political economy, the crucial part played by the developing local-level technocracy has remained largely overlooked.

In accord with our preoccupations throughout this volume, we have focused in this section on the political and economic roles of the state. But we should still not fail to note that development and regulation did not exhaust the activities of the Shulu county government. In Shulu, for example, the local state includes among its responsibilities a certain amount of patronage for culture and the arts. Popular painting movements in the county during the Cultural Revolution decade had drawn some minor national attention. There is also a tradition of folk painting in Shulu, dating back to ancient times but resuscitated during the Anti-Japanese War, and the county Culture Bureau was nurturing it in 1990. Painting and folk arts exhibitions were more or less continually to be found on display in Shulu. The county government also had a hand in promoting the collection of local folktales, songs, poems, and stories for compilation and publication. This was part of a general commitment to recording and preserving examples of local culture.

Then again, like states everywhere, the county government had legal enforcement and coercive roles to perform as well. Law and order were vigorously enforced in Shulu, and both the didactic and the penalizing personas of the local state judicial and coercive apparatuses were much in evidence in everyday life. State laws and regulations were posted prominently in public places around the county, with appended warnings of prosecution for those who failed to comply. The Shulu Justice Bureau was handling approximately 150 civil cases and an additional 50 criminal cases a year at the county level. It was not determined how many police officers were on duty in the county. But while we were there in the summer of 1990, four convicted criminals were executed in Shulu. Before facing their deaths, these four people, along with dozens of others convicted of lesser crimes, were subjected to public humiliation at an open rally downtown. The televised local coverage of the rally revealed an apparently very large uniformed and motorcycle police force assembled for the occasion.

Consequences of State Activity

Though we originally intended it as such at a time when we did not fully grasp the complexity of the Shulu county government, ours ultimately could not be a study that makes a comprehensive judgment about its performance or effects. To do so, we would need to know much more about the resources and alternatives that were available to the Shulu government, the constraints it faced, and the level of real and opportunity costs incurred in achieving what it did. Thus we are unable to adjudicate for the Shulu case the debate over the extent to which local governments' economic interventions are functional for development (for instance, by aiding infant enterprises and sectors, developing markets, and reducing the huge transaction costs set by China's semireformed political economy) or dysfunctional (in producing macroeconomic imbalance and productive and allocative inefficiency).[29] We hope, however, to have contributed to that debate in a different way, by highlighting some of the services that county government provides for Shulu enterprises and the local economy more generally, and that must be added into any balance sheets on the economic role of local governments.

Here we wish to go beyond the debate on economic performance by exploring several outcomes of county government activity that were significant in affecting development yet were not overdetermined by central state policy. One has to do with urbanization. The development of small towns and cities, and the restriction on the growth of major primate metropolises, has been a distinctive feature of Chinese socialist development. Our study of Shulu underscores the very important role of local government in this complex process. The county government took a major initiative in the development of Xinji when in 1984 it began to conceive the building of the downtown development project including Hebei Yiji, the boulevard fronting it, and the large park across the boulevard. This involved the county government in an elaborate set of tasks, including detailed and integrated urban planning, marshaling of investment funds from a variety of sources, complete and original project design and construction supervision, and complex administrative development, coordination, and regulation. All this occurred before Shulu was elevated to the formal status of a *shi* (city) and the county was redesignated a municipality. In this project, the Shulu government surely had the support of the prefectural and provincial authorities. But there is no evidence that the initiative came from above. To the contrary, there is every reason to believe that most of the work was done at the county level. And the upgrading of Shulu's designation to Xinji municipality appears to have been as much if not more a result of its own urban development initiatives than the other way around.

With the Hebei Yiji Market complete and its new urban administrative status in hand by 1986, the Shulu county—now Xinji municipality—government continued to build up its urban center. To the east of the downtown area a planned financial and economic district oriented (somewhat optimistically) to international business was growing up. Here could be found a number of glassy new multistory buildings, broadened roadways, a park and other green spaces. This was but one part of what amounted to comprehensive and detailed urban plans to create distinct residential, commercial, and industrial spaces oriented to the prevailing natural conditions and existing infrastructural and settlement patterns. Integrated into these plans were specific measures concerning environmental protection and urban beautification. As before, this work had the support and now the explicit encouragement and imprimatur of the prefectural and provincial authorities. But it was driven firmly and prominently from the county level.

All this work does mark a sharp break with the Mao era. In those days, national developmental priorities were in agriculture. In the late 1970's, therefore, the Shulu government focused its developmental planning and energies on water conservancy and road building. With the arrival of the reform period, the center preferred to leave agriculture more to its own devices. Industry and commerce became the leading sectors for growth and development. Farmers were permitted to make their way to cities to ply petty trade. Rural towns and cities were to help employ surplus rural labor, contributing thereby to increased labor productivity and to better incomes. Accordingly, the Shulu government shifted its main attention to the expansion and redevelopment of Xinji city.

This shift in focus to the contrary notwithstanding, a second notable aspect of Shulu's development was the general balance the county government has tried to strike, in both the Mao and Deng periods, between its urban and rural areas, and also among its various geographic regions and their widely disparate levels of development. Shulu county leaders were not committed to economic equality or redistribution as goals in themselves. They comprehended the issue in terms of the development of the county as a whole, which they felt would progress best if it proceeded in a balanced way. The 1977-78 water conservancy project was understood not so much as helping a poor region as overcoming a drag on the entire county's economy. The conversion of Shulu county into Xinji municipality reflects an underlying conception also that urbanization would benefit the whole area. In our contacts with Shulu officials throughout the 1980's, they continued to speak of people in Shulu "getting rich together," a very different slogan than the reformist leadership's oft-repeated axiom that "some must get rich first."

Why Shulu leaders maintained something of an orientation to balanced development is a difficult question on which we can only speculate. We believe, as explained in Chapter 3, that it has something to do with the history of this part of Hebei and of Shulu as a revolutionary base area and Communist Party stronghold. Shulu's leaders evinced a style of work and a discourse that reflected the values of the poor struggling to establish a decent and secure livelihood, and of the responsibility of leadership to take care of the more impoverished. Even in the 1980's they often preferred to speak as much of how poor they were, and how far they had to go, as they did of how much they had accomplished. Whatever may have been going on behind the scenes, in public they emphasized the importance of collective effort and unified leadership—this at a time when mere ideological cant of this sort was no longer required or even in fashion. All these values are characteristic of earlier, revolutionary, and immediately post-liberation days.

Shulu leaders' emphasis on balance and a basic level of equality also probably carried some political benefits for county leaders, insofar as it helped maintain good relationships with and relative harmony among the various localities and agencies with which they had to work. Strong emphasis was put by county leaders, in all our interviews with them, on the importance of consensus and cooperation in government. And indeed, there was a detectably consensual atmosphere, generally speaking, in the interrelationships of Shulu leaders whom we encountered. Not infrequently those from different agencies who ran into each other during our busy round of briefings and interviews turned out to be old friends, and sometimes cousins. There was often an air of easy, informal interchange among them, suggesting extended working relationships that bred familiarity and even willingness to disagree with or complain openly to each other. The formal and informal meetings of the county government were, we sensed, probably more often characterized by friendly disagreement than by stern silence and grudging obedience. Insofar as such a style of politics existed in the corridors of the Shulu government, it would have been conducive to outcomes that distribute scarce resources widely rather than narrowly, for reasons that may have as much or more to do with interpersonal relations and pork-barrel politics as with any Maoist commitment to socialist equality.

The commitment to balanced development, to "getting rich together," may ultimately wane in Shulu as it has elsewhere. Such values are certainly under assault from many quarters all over China now—indeed, from all over the world. Even cadres in old revolutionary base areas like Shulu county may soon see their preferred ideals bent beneath the weight of alternative visions of modernization and development. As of this writing, the forces of social change unleashed in China with the reforms appear to remain stuck in the fast-forward mode. The pace and the sweep of change in popular values, especially, have been nothing short of breathtaking. Yet even if, as we suspect many would suppose, it is only a matter of time before the ethos of county government changes in Shulu too, it is important to take note that such older ideals of balanced development achieved through active governmental direction and regulation remained prominent ones locally into the early 1990's. The imprint those ideals have made on the trajectory of economic and political development in the county will be visible, affecting the agenda and partly determining what is possible for a long time to come, we believe, even if the ideals themselves are summarily superseded. Failed visions, too, leave lasting legacies.[30]

The Challenges Ahead for Shulu

The Shulu county government faces major challenges in the foreseeable future. One that looms particularly large for this local state is the continued proliferation of markets. In only the first decade of the reforms, this new set of forces impelled the government vastly to increase its staff, to elaborate its organization, and to carry out a major reorganization and redevelopment of urban space. New pressures and conflicts broke out over the use of water and land. And because those resources are finite and already extremely scarce, the conflicts over them are zero-sum and therefore particularly acute. Other similar conflicts will no doubt arise in the future. As elsewhere in China, state-owned firms were being subjected to competition from collective and private-sector firms through the 1980's. Bureaucratic offices and leaders responsible for county firms were coming into direct and pointed political conflict over this, as in the case of the Eighth Street Brigade's skirmish with the Xinji Chemical Factory. This sort of strife is bound to continue, and may even expand to embroil the workers of endangered firms, a development that could well prove explosive.

A second significant challenge facing the Shulu government is how to absorb the county's labor force and make the best possible use of it. Like much of the north China plain—and the country as a whole—Shulu is very densely populated. By official count in 1990 there were over 48,000 surplus workers in the Shulu countryside, around 20 percent of the total. Unprofitable urban enterprises had begun laying off rural contract workers in the early 1980's, a period of economic adjustment, and there is every reason to expect such pressures for layoffs to continue at least periodically as economic restructuring proceeds. The conflict between regular and contract workers was a flashpoint of popular political contention during the Cultural Revolution, as we have seen. Some national initiatives on labor reform in the mid-1980's could not be implemented in Shulu, no doubt because they were controversial and resisted locally. Even in 1990, a period of political freeze and tightened controls, workers were complaining at labor union meetings about low salaries, uncertain bonuses, the continuing gap between regular and contract workers, slow housing construction, other contract terms, and layoffs. As of 1990 the county government continued to maintain very strict control over the allocation of labor, and it showed no signs of opening up a labor market any time soon. This laid the problems of Shulu labor squarely in its lap. In the Mao period, the commune structure had been integral to the solution of the county's labor problems, but such an institutional apparatus was no longer at hand after 1982. For the foreseeable future, then, the economic, political, and demographic constraints are such that no easy solutions are in sight.

A third set of problems facing Shulu county and its government is that of defining, financing, and living with the future development of the economy. Shulu's leading industrial sector is chemicals, in which there still are apparent opportunities for further expansion. But this could pose serious environmental dangers. Even more threatening may be the further proliferation of rural enterprises. The county's environmental protection officials were competent and concerned, but in 1990 they were working at or near their capacity. Moreover, they were expressing their frustration at being unable to monitor, much less resolve, the environmental problems caused by the large and growing rural industrial sector. The traditional fur and leather trade and manufacturing sector of the local economy was large, highly subject to cyclical movements in the wider economy, and in need of significant technical improvement to upgrade quality in order to remain competitive. Similar improvements were also needed in fruit cultivation, sorting, and shipping. Yet for the production of fruit, as for agriculture in general, water is getting scarcer with each passing day. Very large financial resources and even more political will are going to be required to attack these problems.

The Shulu county government therefore has its work cut out for it. But it also possesses assets that can help it cope and, if luck holds, even thrive. As China's growth has shifted from the inland areas during the Mao period toward the southern and central coastal belt in the reform period, Shulu's location has not been ideal. But we can also share the view of Shulu's leadership that the county's location, on a key railway line not far from the Shandong coast, and in the Beijing-Tianjin periphery, should not be considered a great liability. The county's official elevation and development into a small regional city have given it a distinct advantage over its neighboring counties. Its nationally prominent middle school will continue to be a source of talented technocrats for the middle and upper ranks of government. Its smattering of foreign economic contacts can help too. And if its industries prosper and the tendencies toward enterprise decentralization continue, the Shulu government may also have the financial basis for continued investment and growth.

Perhaps most important of all, however, will be Shulu's political legacies. In both the Mao and Deng periods, the Shulu county government has proved adroit at taking advantage of the possibilities inherent in its complex structure of vertical and horizontal lines of organization and authority. The quality of its leadership has been a major reason why Shulu has stood out among its neighbors. Shulu officials are relatively well educated, and have shown their assiduousness, their capacity for practical vision, and their ingenuity in bringing that vision into reality while generally respecting and even utilizing to local advantage the parameters set by the wider state. Thus Shulu has prospered—not as dramatically as some other localities, but steadily, and under both Maoist and reformist economic and political regimes—in large part because its leaders have managed to make use of what play has remained in those numerous and elaborately crisscrossed threads of authority by which it is not so much bound as tethered within the Chinese state system.

Notes

Notes

1. STUDYING GOVERNMENT AND ECONOMY

1. Studies of local government and politics have tended to focus on coastal sites, including places in Guangdong, Fujian and, more recently, Shandong provinces. For just a few examples of valuable work, see Anita Chan, Richard Madsen, and Jonathan Unger, *Chen Village* (Berkeley: University of California Press, 1984); Philip C. C. Huang, *The Peasant Family and Rural Development in the Yangzi Delta, 1350–1988* (Stanford, Calif.: Stanford University Press, 1990); Shu-min Huang, *The Spiral Road: Change in a Chinese Village Through the Eyes of a Communist Party Leader* (Boulder: Westview Press, 1989); Richard Madsen, *Morality and Power in a Chinese Village* (Berkeley: University of California Press, 1984); Victor Nee, "A Theory of Market Transition: From Redistribution to Markets in State Socialism," *American Sociological Review* 54 (Oct. 1989): 663–81; Peter Nolan and Dong Fureng, eds., *Market Forces in China: Competition and Small Business—the Wenzhou Debate* (London: Zed, 1989); Kevin J. O'Brien, "Implementing Political Reform in China's Villages," *Australian Journal of Chinese Affairs* 32 (July 1994): 33–60; Jean Oi, "Fiscal Reform and the Economic Foundations of Local State Corporatism in China," *World Politics* 45, 1 (Oct. 1992): 99–126; Kristen Parris, "Local Initiative and National Reform: The Wenzhou Model of Development," *China Quarterly* 134 (June 1993): 242–63; Sulamith Heins Potter and Jack M. Potter, *China's Peasants: The Anthropology of a Revolution* (New York: Cambridge University Press, 1989); Helen Siu, *Agents and Victims in South China: Accomplices in Rural Revolution* (New Haven: Yale University Press, 1989); Ezra Vogel, *One Step Ahead in China: Guangdong Under Reform* (Cambridge, Mass.: Harvard University Press, 1989).

Important work has been done on inland areas such as Hebei and Sichuan, but it has focused mainly on subjects other than intermediate government. See Chris

Bramall, *In Praise of Maoist Economic Planning: Living Standards and Economic Development in Sichuan Since 1931* (Oxford: Oxford University Press, 1993); Edward Friedman, Paul G. Pickowicz, and Mark Selden, *Chinese Village, Socialist State* (New Haven: Yale University Press, 1991); Ole Odgaard, "Collective Control of Income Distribution: A Case Study of Private Enterprises in Sichuan Province," in Jørgen Delman, Clemens Stubbe Østergaard, and Flemming Christiansen, eds., *Remaking Peasant China: Problems of Rural Development and Institutions at the Start of the 1990s* (Aarhus: Aarhus University Press, 1990); Louis Putterman, *Continuity and Change in China's Rural Development: Collective and Reform Eras in Perspective* (New York: Oxford University Press, 1993).

2. Most research has focused on provinces or villages. The only major study of county government is A. Doak Barnett, *Cadres, Bureaucracy, and Political Power in Communist China* (New York: Columbia University Press, 1967).

3. See, for example, Sidney Gamble, *Ting Hsien: A North China Rural Community* (Stanford, Calif.: Stanford University Press, 1968).

4. Marc Blecher and Mitch Meisner, "Administrative Level and Agrarian Structure: The County (W)as Focal Point in Chinese Rural Development Strategy." In Gordon White and Jack Gray, eds., *China's New Development Strategy* (London: Academic Press, 1982), 55–84.

5. For example, see Victor Falkenheim, "Provincial Administration in Fukien, 1949–1966" (Ph.D. dissertation, Columbia University, 1972); Ezra Vogel, *Canton Under Communism: Programs and Politics in a Provincial Capital, 1949–1968* (New York: Harper Torchbooks, 1971). A major project on government and politics in each Chinese province, organized by Edwin Winckler, was also underway at the time.

6. See, for example, Tang Tsou, Marc Blecher, and Mitch Meisner, "Organization, Growth, and Equality in Xiyang County: A Survey of Fourteen Brigades in Seven Communes—Part I," *Modern China* 5, 1 (Jan. 1979): 3–40, and "Organization, Growth, and Equality in Xiyang County: A Survey of Fourteen Brigades in Seven Communes—Part II," *Modern China* 5, 2 (Apr. 1979): 139–86, and "The Responsibility System in Agriculture: Its Implementation in Xiyang and Dazhai," *Modern China* 8, 1 (Jan. 1982): 41–106; Friedman, Pickowicz, and Selden, *Chinese Village, Socialist State*.

7. For example, in the early 1970's a movement to encourage peasant artistic production received a modicum of national publicity; see Shulu xian wenhua gongzuo zhan (Shulu County Cultural Work Center), *Shulu xian qunzhong yeyu hua xuan* (Selected amateur paintings by the Shulu masses) (Beijing: Renmin Meishu Chubanshe, 1972). Subsequently, Shulu has been mentioned in the national press for another kind of cultural achievement: the construction of cinemas, libraries, and other cultural centers; see *Beijing Review* 27, 19 (May 7, 1984): 12. Jiujie (Ninth Street) Brigade of Xinji Commune, located in the county seat of Xinji, has attracted some attention in the provincial and even national press for its economically diversified development, and a national keypoint middle school (a school with extra resources and high admissions standards) is located on the outskirts of Xinji. But even these two units were not at the forefront of national developments in their respective areas.

8. For example, when we asked for data on all communes, they could only oblige with a sample, because not every commune had reliable records. Yet they also chose their sample carefully, selecting communes that proved to be well distributed over the economic and geographic ranges of Shulu.

9. By this time, unfortunately for us, our colleagues Stephen Andors and Mitch

Meisner had found it necessary to strike out on new career pathways that took them far away from China studies. And Phyllis Andors was unable to journey to China at the time we had chosen.

10. Marc Blecher stayed two and one-half weeks, and Vivienne Shue more than two months.

2. HISTORICAL AND MATERIAL SETTINGS

1. "Hebei sheng Shulu xian difang shiji qingkuang diaocha baogao" (Report of an investigation into the actual conditions in Shulu county, Hebei province), *Jicha diaocha tongji congkan* 2, 3 (1936): 102. Hereafter cited as "Report."

2. This part of the story finds confirmation in the *Cihai*, China's encyclopedic dictionary. See Shanghai cihai bianji weiyuanhui (Shanghai *Cihai* Editorial Committee), ed., *Cihai* (Sea of words) (Shanghai: Shanghai Cishu Chubanshe, 1979), 1955.

3. In this version, other counties in this part of Hebei were also renamed for events of the An Lushan rebellion. Luchuan county became Huailu (the place where "Lu was captured"), and Fangshan became Pingshan because there An was killed and so peace (*ping*) was restored there. The Shulu and Huailu accounts are subject to doubt because the contemporary character for *lu* is different from the *lu* appearing in An Lushan's name. Shulu people averred that the character had changed over the years.

4. Unfortunately, county gazetteers lack maps, but their detailed descriptions of county transport routes suggest only one small divergence from the present borders, including within the county the little hamlet of Baichikou, which lies about one kilometer west of the present southwestern border.

5. Jiucheng, the old capital, had been abandoned during the Ming dynasty, when it was destroyed by flood.

6. "Report," 104.

7. G. William Skinner, "Marketing and Social Structure in Rural China, Part III," *Journal of Asian Studies* 24, 3 (May 1965): 363–99 (esp. 382 *ff.*).

8. For example, the important north-south connection running along Shulu's eastern edge, which had existed in 1906 but was still cut by 1970, was finally restored by 1980. For further discussion of roadway construction and finance in Shulu, see Chapter 8.

9. Some villages have undergone minor name changes, or have been divided into northern and southern or eastern and western settlements; for example, Zhiqiu has now become Nanzhiqiu (South Zhiqiu).

10. Li Zhonggui and Zhang Fengtai, *Shulu xiangtu zhi* (Local gazetteer of Shulu) (1906), 3rd *juan*, 16–19.

11. Eastern Shulu was joined to Shen county to become Shenshu county; southern Shulu was incorporated with Ji county to form Shuji county; and northern Shulu was joined to Jin county to the northwest to become Shujin county.

12. These included a factory making alkali to be used as inputs for military uniform dyes, and plants producing soap, armaments, and explosives.

13. Throughout history Shulu has experienced frequent, often deadly, drought and flood. Serious famine struck in 1881, and plague in 1903.

14. Li and Zhang, *Shulu xiangtu zhi*, 12th *juan*, 41.

15. Specifically, one-third sorghum, one-third millet, and one-third other grains. Shulu has been upgrading its grain crops during this century. By 1936, millet accounted for 52 percent of grain output by weight, maize 28 percent, wheat 12 per-

cent, and sorghum only 8 percent. By the 1960's and thereafter, wheat and maize predominated.

16. Interestingly, the pattern of agricultural land use in 1906 was almost identical to that of 1978, when 58.9 percent of land was planted to grain, 31 percent to cotton, and 10.1 percent to other crops. By 1986, grain was down to 50.8 percent of cultivated area, and almost all the decline had gone to other crops (oil-bearers, melons and vegetables, hemp, tobacco, and medicinal herbs), which then occupied 17 percent of cultivated land.

17. Zhonggong Xinji Shi Weiyuanhui (Xinji Municipality Committee of the Chinese Communist Party) and Xinji Shi Renmin Zhengfu (Xinji Municipality People's Government), "Xinji shi jingji fazhan zhanlüe (taolun gao)" (Xinji municipality economic development strategy [discussion draft]), June 26, 1986.

18. Li and Zhang, *Shulu xiangtu zhi*, 12th *juan*, 38.

19. This production was also based on imported inputs, in this case wool from Inner Mongolia and Xinjiang.

20. The external orientation of the Shulu economy continues up to the present. In 1978, Shulu supplied nearly half Shijiazhuang prefecture's foreign exports. In 1985, the county Foreign Trade Bureau procured ¥31,984,283 worth of commodities for export, which was 7.8 percent of gross value of industrial output. By 1990, procurements were up to ¥83,360,000.

21. Li and Zhang, *Shulu xiangtu zhi*, 12th *juan*, 38.

22. Xinji had a population of over 7,000, compared with around 8,000 for Jiucheng, Weibo, and Zhiqiu. "Report," 104.

23. Local cotton cultivation has been erratic in the Mao and Deng periods, however. See Marc Blecher and Wang Shaoguang, "The Political Economy of Cropping in Maoist and Dengist China: Hebei Province and Shulu County, 1949–1990," *China Quarterly* 137 (Mar. 1994): 63–98.

24. By 1986 98 percent was irrigated. To be sure, there have always been the odd fragments of land that can still be brought under cultivation. In the late 1980's, for example, responding to burgeoning market demand for fruit, Shulu farmers were planting orchard trees in dried-up riverbeds and along roadsides. But this sort of literally very marginal expansion in fact indicates just how fully Shulu's arable land was already being used.

25. In the central region, grain production averaged 6.88 tons per hectare, compared with 6.12 in the north and 4.97 in the south. Cotton production averaged 288.5 kilograms per hectare, while the north and south only brought in 251. (Normally, grain is measured in [metric] tons per hectare, and cotton in kilograms per hectare [1 metric ton = 1,000 kilograms].)

26. *Zhongguo nongye dili zonglun* (*A general treatise on agricultural geography of China*) (Beijing, 1980). Translated in Joint Publications Research Service (hereafter JPRS) 78034 (May 8, 1981): 126 *ff*. One summary is worth quoting at length for its vivid description of conditions in the Heilonggang, its account of their origins, and the sense it conveys of their long history: "The main reason for the long period of low and unstable yields in the production of food grains in this region is serious damage by drought, waterlogging and alkalinity. This is the region in the province [Hebei] with the most serious damage from drought and waterlogging. Between 60 percent and 70 percent of rainfall are concentrated in July, August, and September. During every heavy rain, the floodwaters from the mountain regions of the Taihang pour into the plains of this region. The river channels in the lower reaches are narrow, the topography is low and flat, and because of the many floods and changes in the waterways of the Yellow River, Hai River,

and their tributaries throughout history, there is a lot of lowland sediment, and water does not flow smoothly, causing floods and damage. Good fields are submerged and the cities and traffic safety are seriously threatened. During the fifteen years from 1949 to 1964, there were nine years of floods and waterlogging. In the big flood of 1963, one-third of the cultivated land of this region was flooded. Because of the frequent damage by drought and waterlogging and improper irrigation, secondary salinization of the soil is widespread and serious. About 18,000,000 mu [1,200,000 hectares] of land were salinized (constituting half of the cultivated land). This type of secondarily salinized and alkalized land has a low ground temperature, the fertility is poor, seedlings cannot be assured of growth in spring, and harvests cannot be assured in autumn; it is said that 'spring is white all over, in summer there is water all over, seedlings are hard to come by in cultivated land, and alkali but not food grains are seen'" (126–27). The translation has been slightly altered here to improve grammar and clarity.

27. We shall have much more to say about this project in Chapter 8.

28. In 1979, four scheduled buses connected Shulu to three regional destinations (Shijiazhuang, Zhengding, and Baoding); by 1986 this had been expanded to seventeen daily departures to nine destinations, now including Beijing and Tianjin. In addition, there were fourteen scheduled intracounty buses (up from six in 1979).

29. "Xinji shi jingji fazhan zhanlüe (xiuding gao)" (Economic development strategy of Xinji municipality [revised draft]). (Xinji: Xinji Municipality Committee of the Chinese Communist Party and the Xinji Municipality People's Government, Aug. 1, 1986), 5, 14.

30. Communes were redubbed townships around 1984; road building, an important developmental activity of the county government, is discussed more fully in Chapter 8.

31. In 1978, the center contained 5.88 persons per hectare, compared with 4.94 in the north and 3.94 in the south. The figures for cultivated land were, naturally, higher: 8.45 persons per hectare of cultivated land, compared with 6.53 in the north and 5.24 in the south.

32. The central region contained 38 percent of the county's surface area, but 46 percent of its total number of settlements.

33. For a brief description of the Chinese household registration system, see Chapter 5. Also see Marc Blecher, "Peasant Labour for Urban Industry: Temporary Contract Labour, Urban-Rural Balance and Class Relations in a Chinese County," *World Development* 11, 8 (Aug. 1983): 731–46.

34. In addition to these, Xinji was also beginning to be crowded with thousands of merchants who came for daily or periodic markets. Some of them took up temporary and often undocumented residence for various periods of time. County officials estimated that there were 8,000 undocumented residents living in the city in 1986.

35. In 1984, population density in downtown Shanghai was 20,239 (State Statistical Bureau, comp., *Statistical Yearbook of China 1985* [Oxford: Oxford University Press, 1985], 57).

36. See Chapter 3.

37. In the early 1980's there had been a problem of street congestion caused by a proliferation of private market stalls. This prompted the county government to build the Hebei Yiji Market, a large shopping center, which basically solved the problem. See Chapter 6.

38. See Chapter 3, n. 11 for details.

39. See Chapter 6 and maps 8 and 9 for a fuller discussion.

40. The former Chengguan Commune became the Chengdong (East City) Urban Administrative District, Tianjiazhuang Commune became Chengxi (West City), Angucheng Commune became Chengbei (North City), Ziyuezhuang Commune became Chengnan (South City), and Xinji Commune became Xinghua (Flourishing China).

41. Guoxi and Hemujing.

42. Indeed, this may have contributed to the relative decline of Guoxi, which had the misfortune to be situated between Xinji and Wangkou. The latter is discussed in more detail in Chapter 5.

43. But as noted above, in 1979 the county government maintained a network of administrative subcenters throughout the county.

44. Vivienne Shue, "China's Local News Media," *China Quarterly* 86 (June 1981): 322–31, and "China: On the Wire," *Intermedia* 8, 2 (Mar. 1980): 18–20.

45. These are in addition to the small clinics in towns and villages.

3. SHULU COUNTY GOVERNMENT

1. As the table indicates, although many new bureaus and offices were set up over this period, none was ever phased out. Even the Second Light Industry Bureau, which was first redesignated a Federation of Cooperative Enterprises and later was technically dissolved, survived as a Light Industry and Textiles Company—still formally a unit of the local government apparatus—after 1987. According to officials of the Shulu Government Affairs Office, no one who had been working for the Second Light Bureau was fired, laid off, or transferred when these redesignations and reorganizations occurred.

2. Direct and deliberate study of the organization and activities of the Communist Party in Shulu was never one of the goals of our research there. Over the years, however, our pursuit of other topics brought us face to face time and again with Party leaders, Party policies, Party organizations, and Party activities. Indirectly, therefore, we were able to ascertain that, in Shulu at least, between 1979 and 1990, one important old axiom of Chinese politics remained firmly in place: the Party was comprehensively integrated into the structure of local government there, and it retained a determining role in nearly all aspects of local political life. This integration of party and government, and its apparent effects on both the style of local politics and the authority of local political leaders, receive some further brief comment below. For the present we should simply note that the Party possessed an organizational apparatus for managing its own affairs in Shulu, including a county Party committee office (*xianwei bangongshi*), a clerical group (*mishu zu*), a dispatch group (*shoufa zu*), an organization department (*zuzhi bu*), a control group (*jiancha zu*), a propaganda department (*xuanchuan bu*), a communications group (*tongxun zu*), a rural work department (*nongcun gongzuobu*), and a Party school (*dang xiao*). As of 1986, there were a total of 57 functional offices, basic-level Party committees, and Party-run mass organizations in operation in Shulu. See *Xinji Shi zhi ziliao xuanbian* (Selected materials from the Xinji gazetteer), 1987: 68.

3. This point is developed further in Vivienne Shue, "State Sprawl: The Regulatory State and Social Life in a Small Chinese City," in Deborah Davis, Barry Naughton, Richard Kraus, and Elizabeth Perry, eds., *Urban Spaces: Autonomy and Community in Contemporary China* (forthcoming).

4. At the commune level (and later at the town and township levels of administration that replaced the communes), by contrast, most local officials have not been on the state's payroll, have not been parts of its personnel system, and have been administratively and functionally responsible in important ways not to state authorities above them but rather to their communities and to the institutions at the commune or township itself.

5. These are explored more fully in Chapter 4.

6. A number of special subsidies available to state administrative cadres and their families are detailed in Chapter 4.

7. There were six townships rated as hardship posts in Shulu in 1990: Mengjiazhuang, Guoxi, Houying, Zhonglixiang, Xiaoxinzhuang and Xizebei. Cadres working in these places received about ¥18 extra as special compensation. But some cadres who were actually working very near to the county seat were also receiving some hardship compensation. These were officials who had previously held positions in county government offices and who, as a result of the expansion of Xinji, were transferred to the new Xinghua and Chengdong urban administrative districts to live and work. Since they were, temporarily, receiving what would have to be regarded as a demotion in status, they were compensated as if for a hardship post.

8. The figure for 1957–78 is 3.8 percent.

9. These figures accord with, and in fact were slightly below, national trends. From 1952 to 1978, total government administrative expenditures nationally rose at an average annual rate of 4.8 percent. From 1978 to 1983 the figure was 16.9 percent. Calculated from State Statistical Bureau, *Statistical Yearbook of China 1987* (Hong Kong: Longman, 1986), 550.

10. See the discussion in Chapter 2.

11. All communes and commune headquarters towns in the 1970's were indeed organized quite similarly. But it is worth noting also that seven commune towns in Shulu—all of them former headquarters of the early, very large communes of the Great Leap—retained a somewhat special character as loci of branch offices of several important county government bureaus. These seven are Zhangguzhuang, Weibo, Hemujing, Nanzhiqiu, Guoxi, Jiucheng, and Xincheng. In 1979 they all had a post office, bank, grain station, cinema, police station, courthouse, and branch offices of the Bureaus of Finance and Tax and of Industry and Commerce Management. Some of these commune towns accommodated county-run productive, commercial, and service units also. Each of these small towns had a contingent of persons classified as nonrural residents living there as well.

A decade of reform did not alter the relative importance of these towns in the Shulu countryside. In 1986, for example, these towns still contained six of the seven regional offices of the Industrial and Commercial Bank. By 1988, these seven small towns outside Xinji still also contained six of the eight outlying hospitals and six of the twelve outlying county-run schools. They also included five of the six officially designated towns (zhen). These little local administrative centers in Shulu did not constitute an intermediate level of government between the county and the commune. They simply served as extensions outward into the countryside of certain routines and functions of county government administration. But this in itself is significant; county government activity in Shulu was not confined to the county seat per se. And the authority of county government was closer to the countryside and to the farming population than some of the traditional formal schematics of China's administrative levels in the literature may suggest.

12. This recent development of town- and township-level tax collection in Shulu receives more detailed consideration in Chapter 4, on county finance. See also Jean

Oi, "Fiscal Reform and the Economic Foundations of Local State Corporatism in China," *World Politics* 45, 1 (Oct. 1992): 99–126.

13. For example, a state grain station (23 employees), an electric power office and transformer station (11), a state cotton purchasing station (9), branches of two state banks (9), a branch tax office (5), a branch office of the court (3), a materials supply station serving enterprises producing for the state plan (4), and so on. Perhaps another way to indicate the actual continuing heavy presence of the state and of state planning in a common *zhen* like Xincheng is to point out also that the *zhen* government annual plan for 1990 was a comprehensive, highly specific, classified (*neibu*) document some 50 pages long.

14. It is important to note, however, that further down—at the brigade or village (*cun*) level—the trend seemed to be moving in the other direction. "Cadres" working at that level had always been classified as regular farmers and were never on the state payroll. There were some 2,429 such village-level cadres in 1979, an average of 7 per village. In 1989 this force was down to approximately 2,000. With decollectivization, in Shulu as elsewhere, there was less work of a purely administrative nature to be handled in the villages.

15. "With further urbanization, we will one day want to change the administrative districts into urban residents' committees [*jumin weiyuanhui*] just like those in Beijing." Interview with Liu Cunzhi, director, Government Affairs Office, July 11, 1990.

16. People living in urban administrative districts do elect their own village committees (*cunmin weiyuanhui*) just as in the towns and townships, however. These committees are generally made up of three to seven persons. In Chengxi district (formerly Tianjiazhuang Commune), for example, which contains ten natural villages (*ziran cun*), the village committees take a leading role in organizing for the Xinji-wide elections, helping, among other things, to find candidates to stand for office. Chengxi elects eight representatives to serve in the Xinji People's Congress.

17. See Chapter 7.

18. As we shall see in Chapter 8, townships generally had to bear some of the cost of local roadway construction.

19. The Chengxi district, for example, then had three leading organs: a Party committee, an economic development committee (*jingwei*), and a district court (*fating*). Under these, it counted four district offices (*suo*) and eight district centers (*zhan*). The offices were an industry and trade office, a tax office, a finance office, and a police station. The centers were an agricultural machinery and electrification management center, an agricultural technology guidance center, a legal services center, a land management station, an enterprise economic management center, a family planning center, a cultural center, and a broadcasting station.

20. But, as Party Secretary Zhang of the Chengxi district noted, this kind of pressure could cut both ways: "Higher standards of work are expected now that we're a *banshichu*. Better quality cadres are demanded now, and better ones are sent here to work. This is considered a somewhat better work assignment, precisely because we're not elected but appointed by the people's congress. . . . We get better personnel to run our enterprises, and better technical personnel are assigned here now. These people get a salary and other perquisites equivalent to those of regular urban personnel" (Interview, July 10, 1990).

21. Specific examples, discussed in Chapter 8, include the 1978 water conservancy project, the pattern of roadway construction, and the complete redrawing of orchard contracts.

22. In chapters to come we will again see examples. One of these concerns the

relationship of the Industry and Commerce Management Bureau to the development of private markets and the activities of private entrepreneurs (Chapter 6). For further discussion, see Vivienne Shue, "State Power and Social Organization in China: From Revolution to Reform," in Joel Migdal, Atul Kohli, and Vivienne Shue, eds., *State Power and Social Forces: Domination and Transformation in Asia, Africa and Latin America* (Cambridge, Eng.: Cambridge University Press, 1994).

4. COUNTY FINANCIAL STRUCTURES

1. We present here the statistics gathered during our fieldwork in Shulu. A comprehensive study edited by the Finance Bureau in Shulu, *Xinji shi caizheng zhi* (Xinji finance gazetteer) (Beijing: Xinhua Chubanshe, 1990), which was published only after the completion of the fieldwork, provides sets of county revenue and expenditure figures for 1949 through 1988 that match ours very closely (see pp. 53–54 ff and 129–130 ff). Where there are discrepancies between our statistics and those published in the gazetteer, they are small ones, varying generally from 1 percent to 3 percent of total revenues or expenditures. Interestingly, the gazetteer does give revenue and expenditure figures for the period of the Great Leap Forward that are much higher than ours. Shulu county's official administrative boundaries were greatly enlarged to take in territory in Shenze and Jin counties during the Great Leap. The figures we obtained from Shulu officials had apparently already been adjusted downward to reflect just the Shulu portion of state revenues and expenditures during those politically and financially tumultuous years.

2. The general principles and practices of the Chinese budgetary process during the Mao period can be found in George N. Ecklund, *Financing the Chinese Government Budget* (Chicago: Aldine, 1966), and in Nicholas R. Lardy, *Economic Growth and Distribution in China* (Cambridge, Eng.: Cambridge University Press, 1978).

3. As Christine P. W. Wong has summarized the situation, "Despite substantial decentralization in many spheres, the budgetary process remained quite centralized throughout the Maoist period. The Ministry of Finance approved not only the consolidated budget but annual revenue and expenditure plans at the provincial level and set the amount of revenue transfers. Provinces in turn supervised formulation of budget plans at the municipal and county levels. Local governments enjoyed little budget autonomy." Christine P. W. Wong, "Fiscal Reform and Local Industrialization," *Modern China* 18, 2 (Apr. 1992): 205.

4. This remained the basic state of affairs in local budgetary relations until the mid-1980's extension of finance authority and responsibility down to the town and township levels when, as explained below, offices in *xiang* and *zhen* governments came to constitute the lowest rung of finance and tax administration.

5. Wong, for example, argues, "Within the budgetary sphere, changes introduced in the reform period have been much less favorable to local governments than commonly assumed, and local budgets have *shrunk* as a share of national income. At the same time, local governments face greatly expanded expenditure responsibilities, many stemming from obligations imposed by national policy. The result is that local governments at all levels are starved of revenue and forced to seek growth." Christine P. W. Wong, "Central-Local Relations in an Era of Fiscal Decline: The Paradox of Fiscal Decentralization in Post-Mao China," *China Quarterly* 128 (Dec. 1991): 693. More information on central-local fiscal share relations during the late 1980's, putting Hebei province practices in a national reform context, can be found in *China: Revenue Mobilization and Tax Policy* (Washington, D.C.: The World Bank, 1990), 87–101.

6. Retained surplus revenues entered the county's extrabudgetary fund, which is discussed below. Revenue shortfalls by the county incurred a *penalty* that, as has been standard practice in PRC finance, was greater than the *reward* for surplus. For example, when Shulu fell ¥2,065,000 short of its revenue target in 1977 due to a disastrous flood, it was compelled to cut its expenditures by ¥1,032,500, exactly half the revenue shortfall.

7. The term "adjusted revenues" referred to the county's "unified industry and commerce tax" receipts. For details on the introduction of these first fiscal reforms, see Wong, "Fiscal Reform," 207–14.

8. See Wong, "Fiscal Reform," 214–19, for an explanation and evaluation of the *ligaishui* (tax-for-profit) reform and its fate. The first phase of *ligaishui* reforms began in June 1983 in Shulu; the second phase in Oct. 1984.

9. Some of these revenues came earmarked for certain purposes, such as pollution control and environmental protection or urban construction and maintenance. But by and large overtarget revenues retained in the county could be spent flexibly by local authorities.

10. Nicholas Lardy, *Agriculture in China's Economic Development* (Cambridge, Eng.: Cambridge University Press, 1983), especially chapter 3.

11. See page 71ff.

12. Shulu had forty-eight county-level industries in 1979; fifty-one in 1986; and fifty-three in operation by 1990. Some of the original forty-eight were closed along the way and new ones opened.

13. In 1978 there were eighteen enterprises in this category. The early 1980's brought one or two plant openings, closings, and mergers, so that there were a total of sixteen enterprises on the books by 1986, and twenty in 1990.

14. In material terms, then, despite their name, these enterprises had little if any "collective" character.

15. The extrabudgetary group also included one commercial enterprise, a transport company.

16. This was the profit share rate up until 1983. After that, 70 percent of after-tax profits went into the county's extrabudgetary fund and 30 percent were permitted to remain in the enterprises themselves for distribution and investment. After 1985, the share rate changed again—to 50 percent/50 percent. Compare the discussion of the extrabudgetary fund, below.

17. By the mid-1980's there was also a very large number of industrial and commercial enterprises operated under "joint" (*lianheti*) and "individual" (*geti*) or private management.

18. For more detailed explanations of how the industry and commerce tax, and other taxes, are levied in China, see the World Bank report *China: Revenue Mobilization and Tax Policy*. Also, A. J. Easson and Li Jinyan, "The Evolution of the Tax System in the People's Republic of China," *Stanford Journal of International Law* 23, 2 (Summer 1987): 339–447. At the time of liberation, there were no fewer than eight separate commercial taxes levied on businesses in Shulu. These were the goods tax, business tax, income tax, deed tax, interest income tax, slaughter tax, transaction tax, and amusement tax. Thus by 1979 the unified industry and commerce tax was the product of successive consolidations and simplifications of the local tax structure, the most important reforms having been implemented in 1958, 1959, 1966, 1967, and 1973. The effects of the 1958 and 1959 tax reforms are already widely understood. In 1966 the amusement tax was suspended. In 1967 the bicycle tax was eliminated, but there remained a tax on motor vehicles. In 1973, four more taxes—the motor vehicles tax, the slaughter tax, the urban land tax, and

the urban industry and commerce tax—were combined into the single unified industry and commerce tax.

19. But note once more that group 4 enterprises, run by higher levels of government, paid this tax directly into higher-level state coffers, bypassing the Shulu county state budget.

20. This scale of tax rates remained in effect through subsequent tax reforms undertaken in the Deng period. In March 1983, the minister of finance, Wang Bingqian, announced that the income tax would gradually replace mandatory profit deliveries. For the meantime, this tax would have eight grades, with a maximum of 55 percent—virtually identical in outline to the tax scale in effect in Shulu in 1978 ("Tax Payment System to Begin June 1," *Xinhua News Agency*, Mar. 28, 1983, 3–4). And in 1986 Shulu Second Light Industry Bureau officials reported that the eight-grade tax scale was still in effect locally.

21. To do the calculations, subtract the cost of doing business from gross receipts. Then subtract the income tax from total taxes paid. (These enterprises were also obliged to pay a business or commodity tax.) Subtract the product of the second calculation from the product of the first. This represents real profits before the income tax levy. Divide the reported income tax by the real profit figure to determine the income tax percentage for the year. Completing these calculations for the series reveals a variation in the income tax from a low of 6.7 percent in 1980 to a high of 15.7 percent in 1984. The average for the period was 11.7 percent.

22. "Other" revenues also included some income from rents on public buildings up until 1958. See *Xinji shi caizheng zhi*, 113–19.

23. These commercial units included nine companies (*gongsi*) like the Foodstuffs Company and the Shulu Department Store, discussed in Chapter 6.

24. How much of Shulu county's drop in revenues from enterprise profits between 1959 and 1963 was due to this reorganization and how much simply to declining profits in that period of economic crisis must remain a matter for future investigation.

25. A 1970 administrative decentralization associated with Zhou Enlai—which may have been similar in scope to the 1957–58 decentralization—brought many important industrial enterprises under "local" leadership (Nicholas Lardy, personal communication). The data gathered in Shulu reflect no such devolution to the county in 1970, however. Shulu officials reported 1969 as the year when several factories came under county administration. It seems likely that Shulu, a leader among Hebei counties in industrial management, was selected in 1969 as an experimental keypoint for the administrative decentralization that at least some national leaders were hoping to press nationwide the following year.

26. "Real profits," in Chinese accounting practice, denotes income minus costs of doing business. Real profits are used as the base for calculating certain tax and profit remission liabilities of an enterprise.

27. It was 30 percent in 1979. The remaining 70 percent of overtarget profits was forwarded to higher levels of the state through the budget process.

28. Here it seems the county government's interest in controlling financial resources, in the ostensible service of fiscal balance and overall economic development, weighed in over the interests of workers in raising family living standards, also a goal articulated by the new Dengist leadership at the time. Note, however, that later, in 1984, a program for funding workers' welfare and bonus payments was begun. (See the column in Table 12 labeled "Workers' Welfare and Bonuses.")

29. A similar diversion of funds from state-owned enterprises to finance investment in the "five small" industries is known to have occurred widely during the

Cultural Revolution. See Christine P. W. Wong, "The Maoist Model Reconsidered: Local Self-Reliance and the Financing of Rural Industrialization," in William Joseph, Christine Wong, and David Zweig, eds., *New Perspectives on the Cultural Revolution* (Cambridge, Mass.: Harvard University Press, 1991), 183–96.

30. In the Finance Bureau, for example, "out of habit" in-budget industry income taxes and adjustment taxes paid to the bureau were still recorded in the state budget as revenue from "enterprise profits." Compare columns 14, 15, and 16 in Table 12 with column 3 in Table 8. What are called "taxes" in Table 12 were recorded as "enterprise profits" in Table 8. The sum of the three columns in Table 12 generally does not coincide exactly with actual revenues collected as recorded in column 3 of Table 8; in some years enterprises did not actually meet their assessed tax liabilities, while in other years they were paying additional sums in back taxes. In 1989, for example, Shulu in-budget enterprises should have paid ¥6,430,000 in income tax, ¥842,000 in adjustment tax, and ¥1,417,000 in profits to the bureau. This is a total of ¥8,689,000. But only ¥8,291,000 was actually collected that year. (These accounting practices are explained in a facsimile communication from Zheng Lanying dated Sept. 16, 1992.)

31. Interview, July 8, 1990.

32. On the expenditure side things seem to have been somewhat more relaxed. Funds not spent by the county in one fiscal year could be carried over to the next, for example.

33. Some funds spent in the category of "Basic Construction and Technical Improvement" were put to use in Shulu's factories and enterprises. But these were special project efforts, far too little and too intermittent to represent the ongoing investment required for county industrial and commercial operations.

34. See Wong, "Central-Local Relations," 702–3.

35. Details can be found in *Xinji shi caizheng zhi*, 176 ff.

36. See Chapter 8.

37. The marked increases in both the staff size of local government and the complexity of local administrative operations in the Deng period are addressed in Chapter 3.

38. A detailed listing is contained in *Xinji shi caizheng zhi*, 219 ff.

39. For ease of display we have combined this line with the old "support for sent-down youth" line in Table 9 and Figure 7. Outlays for sent-down youth in Shulu were finally terminated in 1984. Support for urban unemployed youth began in 1988.

40. The category of "other" expenditures was sometimes used to disguise what amounted to additional administrative expenditures. For example, outlays from this category also included expenditures for industry, commerce, and tax bureau affairs, town and township finance office expenses, and the costs of running the Shulu county jail. But we have moved these, whenever we were able to find them, to the "government administration" column in Table 9. See *Xinji shi caizheng zhi*, 251 ff.

41. While revenue has risen, absolutely, it has declined relative to the growth of the economy, or to GNP. See Barry Naughton, "Implications of the State Monopoly over Industry and Its Relaxation," *Modern China* 18, 1 (Jan. 1992): 14–41; Wang Shaoguang, "Central-Local Fiscal Politics in China," in Jia Hao and Lin Zhimin, eds., *Changing Central-Local Relations* (Boulder: Westview, 1994), 91–112.

42. Wong, for example, points out that "central government policies have in several cases greatly increased the current expenditure obligations that are borne by local budgets" ("Central-Local Relations," 704). And Naughton notes that between

1978 and 1987 "both central and local expenditures have declined as a share of GNP at about the same rate" ("Implications of the State Monopoly," 35).

43. As a World Bank study recently summarized the situation, "China has no regular, formula grant program to support capital projects; all grants are on an ad hoc basis. There is no mechanism or formal program for lending to local governments, and there is no formal mechanism that guides local governments in developing beneficiary financing schemes. Capital financing is done from some combination of current revenues, planned loans or grants, special exceptions to the restrictions on borrowing, and creative, ad hoc approaches to benefit financing." And further, "Provincial and local governments in China cannot borrow. However, there appear to be ways to avoid these restrictions. Short-term borrowing (less than one year) and even some longer term credit financing does occur. It some cases, municipally owned enterprises borrow for infrastructure projects and in some cases the municipal government has pledged its general revenues to secure loans to its enterprises." World Bank, *China: Revenue Mobilization and Tax Policy*, 87.

44. Interview with Zheng Lanying, July 8, 1990.

45. ¥320,000 commandeered by higher authorities from county coffers in 1981; ¥400,000 in 1982; and ¥800,000 in 1987.

46. Christine Wong argues that one of the serious side effects of the uncertain sequencing of the fiscal reform process in China has been to damage the credibility of the center and to create "an atmosphere in which nearly everyone feels cheated, and regional tensions run high" ("Fiscal Reform," 221–22).

47. Interview with Zheng Lanying, July 8, 1990.

48. In 1984, the finance offices (*caizheng suo*) in town and township governments around Shulu employed a total of just 54 persons. By 1986, this number had risen to 131. And in 1989, to help with tax collection and record-keeping during the busy periods, an additional 79 part-time temporary workers were taken on to staff these offices. The new prosperity in the countryside during the 1980's was accompanied by a palpably heightening intensity of official financial planning, control, and tax collection work.

49. Interview, Aug. 20, 1990.

50. In 1989, twenty-three towns and townships in Shulu exceeded their targets while eight fell short. Shortfalls in any given year were expected to be made up (through extra collections if necessary) in the following year, so that the overall three-year fixed target minimum for the township would actually be fulfilled.

51. Interview, Aug. 20, 1990.

52. By far the major source of town government revenues was the revenue-sharing system discussed here. But town governments did also have a few other small sources of income, sometimes including subsidies for special purposes allocated by the county government.

53. See page 82 *ff*.

54. There were eighteen Second Light factories in 1978. Among the largest of these was a clothing factory, a plasticware plant, and a chemical plant. In 1990, Second Light, by that time already reorganized into the Light Industry and Textile Products Company, had a total of twenty enterprises under its leadership. These included the surviving collective enterprises originally governed by the Second Light Industry Bureau, but also several state-owned plants that turned out light industrial and textile products (see the discussion in Chapter 5). The tax and profit-sharing systems applied to these enterprises depended on their ownership status—state-owned or collective. That is, the original investment and ownership conceptions governing these individual factories were not abandoned; on the contrary,

these followed them into their new association with Light Industry and Textile authorities. So by 1990 the Light Industrial and Textile Products Corporation at the county level was actually administering a variety of systems of taxation and profit division in the enterprises under its supervision.

55. The prefecture office, in turn, remitted a portion of its receipts to its system superiors at the province level.

56. There are, in fact, a number of mysterious inconsistencies in the data we collected concerning Second Light. We have elected not to present here materials about which we have serious misgivings.

57. Officials in Shijiazhuang said, in 1979, that the Second Light Industry Bureau at the prefecture also had a ¥10,000 limit on monies it could disburse on its own authority.

58. Detailed data collected on the business of Shulu's banks and credit unions from 1979 to 1989 tend to confirm that these institutions were acquiring greatly enhanced roles in both capital formation and the development of the local economy. The Shulu branch of the Construction Bank, which makes loans on behalf of the State Planning Commission, for example, reported total loans made in 1989 at over ¥36 million. That was nine times greater than the amount loaned by the bank in 1979. The Shulu Industrial and Commercial Bank, similarly, reported total outstanding industrial loans in 1989 of nearly ¥94 million, a figure more than seven times higher than that reported by the Industrial and Commercial Bank in 1979.

59. In most years there were, in fact, a few other "flexible financial resources" (jidong caili) available to the county government, deriving mostly from overtarget revenue collections, county-retained revenue-share divisions, and unexpended funds carried over from the previous year. These flexible funds were usually very small. Xinji shi caizheng zhi, 293–95, presents some detailed figures.

60. In 1985 this category of local surtax was converted to the Urban Construction and Environmental Protection Tax, at which point it also became an in-budget rather than an extrabudgetary revenue source.

61. Xinji shi caizheng zhi, 296, reports a figure of ¥2,516,000. This discrepancy is most likely due to a transcription error.

62. Interview with Zheng Lanying, Aug. 20, 1990.

63. Thirty-eight counties in Hebei province were authorized in that year to levy this category of surtax locally.

64. Because the petrochemicals plant was a joint investment by the county and the prefecture governments, some special profit-share procedures actually had to be applied to it (Xinji shi caizheng zhi, 297).

65. Western analysts in the 1970's, working with far less complete statistics than are available now, had assumed that all county-run industries, since they were in the state sector, were therefore in the state budget. Since the existence, through the 1970's, of a significant county-run extrabudgetary industrial subsector seems unlikely to have been a peculiarity of Shulu alone, certain other working assumptions about the distribution of the profits of county-run industries in China during those years may have to be reexamined. See Nicholas Lardy, *Economic Growth and Distribution*, 168.

66. Note that this is somewhat less than the figures in Table 19 indicate *should* have been forwarded to the county for collection during that period. That total, for 1973–88, comes to ¥10.9 million.

67. This, as explained in the section below on in-budget enterprise profit contributions, was about the time that special allocations were being made out of in-

budget industry profits specifically to assist the extrabudgetary industries, and some Shulu county officials were clearly interested in the plan for conversion.

68. Interview with Zheng Lanying, Aug. 20, 1990. See also *Xinji shi caizheng zhi*, 297.

69. At that point, payable depreciation funds reverted from the Finance Bureau to the various offices (*bumen*) of the county government that held managerial responsibility for each of these local state-run (*difang guoying*) factories.

70. For in-budget factories, higher levels of the state were responsible for making up 80 percent of operating losses. The county government was expected to make up the other 20 percent out of its own resources.

71. *Xinji shi caizheng zhi*, 300–301, gives a factory-by-factory listing of major investments from 1973 to 1983.

72. Audrey Donnithorne guessed as much when she noted that a "local authority known to possess ample extra-budgetary funds might lose some of its advantage through harsher assessments or smaller subsidies" (*China's Economic System* [New York: Praeger, 1967], 393).

73. See Chapter 8.

5. INDUSTRY AND INDUSTRIALIZATION

1. According to official calculations, in 1978 Shulu had only 8.9 percent of the prefecture's population, but accounted for nearly 20 percent of the prefecture's gross value of industrial output (GVIO). Industry in Shulu officially accounted for 55.7 percent of the county's gross value of output (GVO), while in the prefecture as a whole industry contributed only 39.1 percent of GVO. But these official figures understated the total value of industrial production taking place within the county, since they excluded the output of brigade-level industry. Until 1984, it was standard Chinese statistical practice to include only industrial output of enterprises at the commune/township level or above in GVIO. Industrial output value produced by brigade/village-level plants was included in GVAO. This produced considerable distortions that must be kept in mind in analyzing Chinese local industrialization. In Shulu, 1978 industrial output value would rise from 55.7 percent to 65.6 percent of gross output value if brigade-level industrial output were included.

But even this is too low. The official figures for 1978 exclude the output value of several large Shulu plants that before then had belonged to the county government but which had been transferred to prefecture ownership, though they were still located in and employed workers from Shulu.

2. Shulu officials informed us of a state regulation requiring that all publicly announced figures must be in constant yuan. For the years since 1980 the base year was 1980.

3. "Xinji shi jingji fazhan zhanlüe (xiuding gao)" (Economic development strategy of Xinji municipality [revised draft]). (Xinji: Xinji Municipality Committee of the Chinese Communist Party and the Xinji Municipality People's Government, Aug. 1, 1986). Hereafter cited as "Xinji Development Strategy (Revised Draft)."

4. All of these products except perhaps building materials were prominent historically in Shulu ("Xinji Development Strategy [Revised Draft]").

5. The Hebei and national data are calculated from *Guojia tongji ju* (State Statistical Bureau), *Zhongguo tongji nianjian 1990* (Statistical yearbook of China 1990) (Beijing: Zhongguo tongji chubanshe, 1991), 91, 417.

6. An important exception for the Chinese case, however, is Christine P. W.

Wong, "Ownership and Control in Chinese Industry: The Maoist Legacy and Prospects for the 1980's," in *China's Economy Looks Toward the Year 2000: Volume I. The Four Modernizations*. Selected Papers Submitted to the Joint Economic Committee, Congress of the United States (Washington, D.C.: U.S. Government Printing Office, 1986), especially 581–90. She found considerable blurring between "state" and "collective" industry, and little systematic relationship between this formal categorization on the one hand and, on the other, whether it was included in state production planning and material allocation, or whether it was engaged in heavy or light industrial production.

7. Liu Guoguang and Wang Ruisun, *Zhongguo de jingji tizhi gaige* (Reform of China's economic system) (Beijing: 1982), 7; cited in Wong, "Ownership and Control," 574n.

8. This figure would be larger still were it not for the fact that two of the biggest plants in this category—the cylinder-head and chemical factories—had been taken over by the Shijiazhuang prefecture government in 1971.

9. The largest plant was in West Germany. But in 1990 the Xinji Chemical Factory was expecting to overtake its German competitor soon, as a result of an expansion spurred by the rise of a new collectively owned barium salts plant in Shulu with which it was also competing. See Chapter 8 for a discussion.

10. Audrey Donnithorne, *China's Economic System* (New York: Praeger, 1967), 149, 223. This putative upgrading, anyway, was the rationale given for the administrative reorganization.

11. Chu-yuan Cheng, *China's Economic Development: Growth and Structural Change* (Boulder: Westview, 1982), 172.

12. By 1986 this number was down to sixteen, due to one consolidation and one closure. By 1990, with the expansion of light industry, the number was up again, to twenty.

13. GVIO in these plants averaged ¥1,480,000, compared with ¥2,607,000 for the county enterprises as a whole. Profits per plant were lower both in absolute terms (¥111,000 compared with ¥294,500) and as a percentage of GVIO (7.5 percent compared with 11.3 percent). Perhaps the reason may be sought partly in their pattern of labor utilization, since they employed about as many workers per plant (302) as did all county industrial plants (313), despite their smaller output and profits. In other words, their average labor productivity (¥4,900) was far lower than the average for county industry in Shulu (¥8,329). But it must be remembered that all these figures are based on a state-determined price structure that undervalued light industrial products.

14. Christine Wong pointed out in 1986 that "the Second Light Industrial System . . . is less vertically oriented [than state industrial ministries], but its enterprises are subject to greater local control" ("Ownership and Control," 583).

15. See Chapter 4 for further details.

16. Also see Christine Wong's discussion of "'sponsored' or 'affiliated' collectives" ("Ownership and Control," 584).

17. Wong hypothesizes that the source of an enterprise's investment is the criterion distinguishing "state" and "collective" firms ("Ownership and Control," 584). Our findings in Shulu indicate that this is indeed an important criterion, but not the only one used in Chinese administrative practice.

18. It is interesting to note that at about the same time that the Transportation Bureau's Asphalt Felt Factory was being switched to Second Light administrative control another Transportation Bureau enterprise, a vehicle repair shop, was being switched into the county extrabudgetary enterprise category.

19. Michael Bleaney, *Do Socialist Economies Work?* (Oxford: Basil Blackwell, 1988), 51.

20. See also Wong, "Ownership and Control," 584. We argue in the concluding chapter that in Shulu this continued to be the case, even into the Deng period. In conceptual terms, we there theorize this orientation of the local state as more developmental than entrepreneurial.

21. As explained in Chapter 4, though, the extrabudgetary enterprises were not the only ones contributing some of their profits to the extrabudgetary fund.

22. Shulu County Finance Bureau, *Xinji shi caizheng zhi* (Xinji finance gazetteer) (Beijing: Xinhua Chubanshe, 1990), 297 *ff*.

23. See ibid., 298.

24. The details have been explored in Chapter 4. Also see Christine Wong, "Ownership and Control," 574–75, and "The Maoist 'Model' Reconsidered: Local Self-Reliance and the Financing of Rural Industrialization," in William Joseph, Christine Wong, and David Zweig, eds., *New Perspectives on the Cultural Revolution* (Cambridge, Mass.: Harvard University Press, 1991), especially pages 186 *ff*.

25. This is what Schurmann called "decentralization II" to distinguish administrative from enterprise decentralization ("I"). See Franz Schurmann, *Ideology and Organization in Communist China*, 2d ed. (Berkeley: University of California Press, 1968), 175–78, 196–99 and passim.

26. In the category of Shulu enterprises run by higher levels, this left the Shijiazhuang prefecture government with only the electricity generating station. This is consistent with what appears to be a general trend in China toward a reduced role for prefectural governments amid the decentralizing tendencies of the reforms. Likewise, the Hebei province government still had only its grain mill.

27. See the discussion beginning on page 102.

28. An arts and crafts factory—itself an expansion of an earlier jade carving factory—cleaved off two new firms making eyeglasses and signs. Meanwhile, the oxygen bottling plant and the asphalt paper plant that had been established under the Transport Bureau now came under the Light Industry and Textiles Company. And one new factory making composite wood (from glued scraps) was created under the Light Industry and Textiles Company as an offshoot of the existing furniture factory.

29. In addition, the Rural Construction Materials Company ceased production in order to become a purely administrative unit.

30. As in the earlier years of reform, this one too was related to agriculture: the Bureau of Animal Husbandry opened a veterinary medicine firm.

31. In Shulu, as we have seen in Chapter 3, this "streamlining" did not result in any reduction in the complexity of the county government, or in any reduction in its personnel.

32. Interview, Dec. 7, 1986.

33. Data on profitability in Shulu industry are plagued by problems of murky and inconsistent definition (across sectors and over time) and shifting accounting procedures, which preclude systematic or definitive discussion. But it is clear that profits in county industry were dropping through the first half of the 1980's. Second Light Industry enterprise profits showed an average annual decline of 10.2 percent from 1979 to 1985. Between 1979 and 1985 profits of county extrabudgetary industries averaged an annual decline of 5.3 percent, as against an average annual rate of increase of 7.8 percent from 1973 to 1978.

34. Interview, Shulu Economic Planning Committee, June 30, 1990.

35. A discussion of these issues appears below, beginning on page 109.

36. Interview, Wangkou town, July 4, 1990.

37. Interview, Wangkou town, July 4, 1990.

38. See Chapter 7.

39. Christine P. W. Wong, "Interpreting Rural Industrial Growth in the Post-Mao Period," *Modern China* 14, 1 (Jan. 1988): 5–12.

40. For example, see Barry Naughton, "Implications of the State Monopoly over Industry and Its Relaxation," *Modern China* 18, 1 (Jan. 1992): 14–41.

41. See Chapter 4.

42. See Table 12.

43. "Market" is placed in quotation marks here to emphasize the fact that, in the context of China's still partly state-run price and resource allocation systems, enterprise profitability was at best only a very partial function of economic competition.

44. See Chapter 4.

45. See Chapter 4.

46. This by no means represents the total industrial labor force of the county. Town- and village-run industries have developed at an astonishing rate in recent years in Shulu as elsewhere in China. Rural dwellers working in these smaller industries numbered 56,067 in 1990. Rural industry is discussed in some detail in Chapter 8.

47. Shulu was certainly not alone in making such extensive use of contract labor; the practice was widespread around the country.

48. There are two broad classifications that include the vast majority of Chinese: rural households (*nongye hukou*) and nonrural households (*fei nongye hukou*). In the Mao period, only the latter were legally entitled to live, hold regular state employment, obtain social services, or rely upon state grain supply agencies in towns and cities. In the Deng period, with the rise of market forms of allocation of housing, food, and social services, these strictures have been relaxed, and have become somewhat anachronistic. But the classificatory system still prevails, and is occasionally used by local governments attempting to clear rural migrants out of urban areas or, in a more recent development, to attempt once again to regulate the flow of labor from the rural to the urban areas. In 1990, the Shulu Labor Bureau received a new regulation requiring provincial-level approval for any hiring of rural householders by urban enterprises.

49. In the Mao period, even many of those hailing from suburbs of Xinji did not commute on a daily basis, partly because many contract workers were young single people who preferred life in the city, and partly because there was no sufficiently remunerative work there to attract them back. With the rise of the responsibility systems, daily commutation increased as contract workers could put their spare time to productive use on household plots.

50. An increase in the numbers of nonrural householders would indeed put pressure on the distributive capacity of the state grain bureau. More important, it would require an increase in state grain procurement from the rural collective sector, through purchase (which the state could ill afford, since it already heavily subsidizes urban grain supply) or through (politically more unpopular) higher taxes or quotas.

51. Interview, Dec. 9, 1986.

52. The cleavage between contract and regular workers was a major node of conflict in the Cultural Revolution. Nationally, contract workers tended to join or to form their own radical factions during the Cultural Revolution. They vociferously protested not only their lower wages but also their less secure job tenure,

which in normal times placed them at a disadvantage in expressing their discontent over a range of issues. See Hong Yung Lee, *The Politics of the Chinese Cultural Revolution* (Berkeley: University of California Press, 1978), 130–32; Colina MacDougall, "Second Class Workers," *Far Eastern Economic Review* (May 9, 1968): 306–8; Lynn T. White III, "Workers' Politics in Shanghai," *Journal of Asian Studies* 36, 1 (Nov. 1976): 99–116.

53. The rural collective units did not award any work points to the contract workers for these monies. For the majority of contract workers (most exceptions were those from the richest teams with the higher work point values), the new system was a net gain. Those for whom it was not were permitted to retain the old system.

54. In the Shulu Fur and Leather Tanning Factory regular workers with eight years' seniority received 100 percent sick pay, while those with less time on the job were eligible for lower percentages according to a sliding scale. Contract workers who had to purchase food grain in Xinji paid ¥.35 per *jin* (¥.70 per kilogram) for wheat, but regular workers paid the subsidized price of ¥.18 per *jin* (¥.36 per kilogram) for the same grain.

55. The new contract system has been discussed in Gordon White, "The Politics of Economic Reform in Chinese Industry: The Introduction of the Labour Contract System," *China Quarterly* 111 (Sept. 1987): 365–89.

56. And perhaps they did: for example, in 1986, officials of Guanghan county, who had been generally cooperative with our requests for data, said with regret and frustration that they would have difficulty supplying certain rather uncontroversial materials because, under the new employment system, their staff did not have to discharge duties not specified in their contracts.

57. By the mid-1980's, difficulties and inequities had arisen around the ability of county enterprises to meet their responsibilities to retired workers. In the late 1960's, wages of current and retired workers, which previously had been separated financially and administratively—with the retirement fund managed by the labor unions—were collapsed into a single account. As a result, many older firms with relatively larger percentages of retired workers were finding the financial burden onerous. In Shulu's troubled Xinji Agricultural Machinery Repair and Production Factory, to adopt the phraseology of the director of the Labor Bureau, "two current workers had to support one retired worker." This contributed significantly to the plant's financial collapse (see page 103). Moreover, officials of the labor and finance bureaus found themselves having to deal with requests for especially large increases in the wage funds of enterprises with large numbers of retired workers. To resolve this problem, in 1985 a policy of separating wage and retirement funds was undertaken on an experimental basis in several provinces, including Guangdong and Hebei. The Hebei provincial government chose Shijiazhuang city and Shulu as test points. In Shulu, county enterprises were to contribute 20 percent of their workers' wages to a retirement fund administered by the Social Insurance Affairs Management Office of the Shulu Labor Bureau. Subsequently the new policy was extended throughout Hebei.

Regular workers' benefits were: for those with under five years of experience, 50 percent of wages for the first six months, and 55 percent thereafter; 5–10 years, 70 percent and then 60 percent; 10–15 years, 80 percent and then 65 percent; 15–20 years, 80 percent and then 70 percent; over 20 years, 100 percent and then 75 percent.

The retirement benefit scale was: for those with 10–15 years of experience, 70 percent of their highest salary; 15–20 years, 80 percent; 20–30 years, 85 percent;

30–35 years, 90 percent; over 35 years, 95 percent; employed since before liberation, 100 percent.

58. Specifically, the children had to pass a test, be single ("so they'll be better, less distracted workers," according to the Shulu Labor Bureau vice director), and be real children ("not cousins," said the vice director, indicating perhaps some fraudulent abuse of this mode of recruitment into the treasured category of regular worker).

59. As noted above, regular workers were asked to sign contracts, according to Shulu Labor Bureau officials. But these did not place them in the category of contract-system workers. They still retained their job security privileges and superior benefits.

60. Interview, Shulu Labor Bureau, Dec. 9, 1986.

61. Contract-system workers employed over five years were entitled to two years' benefits in the form of a portion of wages, calculated as follows: for the first twelve months, 75 percent if the unemployment resulted from bankruptcy, 70 percent if the enterprise canceled the contract, 60 percent for temporary layoffs; for the second year, 50 percent regardless of cause. Contract-system workers employed under five years could not draw the second year of benefits.

To finance this scheme, enterprises paid one percent of their wage bill into an unemployment insurance fund, which was administered by the Labor Service Company. Despite its name, which its leading official admitted was misleading, this was a noncommercial unit under the Shulu Labor Bureau. It was responsible for overall labor force planning, for administering labor recruitment, training, and retraining, and for the provision of truly temporary ("out-of-plan") workers to certain factories, discussed below. While in some parts of China labor service companies have been used as ways of disposing of surplus regular state workers or disciplining recalcitrant ones (see Andrew Walder, "Workers, Managers and the State: The Reform Era and the Political Crisis of 1989," *China Quarterly* 127 [Sept. 1991]: 478–79), there was no evidence of this in Shulu. One reason for the difference may be that in Shulu regular workers were insulated from the threat of discharge by the existence of contract workers, who could be (and, as we have seen, were in fact being) fired first.

62. Their disability benefits were 100 percent of wages for the first six months, but only 60 percent thereafter. Sick pay benefits had a definite limit according to seniority, after which the worker was discharged: for those with less than 5 years of experience, up to three months of wages; 5–10 years, 6 months; 10–15 years, 9 months; 15–20 years, 12 months; over 20 years, 18 months. As for retirement benefits, those with less than ten years' experience received only severance pay equivalent to two months of salary for every year they had contributed to the retirement fund. Those with ten to fifteen years' experience received 40 percent of their highest salary per month. And those with over fifteen years' experience received monthly benefits of 60 percent of their highest salary plus one percent additional for each year of experience over fifteen.

According to Robert Delfs, the pool for funding retirement benefits for contract system workers is in many places separate from that for funding benefits for regular workers. No mention of this was made in Shulu. But even where this is the case, Delfs points out that with the expansion of the ranks of contract-system workers and the contraction of regular state employment, eventually these separate funds will have to be combined. Thus, the contract-system workers' retirement fund will eventually have to subsidize the benefits paid to regular workers. See Robert Delfs, "Coming of Age," *Far Eastern Economic Review* 150 (Oct. 25, 1990): 17–18.

63. Just what the difference was, and whether or not the increment was adequate compensation for it, cannot be calculated in general. The benefits would depend on the particular employment history and disability, sickness, or retirement situation of each case.

64. Interview, Shulu Labor Bureau, July 6, 1990.

65. Ibid.

66. In fact, but for this goal there was, according to Shulu officials, no difference whatsoever between the old category of temporary contract labor and that of "in-plan" temporary contract labor.

67. Interview, Xinji Fur and Leather Tanning Factory, December 5, 1986.

68. Interestingly, this is approximately the same portion received by the original contract workers after the 1972 compromise, which stipulated that their rural collective units would receive a fee of ¥3–4.

69. The class nature of contract labor is discussed in Marc Blecher, "Peasant Labour for Urban Industry: Temporary Contract Labour, Urban-Rural Balance and Class Relations in a Chinese County," *World Development* 11, 8 (Aug. 1983): 731–46.

70. In the recent past, some enterprises had been circumventing the Labor Bureau by directly hiring relatives of their employees. New regulations discussed in the next section were directed at regulating this (among other things).

71. The reason for this was that many firms had demanded, as a way of dealing with the general thirst for credit, that, under the guise of the newly mooted "shareholding" system, new workers invest ¥3,000 in the enterprise as a condition of being hired. (This requirement was quite legal.) And it was rural far more than urban people who could raise such funds.

72. Interview, Shulu Labor Service Company, July 9, 1990.

73. For a most detailed example, see Wong, "Ownership and Control," 571–603.

6. COMMERCIAL DEVELOPMENT

1. The figure for "leading officials" includes only supervisory personnel, not the large staffs employed by commercial companies and stores.

2. For example, we were shown the Foodstuffs Company's exacting record-keeping of local trade in live pigs and fresh eggs over a twenty-year period.

3. These cooperatives made balancing exchanges among themselves too: around forty of their staff members frequently traveled around the county making contacts and commercial arrangements with other cooperatives and the county company.

4. Until 1976 this agency was known as the Market Management Commission.

5. For a discussion, see Chapter 3.

6. This constituted, of course, a double extension of state power compared with the past, when prices were not only privately negotiated but also kept confidential between the buyer and seller.

7. Traders were generally required to stay in their home counties, to prevent regional private trade.

8. Prices on the free market for pork, chicken, and mutton were about 20 percent higher than state-set prices.

9. As we shall see below, even as late as 1990 the Foreign Trade Bureau remained largely "unreformed" and under strict vertical bureaucratic authority.

10. The formula used was 0.5 percent of industrial and 1 percent of agricultural product value.

11. These were short-term loans, not exceeding three years. Between 1974 and

1978 the bureau had issued a total of ¥3,718,800 in such loans. To put this figure in perspective, the People's Bank extended loans totaling ¥26,867,000 in 1978. The Foreign Trade Bureau was thus a not insignificant source of credit in Shulu.

12. Interview with Liu Jianguo, Shulu Commerce Bureau, July 30, 1990.

13. Interviews with Liu Jianguo of the Shulu Commerce Bureau (July 30, 1990) and with Zhao Zhanbiao of the Shulu Gongxiaoshe, July 19, 1990.

14. Of the six factories, three produced cotton oil.

15. As a matter of general principle, the GXS was intended to handle rural commerce while its old master and now partner in trade, the Commerce Bureau, was to serve consumers and producing units located in the urban districts. This was regarded as a rule of thumb, however, not an absolute division of labor. Some clear crossovers of function were already occurring in 1990 in the crazy-quilt urban-rural mixed economy of Shulu.

16. Interview with Zhao Zhanbiao, Shulu Gongxiaoshe, July 19, 1990.

17. Interview, Vice Director Liu Jianguo, Shulu Commerce Bureau, July 30, 1990.

18. For a fuller discussion, see Chapter 3.

19. Zhili is the historical Manchu name for Hebei; "Xinji shi jingji fazhan zhanlüe (xiuding gao)" (Economic development strategy of Xinji municipality [Revised Draft]). (Xinji: Xinji Municipality People's Government, Aug. 1, 1986).

20. On migration controls in Shulu, see Marc Blecher, "Peasant Labour for Urban Industry: Temporary Contract Labour, Urban-Rural Balance and Class Relations in a Chinese County," *World Development* 11, 8 (Aug. 1983). That article, written in 1982 on the basis of 1979 research, said "[B]ecause of [contract labor, a form of migration control], Xinji is a far less congested place . . . than [it] otherwise would be" (page 738).

21. *Hebei Ribao* (Hebei daily), Jan. 22, 1985: 1.

22. *Hebei Ribao* (Hebei daily), Oct. 23, 1986: 3.

23. On the urban planning aspects of this project, see Chapter 7.

24. Like condominiums in the West, ownership rights to the units in Hebei Yiji were circumscribed in some basic ways. For example, they could not be torn down or expanded. Owners were required to reside and do business in their units, to prevent the market from becoming a set of rental properties. But they could rent out the shopfront portions of their units, so long as they themselves continued to live in the residential portion and the tenant him/herself did some business in the shop. They could also be sold, but new owners were subject to the same stipulations.

25. Shulu officials said that despite the overwhelming demand, they did not expand the project any further at that point because of their concern about their inexperience in running what was already a massive project, and because of the difficulty they would face in receiving the necessary land-use permits from prefecture urban-planning authorities. Of the buyers, 80 percent came from Shulu county, and almost all the rest from other counties in Hebei. Of the local buyers, one-third came from Xinji, one-third from the townships surrounding the city (which were later incorporated into it as administrative districts), and one-third from other parts of the county.

26. Interview, Shulu Industry and Commerce Management Bureau, Dec. 13, 1986. As noted above, the units could be sold to new buyers provided they too agreed to live and do business in them.

27. The Finance Bureau's contribution was most likely intended to be drawn out of revenues from the new urban construction and environmental protection tax that was levied for the first time in Shulu in 1985. This figure for the Finance

Bureau's contribution to the project was a 1986 estimate. Information gathered in 1990, on the other hand, suggested that some of the funds promised by individual investors did not materialize and, in the end, it had fallen to the county government to cover the difference, to the tune of ¥1.8 million.

28. See the concluding chapter for a theoretical discussion of this concept.

29. The market management fee was similar in function to condominium maintenance fees in the West: it covered the collective costs of running and maintaining the market. In setting the fee the bureau had accepted gross sales figures which it knew were well below actual ones (as noted above). So the real fee rate was a good deal lower than this.

30. See Marc Blecher, "Developmental State, Entrepreneurial State: The Political Economy of Socialist Reform in Xinji Municipality and Guanghan County," in Gordon White, ed., *The Chinese State in the Era of Economic Reform: The Road to Crisis* (London: Macmillan, 1991), 265–91; Vivienne Shue, "Emerging State-Society Relations in Rural China," in Jørgen Delman, Clemens Stubbe Østergaard, and Flemming Christiansen, eds., *Remaking Peasant China* (Aarhus: Aarhus University Press, 1990), 60–80.

31. For example, Nanzhiqiu town had a regular pet bird market, with over 2,000 specimens on sale each market day. And on every third day a special market in horse-cart equipment was held at Hebei Yiji.

32. See Chapter 7.

33. Bargaining downward from these maximum prices was, of course, permitted.

34. Interview, Shulu Industry and Commerce Management Bureau, July 9, 1990.

35. These thoughts are developed further in Vivienne Shue, "State Sprawl: The Regulatory State and Social Life in a Small Chinese City," in Deborah Davis, Barry Naughton, Richard Kraus, and Elizabeth Perry, eds., *Urban Spaces: Autonomy and Community in Contemporary China* (forthcoming).

36. These are the permits that have also been used in China by local and provincial authorities to erect trade barriers as part of their efforts to protect and develop their local economies, a phenomenon that became widespread by 1988; see Elizabeth Cheng, "Beggar Thy Neighbor," *Far Eastern Economic Review* 143 (Jan. 12, 1989): 45–46.

37. For more on this organization and its functions nationally, see Willy Kraus, *Private Business in China* (Honolulu: University of Hawaii Press, 1991), 91–93.

38. When the people's communes were established in 1958, their boundaries were drawn to cut across traditional marketing patterns. See G. William Skinner, "Marketing and Social Structure in Rural China, Part III," *Journal of Asian Studies* 24, 3 (May 1965): 382 ff.

39. The exception was located in Xinji.

40. Xinji Shi Gongshang Xingzheng Guanli Ju (The Xinji Municipality Industry and Commerce Administration and Management Bureau), "Shiyige fu tu te chanpin pifa shichang jian jie" ("A brief introduction to eleven sideline, local, and specialty product wholesale markets"), 2.

41. Local officials recounted a ditty from the Ming dynasty—when Shulu was known as Lianguandian—with obvious pride in the past and as an illustration of their hopes for the future:

> When to Lianguandian comes pelt or skin,
> The whole thing is put to good use.
> No matter what grimy shape it's in,
> The whole thing is put to good use.

42. Shulu's proportion of the prefecture's export production dropped from 46.8 percent in earlier years to only around 25 percent in 1986. It bounced back up to about 30 percent in 1990.

43. "Eastern Hebei Opens to the World," *Beijing Review* 23 (June 5–11, 1989): 19–22.

44. These two companies dealt directly with producers, making purchases "more efficiently" than before, according to bureau officials. They also, as companies, were permitted to borrow money from local banks, something that as government administrative offices they were prohibited from doing. This access to credit seemed in the final analysis to be the most important advantage of renaming these offices "companies" (interview, Vice Director Zhang Zhenxiu, Shulu Foreign Trade Bureau, July 19, 1990).

45. Interview, Zhang Zhenxiu, Shulu Foreign Trade Bureau, Dec. 13, 1986.

46. Interview, Zhang Zhenxiu, Shulu Foreign Trade Bureau, July 19, 1990.

47. Ibid.

48. Heilongjiang *is* a border province, of course. Director Lin admitted that this arrangement between the Heilongjiang corporation and Shulu was a highly irregular one. Heilongjiang province authorities normally preferred to keep border trade options entirely to themselves and were loath to share these with suppliers from other regions. Lin attributed the "stretching" of administrative definitions and routines in this particular case to several special factors. First and most important was the high degree of interest the Soviets displayed in certain products such as fur, leather, and pears, which were simply unavailable within Heilongjiang. The implication was that the Soviets would take their business elsewhere unless the Heilongjiang corporation managed to find supplies. Second, Shulu prices for these special commodities were on the low side, so the profit potential was high enough to interest the Heilongjiang corporation. Third, Shulu people (who remained unspecified) already had established some good working relations (*guanxi*) with the Heilongjiang corporation officials. And fourth, the Shulu county leaders were credited by Director Lin with "vision" and with a determination to do all that could be done to improve Shulu trade on all fronts. This inclined them to look favorably upon what would otherwise have been regarded as a most irregular liaison with Heilongjiang. According to Lin, only one other county in Hebei, Zhao Xian, was in 1990 "doing anything like what we do" (interview, Director Lin Jianzhong, Shulu Border Region Trade Company, July 24, 1990). But Zhao Xian was working through another border region trading corporation, not the Heilongjiang outfit.

49. These are the Heilongjiang Guoji Maoyi Gongsi and the Heilongjiang Shangpin Jianyan Ju.

50. Interview, Director Lin Jianzhong, Shulu Border Region Trade Company, July 24, 1990.

51. Visiting Soviet buyers apparently had been bringing long shopping lists with them, and Shulu officials seemed a little shocked by the extensiveness of their needs: shocked, that is, to discover how many consumer goods that they took for granted as being available or inexpensive in China could not be found (legally), for any price, in the USSR. Since the Soviet Union still had no direct trade agreements with Japan, for example, some of these buyers were interested in trying to secure Japanese-made cars and motorcycles through Shulu. Other items they were interested in getting hold of struck Shulu officials as ranging from the embarrassingly elementary (such as student notebooks) to the absurd (such as cracked and broken pottery and ceramics rejects that the Soviet buyers expected to be able to glue to-

gether and then sell for a profit at home). And the Soviets were so eager to buy Shulu pears, they reported, that they were able to unload poor-quality fruit in deals with them, fruit that did not come close to meeting the quality standards applied, say, by trading partners in Hong Kong. "There's almost nothing they *don't* want to buy from or through us," Lin commented about the Soviets (interview, Director Lin Jianzhong, Shulu Border Region Trade Company, July 24, 1990).

52. Interview, Vice Director Feng Huilai, Shulu Office of Economic Cooperation, July 24, 1990. By 1990 it was reported that every Hebei county and municipality government was supposed to have established such an office to identify and facilitate mutually beneficial technical and economic exchanges with other units and localities.

53. Vice Director Feng (interview, July 24, 1990) claimed that the volume of work the office handled actually entitled it under 1990 guidelines to a staff of twelve, but there appeared little likelihood of getting any such assignments upgrade in the near future.

54. It received bulletins and newsletters containing news about exchange possibilities from cities and counties all over north China. Some members of the office staff spent much of their time just reading and making note of these opportunities.

55. Dorothy J. Solinger, *China's Transition from Socialism: Statist Legacies and Market Reforms, 1980–1990* (Armonk, N.Y.: M. E. Sharpe, 1993), 143.

7. URBAN DEVELOPMENT

1. R. J. R. Kirkby, *Urbanization in China: Town and Country in a Developing Economy, 1949–2000 A.D.* (New York: Columbia University Press, 1985): chap. 8.

2. Jiucheng, for example, appeared to us to be a more substantial place than Shenze town, the capital of Shenze county immediately north of Shulu.

3. See Chapter 6.

4. See Chapter 5.

5. On the transition of the county to a municipality, see the discussion in Chapter 1. On the new administrative districts, see Chapter 3.

6. At this time the Shulu county government lacked an office specifically charged with environmental protection. It got one in 1983, when an Environmental Protection Office was established within the Urban Construction Bureau. By late 1986 the Bureau had been renamed the Urban Construction and Environmental Protection Commission, denoting a higher profile for this work.

7. See the discussion below, page 161 *ff.*

8. Actually, it was fourth and sixth largest, respectively, if the polyglot budget line for "other expenditures" is included.

9. "Xinji shi jingji fazhan zhanlüe (xiuding gao)" (Economic development strategy of Xinji municipality [revised draft]). (Xinji: Xinji Municipality People's Government, Aug. 1, 1986). Hereafter cited as "Xinji Development Strategy (Revised Draft)."

10. The county and prefectural bureaus split the remaining 20 percent.

11. Interview, Shulu Urban Construction and Environmental Protection Commission, June 28, 1990.

12. On the use of carrot-and-stick policies by the Chinese socialist state generally, see Marc Blecher, *China: Politics, Economics, and Society — Iconoclasm and Innovation in a Revolutionary Socialist Country* (London: Frances Pinter, 1986), 50 and passim.

13. See Chapter 5.

14. Interview, Urban Reconstruction and Environmental Protection Bureau, Dec. 14, 1986.

15. At that time (until 1986) it was still known as a bureau. Henceforth we will refer to it by its later designation, commission, even when speaking of events before 1986.

16. This facility contained a library, meeting and party rooms, and game rooms (including a pool table).

17. It was used to show films, but also hosted live acts, including rock-and-roll bands from Guangzhou and Hong Kong as well as Chinese opera troupes from Shandong and elsewhere.

18. Marc Blecher, "Peasant Labour for Urban Industry: Temporary Contract Labour, Urban-Rural Balance and Class Relations in a Chinese County," *World Development* 11, 8 (Aug. 1983): 731–46.

19. For a brilliant analysis of how this has been done in Los Angeles, see Mike Davis, *City of Quartz* (London: Verso, 1990).

20. See Chapter 8.

21. The precise amount was set by the street committee or, in the four new administrative districts, the village committees. The bureau kept a 3 percent management fee (*guanli fei*) for its trouble.

22. In one case, a private entrepreneur who made a deal with Chengbei Administrative District to build a store on 1,900 square meters was fined ¥1,400 for not getting the necessary county bureau approvals, even though the transaction took place before the 1987 legislation and subsequent regulations requiring those approvals.

23. For details, see Chapter 8.

24. The corresponding situation in the countryside is discussed in Chapter 8.

25. The company added 10 to 20 percent of the total construction cost to its charges, but out of this it had to pay its own administrative and other operating costs. The average cost of new housing in Xinji was ¥280 per square meter for total area (including surrounding land and walls, but excluding the cost of water and electrical hookups and various permit fees); this came to about ¥15,000 for an ordinary house for a family of five.

26. But these were one-year loans rather than mortgages.

27. Zhonggong Xinji Shi Weiyuanhui (Xinji Municipal Committee of the Chinese Communist Party) and Xinji Shi Renmin Zhengfu (Xinji Municipal People's Government), "Xinji shi jingji fazhan zhanlüe (taolun gao)" (Xinji municipality economic development strategy [discussion draft]), June 26, 1986; "Xinji Development Strategy (Revised Draft)."

28. "Xinji Development Strategy (Revised Draft)."

8. RURAL DEVELOPMENT

1. See Chapter 1, especially Table 1.

2. "Xinji shi jingji fazhan zhanlüe (xiuding gao)" (Economic development strategy of Xinji municipality [revised draft]). (Xinji: Xinji Municipality People's Government, Aug. 1, 1986). Hereafter cited as "Xinji Development Strategy (Revised Draft)."

3. See Chapter 2 for a fuller discussion.

4. The project was enormous for a county of Shulu's size and resources. It involved digging 2 main trunk canals, 13 large branch canals, 43 subbranch canals, and 650 smaller channels, with a total length of 1,690 kilometers. 25,680,000 cubic

meters of earth were moved, in the process creating 3,344 large squared-off fields averaging 10.27 hectares each; 2,600 sluice gates, bridges, and other related structures were also built. In addition, some five million trees were planted along the new canals, to act as windbreaks for adjoining fields and to prevent erosion along the sides of the channels.

5. Interview, July 6, 1979.

6. See Chapter 4.

7. The details of problems encountered, and the considerable work done by the county government to resolve them, were not specified.

8. Interview, Shulu Water Conservancy Bureau, June 29, 1990.

9. Interview, June 29, 1990.

10. According to Shulu Orchard and Forestry Bureau officials, each hectare takes 450 to 900 cubic meters of water per irrigation, compared with about 450 cubic meters for other crops.

11. Shulu Forestry Bureau officials blamed the shortage of land for this slow plan accomplishment, but water supplies were also a constraint that they were reluctant to acknowledge.

12. Gu Chengwen, "State Packs Goods into ¥600m Aid for Poor," *China Daily*, Apr. 27, 1989.

13. County officials in turn attributed Wangkou's takeoff in significant measure to the paving of the highway connecting it with Xinji.

14. The north-south artery was part of the Andong highway (connecting Shulu to Baoding in the north), and the east-west route was part of the Cangzhou-Shijiazhuang highway.

15. More precisely, they passed directly through six communes. Five others were linked to them by unpaved connectors of one kilometer or less.

16. Two of these were only separated from nearby paved roads by short unpaved connectors two kilometers or less long.

17. Put differently, twice as much mileage was constructed from 1970–78 as from 1979–86.

18. There is a small state-run oilfield in Shulu's Junqi township.

19. "In order to raise our municipality's position as an economic center, we must strengthen and perfect the roadway network between our municipality and the towns and countryside of the neighboring counties" ("Xinji Development Strategy [Revised Draft]").

20. This figure is in significant degree so high because of the relative underpricing of crops and animal products compared with industrial and sideline products. Rural industry did not absorb 81 percent of rural labor time or investment. Nonetheless, it was a major rural economic activity and, precisely because of the price distortions, it brought the rural economy a very significant share of its income.

21. On the first two points, see Chapter 2.

22. See Chapter 6.

23. Specifically, it owned two industrial supply companies, a construction materials firm, a construction company, a construction management concern, an agricultural machinery parts plant, and even consumer goods–producing firms such as a fur and leather products plant and a fireworks factory.

24. Interview, July 2, 1990. Probably constraints on input supplies through the state plan, on which Xinji Chemical depended, were a great part of its problem.

25. They are Wangkou, Nanzhiqiu, Xincheng, Jiucheng, Hemujing, Xinleitou, Chengdong, and Weibo. Interestingly, five of these were among the seven county government administrative subcenters in the Mao period, all of which had also

been enlarged townships (*da xiang*) and also seats of the original, oversized communes. See Chapter 3. One was Chengdong administrative district, a former suburban commune. So only two of the eight were rural townships that were not former county government administrative subcenters. One of these was Wangkou, the reform period boom town.

26. The quoted phrase is from an interview with Qi Fachuan, director, Shulu Township Industries Bureau, July 2, 1990.

27. The selection was made in concert with the county government Rural Industry Leadership Task Force (Xiangzhen Qiye Lingdao Xiaozu). This group was chaired by the vice director of the county People's Congress, and included a vice mayor, a Party vice secretary, and representatives of the Agriculture Bank, the Land Management Bureau, the Petroleum Company, the Water Conservancy Bureau, the Tax Bureau, the Bureau of Standards and Measures, the Science Committee, and, of course, the Township Industries Bureau.

28. See the previous note.

29. By contrast, investments under ¥500,000 could be decided by township governments alone, and required nothing more than a business license from the Industry and Commerce Management Bureau.

30. See Chapter 5.

31. In addition, one of three experiments undertaken with the bureau's leadership failed when the test-point enterprise ran into economic difficulties that made it hard to sell shares to the workers.

32. Here we have an example from Guanghan in mind. See Marc Blecher, "Developmental State, Entrepreneurial State: The Political Economy of Socialist Reform in Xinji Municipality and Guanghan County," in Gordon White, ed., *The Chinese State in the Era of Economic Reform: The Road to Crisis* (London: Macmillan, 1991), 265–91, for a comparison based on late 1986 research. Even in 1986, Mr. Qi was rather more reserved than his Guanghan counterparts.

33. Interview, July 2, 1990.

34. Marc Blecher and Wang Shaoguang, "The Political Economy of Cropping in Maoist and Dengist China: Hebei Province and Shulu County, 1949–1990," *China Quarterly* 137 (Mar. 1994), 63–98.

35. The repeaters were Jiucheng and Nanzhiqiu; the others were Xizebei, Fanjiazhuang, Houying, Muqiu, and Xixiaowang.

36. Jiucheng, Nanzhiqiu, and Fanjiazhuang.

37. Blecher and Wang, "The Political Economy of Cropping."

38. Such scattered holdings are not new, and not specific to the Chinese reforms. In many historical and material contexts, small farmers have preferred scattered holdings as a risk-avoidance strategy. In others they have been forced by complex tenancy systems to accept such holdings.

39. This mainly included Xinleitou and Tianjiazhuang (neither of which was identified by the Forestry Bureau as a fruit production keypoint).

40. Interview, Cheng Zhihua, Shulu Foreign Affairs Bureau, June 28, 1990.

41. Interview, Ninth Street Brigade, July 6, 1979.

42. Interview, Ninth Street Residents' Committee, June 27, 1990.

43. On urban land use regulation, see Chapter 7.

44. This depended on the population-land ratio of the village. If the average amount of cultivated land in the township or administrative district was greater than .067 hectares per person, then a lot of 167.5 square meters could be approved. But if there was less, permissible lot size dropped to 134 square meters.

45. For a 134-square-meter plot, this came to an additional ¥335.

46. See Chapter 5; Marc Blecher, "Peasant Labour for Urban Industry: Tem-

porary Contract Labour, Urban-Rural Balance and Class Relations in a Chinese County," *World Development* 11, 8 (Aug. 1983): 731–46.

47. See Chapter 5.

48. This exchange office rented some properties of its own out to temporary residents, and it also monitored the rates charged on the private rental housing market in Xinji.

49. These three communes—Muqiu (poorer), Tianjiazhuang (average), and Fanjiazhuang (richer)—formed a sample of representative statuses.

50. Blecher and Wang, "The Political Economy of Cropping."

51. Liu Huazhen, "Qieji buyao weibei nongmin de yiyuan" ("Don't go against the will of the peasantry"), *Nongye jingji wenti* (Problems of agricultural economics) 6 (June 1989): 10.

52. Terry Sicular, "Agricultural Planning and Pricing in the Post-Mao Period," *China Quarterly* 116 (Dec. 1988): 701.

53. Interview, Dec. 13, 1986.

54. One was Jiucheng, adjacent to Junqi (which had been permitted to reduce its cotton area to raise chives).

55. Specifically, intercropped wheat and cotton brought in ¥9,000 per hectare, compared with ¥6,450 for cotton alone, ¥1,500 for wheat, and ¥2,000 for maize.

9. CONCLUSION

1. Two of the most sensitive and nuanced recent works in this genre are: Helen Siu, *Agents and Victims in South China: Accomplices in Rural Revolution* (New Haven: Yale University Press, 1989); and Edward Friedman, Paul Pickowicz, and Mark Selden, *Chinese Village, Socialist State* (New Haven: Yale University Press, 1991). Other important studies include Anita Chan, Richard Madsen, and Jonathan Unger, *Chen Village* (Berkeley: University of California Press, 1984); and Thomas P. Bernstein, "Stalinism, Famine, and Chinese Peasants: Grain Procurements during the Great Leap Forward," *Theory and Society* 13, 3 (1984).

2. For example, Daniel Kelliher, *Peasant Power in China: The Era of Rural Reform, 1979–1989* (New Haven: Yale University Press, 1992); Jean C. Oi, *State and Peasant in Contemporary China* (Berkeley: University of California Press, 1989); Tyrene White, "Post-Revolutionary Mobilization in China: The One-Child Policy Reconsidered," *World Politics* 43, 1 (Oct. 1990): 53–76.

3. David M. Lampton, "Chinese Politics: The Bargaining Treadmill," *Issues and Studies* 23, 3 (Mar. 1987): 11–41; Kenneth Lieberthal and Michel Oksenberg, *Policy Making in China: Leaders, Structures and Processes* (Princeton: Princeton University Press, 1988); Susan Shirk, *The Political Logic of Economic Reform in China* (Berkeley: University of California Press, 1993); Gordon White, *Riding the Tiger: The Politics of Economic Reform in China* (London: Macmillan, and Stanford, Calif.: Stanford University Press, 1993).

4. Dorothy Solinger, *China's Transition from Socialism: Statist Legacies and Market Reforms, 1980–1990* (Armonk, N.Y.: M. E. Sharpe, 1993); Christine Wong, "Interpreting Rural Industrial Growth in the Post-Mao Period," *Modern China* 14, 1 (Jan. 1988): 5–8, and "Material Allocation and Decentralization: Impact of the Local Sector on Industrial Reform," in Elizabeth Perry and Christine Wong, eds., *The Political Economy of Reform in Post-Mao China* (Cambridge, Mass.: Harvard University Council on East Asian Studies, 1985), and "Central-Local Relations in an Era of Fiscal Decline: The Paradox of Fiscal Decentralization in Post-Mao China," *China Quarterly* 128 (Dec. 1991).

5. Gan Yang and Cui Zhiyuan, eds., *China: A Reformable Socialism* (Hong Kong: Oxford University Press, forthcoming); Jia Hao and Lin Zhimin, eds., *Changing Central-Local Relations in China* (Boulder: Westview, 1994); Cyril Lin, "Open-Ended Economic Reform in China," in Victor Nee and David Stark, eds., *Remaking the Economic Institutions of Socialism: China and Eastern Europe* (Stanford, Calif.: Stanford University Press, 1989), 95–136; Barry Naughton, "Implications of the State Monopoly over Industry and Its Relaxation," *Modern China* 18, 1 (Jan. 1992); Victor Nee, "Organizational Dynamics of Market Transition: Hybrid Forms, Property Rights, and Mixed Economy in China," *Administrative Science Quarterly* 37 (1992): 1–27; Shirk, *The Political Logic of Economic Reform*; Wang Shaoguang, "Central-Local Fiscal Politics in China," in Jia Hao and Lin Zhimin, eds., *Changing Central-Local Relations*; White, *Riding the Tiger*; Paul Bowles and Gordon White, *The Political Economy of China's Financial Reforms* (Boulder: Westview, 1993); Christine Wong, "Fiscal Reform and Local Industrialization," *Modern China* 18, 2 (Apr. 1992), "Interpreting Rural Industrial Growth," and "Central-Local Relations."

6. Jia and Lin, *Changing Central-Local Relations*; Wang Shaoguang, "From Revolution to Involution: State Capacity, Local Power and (Un)governability in China," in Peter N. S. Lee, ed., *Reform and Policy Implementation in China* (Hong Kong: Chinese University of Hong Kong Press, forthcoming); White, *Riding the Tiger*.

7. Here we refer to the classic work by A. Doak Barnett, *Cadres, Bureaucracy, and Political Power in Communist China* (New York: Columbia University Press, 1967).

8. Wang, "Central-Local Fiscal Politics."

9. Jean Oi, "Fiscal Reform and the Economic Foundations of Local State Corporatism in China," *World Politics* 45, 1 (Oct. 1992); Wang Shaoguang, "The Rise of the Second Budget and the Decline of State Capacity: The Case of China," in Andrew G. Walder, ed., *The Waning of the Communist State: Economic Origins of Political Decline in China and Hungary* (Berkeley: University of California Press, 1995); Wong, "Central-Local Relations."

10. Christine Wong, "Material Allocation"; Christine Wong, "Ownership and Control in Chinese Industry: The Maoist Legacy and Prospects for the 1980's," in *China's Economy Looks Toward the Year 2000: Volume 1. The Four Modernizations. Selected Papers Submitted to the Joint Economic Committee, Congress of the United States* (Washington, D.C.: U.S. Government Printing Office, 1986).

11. Wong, "Central-Local Relations," 706.

12. Christine Wong, "Between Plan and Market: The Role of the Local Sector in Post-Mao China," *Journal of Comparative Economics* 11 (1987): 285–398, and "Central-Local Relations."

13. Shulu's gross value of output rose from ¥266.5 million in 1978 to ¥1.4 billion in 1989. Total budgetary expenditures by the county rose from ¥8.9 million in 1978 to ¥37.9 million in 1989.

14. Ezra Vogel, *One Step Ahead in China: Guangdong Under Reform* (Cambridge, Mass.: Harvard University Press, 1989), 193.

15. To recall just one amusing example detailed above, it included fur and leather in the list of sectors of local industry to be emphasized by placing them under the rubric of food products.

16. One example discussed above was the county government's prohibition against private merchants going into wholesale trade in 1987, a time when the center was in general encouraging private commerce.

17. For just two examples, see Chalmers Johnson, *MITI and the Japanese Miracle* (Stanford, Calif.: Stanford University Press, 1982); Robert Wade, *Governing the Market: Economic Theory and the Role of Government in East Asian Industrialization* (Princeton: Princeton University Press, 1990).

18. One theoretical and comparative effort to extend the developmental state to state socialist as well as capitalist countries is Gordon White, ed., *Developmental States in East Asia* (London: Macmillan, 1988).

19. Putting the matter differently, it is not a model of state capitalism, or of what in China has been called bureaucratic capitalism, with particular reference to the 1930's and 1940's.

20. One scholar who has pointed out the existence of significant interregional trade during the Mao period is Wong, in "Ownership and Control," 575–76.

21. We wish to stress that, to our knowledge, there is nothing exceptional about Shulu in this respect. Other researchers have found similar behaviors by county-level officials in other parts of the country. Helen Siu, for example, notes that the government of Xinhui county, in Guangdong's Pearl River delta, was also active in helping rural enterprises to develop, even in some cases at the expense of its own county-level enterprises. See Siu, *Agents and Victims*. Jean Oi also discusses the myriad ways in which county officials helped promote township and village enterprises in the areas she studied, through preferential material allocations, bureaucratic assistance (for instance, to get loans or to train staff), and direct financial support. See Oi, "Fiscal Reform," 120–22.

22. Marc Blecher, "Developmental State, Entrepreneurial State: The Political Economy of Socialist Reform in Xinji Municipality and Guanghan County," in Gordon White, ed., *The Chinese State in the Era of Economic Reform: The Road to Crisis* (London: Macmillan, 1991).

23. Ibid. See also Vivienne Shue, "Emerging State-Society Relations in Rural China," in Delman et al., eds., *Remaking Peasant China* (Aarhus: Aarhus University Press, 1990), where the terms "coordinative" local state and "competitive" local state are adopted to capture the contrast we observed between Shulu and Guanghan.

24. Note that the idea of "developmental Maoism" was first advanced and discussed by Gordon White, in his "Chinese Development Strategy After Mao," in White, Robin Murray, and Christine White, eds., *Revolutionary Socialist Development in the Third World* (Lexington: University Press of Kentucky, 1983), 155–92.

25. Shulu planners understood as much. "We are geographically well situated, convenient to transportation, which is an important condition for developing our productive capacities. We are on the central Hebei plain, near the provincial seat, adjacent to Beijing and Tianjin. We are located at the gateway of the eastward shipment of Shanxi coal, and at the southern part of the North China Oil and Gas Fields. The Shijiazhuang-Dezhou railway, the Cangzhou-Shijiazhuang highway, and the Xinhe-Baoding highway all provide these routes." See "Xinji shi jingji fazhan zhanlüe (xiuding gao)" (Economic development strategy of Xinji municipality [revised draft]). (Xinji: Xinji Municipality Committee of the Chinese Communist Party and the Xinji Municipality People's Government, Aug. 1, 1986).

26. Wuxi county in Jiangsu, Guanghan county in Sichuan, and Anxi county in Fujian.

27. Hong Yung Lee, *From Revolutionary Cadres to Party Technocrats in Socialist China* (Berkeley and Los Angeles: University of California Press, 1991).

28. Johnson, *MITI and the Japanese Miracle.*
29. See the debate between Victor Nee and Christine Wong, summarized in Nee, "Organizational Dynamics," 3–4.
30. Michael Burawoy has made a similar point in *The Radiant Past* (Chicago: University of Chicago Press, 1992).

Index

Index

In this index an "f" after a number indicates a separate reference on the next page, and an "ff" indicates separate references on the next two pages. A continuous discussion over two or more pages is indicated by a span of page numbers, e.g., "pp. 57–58." *Passim* is used for a cluster of references in close but not continuous sequence.

Adjustment tax (*tiaojieshui*), 60
Agricultural Products Company, 147, 246n44
Agriculture: crop diversification in, 19, 170–71, 199–200, 226n16, 251nn54–55; and water/soil conditions, 21–22, 174–79, 225n13, 226n24, 248–49n4, 249nn10–11; taxes on, 54–55, 60, 75, 82, 87, 179; budgetary expenditures on, 67–68, 171–77 *passim*, 190; and land conversion regulations, 165–66, 194–96, 248nn21–22, 250n44; fruit production in, 171, 178–79, 188, 190–91; land contracting system in, 192–98 *passim*, 250n38; cropping policy on, 197, 198–200; local government's influence on, 198–200. *See also* Grain
Agriculture Bank, 178, 185, 187
Agriculture Bureau, 164, 194

Agriculture Ministry, 188
An Lushan, 13, 225nn2–3
Andong highway, 163f, 249n14
Andors, Phyllis, 3
Andors, Stephen, 3, 224–25n9
Animal husbandry, 19
Anti-Japanese War, 14, 18, 20
Asphalt Felt Factory, 97–98, 238n18, 239n28

Barium salts factories, *see* Chemical factories
Barter trade: with USSR, 149–52, 246–47nn48,51. *See also* Commerce
Benefits, *see* Wages and benefits
Blecher, Marc, 225n10
Bohai Petroleum Company, 185
Bonus tax (*jiangjinshui*), 60
Border Region Trade Company, 149–52, 246nn48–49
Boxer Rebellion, 18

Brigade accounting, 193–94
Broadcasting Bureau, 164
Budgetary expenditures: administrative, 37, 39, 68, 229n9, 234n40; as share of revenues, 48, 231n5; target negotiations on, 48, 66, 72, 231nn5–6, 234n32; excluded categories for, 66–67, 234n33; on agriculture, 67–68, 171–77 passim; as local responsibility, 69–70, 231n5, 234–35n42; special grants for, 70–71, 235n43; at town and township levels, 71–75; and extrabudgetary expenditures, 86–88, 237n70; on environmental protection, 158, 247n8
Budgetary revenues: expenditures as share of, 48, 231n5; negotiated targets for, 48–49, 72, 232n6; retention rates of, 48–49, 54, 62, 72, 90, 232nn6,9, 235n50; under ligaishui, 54, 62, 66, 232n9, 234n30; from taxes, 54–60 passim, 232–33nn18–19; from enterprise profits, 60–65, 233nn24,26–28; into extrabudgetary fund, 64–65, 75, 233–34n29; at town and township levels, 71–75, 235nn50,52. See also Extrabudgetary fund; Profits; Taxes
Building permits, 194–95
Bureau-run enterprises, 56, 97–98, 101, 238n17, 239nn29–30
Bus transportation, 227n28
Business tax (yingyeshui), 60

Cangzhou-Shijiazhuang highway, 14, 22, 146, 249n14
Cement factory, 99
Central General Bureau of Handicraft Industry, 96
Chemical factories, 92–101 passim, 153, 159, 161, 184–85, 187, 214, 238nn8–9, 249n24
Chen Yonggui, 194
Chengdong Administrative District (formerly Chengguan Commune), 249–50n25. See also Chengguan Commune
Chengguan Commune, 24
Chengxi district (formerly Tianjiazhuang Commune), 230nn16,19–20. See also Tianjiazhuang Commune
China Environmental News, 159

Chinese Academy of Social Science, 3
Chinese People's Association for Friendship with Foreign Countries, 3
Chinese Revolution, 18
City (chengzhen) designation, 24
Civil Affairs Bureau, 33
Civil mediation committees (minshi tiaojie weiyuanhui), 39
Collective (jiti) enterprises, 94, 232nn13–14. See also Rural collectives; Second Light Industry Bureau enterprises
Commerce: centralization/decentralization patterns in, 122, 125; state-run vs. collective, 123–24, 130–35, 244nn14–15; state regulation of private, 126–27, 243nn6–8; foreign, 127, 129–30, 147–49, 226n20, 243–44nn10–11, 246–47nn48,51; as barter, 149–52, 246n48, 246–47n51; as "friendly city" arrangements, 153–54. See also Private marketplace
Commerce Bureau: GXS's detachment from, 62, 130–32f, 244n15; organization and responsibilities of, 124–26, 133, 243nn1,3; commodity circulation reform by, 134–35
Commodity tax (chanpinshui), 60
Communes: road building in, 22, 180f, 249nn14–16; in late Mao period, 24, 26, 39; township conversion of, 26, 228n40; temporary contract labor and, 110; land contracting system in, 191–93, 250n38; cropping directives to, 197, 251n49; administrative relationships of, 229nn4,11. See also Townships
Communist Party, 18, 31, 191f, 228n2
Composite wood factory, 239n28
Construction and environmental protection tax (chengshi weihu jiansheshui), 60
Construction Bank, 236n58
Contract system employees (hetongzhi zhigong), 110–17 passim, 242nn61–63, 243n66. See also Temporary contract workers
Cotton, 8, 19, 21, 171, 199–200, 226nn16,25, 251nn54–55
County (xian): as focus of study, 3, 5, 204–5

County enterprises: during Mao period, 18, 94–100, 106–7, 225n12; external orientation of, 20–21, 129–30, 226n20, 243–44n11; run by state bureaus, 56, 97–98, 101, 238n17, 239nn29,30; five categories of, 56–57, 94–95, 232nn12–15,17; profits of, 56–66 *passim*, 233nn24,26,27, 234n30; extrabudgetary, 57f, 64–65, 83–85, 99–108 *passim*, 232nn15–16, 233nn20–21, 236n65, 236–37n67; tax revenues from, 58, 60, 232–33n18, 233n19; decentralization patterns in, 62–63, 100, 101–2, 106, 107–8, 120–21, 207, 233nn24–25, 239nn25–26,31; defined, 94; developmental orientation of, 98, 239n20; under Deng reform, 100–102, 107–9, 119–20f, 239nn28–30; employment structure in, 109–17, 240nn46–49, 240–41nn52–54, 241–42nn57–59, 242–43nn61–63, 243n66; environmental issues and, 157–59, 161; urban relocation of, 159, 161–62; housing ownership by, 167. *See also* Rural collectives; Second Light Industry Bureau enterprises; State-run enterprises
County personnel, *see* Shulu government officials
Cropping policy, 197, 198–200, 251nn54–55
Cultural achievements, 214, 224n7
Cultural Revolution, 9, 42, 69, 95f, 112–13, 117, 171, 214, 240–41n52
Culture Bureau, 214
Cylinder-head factory, 62f, 95, 98, 238n8

Decentralization: in China, 1–2, 203–4; of county enterprises, 62–63, 100, 101–2, 106, 107–8, 120–21, 207, 233nn24–25, 239n21; administrative vs. enterprise, 106–9, 239nn25–26; commercial, 122, 125
Delfs, Robert, 242n62
Deng Xiaoping period: governmental structure in, 1, 26–27, 32–33, 228nn40,43; administrative expenditures in, 37, 39, 68, 229n9; urbanization during, 40–41, 230n15; organization of county industry in, 100–102, 107–9, 119–20f, 239nn28–30; decentralization patterns in, 101–2, 107–9, 121f; employment structure in, 110, 114, 118; domestic trade reforms in, 130–31; environmental protection in, 158–59, 161, 247nn8,10; agriculture expenditures in, 170–71, 173; water conservancy problems in, 176–79, 249nn7,10–11; road construction in, 181–82, 249n19; cropping policy in, 197, 198–200; local development promotion in, 210, 253n21
Department Store, 125
Developmental state theory, 209
Districts (*tuan*), 13–14
Donnithorne, Audrey, 123, 237n72

Economic Planning Commission, 34, 101ff, 118–19, 195
Education budget, 67, 87. *See also* Schools
Eighth Five-Year Plan, 178
Eighth Route Army, 18
Eighth Street Barium Salts Plant, 184–85, 187, 214
Eighth Street Residents' Committee, 184–85
Electricity generating station, 98–99, 239n26
Employment, *see* Labor force
Enterprise profits, *see* Profits
Environmental protection, 156–59, 161, 219, 247n8
Environmental Protection Office, 158. *See also* Urban Construction and Environmental Protection Commission
Export trade, *see* Foreign trade
Extrabudgetary enterprises (*yusuanwai qiye*), 57f, 64–65, 83–85, 99–108 *passim*, 232nn15–16, 233nn20–21, 236n65, 236–37n67
Extrabudgetary (*yusuanwai*) fund: in triple-stranded system, 47, 89–91; from enterprise profits, 48–49, 57, 64–65, 83–88 *passim*, 232nn6,16, 233–34n19; from surtaxes, 75, 82–83, 87, 236nn60,63; county control of, 82, 84, 236n59; from depreciation, 86, 237n69; expenditure cate-

gories of, 87–88, 175f, 237n70; and state budget negotiations, 88, 237n72; from enterprise profits, 236nn65–66

Family Planning Committee, 34
Fangshan county (later Pingshan county), 225n3
Fanjiazhuang: battle of, 18, 250n35, 251n49
Federation of Cooperative Enterprises, 228n1
Finance and Tax Bureau, 78, 142–43
Finance Bureau, 39, 231n1; fiscal role of, 48, 66, 72, 119, 195, 234n30; on deficit financing, 70–71; and Hebei Yiji Market, 138, 244–45n27
Finance Ministry, 231n3
Finance offices (caizheng suo), 72–73, 235n48
Financial contracting (baogan), 49, 54, 108, 232n7
Financial structure: triple-stranded model of, 47, 88–91. See also Extra-budgetary fund; State budget; Xitong
"Five small" program, 83, 86, 233–34n29, 236n64
Five Year Plan, 109
Folk painting, 214
Foodstuffs Company, 125, 243n2
Foreign Affairs Bureau, 9
Foreign exchange certificates (FECs), 149
Foreign trade: promotion and regulation of, 127, 129–30, 243–44nn10–11; Shulu county's leadership in, 127, 226n20; fluctuations in, 147, 246n42; as vertical system, 148–49, 190–91; with USSR, 149–52, 246n48, 246–47n51
Foreign Trade Bureau, 34, 127, 129–30, 147–48, 162, 190–91, 243–44nn9–11, 246n44
Foreign Trade Ministry, 129f
Forestry Bureau, see Orchard and Forestry Bureau
Forestry Ministry, 190
Fruit, 171, 178–79, 188, 190–91f, 249nn10–11, 250n39
Fur and leather industry: historical importance of, 19–20, 245n41; transferred ownership of, 96; commercial activity of, 138f, 146, 151; as environmental threat, 157–58, 219
Fur and Leather Tanning Factory, 95f, 137ff, 157–58; employment differentials at, 112f, 117, 241n54, 243n68

Government Affairs Office, 37
Grain: yields and proportions of, 8, 21, 171, 175, 226nn16,25; varieties of, 19, 225–26n15; tax on, 54–55, 82; centralized control of, 56–57, 98–99, 239n26; urban dependence on, 111–12, 240n50; illegal trade of, 127; in Heilonggang, 174f; cropping policy on, 197; intercropping of cotton with, 199–200, 251nn54–55
Grants: for budgetary expenditures, 70–71, 235n43
Great Leap Forward, 46, 62, 96, 124, 171, 231n1
Green belts, 161
Guanghan county, 211, 241n56
Guanghan Rural Credit Cooperative Association, 211
Guoxi, 228n42, 229nn7,11
GVAO (gross value of agricultural output), 8, 92, 188
GVIO (gross value of industrial output): in Shulu county, 8, 92–93, 237n1; per capita, 93; rural industries' share of, 93, 183–84, 249n20
GXS (gongxiaoshe [rural supply and marketing co-ops]), 62, 130–34, 244nn14–15

Hai River project, 175
Han Dynasty, 13
Handicraft industries, 96, 238n10
Health Bureau, 56
Hebei Chemical Industry Bureau, 185
Hebei Electrical Power Bureau, 185
Hebei Foreign Trade Bureau, 185
Hebei Grain Bureau, 56
Hebei province, 8, 13, 92–93, 98–99, 105–6, 209, 225n3, 237n1, 241–42n57
Hebei Yiji Market: historical background of, 136, 244n19; construction and financing of, 136–38, 163, 215–16, 244n25; ownership rights

in, 137, 196, 244n24; county government's motivation for, 138–39f, 156, 208, 227n37; competition in, 139, 245n29; specialized licensing of, 141, 245n31
Heilonggang (Black Dragon Harbor), 22, 174, 226–27n26
Heilongjiang province, 150, 153–54, 246n48
Heilongjiang Province Commercial Products Quality Control Bureau, 150, 151–52
Heilongjiang Province International Commerce Corporation, 150, 151–52, 246n48
Hemujing, 229n11, 249–50n25
Highways, see Roads
Hospitals, 27–28, 35
Household registration (*hukou*) system, 196–97, 251n48
Household responsibility system, 178, 191–98 *passim*, 250n38
Housing Construction Group (Fang Jian Zu), 166
Housing regulations, see Land use and housing regulations
Houying, 229n7, 250n35
Huabei Lianda (*later* Xinji Middle School), 18–19. See also Xinji Middle School
Huang-Huai-Hai Development Office, 34
Hundred Regiments offensive, 18

In-budget (*yusuannei*) industries, see State-run enterprises
In-plan temporary contract workers (*ji-huanei linshi hetong gong*), 114, 116, 243n66. See also Temporary contract workers
Income per capita, 8
Income tax (*suode shui*), 58, 60, 233nn20–21
Individual Household Laborers' Association (Geti Laodongzhe Xiehui), 143
Individual households (*fenhu chengbao*), 192f. See also Household responsibility system
Industrial and Commercial Bank, 150, 236n58

Industrial development districts, 185, 190, 249–50n25, 250nn27,35
Industrial enterprises, see County enterprises
Industrial Products Company, 147, 246n44
Industry and Commerce Management Bureau (Gongshang guanli ju), 39, 68, 136, 230–31n22; organization and responsibilities of, 126–27, 140–42; Hebei Yiji Market project of, 136–38f, 245n29; fruit and vegetable markets of, 143, 146; organization and responsibilities of, 146–47, 167, 212–13, 243nn4,6–8, 245n41
Industry and Commerce Management Ministry, 138
Inner Mongolia, 151
Irrigation projects, 21, 178f, 226n24. See also Water conservancy
Israel, 178

Japanese, see Anti-Japanese War
Ji county, 157, 225n11
Jin county, 225n11
Jiucheng, 14, 18–28 *passim*, 180, 193, 225n5, 229n11, 247n2, 249–50n25
JPRS (Joint Publications Research Service), 226–27n26
Junqi, 146, 199
Justice Bureau, 39, 215

Labor Arbitration Board, 119
Labor Bureau, 112–20 *passim*, 240n48, 241–42n57, 242n61, 243n70
Labor force: state's employment and regulation of, 34–35, 118–20, 243n70; profit retentions to, 64, 107, 233nn27–28; wage/benefit contentions within, 104, 112–13, 115, 240–41nn47,52–54; county's expansion of, 109–10, 240n46; categorical structure of, 109–17, 240nn46–49, 241–42nn57–59, 242–43nn61–63,66; housing and food entitlements of, 111–12, 240nn49–50; 1986 reform policy on, 113–14; as future challenge, 218–19. See also Wages and benefits
"Labor market" (*laodong shichang*), 119, 121

Labor Service Company, 242n61
Land Bureau, 39
Land contracting system, *see* Household responsibility system
Land Management Bureau, 165–66, 194–95, 248nn21–22, 250n44
Land occupation tax (*gengdi zhanyong shui*), 195
Land readjustment small group (*tiaozheng tudi xiaozu*), 191
Land use and housing regulations: on conversion of farmland, 165, 194–95, 248nn21–22; on housing construction, 165–66, 195, 248n25, 250n44. *See also* Household responsibility system
Large towns (*xiao chengzhen*), 24, 26
Law enforcement, 214–15
Li Peng, 150
Lianguandian (*later* Xinji), 13. *See also* Xinji
Licenses, private market, 141, 245n31
Ligaishui, see Tax-for profit reform
Light Industry and Textiles Company, 98, 101f, 228n1, 235–36n54. *See also* Second Light Industry Bureau
Liu Baolu, 158, 176, 198, 213
Loans, 129, 134
Lü Zhengcao, 18
Lucheng county (*later* Shulu county), 13. *See also* Shulu county

Mao Zedong, 193
Mao Zedong period: governmental structure in, 1, 3, 5, 24–29 *passim*, 39, 229n11; economic output in, 8, 92, 237n1, 238n13; administrative expenditures in, 37, 229n9; budgetary process in, 46, 48–49, 90, 231n3, 232n6; organization of county industry in, 94–100, 238nn8,10,13–14,17; local development promotion in, 98, 207–8, 210, 239n20, 253n20; administrative decentralization in, 106–7; temporary contract labor in, 109f, 117, 240nn48–49; commerce arrangements in, 122–30 *passim*, 243n3, 243–44nn6–11; environmental protection in, 157–58, 247n6; agriculture expenditures in, 171–76 *passim*; water conservancy project in, 174–76, 248–49n4; road construction in, 180–81, 183, 249nn13–18; cropping policy in, 197, 251n49
Maoist ethos, 42–43
Market Management Commission, *see* Industry and Commerce Management Bureau
"Market mediators" (*jiao yi yuan*), 126
Market News (*Shichang bao*), 143
Market towns, *see* Towns
Materials Bureau, 34
May Day (1942), 18
Meisner, Mitch, 3, 224–25n9
Mengjiazhuang, 229n7
Migrants (*liudong ren*), *see* Rural people
Ming Dynasty (1368–1644), 13
Mopping Up Campaign (May 1, 1942), 18
Municipality (*shi*) designation, 10
Muqiu, 13, 250n35, 251n49
Muslims, 68

Nanjing Road, 163
Nanzhiqiu (*formerly* Zhiqiu), 153, 225n9, 229n11, 249–50nn25,35
Native Products Company, Foreign Trade Ministry, 129
Net profits, *see* Profits
Ninth Street Brigade of Xinji Commune, 129, 193–94, 224n7
Ninth Street Residential Committee, 165–66, 195
Nonrural residents, 22–23, 39, 111–12, 196–97, 240nn48,50
North China Bureau of the Communist Party, 18
North China Petroleum Company, 99, 165
North China United University (Huabei Lianda), 18–19. *See also* Xinji Middle School
North Korea, 151

Office of Economic Cooperation, 149, 152–54, 247nn52–54
Oi, Jean, 253n21
Oil-bearing crops, 171
Orchard and Forestry Bureau, 179, 190–91f, 198, 201, 214, 249nn10–11
Orchard area, *see* Fruit
Orchard contracts, 191–92

Out-of-plan temporary contract workers (*jihuawai linshi hetong gong*), 114, 116–17, 243n68. See also Temporary contract workers
Oxygen bottling plant, 239n28

Peaches, 188
Pears, 151, 188, 246–47n51
People's Bank, 243–44n11
People's congress (*renmin daibiao dahui*), 41
People's Self-Defense Army, 18
Petrochemical Plant, 115
Petroleum Production Ministry, 183
Petty private trade, see Private marketplace
Pingshan county (*formerly* Fangshan county), 225n3
Planning Committee, 79, 157
Planning Department (*Guihua Bumen*), 166
Political Consultative Conference, 31
Pollution control, see Environmental protection
Population statistics: in Shulu county, 5, 8, 219, 227nn31–32; in Xinji, 22–23, 26, 162–65 *passim*, 226n22, 227nn34,37; in Shanghai, 23, 227n35
Power plant, 62f
Price Bureau, 245n36
Private businesspeople (*geti hu*), 132
Private marketplace: market infractions by, 126–27, 142; regulations on, 126–27, 140–43, 243nn6–8; in Deng period, 130, 135–36; as threat to GXS, 132; county government's development of, 136–40, 143, 245n38; specialized licensing of, 141, 245n31; seasonal, 143, 146. See also Commerce
Profits: as extrabudgetary fund source, 48–49, 57, 61, 64–65, 83–88, 232nn6,16, 233–34n29, 236nn65–66; of Second Light Industry Bureau enterprises, 56, 61, 78–81, 96–97, 101, 235–36n54, 239n33; of state-run enterprises, 56–57, 62–66, 95, 233nn24,26–27, 234n30, 238n8; from detached commercial enterprises, 61–62, 134; labor's retention of, 64, 107, 233nn27–28; from Wangkou-

Xinji plant merger, 104; decentralization policy on, 106–9; GXS's reinvestment of, 131–32; of Border Region Trade Company, 150, 152
Provinces, 105–6, 148, 204. See also Hebei province
Public facilities, 27–28, 35, 44, 67
Public Health Bureau, 34, 97, 157
Public Security Bureau, 34, 161, 167
Public Security Department (*Gonganting*), 153

Qing dynasty (1644–1911), 13, 143

Rail transportation, 22
Real Estate Construction Company (*Fangdi Chan Kaifang Gongsi*), 166, 248n25
Real Estate Management Bureau (*Fangdi Chan Guanli*), 166f, 196, 251n48
Real profits (*shixian lirun*), 63ff, 79–86 *passim*, 108, 118, 233nn21,26. See also Profits
Reference prices (*cankao jia*), 142
Reform period, see Deng Xiaoping period
Regular workers, 104, 109–15, 219, 240–41n52, 241–42nn56–59
Research team: focus of, 3, 5; members of, 3, 224–25nn9–10; government officials' interaction with, 9, 10–11, 42f, 45; statistical findings of, 9–11, 224n8
Residents' committees (*jumin weiyuanhui*), 102, 165–66, 195
Retirement benefits, see Wages and benefits
Revolutionary Committee, 174
Roads, 14, 22, 28, 163f, 180–83, 225n5, 249nn13–19
Rubber factory, 83, 85, 99
Rural collectives, 57, 102, 111, 232n17; share of GVIO from, 93, 183–84, 249n20; Wangkou Town Appliance Factory, 103–5, 186; state's control of, 123–24; commercial activity of, 130–35, 244nn14–15; promotion and regulation of, 184–88, 195–96, 249–50nn25,27,31
Rural contract labor, see Temporary contract workers

Rural Industry Leadership Task Force, 186
Rural people, 22–23, 72, 111, 164–65ff, 196–97, 240n48
Rural periodic markets, 143. *See also* Private marketplace
Rural Work Department, Communist Party, 191f
Russia, *see* USSR

Schools, 18–19, 27–28, 35f, 43, 67, 210, 214
Schurmann, Franz, 239n25
Science Committee, 34, 195
Second Light Industry Bureau, 101–2, 124, 228n1, 235–36n54
Second Light Industry Bureau enterprises: tax liability of, 56, 58, 60, 84, 131; profit retention by, 78–81, 96–97, 106ff, 235–36n54; as blurred category, 94, 123–24, 237–38n6; county's control over, 96–97, 238n14; under Deng reform, 100–101f, 108, 239nn28,33
Second Light Industry Ministry, 56, 96f
Shanghai, 23, 162f, 227n35
Shanxi, 153
Share ownership, 186–87, 250n31
Shen county, 225n11
Shenshu county, 225n11
Shenzhen, 151–52, 210
Shijiazhuang-Dezhou Railway, 22
Shijiazhuang prefecture, 5, 239n26; industrial management role of, 56f, 98–99; and Second Light Industry profits, 78, 236nn55,57; foreign commerce regulation by, 127, 129; GVIO in, 237n1
Shirt factory, 148
Shue, Vivienne, 225n10
Shuji county, 225n11
Shujin county, 225n11
Shulu county: as "tethered deer," 2–3; location and population of, 5, 8, 22, 213, 219, 227nn31–32, 253n25; economic output of, 8, 92–93, 205–6, 209, 237n1, 252n13; press obscurity of, 9, 224n7; researchers' findings on, 9–11; as Xinji municipality, 10, 40–41, 71, 156, 181, 216, 249n19; derivation of name of, 13, 225nn2–3; roads in, 14, 22, 180–83, 225n5, 249nn14–19; warfare in, 18–19; agricultural conditions in, 19, 21–22, 170–71, 225n13, 226n24; foreign trade orientation of, 20–21, 127, 129–30, 147, 149–52, 226n20, 243–44nn9–11, 246nn42,48, 246–47n51; hierarchies of settlements in, 23–27 *passim*; public facilities in, 27–28, 44; hardship posts in, 36–37, 229n7; categories of enterprises in, 56–57, 94–95, 232nn12–15,17; industrial decentralization in, 62–63, 100, 101–2, 107–8, 120–21, 207, 233nn24–25, 239nn25–26,31; and extrabudgetary enterprise conversion, 85, 236–37n67; structure of labor force in, 109–17, 240nn46–49, 240–41nn52–54, 241–42nn57–59, 242–43nn61–63,66; as contract employment test site, 111, 113–14; "friendly·city" relations with, 153–54; water conservancy project in, 174–76, 248–49n4; Mao-Deng period continuity in, 211–12f; state entrepreneurialism resistance in, 211–12f. *See also* Shulu county government; Shulu government officials
Shulu county government: structure of, 2–3, 13–14, 18–19, 24, 26–27, 156, 225nn2–4,11–12, 228nn40,43; background of, 13–14, 156; growth and complexity of, 29, 31–32, 47, 200–201, 205–7, 228n1, 252n13; regulatory role of, 32–33, 165–67, 200, 212–13; vertical and horizontal functions of, 33–34, 47, 86–87, 124–25, 138, 176, 182–83, 187–88, 206; *xitong* offices of, 33–34, 75, 78, 148–49; administrative expenditures by, 37, 39, 68, 229n9, 234n40; fiscal structure of, 47–48, 88–91, 231n3; enterprises run by, 56f, 94, 237–38n6; profit retention by, 56f, 108, 150, 232n16; agriculture expenditures by, 67–68, 171–77 *passim*; deficit financing by, 70–71, 235nn43,45–46; extrabudgetary fund control by, 82–83f, 236n59; in *tiji guanli* relationship, 105–6; commercial responsibilities of, 123; private commerce initia-

tives of, 136–40, 208, 212, 244n25, 244–45n27; developmental orientation of, 138–39f, 176, 199–200, 207–13 passim, 252n15, 253nn19,21; urbanization of Xinji by, 155–56, 158, 162–68 passim, 215–16, 248nn16–17; as environmental issues' mediator, 156–59, 161; land use and housing regulations by, 165–67, 194–95, 248nn21–22,25, 250n44; road planning by, 180–83, 249n19; rural industry promotion by, 184–87, 249–50nn25,27; farm support services of, 198–99; vertical and horizontal functions of, 208–9, 252n16; culture/arts promotion by, 214, 224n7; legal enforcement role of, 214–15; future challenges for, 218–20; Communist Party's role in, 228n2. See also Shulu county; Shulu government officials
Shulu government officials: research team's interaction with, 9, 10–11, 43, 45; state employment of, 33–34f, 229n4; education and competence of, 36, 43f, 89–91, 214, 220; wages and benefits of, 36–37, 68, 229n7; political ethos of, 41–45, 216–17, 230–31n22; developmental orientation of, 213, 216–17
Siu, Helen, 253n21
Skinner, G. William, 14
Socialist Education Movement, 69
Socialist regimes, 122, 209–10
Specialized team contracting (zhuanyedui chengbao), 192. See also Household responsibility system
Spinning factories, 186
Sports Committee, 34
State budget: in triple-stranded system, 47, 89–91; as centralized, 48, 231nn3–4; negotiated targets for, 48–49, 232n6; as fiscal contracting system, 49, 54, 232n7; as tax-based system, 54, 62, 66, 232n8, 234n30; at town and township levels, 71–75, 235nn48,50,52; extrabudgetary fund receipts and, 88, 237n72; statistics on, 231n1. See also Budgetary expenditures; Budgetary revenues
State cadres (guojia ganbu), see Shulu government officials

State entrepreneurialism, 211–12f
State government: and county government, 31–34, 168–69; and town government, 40, 230n13; industry regulation by, 119–20f
State-run (difang guoying) enterprises: ownership and administration of, 56f; taxes on, 58, 60, 232–33n18; net profits of, 60–66 passim, 83, 86, 106–7f, 233n27; under tax-based system, 62, 66, 234n30; in "five small" program, 83, 86, 236n64; extrabudgetary factories as, 83–84f, 236–37nn65,67; heterogeneity of, 93–94, 237–38n6; in Mao period, 95, 238n8; administrative decentralization of, 100, 106–7f, 239nn25–26; direct commercial exchange by, 134–35. See also Extrabudgetary enterprises
Statistics Bureau, 9, 33, 39, 187
Subcounty government, 39–41, 229n11. See also Communes; Towns; Townships
Sugar refinery, 99
Supply and Marketing Co-op network (Gongxiaoshe) enterprises, see GXS
Surtaxes, 75, 82–83, 87, 236nn60,63
Suzhou, 184

Tang Dynasty, 13
Tax-for-profit (ligaishui) reform, 54, 60, 62, 66, 108, 232n8, 234n30
Taxes: four categories of, 54; under ligaishui reform, 54, 60, 62, 66, 108, 232n8, 234n30; on agriculture, 54–55, 60, 75, 82, 87, 179; at town and township level, 55, 72, 75, 235n48; on local industry and commerce, 56, 58, 60, 232–33nn18–21; surtaxes on, 75, 82–83, 87, 236nn60, 63; on GXS, 131; on private marketplace, 142–43; on land occupation, 195–96
Temporary contract workers (linshi hetong gong), 109–17 passim, 156, 219, 240nn46–48,50, 240–41nn52–54, 243n66
Tethered deer metaphor, 2–3
Textile industry, see Fur and leather industry
"Three linkages" policy, 198

Tianjiazhuang Commune (*later* Chengxi district), 250n39, 251n49. *See also* Chengxi district
Tianjin, 22, 188
Tiji guanli ("raising the [administrative] level of management"), 104–6
Towns (*zhen*), 24, 26, 39–40f, 71–75, 235nn48,50,52
Township Industries Bureau, 39, 184–88, 195, 214, 249n23, 249–50nn25,27,31
Townships (*xiang*): historical structure of, 14, 24, 26; as hardship posts, 36–37, 229n7; budgetary collections and expenditures by, 39–40, 57f, 71–75, 235nn48,50,52; as urban administrative districts, 40–41, 230n15; rural collectives of, 57, 102–6, 183–84, 232n17, 249n20; as industrial development districts, 185, 190, 249–50nn25,27,35; land contracting system in, 192–93; cropping patterns in, 197–200 passim, 251n55. *See also* Communes
Trade, *see* Commerce
Trade violations, 126–27, 142, 148
Transportation, *see* Roads
Transportation Bureau, 56, 97f, 100, 142, 164, 180, 181–83
Transportation Ministry, 183

Unemployment benefits, *see* Wages and benefits
Unified industry and commerce tax, 56, 58, 60, 232–33nn18–19
Urban administrative districts (*banshichu*), 23, 26, 40–41, 87, 156, 230n15, 249–50n25, 260nn16,19–20. *See also* Townships
Urban Construction and Environmental Protection Commission (Chengshi Jianshe Huanjing Baohu Weiyuanhui), 34, 136, 141, 158–59, 163, 165, 187, 194, 214, 247n6
Urban Construction and Environmental Protection Ministry, 138
Urban Construction and Environmental Protection Tax, 236n60
Urban Construction Bureau (*later* Urban Construction and Environmental Protection Commission), 158, 161f, 247n6, 248n15
Urban development: of Xinji, 155–56, 161–65, 248nn16–17; pollution control and, 156–59, 161, 247nn8,10; county's regulation of, 165–67, 194–95, 248nn21–22,25, 250n44; governmental relationships and, 167–69
Urban residents, *see* Nonrural residents
USSR: barter trade with, 149–52, 246–47nn48,51

Value-added tax (*zengzhishui*), 60
Vehicle regulation, 142, 245n36
Vehicle repair shop, 100
Vertical ministerial systems, see *Xitong*
Villages (*xiang cun*), 14, 24, 57, 180, 191, 225n9, 230n14, 237n1

Wages and benefits: of county personnel, 36–37, 68, 229n7; of temporary contract workers, 112–17 passim, 240–41nn52–54, 243n68; of regular workers, 114–15, 241–42nn56–58; of contract system employees, 115–16, 242nn61–63; linked to profit index, 118–19, 243n70
Wang Bingqian, 233n20
Wangkou, 26, 28, 103–4, 175, 180, 193, 228n42, 249–50nn13,25
Wangkou Town Appliance Factory, 103–5, 186
Water conservancy, 21–22, 174–79, 219, 226–27nn24,26, 248–49nn4,7,10–11
Water Conservancy Bureau, 34, 56, 99, 175, 176–77ff, 198–99, 201, 212–13
Water Conservancy Law (1988), 177f
Weibo, 229n11, 249–50n25
Wells, 177f, 249n7
Wenzhou, 184
Women employees, 35
Wong, Christine P. W., 231nn3,5, 234–35nn42,46, 237–38nn6,14,17, 253n20
World Bank, 235n43

Xiaoxinzhuang, 229n7
Xincheng, 13–14, 18, 22ff, 26, 40, 180, 229n11, 230n13, 249–50n25
Xinhui county, 253n21

Xinji (*formerly* Lianguandian): industrial base in, 13, 20, 224n7, 226n22; public facilities and transportation in, 14, 22, 28; Japanese occupation of, 18, 20; population density in, 22–23, 26, 162–63, 227nn34,37; administrative status of, 24; commercial traffic in, 136, 156, 244n20; Hebei Yiji Market in, 136–38, 244nn24–25, 244–45nn27,29; urbanization of, 155–56, 158, 162–68 *passim*, 215–16, 248nn16–17; pollution controls in, 159, 161–62; land and housing regulation in, 165–67, 248n25

Xinji Agricultural Machinery Repair and Production Plant, 103–4, 241n57

Xinji Chemical Factory, 92, 95, 185, 238n9, 249n24

Xinji finance gazetteer (*Xinji shi caizheng zhi*), 231n1

Xinji Labor Service Company, 117

Xinji Middle School (*formerly* Huabei Lianda), 18–19, 36, 43, 67, 210, 214

Xinji municipality: Shulu county's redesignation as, 10, 40–41, 71, 156, 181, 216, 249n19

Xinji People's Commune, 23f, 39, 167

Xinjiang, 151

Xinleitou, 249–50nn25,39

Xitong (vertical ministerial systems): intrasystem financial transfers by, 33–34, 56, 75, 78–81, 86–87, 236n58; in triple-stranded system, 47, 89–91; foreign trade as, 148–49, 190–91

Xixiaowang, 250n35

Xizebei, 229n7, 250n35

Zhangguzhuang, 229n11

Zhili, 136, 244n19

Zhiqiu (*later* Nanzhiqiu), 225n9

Zhonglixiang, 229n7

Zhou Enlai, 193, 233n25

Library of Congress Cataloging-in-Publication Data

Blecher, Marc J.
　Tethered deer : government and economy in a Chinese county / Marc Blecher and Vivienne Shue.
　　　p.　　cm.
　　Includes index.
　　ISBN 0-8047-2565-9 (cloth)
　　1. Shu-lu hsien (China)—Economic conditions.　2. Shu-lu hsien (China)—Politics and government.　I. Shue. Vivienne,　II. Title.
HC428.S57B58　　1996
352.94'2'095115—dc20　　95-19174　CIP

⊚ This book is printed on acid-free, recycled paper.

Original printing 1996

Last figure below indicates year of this printing:

05　04　03　02　01　00　99　98　97　96